INTERNATIONAL TEXTBOOKS IN ART EDUCATION
Italo L. de Francesco, Consulting Editor

ART

Search and Self-Discovery

ART
Search and Self-Discovery

James A. Schinneller

Associate Professor
Art Education Extension
University of Wisconsin

INTERNATIONAL TEXTBOOK COMPANY • SCRANTON, PENNSYLVANIA

Fourth Printing, April, 1964

EDITOR'S PREFACE

Whether appreciation of art can be "taught," in the traditional sense of the term, is an old problem to which considerable writing and debating have been devoted. And yet people have somehow learned to respond to painting of various types and schools, to sculpture in the classical and in the contemporary vein, to architecture of the Renaissance as well as to Frank Lloyd Wright's Guggenheim Museum, and to graphic arts ranging from the Chinese to Dürer and Kollwitz. Somehow, people have even acquired a sort of ambivalence—they like the classical for what it is, and they like the modern for what it is. This is as it should be because understanding (or appreciation) does not imply an irrevocable choice.

Professor Schinneller is aware of the problems of appreciation and, therefore, tackles these problems from several approaches: his own poetic descriptions; quotations from men of art; visual presentation; and lastly, by propounding questions and suggesting that personal experience with some form of the arts might lead to one's own answers.

It is rather unusual to find adequately illustrated books. This volume is an exception. The author has spared neither time nor money to procure what is best in order to supplement the word.

This text is unique in another way. The author has actually used this material in teaching students at various levels of understanding—from high school through college graduate courses. What he now presents, however, has been refined on the basis of criticisms made by students as well as from his own observations of the manner in which they responded to what he had to say.

Lastly, here is a perfect blend of history, aesthetics, and criticism. This is a rare combination which should prove effective in leading students to reach their own conclusion, make choices, and arrive at understandings in the field of art.

I. L. DE FRANCESCO

PREFACE

Have you ever wondered why many modern paintings are vastly different from paintings of the past century or what qualities make an interesting piece of sculpture? Why did Greeks centuries ago determine how many American buildings would be designed? How do artists interpret nature and what does organic architecture imply? Do you think experimentation is essential to art or that drawings can tell more than meets the eye? Have you ever wondered where designers secure ideas or how bulldozers and power-shovels can go hand in hand with art? Do you enjoy making things all your own? Have you ever thought that in an age of science man needs the song of a bird?

If you have wondered about such matters, this text is for you. Between its covers you will meet art of the past and the present produced by youths and fully matured artists. Creations by innovators, such as Hans Arp, Willem de Kooning, Pablo Picasso, Louis Sullivan, and Frank Lloyd Wright, are included, along with many other originators who will comment about their work. Rome will be visited at the height of Empire and a cathedral considered, as well as paintings from a recent International exhibit. In addition, suggestions for experiences in design, printmaking, handling carving tools in sculpture, and exciting ventures in crafts will be found within the book along with a host of other creative adventures.

This book has grown out of a desire to foster an increased awareness of art as well as actual involvement, on the part of the reader, with numerous materials, tools, and processes in creative endeavors. To make and to know go hand in hand. Whenever feasible, direct quotes are incorporated into the text to establish a closeness between reader and concepts or artist under consideration. Numerous photographs are included to assist understanding, and a touch of art philosophy and a pinch of history are added to provide sequence and convey the art attitudes and spirit of particular ages.

The placement, following each chapter, of suggestions for actual art experiences in design, architecture, drawing, painting, printmaking, sculpture, and crafts is not to imply that a particular sequence should be maintained in studio activities. Pluck as you wish, for the pattern of use in relating readings and creative experiences is left to the discretion of supervising teachers or the reader. As one example, activities in sculpture may precede graphic or architectural undertakings, as determined by the particularities of specific situations rather than by an arbitrary listing by the author. The structure of this book was formulated as a modest plan, containing an interdependency of parts and organized as a continuum in presenting a somewhat comprehensive yet concise view of art. Regarding the sequence of topics, architecture, for instance, is treated before drawing or painting for it seemed to typify changing design notions and could be closely related to many facets of the reader's environment. Architectural designing on the part of students, however, should not necessarily come before drawing or painting activities; the reverse would probably be more suitable. Thus the framework of the text need not nor should not dictate a specific sequential pursuit of expressions in the varied fields of art. Ideally, the book should serve as a resource guide, and following an initial investigation of its contents, creative adventures should be selected on the basis of interest.

The organization of any book, of course, is a matter of personal conjecture for there can be innumerable solutions in composing a venture which attempts to briefly survey aspects of art which bear on the present and suggest creative activities suitable for familiarizing one with art beyond the freedom and boisterousness of many school art programs. The author, merely taking one stand, hopes that you find the structure and implications of the book to your liking.

Following the grateful recognition of the many who have contributed much to this publication, let's talk about art, let's journey.

JAMES A. SCHINNELLER

Milwaukee, Wisconsin
May, 1961

ACKNOWLEDGMENTS

Recognition is due to a teacher who pointed the way, Professor Frank Wachowiak of the University of Iowa. Friends in the Art and Art Education Departments of the University of Wisconsin and The Pennsylvania State University, Professors Gibson Byrd, Frederick Logan, Edward Mattil, Donald White, John Wilde, the late Viktor Lowenfeld, and many others, extended valuable suggestions and assistance. Professor Edward Zagorski of the University of Illinois was also very kind. Appreciation is extended to the Extension Division, University of Wisconsin, for the use of portions of previous publications. Sections of that material, initially prepared by the author, served as a partial foundation for this present venture. A grant from The Pennsylvania State University also proved most helpful.

The many artists—too numerous to mention here but identified in the text—who contributed photographs of their work and in many cases comments and the museums, historical societies, businesses, universities, and government agencies who rendered assistance are also thanked. The students, junior and senior high school as well as university, whose work is found within this publication are most certainly appreciated. Unless otherwise indicated, all university-student works illustrated were produced at The Pennsylvania State University or the University of Wisconsin. Many of these students were in training for future careers in public school teaching. High school teachers and supervisors who contributed student work also rendered a major service; they are June Baskin, Louise Drumm, Norma Glenn, Dale Kendrick, Mary Adeline McKibbin, Adele Ortmayer, and Arthur Pelz.

Appreciation is extended to Dr. Italo L. de Francesco, former Director of Art Education, now president of Kutztown State College, who offered much helpful advice relating to this publication and served as editor.

JAMES A. SCHINNELLER

CONTENTS

LIST OF ILLUSTRATIONS

Chapter 2. DESIGN, THE ORGANIZATION OF THINGS

Chapter 3. THE DISTANT PAST AND NINETEENTH-CENTURY AMERICAN ARCHITECTURE

Chapter 4. CONTEMPORARY ARCHITECTURE: NEW METHODS OF ENCLOSING SPACE

Chapter 5. DRAWING: RECORDING WITH LINE

Chapter 6. VISUAL REALITIES AND IMAGERY

Chapter 7. PAINTING—THE ADDITION OF COLOR

Chapter 8. GRAPHICS: IMPRESSIONS THROUGH PRESSURE AND INK

Chapter 9. SCULPTURE, DISCOVERIES IN THREE-DIMENSIONAL FORM

Chapter 10. CRAFTS: FEATHERS TO GOLD

ART
Search and Self-Discovery

1 | ART AND WHAT IT OFFERS

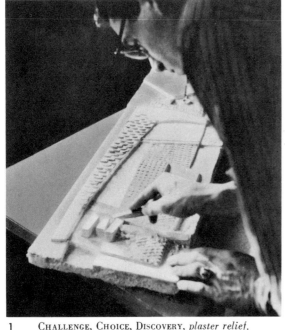

1 CHALLENGE, CHOICE, DISCOVERY, *plaster relief.*

Art Is Dependent on You

Art is an intellectual and an emotional recording of an attitude or an experience presented in a personal manner. The visual arts—painting, sculpture, architecture, and other related arts—are concerned with the creative handling of lines, textures, shapes, colors and space in materials such as paint, stone, and wood. "Creative" implies bringing into existence new constructions through a personal arrangement of existing or new elements.

The uniqueness of art is that it is dependent upon the performer for the final solution. Only he, since the activity is based on self-determination, can provide the answer. This is to imply not that various forms of assistance are unavailable for enlightenment, but rather that, unlike other activities, the conclusion can not be found in following rules and regulations. Instead, it is dependent on invention. Art is unique in indicating the supremacy of the doer, rather than the body of knowledge concerning the field.

An artist once contended that one paints to unload himself of feelings and visions. Art is involved with this experience of living, seeing, thinking, feeling, each in his own way. An experience may be relived, details recalled, and life intensified through art activity. In the face of mechanization, and the fast, complex, and confusing tempo of our time, creativity indicates the value of the individual and what can be achieved by relating the actions of eye, mind, heart, and hand.

The Creative Act

Creative action, which makes up a work of art, is dependent upon an active involvement of the individual during the working process. Through manipulation and constant choice, the idea to be expressed, material, and process combine in a fluid action rather than a rigid sequence. Flexibility is essential to take advantage of newly discovered relationships which may determine new responses; for modifications that derive from work discoveries or intuition frequently change the initial visualization. Thus, art can not be predetermined; the final result evolves through discriminative and constant choices while actively engaged. What are the possibilities of the material (Figure 1)? Would a rough or smooth, light or dark treatment accent a particular area? What should be stressed in an adjacent section? Does the composition require additional details, or would such an action result in unneeded complexities?

It is through the creative process that art challenges the individual and activates what exists within the senses. A more versatile personality should emerge through art experiences. Qualities such as confidence, initiative, and freedom of thought can grow out of creative activity because the constant problem solving that is evident in such undertakings demands independent judgment and personal sensitivity. These combine to expand the horizons of the individual. Art modifies man as well as landscape.

To Open More Than the Eyes

One may wonder what can be secured through creative action and the study of art. What may be the results of combining your imagination with tools and hands to produce something all your own? What can be achieved through the inspiration gained from knowing about the great creative achievements of mankind? Can there be joy in discovering the subtle coloring of a leaf or becoming aware of the interesting proportions of a building?

What one can expect from art is, of course, dependent upon what one is willing to give to the field. Effort and study increase knowledge, and active participation — from drawing and painting to carving or designing architectural forms — provides valuable insights and develops skills. Art activity should not be limited to only those who are preparing for a potential profession or career in art; for it can provide enrichment to all students no matter what their future vocations. It should aid those confronted with problems in building, selecting, enjoying, and evaluating. Knowledge of art should develop an awareness and appreciation of both nature and well-designed man-made objects that range from paintings and houses to kitchen utensils. Art should aid in developing a belief in oneself and a desire for creating a more beautiful and meaningful world in which to live.

An intriguing duality exists in art, for while it can assist a lone individual by adding new dimensions to his life, it can also serve to enrich an entire society.

Beyond the Obvious: Toward a Better World

While some men create on canvas and others carve in stone, it would be fictitious to think of art as confined only to problems of studio or museum. Art may move outdoors and bring forth effective solutions for play, for comfort, for worship; it may stimulate the senses, activate the mind, and warm the heart. Through art man creates ideas which may result in small book jackets or cause tremendous changes in the pattern of the land.

Bulldozers, steam shovels, trucks, and men — the paraphernalia of building — are gouging out new shapes in the contour of the earth. Welder, crane operator, rigger, and construction engineer are raising the products of industry to formulate new city landscapes. Art plays its role through the germination of ideas which offer visual sensitivity and practicality to these new growths of concrete and steel and thereby provide man a new season warm with the promise of things to come.

Master plans are emerging through the contributions of artists and architectural engineers, civic planners, and traffic engineers which offer solutions to the complicated problems of urban living. Slums, inadequate streets and lighting, and business and industrial congestion are several critical urban problems currently confronting man. Difficulties in traffic flow, for example, cost large cities millions of dollars in lost revenue yearly. Several decades ago a survey revealed that the losses due to delay and lost motion in street transportation in the metropolitan area of New York reached a million dollars a day. Creative thinking on the part of designers can solve these critical problems and provide grandeur to entire cities. Such is the case in Pittsburgh, Pennsylvania, as well as innumerable other cities throughout our land and across the seas.

2   *Business Area of Pittsburgh, Pa., 1945. (Courtesy Allegheny Conference on Community Development)*

3   MASTER PLAN FOR PITTSBURGH, PA. IN 1965. *(Courtesy Allegheny Conference on Community Development)*

A Change of Face to Benefit Society

Pittsburgh was until recently a grim, disjointed, and chaotic area (Figure 2). Defaced by its heavy industry and bearing the scars of previous unrestricted expansion and the flight to the suburbs, the city demanded rejuvenation. Otherwise, it was doomed, linked to the past, strangled by confusion and urban complexities. Through recent and determined action by men with vision, Pittsburgh is rapidly becoming a gateway to the future (Figure 3). Its heart has been transformed through the removal of old arteries and tissue and the introduction of park areas with patches of greenery and trees. These areas, flanked by new, wide boulevards and imposing contemporary buildings and parking areas, eliminate congestion and provide beauty to the center of a great metropolitan area. Wide concrete roadways that cross new bridges and eliminate steep grades by cutting through recently constructed tunnels also fan out to serve the fringes of the city and the surrounding landscape efficiently. Pittsburghers now enjoy freedom of movement and richness of view.

Plato's contention can once again become a reality for many communities throughout the land. Twenty-three centuries ago, the great Greek philosopher implied that a society is sensitized and influenced well by every sight and sound of beauty; he compared the effect to that of a pure breeze blowing across a good land.

What can art do for your area?

To Brighten the Home

The purpose of art can be manyfold; for it offers artists diversified opportunities ranging from serving the homemaker or assisting religion, business, and industry to entertaining children or speaking to men of justice.

Art can provide elegance to the products which make up a civilization, from skyscrapers to houses, furniture (Figure 4), to kitchenware (Figure 5). Existence may be intensified, feelings aroused, and comfort assured through art. The labors of housework may be lessened and ease of maintenance secured through visually pleasing, lightweight, and versatile furniture created by artists such as Harry Bertoia. Elegant dinnerware may add excitement to a table setting and brighten the day. Through creative ingenuity, products of an age rise above the ordinary and commonplace and offer joy and comfort to living.

4   *Metal Chair, Harry Bertoia. (Courtesy Knoll Associates)*

5   *Ceramic Dinnerware, Kaarina Aho. (Courtesy the Embassy of Finland)*

6   *Saint Edmond's Episcopal Church, Elm Grove, Wisc. A soaring hyperbolic para-
boloid roof serves to shelter curved and straight brick, glass, and wood masses.
Designed by William P. Wenzler. (Courtesy the Architect)*

7   *Staircase, G. M. Technical Center, Detroit, Mich., white
terrazzo slabs, stainless steel rods, teak, designed by
Eero Saarinen. (Courtesy General Motors Corporation)*

For Church, Industry, and Business

Art may serve religion, industry, and business in
many ways. William Wenzler, Eero Saarinen, and
many other architects, through new engineering feats,
attain exciting sculptural forms and dramatic compositions of materials. These artists erect inspirational
shelters in which to worship or work in many sections
of our land (Figures 6 and 7). Painters add interest
to the walls of many business buildings (Figure 8).
Portraying a whimsical view of the forms and activities which make up a city, Saul Steinberg's mural
conveys exuberance while harmonizing with the intentions of the surrounding ballroom.

Impact is gained in the communications of industry and business through the ingenuity of other artists such as Louis Dorfsman (Figure 9). His presentment with superimposed question marks invites
inquisitiveness, thereby encouraging a desire for
additional examination which assures communication. Symbols of the partially covered fish and randomly sliced melon also provide interesting interplays of shapes, valves, and textures, which contribute
toward a novel advertisement.

Play and More Serious Matters

Art may fulfill its purpose by providing exciting
implements of play or offering the means of crying
out against man's inhumanity toward man. Located
in a park, items such as the *Play Sculpture* (Figure

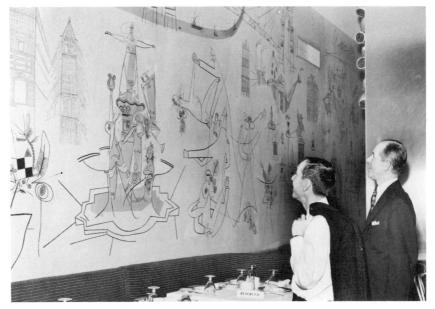

8   *Ballroom Mural, oil paint on canvas, Saul Steinberg. (Courtesy Terrace Hilton Hotel, Cincinnati, Ohio)*

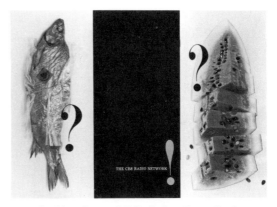

9   *Booklet Cover, C.B.S. Radio, Louis Dorfsman. (Courtesy Lithographers and Printers National Association, Inc.)*

10) stimulate youngsters to climb, crawl, jump, and invent various means of ascending and descending. Placed in a park, a sculpture such as *Social Consciousness* (Figure 11) may communicate to the more matured, demanding contemplation and reflection. The center figure of this monumental group appears to seek social compatability through a consideration of the forgotten, the ignored, the destitute, the mutilated, and the crippled. The sculpture implies that you are your brother's keeper, be he rich or poor, humble or feeble, and regardless of race, creed, or color.

Art Can Tell of Many Things and Perform in Many Ways

By pointing out a star, fingering the strange, or commenting about the known, art may suggest happiness; or sadness, a nod, tear, or smile may be its response. By dealing with man's heroics or degradation or just his day-by-day routine, it structures the products and conveys the spirit of its age. The versatility of art is endless and ageless and is limited only by the vision of each age. In the present it serves man, and it will continue to serve him; for it has always been so. Because of its visual form, which is universal, art eliminates geographic and historical boundaries and the barriers of language to speak in a manner common to all men.

10   PLAY SCULPTURE, *hexapod, cast concrete. (Courtesy Play Sculptures, Inc., New York, N. Y.)*

11 SOCIAL CONSCIOUSNESS, *bronze sculpture in Fairmount Park, Philadelphia, Pa., Sir Jacob Epstein. (Courtesy Fairmount Park Art Association)*

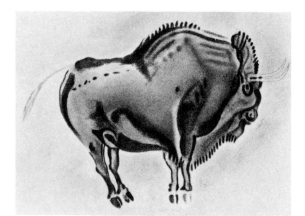

12 THE BISON, *painting in Cave of Altamira, Northern Spain, Palaeolithic Period. (Courtesy American Museum of Natural History)*

Illuminating the Pages of History

Long before the written word, man used his ability to carve, draw, and paint as means of communication. In the early dawn of mankind, before man emerged from caves, art played a vital role in extending his concept of life. Representations of men as well as beasts appeared on cave walls twenty-two thousand years ago (Figure 12). Possibly created to gain a magical control over the form represented, cave paintings illustrate prehistoric man's skill in an art activity. Such paintings as *The Bison* shed light on an otherwise dim past and, through directness of presentment and sensitivity of execution, harmoniously link art of the past with current creative efforts.

What can art tell us? It can tell us of the aspirations and deeds of past civilizations. It can relate the grandeur of man long before the birth of Christ or the march of Roman warriors into Gaul. Twenty-one centuries before the Santa Maria, Pinta, and Niña sailed westward from Palos or before Nicolaus Copernicus looked toward the sky, Greeks searched for and found a universal beauty within stone (Figure 13). Fragments of their works provide insight into their skills, accomplishments, and dreams. The Grecian concern for richness through idealized proportions and serenity has given both seeds and fruit to nourish innumerable men in succeeding centuries. Art provides a civilization the means of achieving immortality; for through the future unfolding of its products, its period and contribution live once again in the mind of man.

Reaffirming Constant Interests

What can art tell us? It can tell us of man's constant interest in nature, his inherent greatness and his Gods, and his concern with death, as well as the events which contributed toward the birth of his society.

Far from the Mediterranean basin, artists viewed nature rather than man as the center of things. Eastern winds and the rhythm and essence of natural forms have long been recorded by innumerable Oriental artists. Their interests have been presented by the works of poets, such as Li T'ai-po "and the earth belongs to no one. The peach trees blossom and the waters flow and flow," as well as by drawings, prints, and paintings of artists such as Ni Tsan. His *Landscape* (Figure 14), inscribed as being completed on the second day of October, 1362, reveals both the vitality and tenderness of living things. Ni Tsan embraced nature completely and through choice lived amid the mountains and waterways of China recording the experiences he knew and loved.

Five centuries later, painters such as John James Audubon and George Catlin followed a similar way of life in America. While wandering throughout the west, they portrayed the living creatures and the vastness of our land.

13   YOUNG HORSEMAN, *marble relief, from Rhodes, Greek, 4th century* B.C. *(Courtesy Metropolitan Museum of Art, Rogers Fund, 1912)*

14   LANDSCAPE, *illustrated scroll, watercolor, Ni Tsan, Yuan Dynasty. (Courtesy Freer Gallery of Art, Washington, D. C.)*

15   Sᴋᴇᴛᴄʜᴇs ғᴏʀ ᴛʜᴇ Mᴀᴅᴏɴɴᴀ, *pen and ink, Leonardo da Vinci, Italian Renaissance. (Courtesy Metropolitan Museum of Art, Rogers Fund, 1917)*

16   Jᴀɢᴜᴀʀ, *carving in volcanic rock, Aztec, 15th century. (Courtesy Philadelphia Museum of Art)*

SIVA, *bronze sculpture, Southern India, 16th century.*
(Courtesy Philadelphia Museum of Art)

17

Conveying the Greatness of Man and His Beliefs

Art can introduce us to the giants of the past who once again may inspire through their heroic accomplishments. For instance, the genius of individuals such as Leonardo da Vinci can become apparent. That Renaissance man, celebrated as painter, sculptor, architect, musician, engineer, and scientist, proved to be one of the most versatile members of mankind. His interests ranged from designing military fortifications and flying machines to decorating walls of monasteries with paintings such as his *Last Supper*. He labored four years in creating the *Mona Lisa*, perhaps the most celebrated portrait in the world. He discovered scientific truths and exposed spiritual values. Leonardo's studies, such as the sheet of *Sketches for the Madonna* (Figure 15), indicate a mind eagerly searching and discovering. Keen observation, great intellect, and sensitivity of draftsmanship enabled Leonardo to produce great works which continue to strongly communicate through the ages.

In addition to insight into the beliefs of Christians, art provides an awareness of the gods of other peoples. Early Spanish accounts relate that the Aztecs worshiped many gods, one of which was presented in the form of a jaguar. This jungle beast, found in the dense forests of Mexico, represented Tepeyollotl, the earth god of the night hours. In 1521, upon their

victorious entrance into Tenochtitlan, now called Mexico City, Hernando Cortez and his conquistadors probably viewed such Aztec sculptures as the *Jaguar* (Figure 16). The carving of reddish volcanic rock presents the jungle cat in a compact and economical manner. Through such examples contemporary man is provided a view of long-vanquished empires. The past can be partially reconstructed and the skills, interests, and beliefs of foreign cultures can be understood through art. Religious art imagery, depending on man's experience, may be in the form of a jungle beast or even a dancing figure.

Crushing an enemy beneath his foot and suggesting unlimited and divine strength, the Hindu god Siva is represented as the dancer Natarāja (Figure 17). In portraying the dance of creation and destruction, the multiarm sculpture indicates the comprehensive powers of Siva. Particular gestures of the hands, such as the palm extending, denotes that fear is unwarranted; the grasped instrument representing the first sound in the universe and the destructive flames portrayed in another hand indicate the extensive provinces of this Indian god. Such works of art provide insight into the beliefs of approximately two hundred and fifty million Hindu worshipers in India and also illustrate the great skill of Indian artist-craftsmen of long ago.

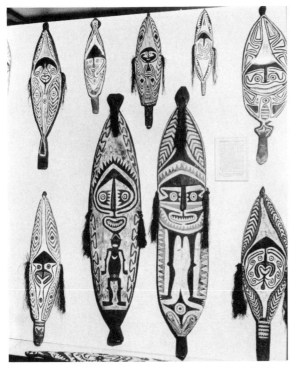

18   *Memorial Tablets, carved and painted wood, New Guinea. (Courtesy Chicago Natural History Museum)*

19   WASHINGTON AT PRINCETON, *oil painting, M. M. Sanford, early 19th century. (Courtesy New York State Historical Association)*

For the Living and the Dead

Art has many ways and many unusual reasons; it has long served strange, as well as common, needs of both the living and the dead. Egyptians erected huge, somber, commemorative pyramids to protect the dead from the living; other societies have produced bright decorative markers to protect the living from the dead. In a highly prolific center of primitive art, the Papua Gulf area of New Guinea, natives created ornate memorial tablets (Figure 18). The carved wooden plaques, accented with color, were thought by the natives to possess supernatural powers. When placed adjacent to the skulls of dead enemies, the tablets acted to protect the living from the evil spirits of their former adversaries. A boldness of concept is prevalent in the art of that region; it results from the skillful combination of stylized human forms and geometric shapes that create dramatic patterns. Natural materials, such as sharp sea shells that serve as carving tools and the tough, rough skin of sting rays that act as sandpaper, were frequently employed by the natives of New Guinea when working with wood. Art served to fulfill their social and religious needs and added richness to the products of their society.

The Retelling of Heroic Endeavors

By passing down pictorial images, art comprises part of a nation's heritage. History may be captured to inspire future generations through recordings with brush and paint. Events such as the Battle of Princeton, which saved New Jersey for the American revolutionists, may again be perceived by man. The flutter of flags, the battle formations and tactics, the roaring muskets and rearing horses, and the living mingled with the dead can be readily imagined when viewing *Washington at Princeton* (Figure 19). The price of a nation's birth and the decline of empire are vividly portrayed in the benevolent painting by M. M. Sanford.

Art is truly a comprehensive language which relates the dreams and accomplishments, the activities, beliefs, and desires of humanity in inspirational, understandable, and universal terms.

From Paper to Steel: The Materials of Art

Creative potential is limited only by one's ability to conceive of possibilities in materials and processes. Paper, metal or stone, ink transferred from a copper plate or paint forced through a screen, these and all other materials and processes, contain both limitations and unique opportunities for expression.

When considering the suitability of a material for expressing an idea, both an experimental attitude and truth to the material are important factors. These notions tend to conflict and limit each other; frequently, they operate in opposition to each other. It is the responsibility of the individual to maintain a balance, based on personal sensitivity, between experimentation, investigating what can be achieved through unique means, and truth to material, which implies a consideration of the inherent richness and potential naturally obtainable within the material. Timidness prevents creative vitality, while stretching a material beyond its natural limits results in bedlam and artificiality.

Answers in art are dependent on a fusion of inquisitiveness and respect combined with feeling and knowledge. Paper may be drawn or painted upon, cut, torn, creased, folded, to express an idea (Figure 20). The possibilities in metal differ from those in stone. Metal, obtainable in sheets and rods, can identify form through linear means, thereby providing spaciousness, fluidity, and lightness as well as suggesting bulk through implied mass (Figure 21). Weight and immovability are apparent features of a block of stone. Monumentality, rigidity of mass, bulk, and a somewhat unyielding surface are natural characteristics to be both exploited and retained in stone (Figure 22). Man may even tell of ideas through an inscribed copper plate inked and pressed against paper. The expression is recorded through line and subtle and bold gradations of dark and light areas (Figure 23). Through different materials and processes, forcing paint through a silk screen results in a pattern of flat shapes and segments (Figure 24). Each material and process contains specific characteristics which offer rich and distinct results.

20　*Mask, Paper, Junior high school student, University High School, Iowa City, Iowa.*

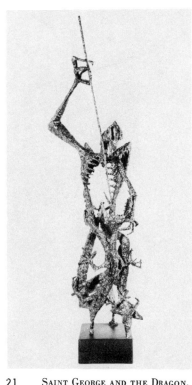

21　Saint George and the Dragon, *welded steel, Michael F. Andrews. (Courtesy the Artist)*

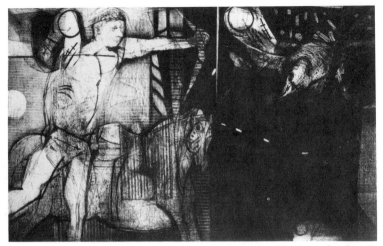

23   SAGITTARIUS, *intaglio print, Mauricio Lasansky. (Courtesy the Artist)*

THE GUARDIAN, *limestone carving, Leonard Baskin.
(Courtesy Grace Borgenicht Gallery Inc., New York,
N. Y.)*

22

24   SINGING AND MENDING, *silk screen print, Robert Gwathmey. (Courtesy
Addison Gallery, Phillips Academy, Andover, Mass.)*

25   Spring Thaw, *watercolor, Yar Chomicky. (Courtesy the Artist)*

Details and Features: The Structure of Art

The transparency and fluidity of the medium are fully realized in the watercolor painting by Yar Chomicky, *Spring Thaw* (Figure 25). The artist portrays the decline of winter through the exposure of earthen colors and symbols of trees, devoid of foliage, that appear anxiously to await rebirth. Keen and subtle segments complement one another and provide a tempo indicative of the coming season.

An extensive number of lines are apparent in the painting; they range from delicate lines representing tree branches to a thick sweeping line identifying the foreground. Many shapes are evident, such as the small dark areas in the foreground and the larger masses in the background. Texture, a sense of smoothness or roughness of surface, is implied in the active grouping of lines representing trees, the mutations of color, and the scattering of shapes in the foreground. The grain effect obtained through paint partially superimposed over paper in the foreground also suggests a roughness of surface. Attempt to visualize the light and dark values, white to black, as a color range and it becomes obvious that extensive contrasts occur. Notice how the small dark passage of color above the trees acts to extend interest as well as identify space.

The components which make up a work of art — line, shape, texture, value, and color — are termed elements of art. The activity of combining these elements into unified structures is a creative design process. The artist selects and arranges the elements, thereby designing what he considers to be the most effective form in which to express his ideas. Qualities such as rhythm, balance, harmony, emphasis, subordination, variation, and unity result from combining the elements into compositions. To draw a parallel with music, the element of "sound" gains a rhythm when it is repeated. The rhythm may emerge as unified or contrasting passages of sound with a rapid or tranquil movement, depending on time sequence. Similar relationships hold true for the visual arts, but rather than being organized in time, they are arranged in two- or three-dimensional space.

Rhythm, balance, harmony, emphasis, subordination, variation, and unity are contained in the painting *Spring Thaw*. Rhythm is suggested by the placement of lines and the action of dark and light values implying movement through sequence. Harmony, in kinship with unity, is evident in the similarity of shapes and values and the repetition of related lines and surfaces. Emphasis is found within areas which assume major importance, while subordination is of a reverse nature. Dark or large areas usually contain emphasis, while less evident areas act as subordination. Variation is obtained through contrast or placement. Unity can also result from placement or repetition.

Trees, Imagery Changes with Species, Time, and Point of View, photographs, University student.

26

Trees; Even an Insect

The elements of art and the qualities or principles of design are found in nature as well as in art. Consider trees for a moment (Figure 26). Line is found in branches, shape in limbs and leaves, and texture in smooth surfaces of leaves and also in rough bark. Value, light and dark, is apparent in the pattern of shadows. Color, while lacking in a black and white photograph, is obvious in trees, even changing with the seasons from lush green to golden brown. All the elements unite to comprise form. One may speak of the form of the tree and thereby imply the sum total of the parts. A shape divorced from form, such as a leaf from a tree, may also be considered form when viewed in its entirety. Components frequently possess all the elements of art, as witness a leaf. The linear veins provide texture and indicate shapes, and patterns of dark and light and color are readily visible.

The most inconsequential of subjects, even an insect, may achieve grandeur of form through a wise use of the elements of art and principles of design. Knowledge of natural form and the welding process, combined with imagination, enabled Cesar Baldaccini to create *Animale Organico* (Figure 27). The iron sculpture, an expressive distortion of conventional form, extends and deepens the spectator's awareness through its unusual treatment. Active segments of metal adjacent to subdued areas provide the

sculpture with vitality and impact. Strong interplays of texture and shadow within the three-dimensional form result in an active balance and unity. Examine the sculpture for insight relating to its use of line, shape, and texture. Do you notice qualities of rhythm and areas of emphasis and subordination? How would you express your idea of a fantastic creature?

The Importance of Personal Feelings and Personal Interpretations

A factual recording, merely imitation or a photographic-like copy, is not sufficient to be considered art, since the interpreter contributes nothing but an indication of patience and skill. A feeling, a mood, the reaction of the observer must be evident in a work of art. A creative act goes beyond rendering facts or formulas. Art lies beyond nature, science, and man-made laws, somewhere midway between mechanics and chaos. It represents the uncensored statement of its author, who must think, feel, and improvise for himself.

The paintings of John N. Colt are usually derived from an intimate contact with nature. His painting *Along a Path* (Figure 28) resulted from an invigorating journey comprising both actual and imaginative aspects. Noting unusual roots, leaves, twigs and blossoms, Colt, through rapid pencil sketches, captured impressions of these natural forms. Later he modified, fragmented, interchanged, and regrouped these images into an original pageantry suggestive of the fleeting moods and essence of nature. Relating to his method of creating paintings and their relationship with the realm of nature, Colt states that:

Ideas that evolve in my paintings are derived from a close observation of nature. I do not imitate nature but I am goaded by her multiple facets of structure, surprise, order, idea, repetition and variation.

To be spurred by nature's order is also to be acutely aware of the vast interrelatedness of her forms from microscopic organisms to structures cosmic in scope. From the embryo to decay. Leonardo da Vinci, in his notebooks, remarks of seeing great battles in rock formation and structure, even to the action of horses and expression in men's faces; and the same shapes and visual impressions restated in dry mud, embers, flames, and again in clouds. These similarities of structure never cease to be startling.

Nature is, for me, the source of richness and vitality; the painting in turn becomes a metaphor of nature.

The artist creates by taking a germ of an idea and playing with it—twisting it, reversing, multiplying, revising and reordering within the dictates of his media, but he is often rendered breathless by the inexhaustible groupings; the juxtapositions of nature, the master innovator.

Individuals most effectively treat that which touches their hearts and inspires visions in their minds. Art demands such an emotional involvement. John Ruskin, the nineteenth-century art philosopher, clarified this role of the emotions in art in contending that[1]

All the rules of aerial perspective that ever were written will not tell me how sharply the pines on the hill top are drawn at this moment. I shall know if I see them, and love them, not till then.

Ruskin's comment is most certainly true. For instance *Forest Traveler* (Figure 29) contains evidence of feeling and a lyrical freshness; for it represents what is known and probably loved. The drawing was created by a student living in a Pennsylvania town which is ringed by mountain ranges covered with green forests. These timber tracts house chirping squirrels, bear, graceful white-tail deer, turkey, grouse, and many other elusive creatures. With crayon and paper the student presents his impressions of wandering within a somber segment of these woods. One senses that the student reveals his reaction toward what is known and has been often experienced on his part.

[1] William Sloan Kennedy, *Art and Life—a Ruskin Anthology* (New York: John B. Alden, 1886), p. 294.

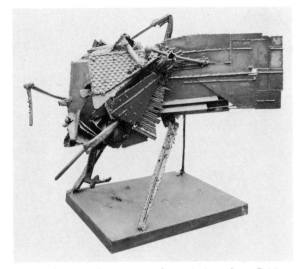

27   ANIMALE ORGANICO, *sculpture in iron, Cesar Baldaccini. (Courtesy Carnegie Institute, Pittsburgh, Pa.)*

28   ALONG A PATH, *oil painting, John N. Colt. (Courtesy the Artist)*

29   FOREST TRAVELER, *crayon drawing, student, Williamsport High School, Pa.*

30 SHOOTING FOR THE BASKET, *pencil drawing, student, Oak Park and River Forest High School, Ill.*

31 REARING STALLION, *sculpture in welded steel plates, Leo Steppat. (Courtesy the Artist)*

He flavored his presentment with a vigorous treatment of lines, shapes, and placements and handled his crayon in a personal and inventive manner.

Interest, desire, and a sense of participation are also clearly shown in the drawing *Shooting for the Basket* (Figure 30). Produced by another young student, it stresses joyful but intense involvement as a basketball game, through the art experience, is lived once again. The hopes and expectations of and the eagerness for a successful basket are vividly portrayed. Notice how the background treatment permits only a short recession in depth and provides a minimum of details. Thus, interest is focused on the players.

Leo Steppat, a contemporary sculptor, speaks of the importance of feeling or intensity of emotion to the artist when, in regard to his *Rearing Stallion* (Figure 31) he says:

Somebody might want to write a poem because he becomes strongly moved by some aspect of life. Inspiration may range from a flower or a day in spring to love, death or any of the emotions and concepts which stir the soul of mankind.

What applies to poetry applies also to all the other arts. Intensity of emotion is the first indispensable prerequisite for creativity. However, emotion is simply raw material, for properties of form will determine how much of a work of art the final product is. Creating as well as understanding of art depends on the presence of this awareness of artistry of form. This awareness can be developed best by looking at much art of all the ages and all the cultures of man, seeing helps much more than reading and philosophizing about art. To give comparison, one learns to appreciate fine foods by eating rather than by reading cookbooks.

With respect to my *Rearing Stallion*, I am not quite sure what induced me to make this sculpture. Maybe I was concerned with the simultaneity of finely knit grace and complete virility embodied in a stallion. In doing this piece, as in doing any other sculpture regardless of how realistic or how abstract it might be, I was continuously concerned with relating contours to volumes, curvatures to planes, lines to areas while trying to retain a constant awareness of the totality of shape and spirit of the work.

The artist's inventing, thinking and using of judgment is fundamentally different from the manner of thought which goes into solving an arithmetic problem. I would rather compare the artist's awareness of form with the athlete's awareness of how to use his body. I would also compare it to the kind of inventiveness and judgment which goes into cooking when one uses and tries ingredients and seasonings until the dish "tastes right."

As to my working in steel, I like that medium because of the great possibilities of design its resilience and strength permit.

TOPICS FOR CONSIDERATION

1. In the past, how did societies make extensive use of the arts?
2. Why does our modern civilization need art?
3. What are the purposes of art in a school program?
4. How does producing art cause one to think for oneself?
5. What does the term "creativity" imply?
6. Are there evidences of the use of art in your community?
7. What art elements and materials are used in painting, sculpture, and architecture?

SUGGESTED ACTIVITIES

1. Make as extensive a list as you can of activities from architecture and landscaping to costume design and window decorating which involves creative action.
2. Start a collection of photographs and articles relating to the arts. Excellent reproductions may be secured from issues of *Life*, *Time*, and a host of other magazines. Classify visual material as to area and keep in appropriate folders or scrapbook.
3. Visit your school and public library and become familiar with the available art publications, both periodicals and books.

APPROPRIATE REFERENCES AND READINGS

FAULKNER, ZIEGFELD, and HILL. *Art Today,* New York: Henry Holt & Co., Inc., 1956.

FLEMING, WILLIAM. *Arts and Ideas,* New York: Henry Holt & Co., Inc., 1956.

GOMBRICH, E. H. *Art and Illusion,* New York: Pantheon Books, Inc., 1960.

KUH, KATHERINE. *Art Has Many Faces, The Nature of Art Presented Visually,* New York: Harper & Brothers, 1951.

NEUTRA, RICHARD J. *Survival Through Design,* New York: Oxford University Press, 1954.

Praeger Picture Encyclopedia of Art, New York: Frederick A. Preager, Inc., 1958.

ROOS, FRANK J., JR. *An Illustrated Handbook of Art History,* New York: The Macmillan Co., 1954.

2 | DESIGN, THE ORGANIZATION OF THINGS

The beautiful rests on the foundations of the necessary.
RALPH WALDO EMERSON[1]

32   THE OLD KING, *oil painting, Georges Rouault. (Courtesy Carnegie Institute)*

[1] *A Modern Book of Esthetics,* edited by Melvin M. Rader (New York: Henry Holt & Co., Inc., 1935), p. 405.

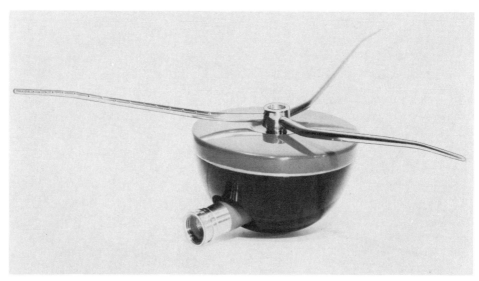

33   *Lawn Sprinkler, metal, Industrial-design student, University of Illionis. (Courtesy Professor Edward Zagorski, Department of Art, University of Illinois)*

Meanings and Implications

Design is a process of building by selecting the elements of the visual arts — line, value, color, and texture — and arranging them in unified two- or three-dimensional structures. It is basic to all creative activities, because it relates to organizational method in all areas of the arts. Sculptors, painters, architects, and all other creative individuals may be considered designers because of their concern in producing unified structures. A sculptor designs his forms through building, modeling, or carving. A painter, employing paint, brushes, and canvas, designs by combining colors and shapes into a composition in order to convey an attitude toward experience. The architect, working with wood, stone, metal, or similar material, creates structures suitable for dwellings.

The designer regulates elements in space to devise effective visual relationships. Problems in design may relate to an artist's endeavor to present an expressive and revealing pattern in lights and darks within a drawing or painting (Figure 32) to an industrial-design student's search for a pleasing and practical form for a lawn sprinkler (Figure 33). A high school student often designs when manipulating and organizing various materials to express an idea (Figure 34). The designer's efforts may range from producing a pleasing table to solving problems pertaining to city planning.

34   *Abstract Pattern, cut paper, student, Wisconsin High School, Madison, Wisc.*

35 *French Comfort Chair, indicative of a popular design practice of the latter portion of the 19th century.*

37 *Danish Chair, contemporary. (Courtesy the Danish Embassy)*

36 *New England Chair, early 18th century. (Courtesy United States Natural Museum, Division of Cultural History, Smithsonian Institution)*

Current Influences

Periods of history produce design images and products in part indicative of the attitudes and experiences held by their artists. The following influences, at times in contradiction to one another, tend to develop mid-twentieth-century attitudes and characteristics:

1. The nature of contemporary art, with emphasis on the importance of personal expression and experimentation.

2. Machine technology and the development of new materials and processes; resistance to the overemphasis on nonessentials relating to surfaces and organization of form; stress on control, logic, economy, and function.

3. Impact of revivals, interest in design notions and products of other nations, past and present. Current

interest in Scandinavian, Italian, classical, Victorian, and early American art forms.

4. The influence of organic and international architecture and the teaching approach developed by the German design school, the Bauhaus.

5. Desires for frequent design change in certain areas of industrial and commercial design to entice consumer purchase. Planned obsolescence, often artificial or trite modifications.

Consider Your Design Judgment

Good design is not dependent on applied decoration, but rather is concerned with common sense. As a simple test of your design judgment, refer to Figure 35 and consider the following questions:

1. Do patterns covering the chair demand undue attention? Are needless details in evidence?

2. Does the fringe function as a structural detail, or is it only a dust catcher?

3. Is applied decoration an assurance of beauty?

4. Does the chair suggest comfort and rest or activity?

5. Is the chair's form pleasing; does it possess interest and grace?

6. In order for the chair to complement and harmonize with its surroundings, what type of visual environment should be in evidence?

Taking into account the prime purpose of chairs as providing both visual and body comfort, compare the New England and Danish chairs (Figures 36 and 37). Consider simplicity of form, surface, construction, and compare practicality of manufacturing and ease of maintenance. What differences between these forms seem apparent?

It should not be thought, however, that only the present offers opportunity for observing sound practices in design, because many of the utilitarian forms produced in the past possess the attributes of good organization. The direct, simple solution evident in the plow (Figure 38) provided a form ideally suited, in time, for its intended purpose of piercing the earth to feed a nation. The Shaker Blanket Chest (Figure 39) provides visual impact through evidence of excellent craftsmanship and a direct use of wood that permits the natural grain to emerge and contribute interest. Both the plow and chest appear naturally suited for their intended purposes. Good design depends not on applied decoration or on frequent trite and incidental change, but rather on personal ingenuity and the wise use of material available to the age.

38   *Connecticut Plow, early 19th century. (Courtesy Department of Science and Technology, Smithsonian Institution)*

39   *Shaker Blanket Chest, pine, Canaan, N. Y., 1836. (Courtesy National Gallery of Art, Index of American Design)*

40   OWL, *stone carving, Archaic Greek. (Courtesy Art History Department, University of Wisconsin)*

42   OWL, *bronze sculpture, Pablo Picasso. (Courtesy Mrs. John D. Rockefeller, III)*

41   OWL, *plaster carving, Junior high school student, Wisconsin High School, Madison, Wisc.*

Good Design Is Ageless

Effective design solutions are limited neither to particular periods of history nor to specific levels of maturity. This contention can be illustrated by considering a common subject illustrated by three distinct design solutions (Figures 40 to 42). One form emerged twenty-five centuries before the other two. Another differs in being produced by a youth. The third is unique, in relationship with the others, as a production by a mature contemporary artist. The three forms, while differing in certain respects, share a common relationship of good design. All are fully realized expressions that are designed in direct forceful manners and function as excellent sculpture. Good design is ageless.

The term "universal," which implies "timelessness, suited to all purposes and conditions," may be applied to many designs of the past. Much art, ranging from great sculptural or architectural forms and paintings to pottery, functioned in its day and proves harmonious with current design standards. The Greek temple, Greek and Gothic carvings, pre-Columbian pottery, paintings of the Renaissance, Rembrandt's prints, all possess a universal quality through good design. Executed with the most effective means available to achieve intended purpose and strongly stamped by the personalities of the creators, such designs, achieved ages ago, stand as great statements. They join many contemporary forms, in a comprehensive field, representing the finest attainments of man.

Design Logic: Function in Nature and Objects Man Makes to Fly

To understand design, the terms "function," "simplicity," "directness," and "originality" must be considered; for they are prime requisites. These terms do not always operate independently; frequently, they depend upon each other for attainment. For example, a functional design is usually simple and direct as regards form, surface, structure, and organization, because function is concerned with proper employment of parts to obtain the direct fulfillment of desired purpose.

Function in nature is obvious, because all living organisms possess logical forms for explicit and intended purposes. Poorly designed forms—those unable to adapt—soon perish, for the laws of survival constantly function. However, great differences in shape, surface, and structure still exist in nature. Certain fish such as pike and barracuda are provided with slick, simple forms that offer little resistance to movement in water. These forms function; they are suitable for intended purpose. It can not be concluded, however, that simplicity or streamlining is essential to obtain functional forms. The sargassum fish, a voracious carnivore, possesses a complicated form covered with knobs, tassels, and ribbonlike parts (Figure 43). Its environment is the Sargasso Sea and reef areas of the Caribbean, which abound with floating patches of sargassum weeds. The function of its complicated form is to permit the fish to cling to and assume a form similar to that of the surrounding weeds in which it hunts its living prey. Thus, forms may be complicated or simple yet prove logical or functional depending upon needs and environment.

Natural organisms, in addition to their logical forms, possess structures which are functional. Consider the Ruffed Grouse (Figure 44). Its hollow bone structure and light feather surface provide a minimum of weight for ease in flight. Short, powerful

43   *Sargassum Fish. (Courtesy American Museum of Natural History)*

44   *Ruffed Grouse. (Courtesy Pennsylvania Game Commission)*

45   *Atlas Missile. (Courtesy U. S. Department of Defense)*

wings also provide great lift and thrust. Its surface pattern also proves to be functional; for the grouse is provided with a somber plumage of white and brown barred and speckled with black. This natural camouflage enables the bird to blend with its environment for protective purposes. Strong, stubby legs assist the grouse in rapidly leaping into flight and, combined with compact body and short powerful wings, enable rapid movement in the bird's forest environment. Even design modifications due to climatic change occur in the grouse. As winter approaches, with its threat of deep snows, feathers in abundance begin to appear on the bird's legs and a few appear within its claws. Why? They function or serve as natural snowshoes that enable the grouse to scamper across the white crust of winter. With the advent of spring, many of the leg feathers, no longer essential, flutter to the forest floor.

An endless variety of design solutions, obvious in nature, illustrate the complete attainment of functional design in organic forms. Can you think of several?

Man-made shapes and forms also prove functional when their intended purpose is fully realized (Figure 45). Jet aircraft and rockets are functional; for nonessentials have been eliminated and all portions separately and combined fulfill essential purposes. In machine-made products, design should be in harmony with manufacturing processes and should take advantage of machine precision and capabilities.

Authorities have stated that good design within our machine age should grow out of the machine, the results being determined by what machine tools and processes can naturally provide. However, many products, for example, in aircraft and rocket manufacture, require the building of new machines and new production methods before the designs can be fully realized through manufacture. Thus, particular designs may determine the subsequent designing of new machines or may be produced by existing methods. Whichever the case, machine technology and procedure influence the form. Lewis Mumford's statement[2] sums it up quite well:

> The elegance of a mathematical equation, the inevitability of a series of physical inter-relationships, the naked quality of the material itself, the tight logic of the whole — these are the ingredients that go into the design of machines, and they go equally in products that have been properly designed for machine production.

[2] *Ibid.*, p. 413.

Tools, Cans, and Shelter

The soldering iron (Figure 46) indicates how an industrial-design student has solved the problem of providing functional elements in a tool. The pronged base provides security in a practical manner; the plastic handle provides ease of grasp and cleaning. The point of the tool is located a sufficient distance from the handle to protect it from heat. The sloping curve of the neck permits the tip to be easily seen and handled while holding the tool. Each element functions, and the visual effects are pleasing. Beauty of form grows out of the practical.

Rounded corners of the Reynolds aluminum containers (Figure 47) provide ease of contents removal. The direct, simple advertising on the face of the container possesses unity in its relation to the container's form and impact through contrast and variation.

The house designed by Herb Fritz (Figure 48) exposes its basic structure and stresses the natural quality of wood, glass, and concrete for visual enrichment. The warm tones and grain pattern of wood, the slickness and transparency of glass, and the solidity of concrete block are related through harmonious proportions which contribute naturalism and appropriateness to the structure. Exposed beams, the interplay of interior and exterior space, and simplified constructional methods also provide a logical directness to the design. All segments are essential and related; they culminate in a practical form which functions as inspirational shelter. Good design is secured through the elimination of nonessentials. Lasting interest is gained not through applied decoration, but rather through inspiring construction methods and the wise use of materials.

Function in Art

Function or purpose varies within the arts. For instance, it is obvious that the purpose of architecture — to provide pleasing, logical dwellings — is different than the purpose of painting. The role of a poster also differs from the role of a table as regards purpose and use. When an understanding of the purpose of an art is possessed, one can judge its design in terms of functioning in a suitable manner. The effectiveness of the artist in stating his idea, meeting the needs of the problem, and eliminating the superficial are means of evaluating his design.

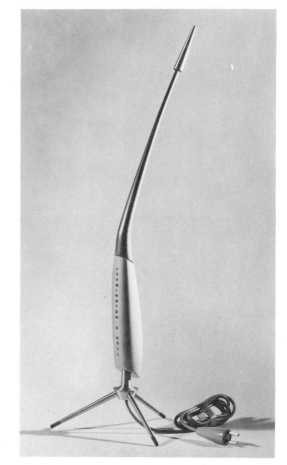

46 *Soldering Iron, Industrial-design student, University of Illinois. (Courtesy Professor Edward Zagorski, Department of Art, University of Illinois)*

47 *Storage Units. (Courtesy Reynolds Metals Company)*

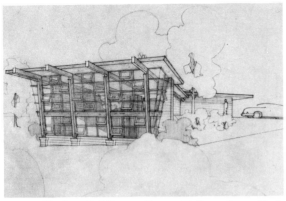

48   *Charles Hiedelberger House, Madison, Wisc., Herb Fritz. (Courtesy the Architect)*

49   THE PEACEABLE KINGDOM, *oil painting, Edward Hicks, 1830. (Courtesy New York State Historical Association)*

50   *Ceramic Pottery Forms.*

The function of drawing, graphics, sculpture, and painting is to provide the means of visually commenting on one's attitude and feelings regarding experiences or environment. The expression of the self — personal interpretation — is the main purpose of these arts. Notice the whimsical charm and the direct and personal expression in Edward Hicks' painting *The Peaceable Kingdom* (Figure 49). Hicks' desire was to convey a dream or wish regarding a new land which unfolded westward from America's eastern seaboard. Hicks employed personal ingenuity in arranging and rearranging shapes and colors in order to comment about his imaginary world in which love and understanding were supreme. In the arts, originality, the mark of the doer, must be in evidence.

Naturally, all functional designs and man-made products cannot be considered works of art. Even within one particular activity, purpose may vary between producing utilitarian products and producing creative works. Contemporary pottery illustrates this fact in an obvious manner. Pottery may meet basic needs by providing roof or floor tile or simple containers for manufactured goods such as jelly and jam. Such products are functional and utilitarian; they meet the obligations of intended use in a precise manner. Identical forms are produced endlessly; the human element is controlled, expression is restricted, yet purpose is fulfilled. While the design of these forms may be excellent and functional, such qualities are not the main ingredients of art. Pottery functions as an art area only when the potter's concern is in the discovering of new shape and surface possibilities in the designing of personal forms in clay. Only then can pottery be considered an art form.

Figure 50 illustrates that in relationship to a basic cylindrical clay form numerous modifications are obtainable. Design possibilities are unlimited, far beyond what a photograph may imply. It is conceivable that as many designs could exist as there are individuals engaged in creating such forms; for no two individuals would design identical forms. This is not to imply that all such forms would necessarily be well designed; many possibly would appear clumsy or poor in proportion, lack consistency between form and surface glaze, or indicate poor craftsmanship. However, the design possibilities for producing well-designed objects would be unlimited, provided sensitivity toward material and proportion and skill in execution were apparent.

Originality in Design: The Emergence of Self

The American Romantic, Henry David Thoreau[3] once said,

> If a man does not keep in pace with his companions, perhaps it is because he hears a different drummer. Let him step to the music which he hears, however measured or far away.

In our present age, with rapidly expanding cities resulting in complex traffic and housing problems, with growing technology, group pressures, the impact of scientific method, and mass media forming unified tastes, the visual arts — whether pottery or architecture, crafts, or graphics — serve as a bulwark, a refuge, for individuality. The arts may be considered the Walden Ponds of our century, where man can find unique solutions and freedom within himself. Each profession in its own way adds to man's movement from the shadows of ignorance to a proper plateau beneath the sun. The artist-designer is concerned with the design practicality and beauty of that plateau.

The following comments by artists with reference to their creations provide insight regarding their attitudes toward design.

TWO WAYS IN CLAY AND BRONZE AND MARBLE

To me, pottery is a three dimensional form using clay as its medium and pottery making is merely an expression of the potter's sensitivity toward this very medium. As a designer-craftsman, I feel that a realization of the limitations of the material is of prime importance. Equally important is an awareness of the "fitness" of the design. That is, the design should fit the purpose of the work — be it utilitarian or purely decorative. In the matter of form, I strongly believe that a good form in pottery should have rhythm and movement. In other words, it must give a feeling of continuous growth. Another vital element of good form is unity. By unity, I mean simply the harmonious relations of the various parts within the created form. In short, a good form is a fully realized expression of rhythm, movement and unity. (Figure 51)

HENRY H. LIN

In their wheel origin, experimental pots such as this retain some of the humility of simple more direct vases, bottles, jars and bowls. I value the plastic nature of clay, the quality of fingers feeling,

51   *Stoneware Bottle, clay, Henry H. Lin. (Courtesy the Artist)*

[3] *Walden and Selected Essays* (Chicago: Packard & Co., 1947), p. 295.

52   *Experimental Pot, clay, Kenneth
R. Beittel. (Courtesy the Artist)*

53   Animal Amphora, *bronze and mosaic pot, Marjorie
E. Kreilick. (Courtesy the Artist)*

thinking and drawing in motion around a volume
of air as the live wall spins between them. Pressure
marks and even smudges are left so that any
decisiveness arises with authority from the wet clay.
Here the working process was synthetic. Several
pieces were thrown and set together according to
idea and trial and error. I originally made a smaller
spouted bottle much like the top section of this one
and from it got the idea of raising a similar form up
into the air much like the hand on the end of an
upraised arm. There was a definite feeling of
gesture intended. I hoped it would also have the
organic sense of growth and simple grace that seed
pods and terminal buds possess, but only in a symbolic, not an imitative way. The pot was thrown of
clay dug locally. It was left unglazed on the outside.
Areas of the surface were decorated with a slip
made from a white clay found nearby into which
was introduced a large quantity of iron-bearing
sand. It was fired in open flame in a home-made
kiln. Thus was completed a process which hoped to
unite simply, directly and permanently, in unpredictable ways, a product of earth, water and fire.
(Figure 52)

KENNETH A. BEITTEL

In building, I often begin with no preconceived
problem but proceed with the desire of coaxing to
the consciousness a still vague form-idea. Control
and order then solidify the concept. Sometimes I
begin with a subject to solve a sculptural problem.
This process is more than a technical exercise and
unexplainable jumps in the process of thought are
interwoven with deliberate imagination.

My intention was for this animal amphora to be
a proud pot. Equally natural and noble in profile,
the form has an animal's bulkiness and body-
waddle. The carriage of the neck terminates in the
impertinent beak of a spout. From the internal
workings of the pot the marble inlay rises to reveal
an emotional calligraphy. Marble and bronze unite
in inlay to form a stronger expression than is possible with shallow surface decoration. (Figure 53)

MARJORIE KREILICK

A CENTER FOR WORSHIP

An architect speaks of his church design and problems relating to its form (Figures 54 to 56):

A church to seat 1,000 takes about 10,000 square
feet of floor area. The early design for a nave type
Church would have been a form 50 feet wide and
200 feet long with 500 lineal feet of outside wall.
A cruciform plan church with an altar at the center
(similar to St. Peter's in Rome) would have had the
same length of exterior to house 1,000. Two other
forms were also considered, a square 100 feet on
the side of 400 feet lineal of outside wall or a circle
113 feet in diameter and 355 feet in circumference.
The circle was immediately discarded because of
site restrictions. However, a modified square in the
form of a fan seemed a desirable approach. This

54

Interior, Queen of Peace Roman Catholic Church, Madison, Wisc., Joseph J. Weiler. (Courtesy the Architect, photographed by William Wollin Studio, Madison, Wisc.)

Southern View, Exterior, Queen of Peace Roman Catholic Church. (Photographed by William Wollin Studio, Madison, Wisc.)

55

56

Eastern View, Exterior, Queen of Peace Roman Catholic Church. (Photographed by William Wollin Studio, Madison, Wisc.)

57

plan required 420 lineal feet of wall to surround the 10,000 square feet of floor area. Three complete designs were made for this project, namely, nave plan, cruciform and fan. Later models were made for the latter two. When presented to the parish, the fan approach was chosen, not only for its obvious economies in construction, but because seating would be close to the altar, giving a feeling of nearness to the religious service.

In placing the fan shaped church on the lot it was decided to face the structure south, for the reason that the sun would help remove most of the ice and snow in the winter. Also, the building would be more accessible to a parking lot. Parking along an existing road with fast moving traffic to the north would be undesirable.

The roof of the sanctuary is raised above the general roof area in order to admit direct sunlight to the sanctuary during the winter months. The overhang of the roof of the sanctuary is so designed to eliminate direct sunlight during the hot summer months.

Two large windows at the south admit natural light but are shaded with a long overhung roof. This overhang likewise shelters two ramps from the driveway at the south leading to the church auditorium, thus eliminating the customary high steps which prove difficult at funeral services and are hazardous to elderly people and invalids.

A large tower is provided at the south elevation. This tower of two-inch stone slabs supported by a structural steel frame is crowned with a stainless steel cross which is visible for miles. In front of the tower is a small formal garden. The church building is of reinforced concrete and steel up to and including the ground floor. The roof construction

is of laminated wood arches. The shape of the church dictated the use of tripod construction, where the thrust of each pair of arches is balanced by one large center arch. All arches are tied together by steel beams which support the first floor, thus giving an unusually stable building.

The walls of the church are brick inside and out. Smooth stone trim is used on the exterior and the edges of the roof construction are trimmed with aluminum. Windows are of plate and stained glass and the roof is of light colored shingles. Natural finish is on all wood construction and the interior trim is of aluminum. Doors and frames throughout are also aluminum with the view to low maintenance.

JOSEPH J. WEILER

METAL AND WOOD

A designer of contemporary jewelry (Figure 57) states:

Design in art is similar to good composition in English, whereby the individual removes all words and punctuation which distract from what he is wishing to communicate. In designing the artist also removes all forms, textures, lines and spaces which would confuse or destroy his desired expression.

Jewelry being small and usually seen at a glance creates a particular problem for the designer. He must keep the piece clean by limiting the number of forms, lines and textures used; clear by developing good definite forms, utilizing the textures, colors, and properties of the media; and technically proficient so as not to destroy the directness of the desired expression.

IRV KINNEY

A DIRECT COMMUNICATION

Regarding the design of his Container Corporation of America advertisement (Figure 58) an artist contends that:

Obviously, Jane Addams seemed to be preoccupied with the four races living in our world: The White, Black, Yellow and Red. The important objective was to symbolize these men, and in such a way that would clearly show their willingness to "hold together."

Naturally, these four elements had to be human, nonabstract symbols of men. Therefore the hands, each one being held by another hand and each one holding a hand, forming an indestructible pattern of strength, convincing but not brutal. I was careful to follow the purely human approach: I did that, I believe, by ways of strong, yet gentle action in the design itself and by using powerful but not primitive colors.

The task of the designer is to translate thoughts and words into pictures. For instantaneous communication in advertising design, the process of subtraction and elimination is of primary importance.

Strengthening a layout means shaking out superfluous material that creates complications and causes delays in message communication.

GEORGE GIUSTI

58   Advertisement, George Giusti. (Courtesy Container Corporation of America)

TO PLACE ON A TABLE

Problems pertaining to design and industry are discussed by an artist who produces silverware forms (Figure 59) for mass production.

The industrial designer is confronted with many problems in designing a contemporary sterling silver flatware pattern. For hundreds of years, artisans and craftsmen have designed and executed unbelievingly beautiful flatware designs in silver. On this tradition, and using one of man's most cherished metals, the industrial designer must create a design to be manufactured by modern machines for a mass market. The designer must be aware of the properties and limitations of the metal and must be familiar with the various machines and processes used to manufacture the product. While the design is being conceived, the designer must continuously be aware of the total visual aspect of the design, and perhaps most importantly, the form itself. The design with its form and decoration, if used, must present a total concept. The individual pieces must be considered from the human-engineering aspect as well. They must fulfill their function and be pleasing to see and to hold. In the *Stardust* design there are light decorative incised stars, from whence the design gets its name. The application of a basic geometric motif to a well-balanced form produces a contemporary, and aesthetically pleasing design.

RICHARD L. HUGGINS

59   Silverware, Richard L. Huggins. (Courtesy Gorham Company)

60 *Birch Desk, James A. Schinneller.*

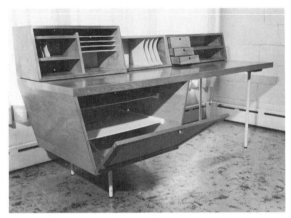

61 *Storage Facilities in Birch Desk, James A. Schinneller.*

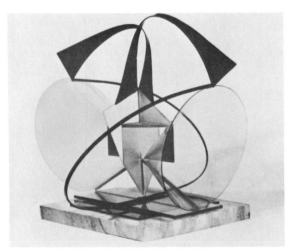

62 CONSTRUCTION IN SPACE, *Plexiglas, Naum Gabo, 1928. (Courtesy Philadelphia Museum of Art)*

FOR STORAGE AND WORK

Figures 60 and 61, which illustrate a desk produced by the author, indicate certain personal design solutions. A large desk, without apparent bulk, containing an extensive work surface and storage area was desired. The over-all form consists of a main section which supports interchangeable storage units upon its top surface. Massiveness, without bulk or suggesting great weight, was gained by employing diagonals, similar proportions, birch of a light value, and the subordination of legs.

Unity was gained by birch repeated in all units, the use of similar surfaces on the sliding doors, and the repetition of diagonals in creating form. The slope of the sides of the large lower storage unit is restated in the fronts of the upper units. The sloping of the upper units provides a sense of additional work surface. White painted surfaces on legs, partitions, and shelving also tend to unify the form. Contrast or variation is obvious in differences in shapes and sizes of the various units and the dark surfaces of the sliding doors.

The bottom compartment, with wide uncomplicated shelving, permits the housing of large papers, illustrations, and miscellaneous flatware which an individual interested in the arts often stores. The semirough cloth-surfaced storage doors add a difference in texture to complement the adjacent semigloss wood surfaces. The upper-right unit contains compartments for envelopes and stationary and shelving for correspondence, pamphlets, and related materials. The center unit functions as a general storage area for work underway. Books, pamphlets, and notes can easily be stacked or cubbyholed for immediate reference. Drawers for pencils, pens, brushes, inks, tape, scissors, and incidentals are located in the unit to the far right; adjacent to the drawers are additional storage areas, the bottom one for printed matter and the top one for small, three-dimensional supplies.

Where Solutions Are Found

The artist-designer may derive design ideas from numerous sources. Observation of man-made products or organic matter often provides ideas. Insight may also result from experimentation with material or from the development of new materials and manufacturing processes. A design notion, while obtainable from a single influence, usually is achieved by combining sources. For example, a designer may secure ideas from nature and contemporary art or art of the past, experiment with materials and tools, employ a traditional or contemporary process, and thereby have a design emerge from a fusion of sources.

The following areas are intended not to rigidly categorize or erect artificial barriers, but rather to indicate sources which germinate design ideas.

Expression through experimentation
Experimentation: the Bauhaus approach
The development of new materials and processes
Nature
Art of the past
For clarity, each source will be discussed separately.

Experimentation: It Always Seemed To Be

Artists have experimented, in order to secure good designs, throughout the history of art. The creative process implies experimentation, the discovery of new possibilities through the manipulation of the elements, media, and materials of art. The Renaissance, an age of discovery, found painters deeply concerned with investigations and experiments with line to develop lienar perspective, with value to imply solidity, and with paint washes to further glazing techniques.

Century followed century, and artists continued their search for new methods in expression. Rembrandt experimented with darks and lights to define form, and a host of others searched for solutions to particular problems relating to design in composition.

John Constable and Joseph Turner, Englishmen of the past century, experimented with the plasticity of paint and the effects obtainable through the fusion of colors. A fellow countryman, Joseph Paxton, produced a Great Crystal Palace through experiments with glass and iron. Several years later the French Impressionists investigated natural light and experimented with color in order to suggest the vitality of light in nature. French sculptors such as Auguste Rodin experimented with distortions in form in order to provide vitality to their three-dimensional designs. Within our country Louis Sullivan conducted experiments with new building materials and construction methods.

Unique Explorations of Our Century

The present century finds artists continuing the search for new methods of interpreting and presenting experiences through highly inventive and personal means. Recently developed as well as traditional materials are explored, and new attitudes regarding design are constantly emerging. Man now speaks of painting with colored lights, sculpture that moves, and houses of plastic as creative thinkers extend the frontiers of design possibilities. Unusual concepts regarding organization, space, movement, and technique are born. A consideration of several twentieth-century artists reveals that our age is a period of personal inventiveness.

INVESTIGATIONS WITH SPACE

Naum Gabo, born in Russia in 1890, and later residing in the United States, was one of the founders of Constructivism. The movement, which emerged in 1913, stressed three-dimensional organizations of metals, plastics, glass, and wire arranged in abstract manners (Figure 62). These experimental exercises identified space without the sense of weight and solidity of traditional sculpture. Gabo, through previous study in physics and mathematics, frequently implied relationships between his constructions and science. He contended his work was shaped as an engineer forms a bridge or a scientist plots a planetary orbit. Employing such terms as "dynamic rhythm" and "kinetic movement," he produced designs which treated space in active and unique manners. His space constructions, in emphasizing the transparency of materials and defining space through suggestion as well as enclosure, have formulated attitudes and suggested experiences to many designers. Gabo's constructions led to additional investigations in the identification of space by the Bauhaus and other schools which followed. The findings of such ventures influenced sculpture and theater and furniture design, especially in Germany and Russia and later in the United States, by an emphasis on economical means and new materials arranged to provide direct communication or meet intended need.

63   MERZ KONSTRUCTION, *painted wood, wire, and paper,
Kurt Schwitters, 1921. (Courtesy Philadelphia
Museum of Art)*

EXPRESSION WITH SCRAP MATERIALS

No longer need design be limited to a hierarchy of materials in which marble, for example, had more value than wood or wire. What began as protest was channeled into a logical stream.

Kurt Schwitters, 1887–1948, a German artist, was an active member of the Dada movement in art. His designs indicate that art can be composed of most anything if organized in a personal and interesting manner. Schwitters searched for common and frequently valueless elements, such as scraps of wood, wire, and twine and bits of glass and paper, and transformed his findings into unified designs. Unusual relationships of texture and shape and passages of subtle and bold colors and values combine to form his relief *Merz Konstruction* (Figure 63). Odds and ends selected by observant eyes and arranged with sensitive hands can communicate with authority.

The Dada movement, founded in 1916 and lasting less than a decade, was originally established as a complete rebellion against intellectualism and logic in art and life. Novelty, and often nonsense, was stressed to compensate for man's disillusionment with society. What was the condition in Europe which would stimulate such attitudes? Dada emerged at a period in history when millions of men were deep in combat. Thousands, aboard ships of steel, patrolled the seas or perished off the Jutland Banks. Stretching from the North Sea far inland, trenches housing men, both living and dead, deep in the earth, patterned the landscape. Battles such as Tannenberg and Verdun were vivid memories; ruined cathedrals and hungry children were realities. If man, through benefiting from centuries of an intellectual background, reaped such rewards, it was apparent that no worse could come through a complete denial of logic and tradition. Pure experimentation flourished during the Dada era, with efforts directed toward a deliberate ignoring of reason. The Dada artist searched for the unusual which would divorce him from traditional art and his time in history. Through his efforts he discovered new ideas regarding both materials and organization and formed a segment of this century's design tradition. Art can be most anything if done in a certain way.

DESIGN THROUGH CHANCE

Hans Arp, French painter, sculptor, and poet believes that reason has separated man from nature. One of the founders of the Dada movement, he influences many who are currently active in the arts. He stresses an irrational, antiscientific approach based on intuition or unpreconceived means. Breaking radically with the believers in organizing through established and accepted rules and procedures, Arp provided a new insight hitherto denied by intellectual inhibitions. His design approach is of utmost simplicity; frequently, it is completely dependent upon chance; yet to contend it is unnatural or superficial would be foolish. His means are as natural as the arrangement of pebbles organized by tides, the outcropping of rock on a hillside, or wild flowers emerging from seeds randomly deposited by the winds.

Many of Arp's designs, such as *Objects Arranged According to the Law of Chance or Navels* (Figure 64), result from a random scattering of material without deliberation. The relief possesses a purity of form and a crisp monumental quality. As the title implies, the method of designing is adventurous and tends to offer unique possibilities. Frequently Arp drops, without thought, objects upon a surface and permits the haphazard result to determine arrangement. Cut and torn paper are often used by the artist, who releases the material several feet above a horizontal background and permits the papers to flutter down and automatically acquire interesting relationships upon the background. Lucid and exciting results are achieved through pure discovery and a direct approach in organization.

Hans Arp is strongly inspired by natural substances and gains insight into shapes by observing uncomplicated organic matter such as eggs, leaves, and clouds. The term "biomorphic," living form and structure, can be applied to many of his forms. His unique inventiveness tends to liberate many designers from restrictive practices devoid of potential. Arp has influenced many artists in areas such as advertising, painting, and sculpture; he offers an element of excitement to all who are concerned with design practices.

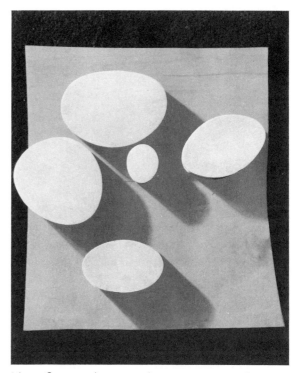

64   OBJECTS ARRANGED ACCORDING TO THE LAW OF CHANCE OR NAVELS, *varnished wood relief, Hans Arp, 1930. (Courtesy Museum of Modern Art)*

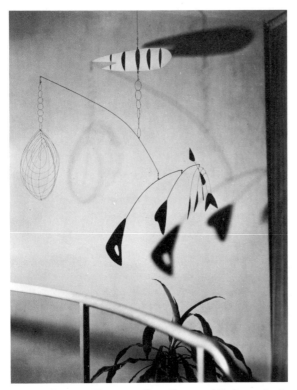

65 LOBSTER TRAP AND FISH TAIL, *mobile in steel wire and sheet aluminum, Alexander Calder, 1939. (Courtesy Museum of Modern Art)*

SCULPTURE THAT MOVES

I want to make things that are fun to look at. . . .

So says Alexander Calder[4], the creator of mobiles:

Have you ever watched branches and leaves flutter and dance in the wind or a bird soar high overhead? Would it be possible to design forms which, through suspension in space, create exciting movements of color and pattern? The American Alexander Calder thought so and, by combining the skill of an engineer and the sensitivity of an artist, discovered new possibilities for design (Figure 65). His mobiles, playful sculptures that move, provide motion to a traditionally static art. Mobiles are usually constructed of sensitive wire, prone to the slightest pressure, and brightly painted light materials that are responsive to circulating currents of air. The perfectly balanced form, highly susceptible to movement, produces changing patterns composed of poetic arrangements of shapes in space.

Calder's design approach is relatively uncomplicated. He cuts simple shapes from thin aluminum, discarding some, retaining others, until numerous shapes are available for selection. He then seeks various possibilities for organization by arranging the segments on a table. Upon achieving a pleasing relationship, he attaches the shapes to wire, suspends

[4] Selden Rodman, *Conversations with Artists* (New York: The Devin-Adair Co., 1957), p. 140.

66   CONVERGENCE, *oil painting, Jackson Pollock, 1952. (Courtesy Albright Art Gallery, Buffalo, N. Y.)*

them in space, paints them gay colors or black or white. Calder[5] contends,

> I know pretty well what will happen but it's all "cut and try" and sometimes they surprise me.

Mobiles offer opportunities to enrich overhead space conventionally viewed as devoid of possibilities. They extend a creative challenge to treat space with accents of shapes and colors, which, through movement, present interesting and ever-changing designs overhead.

AWAY WITH THE BRUSH

Inquisitiveness and a willingness to try, to venture toward the unusual, are mandatory for the designer. By dripping paint from sticks and pouring from cans, the American painter Jackson Pollock devised an experimental approach which assured new design results (Figure 66). His novel means of applying paint to surfaces eliminated the traditional method of brush application and conveyed a sense of spontaneity and freedom difficult or impossible to obtain through brush use. His active designs, composed of swirling linear patterns, extend an invigorating means of producing surfaces through a semicontrolled technique. Pollock's pulsating style has influenced designs in advertising and textiles as well as painting. His experimental approach encourages a more flexible attitude on the part of the timid.

[5] *Look Magazine*, Vol. XXII, No. 25 (Des Moines: Cowles Publishing Co., Dec. 9, 1958), p. 56.

THE BAUHAUS, AN ORGANIZED APPROACH TO EXPERIMENTATION

It is obvious that the process of experimentation is not unique to our century; however, a certain attitude toward its value and an approach toward developing it within a school program is most certainly a twentieth-century product. The first artists to develop an influential and contemporary system relating to design experimentation were the founders and teachers of the Bauhaus. It remained for this school to clarify the role of experimentation as a means for acquiring design experience and also to provide practical steps for the training of creative designers for this century.

The Bauhaus was a German school of design originally established in Weimar, Germany, in 1919, and later moved to Dessau, Germany, in 1925. In 1933 it was disbanded. Many of its teachers later moved to the United States and introduced its principles into the schools of America. For example, Walter Gropius, the founder, became associated with the School of Architecture at Harvard University and L. Moholy-Nagy established an institute of design in Chicago.

The Bauhaus resulted from the combining of an existing art academy with an arts and crafts school. Its intent was to serve as a consulting art center for industry and the trades and to produce artist-craftsmen. Architecture, sculpture, pottery, metal work, stained glass, furniture, textiles, typography, advertising layout, mural painting, and stage design were offered as areas for concentration. All students, no matter what their future specialties, were required to take the same primary courses in the first year.

Thus future architects, painters, sculptors, and industrial designers received identical design foundations in a preliminary course which stressed pure experimentation.

The Bauhaus, staffed by many of the great artists of Europe, proved unique in its attitude toward teaching design. A classical attitude owing allegiance to previous findings prevailed in other schools throughout the world, with instructors and students of design strongly dependent on the notions advanced by experimenters of long ago. In no other school were students encouraged to create on such a scale, instead of repeating designs previously produced. In the Bauhaus, technique was acquired as needed and a freedom of approach was evident. Self-confidence was stressed as an important factor, and an experimental attitude was encouraged.

The Bauhaus developed a systematic approach toward experimentation which can be illustrated by considering the Preliminary Design Course in the school's curriculum. In 1926, an instructor of the course, Joseph Albers[6], indicated its procedure and aim:

> The ability to construct inventively and to learn through observation is developed — at least in the beginning — by undisturbed, uninfluenced and unprejudiced experiment, in other words, by a free handling of materials without practical aims.
>
> To experiment is at first more valuable than to produce; free play in the beginning develops courage. Therefore we do not begin with a theoretical introduction; we start direct with the material.
>
> . . . .
>
> As the course advances the possibilities in the use of various materials as well as their limitations are gradually discovered. . . . Our aim is not so much to work differently as to work without copying or repeating others.

The materials used for experimental purposes in the Preliminary Design Course were sheets of paper, cardboard, corrugated paper, wire, screen, tin, glass, wood, match boxes, phonograph needles, and other miscellaneous materials. The experimental projects often dealt with building collages and various paper, wood, plaster, tin, or wire structures. The aims of such activities were to become acquainted with the properties and building potentials of materials, increase one's sensitivity to form, color, texture, and space relationship, and develop the power to invent. Designs possessing qualities of economy and simplicity grew from the potentials in materials and the

creativeness of the producer. A folded-paper experiment illustrates one example of a student project within the Bauhaus. The purpose of this undertaking was to provide insight into the properties of flexibility and rigidity possessed by paper. Sheets of paper were folded until an intricate form capable of bearing great weight resulted. A heavy book, for example, could be supported by this paper form. Not only would an awareness of the strength and structural potential of paper result, but the undertaking would have additional benefits. Students would have gained an awareness of the logic of economy and the importance of ingenuity. These attributes could, therefore, influence future endeavors in any material.

Students and Their Work

Countless private art schools, elementary and secondary art programs, and college and university art departments employ design practices which have their source in the Bauhaus. The impact of the German school is obvious in most any design curriculum with a stress on discovery through the manipulation of materials. Paper and wire constructions, collages, hand sculptures, and related activities link our schools with that first contemporary design school across the sea.

Currently in America student design experiments range from cut and torn paper to collages, space dividers, and hand sculpture. While they could be considered ends in themselves, their main purpose is to develop an awareness of design principles. Sensitivity toward form, texture, and space relationships and methods of organizing qualities of unity and variation within structures are objectives to be achieved within these design projects. Emphasis is placed on learning through experimentation and the value of self-discovery.

An explanation of the nature and purpose of the following projects will illustrate intent.

Figures 67 and 68, Twisted and Folded Paper and Cut Paper Design, are projects dealing with form investigation. The first project is concerned with the construction of a three-dimensional form by cutting and manipulation. The structure is built by overlaps and interlocking cut joints which are not dependent on adhesives, clips, or pins. An awareness of the flexibility and structural possibilities of a material is a prime goal. Figure 68 deals with two-dimensional paper organization with both positive space and negative or unoccupied space contributing interest and defining form. A feeling of unity is suggested by shape and color repeat. The long strands of paper, acting as lines also tend to unite. Contrast or varia-

[6] *Bauhaus*, edited by Herbert Bayer (New York: The Museum of Modern Art, 1958), p. 116.

Twisted and Folded Paper, student experiment, West High School, Madison, Wisc.

67

tion is acquired through placement and value differences, while movement and rhythm are gained through repetition and the flowing quality of the cut paper shapes.

Figure 69 is a collage, an arrangement of three-dimensional materials possessing various surface qualities. Miscellaneous materials are organized on a two-dimensional surface in collage undertakings, with the objective being the creation of an interesting pattern. Such a design activity develops familiarity with organizational and surface potentials. Rough, semismooth, slick, opaque, translucent, and transparent materials are usually used, and the result, frequently nonobjective, possesses a complete abstract design. The term "collage" is also applied to a process which combines painted surfaces and miscellaneous material. Cubist and Dada painters, during the first quarter of this century, often pasted pieces of paper, newspaper, photographs, or other textured and figured material within portions of their paintings.

Figure 70, Space Divider, deals with the arrangement of three-dimensional relationships in space. Simplicity of construction, the placement of shapes resulting in interesting space relationships, and qualities of unity and variation are goals. Note how unity is suggested by the repetition of similar shapes and variation is secured through space relationships and size contrasts. Can you see additional evidences of unity and variation in the Space Divider?

Have you ever handled a rock, a golf club, or a bow which naturally seemed to relate to or fit into the hand? Hand sculptures (Figure 71) are designed to properly adjust to the grip of the fingers and palm when handled. They are usually constructed from wood or plaster. The term "feelies" is also used to describe these sculptural explorations.

68 *Cut Paper Design, student experiment, West High School, Madison, Wisc.*

69 *Collage, student exploration, West High Schoool, Madison, Wisc.*

70 *Space Divider, student experiment, West High School, Madison, Wisc.*

Hand Sculpture, student exploration, University of Illinois.

71

A YACHT CLUB FOR LAKE MINNETONKA

AN UNDERGRADUATE THESIS
SUBMITTED BY
WILLIAM L. GUERIN
UNIVERSITY OF MINNESOTA
FALL QUARTER, 1957

72 A Yacht Club for Lake Minnetonka, *proposed design, architecture student, University of Minnesota. (Courtesy Department of Architecture, University of Minnesota)*

Beyond Design Experiences: The Results of Experimentation

Enriched works of art can be achieved through a design sense cultivated, wholly or in part, by activities such as cut paper designs, collages, mobiles, and hand sculpture. It may prove difficult to conceive of the transfer of knowledge from one art area into another; for influences can be subtle rather than obvious. However, the benefits derived from experimental design projects can not be denied. As one example, an understanding of the concept of space and the means of creating interesting space relationships gained from constructing space dividers may be transferred into an ability to control space in architecture. Both are dependent on pleasing space arrangement; therefore, activity in the former area can affect subsequent experiences in the latter.

The architectural drawing, *A Yacht Club for Lake Minnetonka* (Figure 72) contains a roof structure suspended in a clever manner. This method of supporting the yacht club roof possibly resulted from insight gained by the suspension of abstract forms in an experimental design undertaking. Within many contemporary schools of architecture, including the University of Minnesota, students build abstract space dividers and constructions within design courses. These experiments, often similar to current

explorative ventures in many high school art programs, may suggest unusual methods of construction which can be incorporated into architectural designs (Figure 73).

Handles and related grips for tools and household utensils can grow out of experiments with hand sculpture (Figure 74).

Lorraine Krentzin, influenced by previous experiences with collages and two-dimensional paper compositions, brought a design sensitivity to bear in creating the abstract wall hanging (Figure 75). She often experiments with cut-paper designs before cutting cloth forms for her decorative hangings.

Previous experiences such as organizing shapes in space or exploring the possibilities of color, value, and texture through cut paper or collages may greatly assist subsequent ventures in advertising design as well as crafts, painting, sculpture and all other areas of the visual art. Even such simple procedures as folded-paper investigations may serve as the foundation upon which may emerge new forms for packaging (Figure 76). The benefits of creative design experiences can be manyfold in developing form, awareness, sensitivity, and powers of invention.

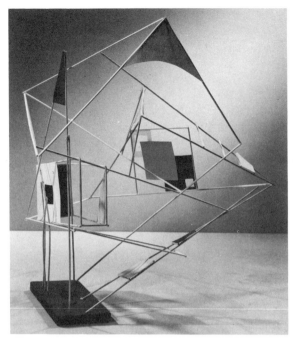

73   *Spatial Construction, student experiment, Wisconsin High School, Madison, Wisc.*

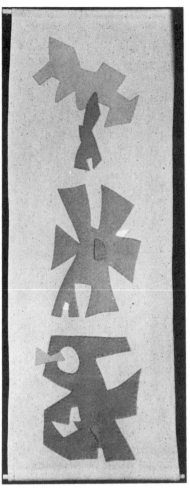

75   *Wall Hanging, felt and tobacco cloth, Lorraine Krentzin. (Courtesy the Artist)*

74   *Woodworking Plane, proposed model, Industrial-design student, University of Illinois. (Courtesy Professor Edward Zagorski, Department of Art, University of Illinois)*

The Fruits of Our Age: New Materials and Processes

Twentieth century technology greatly affects many areas of design. Recent technological advances offer a source for developing design ideas. Countless new materials are being developed in our age. Aluminum, numerous alloys, plastics, synthetic fibers, laminated woods, improved concrete, various bonding and building materials, and a great range of allied materials have been produced in our research laboratories. These materials often advance unique opportunities for the designing and building of forms which were often unobtainable or inadequately realized by the employment of traditional materials. Thus a design solution is often determined or strongly influenced by the inherent characteristics of these new materials.

Plastics, as one example of a recently developed material, provide a new source for expressing design ideas. Possessing great flexibility and strength, they offer unique potentials for creating functional surfaces, shapes, and forms. Jack Collins, industrial designer, says that:

> Use of plastics in industrial design has risen steadily over the past ten years. Plastics in some form are now used in about 75% of my work. Plastics provide easier maintenance, better functionality, and more beautiful products through graceful lines and smooth textures. The use of this material improved many of the old-fashioned methods of production, and our design range extends from tiny control knobs to large clothes hampers. Plastic bowls, spatulas, cereal dishes, mixed decanters, tape dispensers, cups, basting brushes, picnic accessories, photographic equipment, and packaging have not even begun to utilize the potentiality of plastic materials and processes.

A consideration of the features of plastics readily indicates inherent characteristics which offer numerous structural applications. Plastics possess lightness of weight, a high strength-to-weight ratio, resistance to corrosion and wear, controllable thermal and electrical resistance, complete color penetration, and ease of formation. Plastics are also extremely versatile; their properties can be easily modified by molecular rearrangement, pigmentation, or fusion with other materials. Many materials have been altered and improved by combination with plastics. The resin impregnation of wood resulted in plywood and wood laminates; the lamination of glass and plastic produced safety glass; textile fabrics have been improved by impregnation with plastics; even metals have been laminated with plastics to more adequately fulfill intended purpose. Designers now create new forms from plastics and related compounds ranging from radio knobs to houses.

The plastic house (Figure 77) is composed of eighteen hollow plastic sections or modules, each 8 by 16 feet, which produce ceiling, wall, and floor. Two modules are centered to serve as a utility core containing bath, kitchen, laundry, and heating. Projecting out, through cantilevered construction, are four 16-foot square wings containing living, dining, and sleeping areas. The entire form is composed of preformed plastic shells, and the interior (Figure 78) indicates an extensive use of plastics from floor coverings and counter tops to furniture and room dividers. Such design solutions were unobtainable until the introduction of this new material, which along with many other new substances extends challenging sources for the imaginative designer.

76 *Tripod Milk Containers, designed by Harley Earl, Inc. (Courtesy Aluminum Company of America)*

77 *Plastic House. (Courtesy Monsanto Chemical Company)*

78 *Interior of Monsanto Plastic House. (Courtesy Monsanto Chemical Company)*

79 *Alcoa Forecast Chairs, aluminum, Paul McCobb. (Courtesy Aluminum Company of America)*

Advances in industrial productional methods and machine technology also strongly influence many designers. New stamping presses, lathes, various cutting and forming tools, and advanced manufacturing techniques act to expand design frontiers. New and complex machine operations may produce practical and exciting forms previously unobtainable. Alcoa Forecast chairs, designed by Paul McCobb, can be cited as a form development obtained through new industrial processes which brought forth means for casting and molding aluminum (Figure 79). Paul McCobb saw a great potential in this industrial process for producing elegant furniture, and by employing the sensitivity of a sculptor, he created a range of new functional forms.

The future holds great promise for design as man, in studio and laboratory, seeks more practical and exciting means to treat the products of his age. Concrete play sculptures, buildings that float, toys moved by the sun — yesterday's dreams — are now realities.

Designers now create play sculptures to bring joy to youngsters throughout the land. Sturdy and durable materials — galvanized tubular steel, fiberglass, aluminum, and concrete — combine to produce fantastic play houses or villages (Figure 80). The design solution enables constant modifications in arrangement with each new grouping stimulating added interest in the concrete slabs, ladders, and bars which encourage crawling, climbing, and creative play.

In proposing a *Building That Floats* (Figure 81), Herb Fritz visualizes a design that unites lake and shore. A broad passage permits ease of entrance, and unhampered lake breeze and view present invigorating sensations. New lightweight reinforced concrete and creative imagination make the building a possibility. Experiments with concrete during World War II resulted in seaworthy barges, so the buoyancy of the material, if properly structured, is apparent.

A whimsical moving display termed *Solar Toy* produces a joyful visual treat of whirling shapes and passages of color (Figure 82). Designed by Charles Eames, the brilliant shapes, spinning wheels, and crankshafts combine visual pageantry, motion, and sound to create an exciting display. Completely powered by the sun's rays in drawing electric energy from selenium cells in an aluminum-sheet reflector, the toy plants joy in the world through colorful seeds nourished by a recently developed means of capturing and storing solar energy. The future holds great promise for the development of a massive range of unique solutions and new forms as scientists, engineers, and artists constantly expand the field of design.

FANTASTIC VILLAGE, *reinforced concrete and galvanized metal. (Courtesy Play Sculptures, Inc., New York, N. Y.)*

80

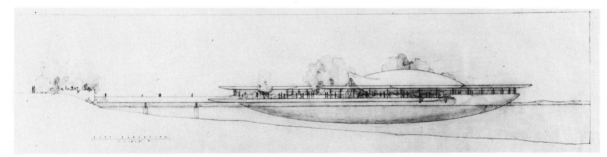

81   BUILDING THAT FLOATS, *concrete, proposed music auditorium, Herb Fritz. (Courtesy the Architect)*

SOLAR TOY, *plastic and aluminum, Charles Eames. (Courtesy Aluminum Company of America)*

82

83   PEERING DOWNWARD FROM ABOVE THE CLOUDS, *aerial photograph. (Courtesy Eastman Kodak Company)*

84   THE HAZE, *wool hooked rug, Lotta Ring. (Courtesy Bigelow-Sanford Carpet Company, Inc.)*

85   *Cuff Links, silver and wood, John Frase. (Courtesy the Artist)*

Another Source: Nature, Even a Cow

A panoramic view comes to mind in considering William Wordsworth's description[7] of nature as a vast universe full of wonder and beauty (Figure 83).

Whose dwelling is the light of setting suns,
And the round ocean, and the living air,
And the blue sky, and in the mind of man;
A motion and a spirit, that impels
All thinking things, all objects of all thought,
And rolls through all things. Therefore am I still
A lover of the meadows and the woods,
And mountains; and of all that we behold
From this green earth; of all the mighty world
Of eye and ear, both what they half create,
And what they perceive; well pleased to recognize
In nature and the language of the sense,
The anchor of my purest thoughts, the nurse,
The guide, the guardian of my heart, and soul,
Of all my moral being.

The artist, be he poet, painter, or musician, has always rendered homage to nature. It has provided him with a source of wonderment, inspiration toward attainment, and the basic materials of art from clay and fiber to pigment, marble, and wood. Through observation and related experiences with nature innumerable artists, past and present, have achieved knowledge, sensitivity, and awareness relating to design possibilities. Subjects and structural solutions are revealed through unlimited examples existing in nature.

What is nature? It is bright sunlight, dull shadows and scattered stars, soil, movement, and texture, panoramic landscape or minute thistle, a flower, shell, fish, or leaf. Nature is also a process; for it caps the mountains, rustles the fields, pounds the shore, splashes colors across the evening sky, and both nourishes and destroys the young and old. It indicates great passageways for geese on southward flight, suggests time for caribou migrations, encourages the snail to seek cover within itself, and unfolds the bud to blossom.

The charm of natural colors and the atmospheric effects of mist provide the design idea for a rug, *The Haze* (Figure 84), by the contemporary Finnish artist, Lotta Ring. The emerging irregular pattern, both obvious and obscure, conveys the sensation of mist or haze through variation in color intensity. Unity is gained through absorption, as background and foreground permeate, resulting in a rhythmical penetration throughout the pattern. The obvious unity and the consistency between design and theme completely fulfill the intended purpose of revealing the artist's idea.

A reproduction of a fish (Figure 85) suggested form possibilities for cuff links to John Frase. Surface contrasts enrich the simple forms of the jewelry. Frase frequently refers to nature and treats its offerings in a highly personal poetic manner.

[7] From *Lines on Tintern Abbey.*

86   CLIFF HOUSE, *The Carl Bauman home, designed by James Dresser, Village of Shorewood, Wisc. (Courtesy Carl Bauman)*

A particular locale, a segment of nature, can even offer suggestions for exciting structures to many architectural designers. The *Cliff House* (Figure 86) indicates the influence of nature in being harmoniously related to a projected environment of trees, rocks, and soil. The house, designed by James Dresser, is perched on a rocky cliff and rises from the peak of its setting in a logical sequence of movements determined by the contour of the land. The house assumes the character of its surroundings owing to its related form; it is built of stone taken from the cliff and local lumber, which relates to the adjacent trees. The peak of the cliff is also repeated in the pitch of the roof, a portion of which is pierced to enable a tree, secure in the earth, to pass through the roof line into the sky.

Within the cliff house, exposed ceiling beam construction symbolizes an oak leaf; for secondary beams radiate out from a main beam to suggest a leaf pattern. One corner of the living room's concrete slab floor remains unpoured, and the exposed underlying earth serves as a natural planter. Exterior stone walls reappear in the interior, and natural light is assured in various areas by the use of skylights. Space is both retained and released by variations in floor and ceiling levels. The entire structure, exterior and interior, possesses an interdependence of parts which together function as an organic design in harmony with its natural environment.

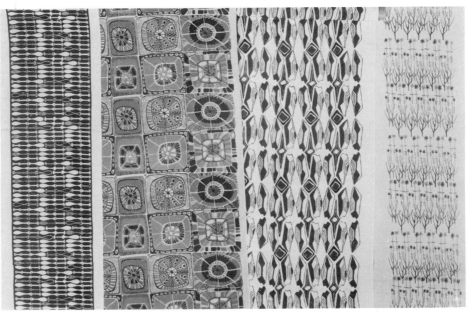

87   *Textile Prints, silk screen on cloth, Mathilda Vandenbergh. (Courtesy the Artist)*

Mathilda Vandenbergh is also keenly aware of design potentials in nature. Her textile designs (Figure 87), often developing from man-made or natural forms, possess sensitivity and charm. She acknowledges her sources of subject matter in saying:

A silhouette of a wooden bobbin used for lace-making provided the basic form for my print *Lace Bobbins.* The arrangement of contours provided opportunity for associating both positive (occupied) and negative (unoccupied) shapes.

Experiments in beginning with a nucleus center and working outward to join adjacent shapes served as the design approach for *Radial Squares.* The design grew from this imaginary center, possibly originally associated with elements observed in natural forms.

The textile print *Brown and Black Bark* developed from shapes observed in pieces of bark. The mirrored position of shapes and a rearrangement of lights and darks are stressed in this design.

A line drawing of dry plants provided subject matter for *Floral Row.* Through overlapping and the reversing of the basic motifs I attempted to gain added interest. The arrangement of layout with noticeable bands of density provides contrast to the pattern.

Sources in nature which stimulate ideas may range from an interior section of fruit, to sea life, a root, even a cow (Figure 88). The only limitations are the bounds of man's experience and imagination.

88   LA VACHE (THE COW), *oil painting, Jean Dubuffet. (Courtesy Pierre Matisse Gallery)*

89   *State Capitol Dome, Harrisburg, Pa. (Courtesy Pennsylvania Department of Commerce)*

Looking Over One's Shoulder: Art of the Past

Designers of the last century in all fields of art showed great interest in reviving and repeating art forms of the past. Painters formed brotherhoods such as the Pre-Raphaelites to escape the problems of their era by returning to methods and notions of a bygone age. Numerous furniture designers repeated earlier forms; sculptors and architects concerned themselves with Greek and Roman designs. The century was known as the Age of Revivals, with Greek, Roman, and Gothic designs providing the major inspiration. Designers looked not within themselves but toward the grand manner, proven styles, and ancient authorities such as the Roman Vitruvius or the Italian Palladio for laws relating to building.

The glory of the past was attempted to be transferred to the present. Innumerable government buildings constructed in the last century illustrate this trend. They indicate, among other traditional features, a direct linkage with Roman domes conceived twenty centuries ago (Figure 89). For ancient Roman dome solutions served for numerous structures during the Italian Renaissance and later periods in Europe and America. These duplicative tendencies, by placing a premium on recapturing the past, ignored original and direct solutions relating to the problem at hand.

At the turn of the twentieth century Oswald Spengler[8], the German philosopher and art historian, reaffirmed a traditional design attitude by contending that "tradition is not just a collection of recipes borrowed from the exterior aspects of work; it is the funded wisdom of innumerable creators, the ideas and symbols expressive of the genius of the culture. An absence of traditions, or a search for them, means not health but decadence." A contemporary of Spengler, Henry van de Velde, Belgian artist and educator, tended to refute Spengler's contention. Van de Velde[9] stated, "As long as there are artists . . . they will protest against any proposed canon and any standardization. The artist is essentially and intimately a passionate individualist, a spontaneous creator. Never will he, of his own free will, submit to a discipline forcing upon him a norm, a canon."

Logic seems to dictate that both men were correct in their view, because both knowledge and rejection of tradition are essential to the designer. Tradition should be accepted when providing enlightenment, rejected when binding or limiting the emergence of possibilities.

André Malraux[10], the contemporary French art historian and philosopher, speaks of the present as a "museum without walls."

> Nowadays an art student can examine color reproductions of most of the worlds' great paintings, can make acquaintance with a host of second rate pictures, archaic arts, Indian, Chinese and Pre-Columbian sculpture of the best periods, Romanesque frescoes, Negro and "folk" art, a fair quantity of Byzantine Art. . . . We . . . have far more great works available to refresh our memories than those which even the greatest of museums could bring together. For a "Museum Without Walls" is coming into being.

[8] *The Decline of the West*, Vol. 2 (New York: Alfred A. Knopf, 1929), p. 444.
[9] Nikolaus Pevsner, *Pioneers of Modern Design* (New York: The Museum of Modern Art, 1949), p. 18.
[10] *The Voices of Silence* (Garden City, N. Y.: Doubleday & Co., Inc., 1953), p. 16.

Archaeological and art historical studies which cover all phases of the arts, the growth of local museums and art galleries, well-established world trade, numerous references to the arts in popular publications, the art film, certain evidences of tasteful design within television programing and advertising, and well-designed objects within our markets, provide innumerable opportunities for viewing numerous design practices. Profound influences on the designer are apparent on both a conscious and an unconscious level. Numerous designers, however, still follow traditional trends in merely reproducing past styles or accepting current foreign influences. This is indicated by the constant revision of styles in women's fashions, the reemergence of early American or period furniture, the copied Scandinavian style emerging from the south. On the other hand, there currently exist many designers who are both aware and respectful of tradition and yet retain an individualistic expression. Contemporary art, in many respects, is built upon the past, but it is vitality concerned with expression centered in the self, the uniqueness of each personality. While the true artist is not now concerned with the direct copying of designs of the past, to deny the influence of the past would indeed be both ridiculous and impossible.

The present is merely an extension of the past; thus, both past and present provide fertile grounds for the excavation of ideas. Sources of inspiration or design ideas may exist in past visual art forms, processes, and techniques, in traditional literature, or in any area relating to man's past. Quality in design is related not to source but to the ability of the designer in handling materials in a personal manner and logically solving the design problems in the activity undertaken.

When designing modern forms, the architect Edward Durell Stone often draws upon his knowledge of art of the past for ideas upon which to build. But one important difference exists between his designs and those conceived of by the majority of designers of the last century. Stone finds traditional solutions inspirational but not binding. He does not produce replicas, nor does he duplicate previous notions, but rather he uses historical sources as a starting point for developing personal forms. His architectural solutions, in harmony with current constructional methods and materials, tend to echo man's rich design heritage in contemporary terms.

In creating the United States Pavilion at the Brussels World's Fair, in 1958, Stone's main purpose was not to imply association with past grandeur but

United States Pavilion, Brussels Fair,
aerial view of bicycle wheel roof, plastic
panels, and metal spokes. (Courtesy U. S.
Department of State)

90

Interior of Pavilion. (Courtesy U. S.
Department of State)

91

Plaza and Front of Pavilion. (Courtesy
U. S. Department of State)

92

to solve the needs of exciting shelter for visitors and displays in the pavilion. However, a form similar to the Roman Colosseum, a high circular amphitheater, suited Stone's purpose of enclosing a huge amount of space with a minimum of means. The Colosseum, constructed as a sports arena in A.D. 80, during the heights of the Roman Empire, afforded 50,000 spectators seating from which to witness spectacles. Stone, well aware of this Roman solution and admitting its influence, followed its circular form. The methods devised long ago by Romans to cover portions of the Colosseum also suggested a suitable structural approach toward roofing the United States Pavilion (Figure 90). The Pavilion proved to be the largest free-span circular building ever constructed. Designed as a huge drum with translucent walls and plastic panel roof, the entire form was supported by thin columns. The columns, in addition to the translucent walls and roof, provided a quality of elegant lightness to the interior (Figure 91).

A plaza (Figure 92) located in front of the Pavilion contained a reflecting pool and 130 flowering apple trees. An article in a popular magazine[11] described the structure as follows:

> Nearly as vast as the width of Rome's Ancient Colosseum, which inspired it, combining dignity, symmetry and an inviting holiday glitter, the pavilion is the finest showcase the United States has built abroad at a major worlds fair. Spectacular in its daring engineering and inspired in its architecture, it is already recognized as the number one United States exhibit at Brussels and a leading contender for world architectural honors.

A comparison of *Fragments d'Hesiode* (Figure 93) by the French artist Georges Braque with the Cypriote statue *Pair of Horses* (Figure 94) indicates apparent relationships. Although separated in time by thousands of years, both sculptures contain an economical rigidity devoid of superficial details. Both also possess a clearness and sincerity of vision which unites men of many periods in their efforts to communicate beliefs or aspects of their world.

Many contemporary artists are interested in qualities which are frequently apparent in archaic or primitive design. To attain the essential, akin to a primeval expression is a major goal for these artists. Their designs are uncluttered, free of the innovations which have superimposed a veneer of classical respectability or intellectual refinement upon conventional forms.

[11] *Time Magazine*, Vol. LXI, No. 13 (Chicago: Time, Inc., March 31, 1958), p. 56.

93 FRAGMENTS D'HESIODE, *bronze sculpture, Georges Braque, 1957. (Courtesy Carnegie Institute)*

94 PAIR OF HORSES, *terra cotta, Island of Cyprus, 1000 B.C. (Courtesy Metropolitan Museum of Art, the Cesnola Collection; purchased by subscription, 1874-1876)*

95   TROJAN HORSE, *silk screen print, Dean Meeker. (Courtesy the Artist)*

To touch again the spirit, to partake of unhampered feeling is desired. Therefore, a sense of naïvete, a childlike directness, is often evident in their work owing to solutions which seem fundamental, enduring, and essential.

The artist-designer is frequently devoted to the destruction of current values in searching for the original. Discarding the immediate as a design source, he refutes popular ideas and theories, thereby rejecting segments of past art which have greatly influenced the preceding generation of designers. This constant revitalizing process creates a never-ending source through revivals. Aspects of antiquity that harmonize with the designer's personality or intentions prove influential and are rescued from obscurity. The characteristics of the past permit such a procedure; for the past is a magnificent and comprehensive source of unusual solutions. Man, no matter what his mode of expression, can usually find parallels or stimulation in previously produced

examples of art. Inspiration is not limited exclusively to ancient forms in architecture, sculpture, painting, or the other visual arts. Even ancient literature can inspire contemporary expressions.

The great epic poem, the *Illiad* — derived from Ilium, another name for Troy — is attributed to the Greek poet Homer. In this artistic masterpiece, produced approximately one thousand years before the birth of Christ, the episode of the fall of Troy is narrated. The ancient stronghold in Asia Minor was captured and destroyed in 1184 B.C. through an unusual and deceptive action, with which you are probably familiar. In the tenth year of the Trojan War between Greece and Troy, following an arduous siege, the Greeks appeared to depart, leaving a huge wooden horse, supposedly a gift, outside the recently besieged city walls of Troy. Greek warriors hidden in the hollow interior of the horse gained admittance beyond the stout walls when the horse was drawn into Troy by the unsuspecting defenders. Upon springing out of concealment, the Greeks over-powered the Trojan warriors and opened the gates of Troy to their companions who had remained secreted outside the city walls.

Inspired and enlightened by Homer's historical work, Dean Meeker, a contemporary artist, designed a version of the great Trojan horse (Figure 95). Bold linear movements and an active pattern of dark and light values create a rhythmical and forceful presentment. The interior of the wooden horse is portrayed in a highly decorative manner with passages of symbols representing Greek soldiers arrayed with implements of battle. The artist employed visual penetration in his design to expose the interior of the wooden horse structure. Such an X-ray solution affords the contemporary viewer a glimpse of hidden warriors denied Trojans, perched on fortified walls, ages ago.

Traditional portraits by early American painters, such as Charles Willson Peale and Gilbert Stuart, undoubtedly provided insight regarding George Washington's facial characteristics to Chuck Ax. Can you imagine a more simplified version of the father of our country than that found in the Container Corporation layout (Figure 96)? Would it still adequately identify Washington?

The function of a poster is to provide an immediate transfer of imagery. Communication must be positive, simple, and unique. With a bare minimum of lines Chuck Ax attains this goal. His dignified and legible presentment suggests security and strength, and one clearly perceives George Washington through an explicit and novel interpretation. One tends to notice the unique rather than the commonplace.

In addition to historical subject matter, artists often create new designs through a knowledge of ancient art processes. Ilonka Karasz modifies the mosaic process, an historical art form used centuries ago by many civilizations. By substituting multicolored aluminum foil for traditional tile, glass, or marble, she creates an outstanding means for adding visual enrichment to a wall (Figure 97). Her work, expressed in a personal manner, is tempered by both past and present influences.

One can taste in diversified manners from the river of art. The stream remains the same, but the water constantly changes as men from all the yesteryears replenish the headwaters. What is done today becomes an historical current of tomorrow and joins the influential flow as an additional design source to be assimilated or rejected by those who follow.

96   GEORGE WASHINGTON, *advertising design, Chuck Ax. (Courtesy Container Corporation of America)*

97   *Mosaic Wall Covering, colored aluminum foil, Ilonka Karasz. (Courtesy Aluminum Company of America)*

TOPICS FOR CONSIDERATION

1. In your own words, what is design?
2. What qualities should be present in effective designs?
3. Why does design change? Consider airplanes, chairs, clothes, etc.
4. Do you think some design changes are uncalled for? If so, in what areas and why?
5. Does a creative person rely on art of the past? If so, how?
6. What importance does the realm of nature hold for the designer?
7. Why are experimentation, economy, function, and originality important aspects in design undertakings?

SUGGESTED ACTIVITIES

1. Collect several objects or photographs of man-made forms which you consider well designed and evaluate their design qualities and merits. Your choices can be made from innumerable objects ranging from ash trays and flashlights to hammers and posters.
2. Considering how writing tools have progressed from quills to ball-point pens, sketch several designs of effective writing instruments which remain for the future. Or if you prefer, design a lamp or a chair which you think will be popular ten years hence. Present your selection in pencil, in pen and ink, or as a three-dimensional model.
3. Collect textured and transparent materials, such as bits of cloth, sandpaper, cellophane, and screen, and create a collage. For background, use an 18 by 24 inch sheet of construction paper or cardboard. Upon completion, consider how different surfaces exist in nature and also how textures are employed in furnishings and houses.
4. Design a book jacket or recording cover. Decide on appropriate size and theme, following an examination of an actual book or phonograph record. Employ cut construction paper and either ink or tempera paint.
5. GIRLS: Create sketches of a wardrobe suitable for a trip to your favorite city or a summer vacation in Bermuda or Hawaii. BOYS: Design a racing car. Imagine it as being prepared for entry in a coming 500-mile race at the Indianapolis Speedway. Display your designs, along with the works of other members of the class, and note the variety of solutions.
6. Produce a space divider or stabile approximately fifteen inches in height. Cardboard, plastics, light metal, wood, and wire, singularly or combined, should be suitable for this purpose. Stress open construction, unusual joints, and intriguing shapes. Following its creation, think, for a moment, how such forms could influence architecture, serve as outdoor sculpture, or indicate new methods for furniture.

APPROPRIATE REFERENCES AND READINGS

ALLNER, W. H. *Posters*, New York: Reinhold Publishing Corporation, 1952.

America's Arts and Skills, by the editors of *Life Magazine*, New York: E. P. Dutton & Co., Inc., 1957.

ANDERSON, DONALD M. *Elements of Design*, New York: Holt, Rinehart, and Winston, 1961.

Annual of Advertising Art, New York: Art Directors' Club.

Bauhaus: 1919-1928, edited by Walter Gropius, New York: Museum of Modern Art, 1938.

Chairs, edited by George Nelson, New York: Whitney Publications, 1953.

DREXLER, ARTHUR, and DANIEL, GRETA. *Introduction to Twentieth Century Design from the Collection of the Museum of Modern Art*, Garden City, N. Y.: Doubleday & Co., 1959.

EMERSON, SYBIL. *Design: A Creative Approach*, Scranton, Pa.: International Textbook Co., 1953.

Industrial Design in America, edited by the Society of Industrial Designers (Annual Publication), New York: Farrar, Straus, and Young, Inc.

KEPES, GYORGY. *Language of Vision*, Chicago: Paul Theobald, 1949.

MOHOLY-NAGY, L. *Vision in Motion*, Chicago: Paul Theobald, 1947.

MUMFORD, LEWIS. *Art and Technics*, New York: Columbia University Press, 1952.

PEVSNER, NIKOLAUS. *Pioneers of Modern Design from William Morris to Walter Gropius*, New York: The Museum of Modern Art, 1949.

READ, HERBERT. *Art and Industry*, New York: Horizon Press, Inc., 1954.

THE DISTANT PAST AND NINETEENTH-CENTURY AMERICAN ARCHITECTURE

Gone, glimmering through the dream of things that were.

GEORGE GORDON BYRON[1]
19th Century Romantic

The Roots of the Matter

Have you ever wondered why our nation's Capitol was designed to imitate a Roman temple or why innumerable American homes were built, a few decades ago, as miniature Gothic cathedrals or medieval castles? The answers, found in understanding the principles guiding designers of the past century, unfold in close relationship with the beliefs and skills of ancient foreign civilizations. The story consists of fantastic as well as logical qualities; for the Republic's architecture, appearing immediately following the American Revolution, actually started in distant lands thousands of years before the flag was born.

A diversity in architectural solutions, an apparent feature of the present, did not always exist in America. During the last century, tradition frequently limited possibilities owing to edicts from antiquity. To recognize these bindings involves a survey of a multiplicity of design practices and social customs; for numerous factors warrant consideration. The most important of these are to be found in the classical and Romantic architectural traditions which developed through the centuries in Europe and later upon our shores. Both traditions served as fountainheads for design practices during our immediate

[1] From *Childe Harold.*

lake dwellers designed large sloping wooden structures; and in China, the pagoda form appeared. The inhabitants of India carved into cliffs of solid rock and formed huge, ornate temples; high in the mountains of Peru monumental structures composed of huge stones were erected by the Incas; and a civilization in Greece created temples of marble. These marble temples were to become of utmost importance to America; for they provided the design foundation upon which a great portion of Western civilization was erected.

The Roman Empire accepted Greek design and added monumental and ornate characteristics. Following the decline of Rome, Roman design provided the basis for Romanesque architecture. This style, in evidence from the fifth to twelfth century, retained the round arch and general massiveness of Roman designs but possessed a simplicity more in kinship with Greek architecture. Following the Crusades, Gothic architecture, during the twelfth century, grew, in part, out of Romanesque architecture. Gothic design, most evident in France, England, and Germany, resulted from the breaking up of the feudal system and the subsequent growth of towns. Expanding centers of population demanded local church architecture, and elaborate constructions sponsored by local civic pride and church wealth were undertaken. The style, unique for its time, differed vastly from the earlier Greek architecture in construction methods, details, and final form.

In the fourteenth and fifteenth centuries, during the Southern Renaissance, Italians denied the happenings in the lands to the north. In an attempt to revitalize their homeland they peered back in time, beyond Gothic and Romanesque designs, and selected ancient Roman architecture as a fitting expression for their period of history. Several centuries later, Roman architectural designs were traced back to earlier Greek forms and both Greek and Roman styles were revived and employed, along with the rejuvenated Gothic, throughout the Western World.

The past century was an age of extensive revivals in both Europe and America. Owing to constant fluctuations of interest between the renewal of Greek, Roman, and Gothic forms, all three styles, as well as others, patterned the period. Since each style possessed particular design characteristics, authorities constantly disagreed; each cited the period which was in harmony with his personal notion or taste. Thus, strong tendencies toward duplicating both classical and Romantic forms were major design features of the century.

past, and their influences continue into the present, though on a smaller scale. To be aware of these movements is to recognize both the greatness of man and art; for the story of architectural design is also the history of man and his art.

Getting Out of the Rain and Then Some

Architecture, the art of building structures which suitably house and inspire man, has a long and varied history. Its beginnings immediately followed prehistoric men's emergence from caves or jungle underbrush or their descent from trees, huge rocks or chunks of soil which provided partial cover from the terrors of the age. During this transition, men naturally began to concern themselves with constructing crude structures for protection against weather, beasts, and other men. Some turned to hides stretched across sticks, others to woven grasses and leaves, blocks of sun-dried mud, or chunks of ice. The availability of local materials, man's innate creativeness, and, later, group modifications deriving from tribal customs were determining factors in design. Following great passages of time and at varying periods architectural styles were established. Probably, many later perished, while others remained to pass on a variety of traditions through the ages. In the far north, Eskimos developed igloos; in Malay,

Two Schools and Their Followers

"Classicism" relates to adherence to or imitation of Greek or Roman art, and the term "classic" in its finest sense implies purity and excellence. When and if used in a derogatory sense, it implies imitative and academic qualities, devoid of feeling. "Romanticism" is usually more experimental and emotional and therefore less restrained than classicism. Its appearance in architecture during the nineteenth century was largely related to the revival of medieval Gothic architectural forms and thus was in opposition to the classical style of Greece and Rome. Irving Babbitt[2], an authority on Romanticism, differentiated between classic and Romantic attitudes in a comprehensive yet concise manner. He contended that something is in the Romantic spirit,

> When, as Aristotle would say, it is wonderful rather than probable; when it violates the normal sequence of cause and effect in favor of adventure. A thing is romantic when it is strange, unexpected, intense, superlative, extreme, unique. A thing is classical when it is not unique, but representative of a class. In this sense medical men may speak correctly of a classic case of typhoid fever, or a classic case of hysteria. One is even justified in speaking of a classic example of romanticism. By an easy extension of meaning a thing is classical when it belongs to a high class or the best class.

In its conventional art usage, however, because of long association, "classical" usually relates to Greek and Roman art or their derivatives.

One may wonder, regarding the classical and Romantic design movements, which is superior. The answer is to be found within oneself. After gaining insight into their attributes, one must judge each style in terms of personal logic and appeal. It is a question not of selecting one at the expense of the other, but rather of becoming aware of each movement's unique accomplishments. Many creative individuals possess a duality of taste, appreciating and employing aspects of both design traditions. John Ruskin[3], the strong advocate of Gothic design during the past century, possessed many classical views. His utterances regarding the importance of personal interpretation in the arts, plus his supposedly Romantic spirit, lead one to believe he would be sympathetic toward the emergence of new forms in design. On the other hand, his comments regarding the Crystal Palace, a huge glass and iron structure built in London for the Great Exhibition of 1851, illustrate a lack of appreciation of experimental forms. Upon viewing this unusual building, highly unique for its day, he remarked,

> The quantity of thought it expresses is, I suppose, a single and admirable thought . . . probably not a bit brighter than thousands of thoughts which pass through an active and intelligent brain every hour — that it might be possible to build a greenhouse larger than ever a greenhouse was built before. This thought and some very ordinary algebra are as much as all that glass can represent of human intellect.

Such an utterance is more in tune with a classical than a Romantic attitude.

There are many other examples of creative individuals who possessed both Romantic and classical tendencies. For instance, as early as 1800, Benjamin Henry Latrobe introduced both classical and Gothic notions into American architecture. Louis Sullivan, another great American architect active at the turn of the century, bitterly opposed the classic revival in America; yet his notions of simplicity in design were often more in harmony with the classic than Gothic style. The great West Coast architect, Bernard Maybeck, designed both Romantic and classical architecture. His Romantic masterpiece, The First Church of Christ Scientist, built in Berkeley, California, in 1910, is composed of both Japanese and Gothic elements tempered with Maybeck's sensitivity and inventiveness. Five years later he created The Palace of Fine Arts in San Francisco in a classical style patterned after Roman structures. Maybeck's versatility indicated an individual who, rather than be restricted by traditional edicts, considered them adaptable to helping him fulfill his intentions. Frank Lloyd Wright, considered by many to be one of the greatest architects of all time, combined qualities of both Romanticism and classicism with great creative ability. He stressed the naturalism of the Romantic tempered by the awareness of simplicity and proportion of the classicist.

Mid-twentieth-century architectural design consists of an extensive variety of forms; for art is currently in a period of ferment. Numerous structures produced for contemporary man have their roots imbedded in past notions of design, while many others have resulted from the distinct architectural design movements native to our century: organic

[2] *Rousseau and Romanticism* (New York: Meridian Books, 1957), p. 18.

[3] *Nikolaus Pevsner, High Victorian Design* (London: Architectural Press, 1951), p. 11.

98   The Parthenon, Athens, Greece, after twenty-three centuries of ravage by weather and man. (Courtesy Art History Department, University of Wisconsin)

architecture and the international style. If an understanding is acquired of the latter two movements, discussed in the next chapter, in addition to an awareness of classical and Gothic architecture and their derivative forms, a knowledge of architecture and a definite design attitude should result.

Ancient Grandeur on a Hilltop

Greek architecture resulted from Egyptian, Cretan, and Dorian influences modified by Grecian innate sensitivity. Numerous architectural traditions have been produced by man since time began; however, the influence of the Greek tradition on Europe and subsequently America has been the most profound. Designers in Greece, centuries before the birth of Christ, produced architectural forms which proved to be a basic source for designs for the following twenty-five centuries throughout the Western World.

The Parthenon (Figure 98), a temple honoring the goddess Athena, was erected on the Acropolis, a fortified hill in Athens, between the years 447 and 432 B.C. Constructed in marble, with ingenuity and sensitivity, it stands, even in ruins, as one of man's most noble expressions. Possessing ideal proportions, a grandeur of form, and a perfect harmony between an absolute simplicity and ornateness, this Greek temple achieved classical design perfection. The Parthenon's

designers, Callicrates and Ictinus, obtained a visual perfection within the temple through both a harmony of proportions and numerous subtle compensations for proper visual reactions in viewing an elongated rectangular temple (Figure 99). In the lower area of the Parthenon the long horizontal steps were curved slightly upward to refute a natural optical illusion which would imply a slightly concave movement in perfectly straight steps. The Doric columns were designed to lean gently inward; for perfectly straight perpendicular pillars would appear to slant forward. The columns also deceived and satisfied the eye through a slight swelling in the shaft which provides a visual sensation of regularity in taper when viewed from below.

Metopes, carved relief panels in the Doric frieze which encompassed the Parthenon above its columns, portrayed men in combat with centaurs. These creatures, half man and half horse, were prime symbols in Greek mythology. The pediments, the triangular areas above the metopes, also contained themes pertaining to Greek myths. The birth of Athena on Olympus was conveyed in the east pediment, and the west pediment portrayed the struggle of Athena and Poseidon for the possession of Attica. Thus were presented to Grecian eyes stories of their gods and goddesses.

99   *Model of Restored Parthenon. (Courtesy Metropolitan Museum of Art)*

The interior of the Parthenon contained a huge statue, nearly forty feet in height, composed of gold, wood, and ivory. Created by Phidias, who also directed the creation of surrounding statuary and the bas-reliefs of the exterior, it depicted Athena, the patron goddess of Athens. Upon the monumental sculptural form, riveted gold plates suggested drapery and ivory portrayed the flesh of the Athenian goddess. Unfortunately, the statue disappeared centuries ago following its transportation to Constantinople in A.D. 435. It was moved after a decree by Emperor Theodosius II banned heathen imagery in the Parthenon. However, insight into Phidias's skill as a sculptor, as well as the excellence of Grecian sculpture of the Golden Age, can be recognized through copies such as the *Athena Lemnia* (Figure 100) originally attributed to Phidias and found upon the Acropolis.

Throughout later history the Parthenon's design has been repeated, distorted, mutilated, or sensitively reinterpreted in an endless number of derivative forms; yet the original remains to be surpassed. Roughly five centuries following its construction, Plutarch[4], a famous Greek philosopher, wrote regarding it and adjacent structures on the Acropolis that

They are created in a short time for all time. Each in its fineness was even then and at once age-old; but in the freshness of its vigor it is, even to the present day, recent and newly wrought.

The words of Plutarch, recorded twenty centuries ago, still ring true. The era in which the Parthenon was created is even now referred to as the Golden Age; for its designs remain untarnished.

One may wonder why the forms of the Grecian Golden Age perpetually remain as high watermarks in the history of man's expression. The answer is found in that era's concern with serenity, idealism in proportion, skillful execution, and a stress on the universal rather than the particular in art. Its ventures in dramatics, literature, philosophy, science, pottery, painting, and silverwork as well as architecture and sculpture still communicate to man meaningful aspects of his constant search for logic, universal truths, and visual harmony. The Greeks of this Golden Age even now, through written words as well as visual creations, convey the greatness of man. Aristotle, Herodotus, Pericles, Plato, and Socrates still speak and provide meaning to us, and Phidias, as well as others, continue to touch men's hearts and minds through stone.

A Touch of History

The cities of Rome and Greece developed somewhat simultaneously. While Rome was establishing herself as the dominant force in Italy, Athens con-

[4] From *Life of Pericles.*

tinued as a self-contained city-state and reached its age of greatness between 480 and 430 B.C. under the leadership of Pericles. Within the following century a new age was born; it served as a transition between Greece and Rome. Macedonia, a land north of Greece, emerged as a world power through the exploits of its young king, Alexander the Great. That ruler of the small northern kingdom conquered the entire Hellenic (Greek) peninsula, in addition to Egypt, Asia Minor, and Western India, before dying of fever at the age of thirty-three in Babylon. His triumphs ushered in the Hellenistic Age, a period which carried Greek design throughout the Mediterranean basin and beyond to the lands of India. Many art centers sprang forth during this period of expansion and produced numerous works which, while basically Greek, were often marked with foreign ornateness. An emphasis on nonessentials and a stress on the particular, such as, in sculpture, muscular studies of a specific figure, became apparent in much art of this period. Authorities have referred to Hellenistic art, a period which greatly influenced late Roman art, as a moonlight reflection of a sun that had set.

While the Hellenistic Age flourished in the east, the Roman republic was in the latter stages of consolidating her strength on the Italian mainland. Her conquests of the Etruscans, Volscians, Latins, Hernicans, and Samnites, as well as other Italian tribes, were completed in 265 B.C., and Rome, following the earlier Macedonian policy, undertook world conquest. After sixty-three years of intermittent campaigns against Carthage, Rome in 202 B.C. gained firm control of the western Mediterranean. The Greek city-states in southern Italy and Sicily, which for several centuries had, along with the Etruscans, influenced Roman notions of art, were now completely within Rome's control, and the eyes of empire looked eastward. The battles of Cynoscephalae and Pydna followed, and in A.D. 148 Rome proclaimed Macedonia a province. Within two years Corinth fell, Athens was incorporated into the Roman Empire, and the entire peninsula of Greece was conquered. In another thirteen years Syria and adjacent areas of Asia Minor and northeastern Africa stood beneath Roman battle banners, and the claws of the imperial eagle clutched a huge empire. Rome had now absorbed Alexander's Hellenistic world, and with an armored fist molded an architecture suitable for a world power.

100   ATHENA LEMNIA, *cast of original marble carving, attributed to Phidias, ca. 450-440 B.C. (Courtesy Metropolitan Museum of Art)*

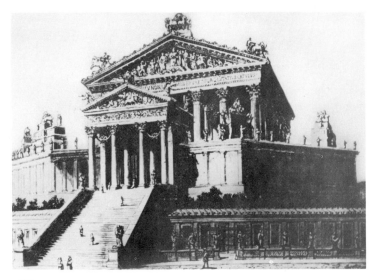

Temple of Jupiter Capitolinus, Rome, Italy. (Courtesy Art History Department, University of Wisconsin)

101

Not to Be Outdone: The Forces of Empire

Many seeds, derived from early Grecian and Etruscan designs, had already been sown in Rome with the erection of temples such as Jupiter Capitolinus in 509 B.C. Destroyed by fire in 83 B.C., Jupiter Capitolinus was reconstructed (Figure 101) by the emperor Domitian during the first century A.D. Its stress on decorative detail and applied ornamentation brings to mind a comment by J. Huizinga[5], a noted authority on the arts. His comment, while directed toward French design of the late Middle Ages, may prove equally appropriate to describe the Temple of Jupiter Capitolinus as it:

> Tends to oust beauty by magnificence. A tendency to leave nothing without form, without figure, without ornament. The flamboyant style of architecture is like the postlude of an organist who can not conclude. It decomposes all the formal elements endlessly, it interlaces all the details, there is not a line which has not its counterline. The form develops at the expense of the idea, the ornament grows rank, hiding all the lines and all the surfaces. A horror vacui reigns, always a symptom of artistic decline.

The term "horror vacui" indicates an overemphasis on applied decoration with chaos resulting because all surfaces scream for attention. To the Roman such a visual display undoubtedly signified the richness and grandeur of his civilization; however, centuries later, man employed such a discordant design approach for a different purpose. Medieval man viewed simplicity or unoccupied space as a

[5] *The Waning of the Middle Ages* (London: Edward Arnold & Co., 1924), p. 228.

horrible vacuum which permitted occupancy by the devil, and if all such empty spaces were filled with a maximum of details, evil forces were denied shelter. Such decorative tendencies, evident in areas of both classical and Gothic art, cause visual confusion and strain; the eye is forced to attempt to digest more than is visually comfortable and is denied enjoyment of the entire form.

Designers in Rome aimed at an imperial magnificence, at its best grandeur, at its worst grandiosity and vulgarity. In temple design and sculpture the Romans, in kinship with the Hellenistic Greeks, usually lacked the restraint and clarity which make the earlier Greek forms supreme. It should not be concluded, however, that Roman architecture is inferior to Greek architecture as related to ingenuity and building skill. The Romans proved highly inventive, and, while more excessive in detail, they were also more experimental than the Greeks in their temple construction. Modifying and expanding earlier forms to suit their purpose, Romans often used nonsupporting columns for decorative effects, exposing them completely or partially embedding them in walls, and they also made an extensive use of a wide range of colored marble. They were master builders, further developing methods of vaulting large areas with the round arch and the dome as well as producing well-engineered bridges, aqueducts, and roads. At its height the Empire had fifty thousand miles of excellent roads serving as innumerable fingers of influence which carried Roman law and customs into the universe of the ancients: distant provinces from England and France to northern Africa and Asia Minor.

Both the Etruscan influence, which led toward the use of round arches to secure vaulting and dome construction, and Grecian influence are apparent in the Pantheon (Figure 102). The original structure, built in 27 B.C. during the reign of Octavian by Agrippa, a consul, was probably constructed to commemorate the naval battle of Actium fought on September 2, 31 B.C. In A.D. 120 the Pantheon was modified by the emperor Hadrian, who added the present rotunda and dome. This circular temple has brick and concrete walls twenty feet in thickness crowned by a huge pierced concrete dome which permits natural light to flood the interior. The interior, measuring 141 feet in height and width, with its highly organized system of arches incased in the walls, supports the huge dome which contains an oculus, or opening, 29 feet in diameter. The temple's logical and exciting method of construction illustrates the engineering skill and ingenuity of Roman designers. In 610 the Pantheon was consecrated as a Christian church, the Santa Maria della Rotunda, and it now stands as the only pre-Christian Roman temple still in a well-preserved condition.

A sketch of the interior of the Baths of Caracalla (Figure 103), constructed in Rome in A.D. 217, indicates the Roman's ability to grandly enclose a huge amount of space. Vast spaciousness and splendor were evident in the bathhouses of Rome, and they usually contained libraries, lecture rooms, and stadiums in addition to facilities for hot or cold baths. Over nine hundred of these structures were erected before the decline of Rome in the fifth century A.D. Approximately fourteen hundred years later the Baths of Caracalla served as inspiration for the design of the Pennsylvania Railroad Station in the heart of New York City.

Though the Roman designer often lacked the lightness of touch and sensitivity of proportion native to the earlier Greek, his greatness lay in building for empire beyond the city-state. Such intentions naturally culminated in notions of monumentally enclosing great spaces and organizing numerous decorative details within elaborate forms to suggest the pomp and grandeur of Roman civilization. The architecture of Rome had a profound influence in America; for even our football stadiums, as well as our national Capitol, can trace their roots to Rome. While Greek forms remained hidden from the Western World until late in the eighteenth century, owing to the Turkish occupation of Greece, Roman forms remained exposed for the wonderment and stimulation of future generations.

102   The Pantheon, Rome, Italy, model. (Courtesy Metropolitan Museum of Art, Bequest of Levi Hale Willard, 1883)

103   Baths of Caracalla, Rome, Italy, sketch. (Courtesy Art History Department, University of Wisconsin)

Young America Finds Reasons for Planting Temples in Its Land

It is by no mere chance that the Roman eagle came to roost again in America and, in a new form as the American eagle, became next to the flag itself the universal symbol of the United States. (Figure 104)

The comment by the contemporary historian Talbot Hamlin[6], as well as the magnificent early nineteenth-century carving by William Rush, indicates the extensive influence of Rome within young America.

Many centuries following the decline of the Roman Empire, its design concepts were transferred to our shores by way of England, where men such as Inigo Jones and Sir Christopher Wren had previously reinterpreted classical forms. During the American Republic's birth, individuals such as Thomas Jefferson and Benjamin Henry Latrobe, under the influence of English taste, preached the virtues of Roman and Greek architecture, and columns and domes began to emerge throughout the Eastern landscape. Thomas Jefferson, in 1785, suggested an imitation of the Maison Carrée, a Greek-inspired Roman temple built in Nîmes, France, during the second century A.D., as a fitting design for the Virginia state capitol (Figure 105). Twelve years later, Benjamin Henry Latrobe produced the Bank of Pennsylvania in Philadelphia in the form of a Greek temple. Latrobe later followed William Thornton in designing portions of the nation's Capitol, which was derived from the Roman architectural style. However, the final form of the nation's Capitol has been composed through the contributions of subsequent designers as well as the original contributors. For instance, its present huge iron dome, which is painted white, was conceived by T. V. Walter and completed at the close of the Civil War. In 1819, Latrobe followed the design of the Parthenon in designing the Bank of the United States, currently the Philadelphia Customs House. Two decades later the ancient Temple of Neptune in Paestum, Italy, served as the model for the subtreasury building in New York City, and somewhat later a copy of the Roman Pantheon appeared, in the same city, to serve as a library for Columbia University. Such structures joined numerous other classical revival forms sprouting in the nation's Capitol, along the settled seaboard, and inland to the frontier.

104   THE MIGHTY EAGLE, *wood carving, William Rush, 1808. (Courtesy Pennsylvania Academy of the Fine Arts)*

[6] *Greek Revival Architecture in America* (New York: Oxford University Press, 1944), p. 5.

105   *Virginia State Capitol, Richmond, Va., Thomas Jefferson, 1785. (Courtesy Virginia
Department of Conservation and Economic Development)*

One may wonder why the Founding Fathers accepted and advocated both ancient and foreign architectural styles for a nation in its infancy. Why would the father of our country, George Washington, be portrayed in sculpture as an ancient Roman dressed in toga, and why would our government buildings be capped with Roman domes? The answer is evident in the needs and atmosphere of the day. To many patriots during the early period of American history, Greece served as the first example of a democratic city-state, while Rome represented the mother of Republics. Since the ancient Roman citizen symbolized the perfect republican and the Roman tribune an excellent system of government, many characteristics of the political system as well as the visual imagery of the American Republic were developed from Roman practices. In American politics aspects such as senators acting as representatives indicates a Roman influence. Even poets of the period, for instance Edgar Allan Poe[7], paid homage to the classical world with such utterances as

To the glory that was Greece and the grandeur that was Rome.

Citizens faced with the innumerable problems of a young and growing nation looked hopefully toward Rome and Greece for inspiration. It seemed that, since those ancient civilizations had prospered, their ancient trails should be followed. Therefore, it was

natural for numerous architectural designers to turn toward classical forms for inspiration and the opportunity of capturing and associating with the glory that was Greece and the grandeur that was Rome. The classical world provided a young America with a sense of stability and a wonderful suggestion of a possible golden age.

The naming of towns such as Athens, in Maine; Syracuse, Rome, and Troy, in New York; Alexandria, in Virginia; and Sparta, in North Carolina indicates the extensive Eastern interest in Greek and Roman cultures. As American civilization moved beyond the Ohio territory, towns such as Alexandria, Macedonia, and Sparta appeared in the Midwest. Later, reaching the Far West by way of prairie schooners across the midcontinent and ships around the Horn, the influence of the ancient classical world spread from shore to shore and covered the land. From Olympia, in Washington, and Antioch, in California, to Athens, in Georgia, architecture now assumed the guise of temples of long ago. Greek-columned structures now stood adjacent to Spanish adobe buildings in the Southwest and, in the Southeast, met the French-derived grille-faced forms which had emerged in the southern regions of the old Louisiana Territory.

Innumerable small homes as well as huge public buildings designed during the last century were strongly stamped by the classical influence. The Kilbourntown house (Figure 106), erected in the Midwest in 1844, ideally illustrates the design tendencies of the Greek revival in small home construction. It

[7] From *To Helen*.

106   *The Kilbourntown House, Milwaukee, Wisc., 1844. (Courtesy State Historical Society, Wisc.)*

possesses the restraint of details and harmony of proportions originally found in the Parthenon and reflects the temple's characteristics with dignity and charm. Such houses were later to be followed by houses inspired by Gothic churches and medieval castles as Americans continued to search for significant architectural expression.

The revival of classicism continued throughout the nineteenth century, with public buildings, houses, and even barns following designs created ages before. Many variations in classical interpretations appeared; they ranged from the conventional rectangular form to square, octagonal, and circular structures. Individuals who favored octagonal and circular schemes, motivated by desire for unity and order, frequently indicated that, by eliminating the sharp corners of a square architectural plan, an equal amount of space could be enclosed with a substantial saving in building material. Such approaches were derived from plans employed in the Roman Pantheon and the villa rotunda schemes of the Renaissance.

A most obvious indication of the impact of the classical revival during the past century can still be viewed in a multitude of Federal, state, county and city government structures. Similar forms, often of less magnitude, were constructed on many college and university campuses to imply a link between the contemporary scholar and the wealth of knowledge flowing from previous generations. Can you recall several classical revival buildings in your region?

Classical Architecture in Our Century

Though partially replaced by Romantic architecture, especially Gothic, in the latter portion of the nineteenth century and later by organic and international design attitudes in our century, the classical tradition in design continues into the present. Its influence was carried into this century through beliefs, identical or similar, to those advanced by the architectural scholar W. A. Eden[8]. His writings, undertaken at the turn of the century, clearly stressed a classical point of view:

> From the Romans of the Augustan period . . . we may learn how to reconcile the classical idea . . . it was the Augustan Vitruvius who provided us with an authoritative canon of proportions . . . a knowledge and understanding of the essence of architecture. Having reached Vitruvius in our quest for architectural understanding we cannot but follow him back to ancient Greece, the fountainhead of all our knowledge.

Many Greek and Roman adaptations, ranging from the San Francisco Palace of Fine Arts to the more recent Supreme Court Building, in Washington, D.C., have been produced in this century. The San Francisco Palace of Fine Arts, created by Bernard Maybeck for the Panama-Pacific Exposition of 1915, was designed as a huge Roman ruin. The domed major structure, adjacent to a lagoon which

[8] *The Process of Architectural Tradition* (London: Macmillian & Co., Ltd., 1942), p. 113.

provides shimmering reflections, is a highly popular public monument to many Californians. The Supreme Court Building, imitative of a Grecian temple, contains impressive sculptured pediments high above its dignified entrances. Another excellent example of Greek revival architecture which incorporates rich pediments in its design is found in the huge Philadelphia Museum of Art. Designed by Traumbauer, Borie, and Zantziger, associated architects, and opened in 1925, the museum is grandly located on a knoll, flanked by wide thoroughfares, in the heart of the city. The pediment of the north wing contains polychrome glazed terra cotta decorations (Figure 107) derived from the Greek practice of painting over marble sculpture.

The Mellon Institute, a classical structure built in Pittsburgh, Pennsylvania, in 1937, may serve as another example of a rather recently constructed form clearly derived from traditional classical design (Figure 108). In this Institute devoted to advanced scientific research are contained some of the most advanced and fully equipped scientific laboratories in America. There are eight floors in the structure: the three lower floors contain an auditorium, shops, utility plants, and mechanical equipment; the fourth, or main, floor has administrative offices, library, and museum; and the four upper floors contain scientific laboratories. The following quotation from a descriptive pamphlet issued by the Institute provides interesting factual information regarding the building.

> Those statistically minded will be interested in the fact that, in the construction of Mellon Institute's home, there were used 269 carloads of Indiana limestone, 62 carloads of granite from Vermont, 932 tons of reinforcing steel, more terra cotta (inside and in the courts) than in any other building ever constructed, and much aluminum for doors, window frames, ornamentation, and other architectural details. There are 62 monolithic columns around the building; these columns, with bases and capitals, have an over-all height of 42½ feet. Each column shaft is 36½ feet in height and 6 feet in diameter and weighs 60 tons. There are 1151 windows in the court walls alone, and 30,000 square feet of plate glass in all parts of the building. Although the height from the sidewalk level is about 85 feet, there are two full floors beneath that level. As for the general dimensions, the building is approximately 306 feet wide at the front, 227 feet at the rear, and 334 feet from front to rear, and all sides are treated alike architecturally. Its volume is more than 6 million cubic feet and the total floor area is over 400,000 square feet. There are 488 rooms. The style is the architecture of ancient Greece, which combines great beauty with a simplicity that is fitting to a home of science.

107 *North Wing of Philadelphia Museum of Art, completed 1944. (Courtesy Philadelphia Museum of Art)*

108 *Mellon Institute, Pittsburgh, Pa., 1937. (Courtesy Mellon Institute)*

109   *American Embassy, New Delhi, India, model, 1959. (Courtesy U. S. Department of State)*

Unity between the exterior and interior of the Mellon Institute is gained by the repetition of materials and the frequent use of classical-inspired decoration within the interior. Subject matter in bas-reliefs, on pedestals, and on elevator doors ranges from symbols representing contemporary scientific organizations and the fruits of science to Greek mythology. One bas-relief, a shallow wall carving, in the rear of the main lobby represents the birth of Athena. This goddess of knowledge is portrayed, true to Greek mythology, springing forth, fully armored, from the head of Zeus.

Mellon Institute, designed by the architectural firm of Janssen and Cocken, represents the fully transplanted classical style. Ancient glories apparently cannot be forgotten. The design is almost totally dependent on past design concepts; however, other classical-inspired buildings produced in this century deviate greatly from a rather exact reproductional process yet suggest the simplicity and elegance of early classical design.

The American architect, Edward Durell Stone[9], a highly creative and versatile designer, combines his knowledge of classical art with contemporary materials and construction methods in producing original and exciting modern forms. In protest against the severity of many modern buildings, with their acres of glass façades and harsh rigid structure, he incor-

porates classical features within his architectural solutions. Speaking of classical architecture he says,

> These great monuments of the past were an inspiration, not to copy, but to enrich your vocabulary. The Pompeian house and the romance of the classical — why, I harken to them even now.

Edward Stone's Embassy Building (Figure 109), in New Delhi, India, designed for the State Department, possesses both compactness and a quality of grandeur that much modern architecture lacks. The influence of the classical temple form such as the Parthenon is apparent in the horizontal stress and general proportions. The building also blends into the design tradition of India in being faced with decorative tiles and incorporating arabesque grilles in the façade; both features are native to Indian architecture. The building also contains fifty gold leaf columns and an inner garden under a mesh roof. The meshed roof and the extensive use of grille in the façade, permitting a free flow of light and air, compensate for the warm New Delhi weather.

Designers such as Edward Stone can carry classical influences into our age in both sensitive and sensible manners, provided their creative judgment, and not tradition, determines the final form.

[9] *Time Magazine*, Vol. LXXI, No. 13 (Chicago: Time, Inc., March 31, 1958), p. 62.

The Start of Another Trail: Toward the Gothic

The Visigoths, fierce northern warriors, crossed the diminishing borders of the Roman Empire early in the fifth century and moved southward. Only ruins remained following their march through Rome; for the imperial Roman eagle had been plucked and its feathers scattered to the winds. The Colosseum lay deserted and the triumphant arches of Rome were now a mockery, and huge temples, bathhouses, and entire forums dissipated into the mists to remain in the haze of antiquity until revived through a rebirth of memories in Italy many generations later. Following the destruction of Rome, Western civilization was mainly sheltered, for the next few centuries, within monastery walls.

Long after the decline of Rome, but before the Italian Renaissance reawakening, exciting and unusual architecture began to appear in lands to the north of Italy. This new style grew out of Romanesque design, which consisted of Christian church architecture modified from earlier Roman basilicas and interpreted in a direct manner. The relatively simple Romanesque structures, with their uncomplicated surfaces and details, were in keeping with the austerity of the early Christian faith. The newly emerging Gothic style, however, was to prove vastly different from Romanesque.

The term "Gothic" can prove misleading, but its acceptance continues because of long usage. The word was coined by Italians to describe the architecture of France and subsequently Germany and England, but the style was not derived from the Goths, nor the Visigoths, a subdivision of that Teutonic tribe; rather, it was developed by a French civilization composed of a fusion of Gauls, Celts, Franks, and related tribes. The Italians originally employed the term "Gothic" as a mark of disrespect for the builders of the north, because the Renaissance Italians were concerned with reviving the classical style through a rebirth of the old Roman Empire. The holding of contempt for French designers and the belief that nothing good could come from the vandals of the north were natural reactions on the part of fifteenth-century Italians; for had not the Visigoths, under Alaric, plundered Rome in A.D. 410? The term "Gothic" thus was synonymous with barbarianism and desolation; for the Visigoth butchery of Rome marked the total decline of the ancient world and closed the age of the southern caesars. Fortunately, contemporary man does not share the fifteenth-century Italian's negative notion of Gothic art, but rather views the style as representative of an era of magnificent architectural accomplishment in church construction. Art produced in France, Germany, and England from approximately 1200 to 1600 is still classified as Gothic and is considered to be Romantic rather than classical in concept.

Touching the Clouds in Reaching for Heaven

The first building incorporating Gothic characteristics was the Abbey of Saint Denis, constructed in 1140 near Paris. It marked the beginning of a great movement in religious construction with the finest period attained during the twelfth century in the form of the cathedral, which proved the greatest design achievement of its age. Construction was a complete community venture, with priest, prince, merchant, and artisan all actively engaged. Craftsmen were replaced by sons followed by their sons, because creative energy was expended over an extremely long period of time in erecting these monuments to Christianity. These ornate structures, with their great emphasis on vertical movement, paid visual homage to the Christian God through forms vastly different than those previously raised to honor pagan gods of Greece and Rome. Gothic designers created a unique means of enclosing huge areas of overhead space and attained great heights through the development of pointed arches and buttresses. Pointed arches, with their steeple effects, permitted greater heights than were obtainable with the round arch previously employed by the Romans or with the Greek post and lintel method of construction, which consisted of vertical posts supporting overhead horizontal beams. It also made possible ribbed vaulting composed of a framework of arches which acted as ribs. The vaulting yielded structurally decorative overhead interiors and added a minimum of weight to the building. Buttresses, masses of masonry which acted as exterior side ribs, were devised to permit the cathedral to be sheathed with thin masonry and stone walls which could be frequently pierced to admit light. Both pinnacled and solid buttresses, as well as flying buttresses (Figure 110) which acted as half arches, were incorporated into Gothic construction. They played a prime role in supporting and reinforcing the cathedral walls by counteracting the thrust exerted by rib vaulting and roof against the thin walls. All structural portions of the Gothic church were highly dependent upon one another; the interdependence resulted in a logical and organic relationship of all parts to the whole. Designers usually treated all surfaces of this unified form with a mass of details which provided an apparently inexhaustible amount of visual excitement (Figure 111).

The Rheims Cathedral, erected between 1211 and 1430, illustrates one of man's most noble ventures and serves as an excellent example of the structures late medieval man raised to praise his God. The French architectural scholar Emile Mâle[10] says that Rheims

> is the national cathedral. Other cathedrals are catholic, that is to say universal; but Rheims is French . . . so rich is the façade that any further decking out for coronation days was superfluous. Canopies of stone are inalterably in place above the door, and Rheims is forever in readiness to receive monarchs.

An examination of the façade indicates certain qualities inherent in Gothic church design. The lower portion of the façade contains huge portals which prove to be grand and imposing entranceways. Directly above the main portal a huge rose window appears, flanked by monumental towers which reach far above the main portion of the cathedral. The towers create vertical thrusts compelling the eye to follow the form deep into the heavens. In the original designs, spires were to be included to further increase the aspect of height achieved by the towers. The circular stained-glass rose window possesses a bar tracery symbolic of a flower's form. Tracery consists of stone bars or moldings which when fitted together provide decoration and a means of supporting large areas of stained glass. The rose window and the stained-glass windows along the cathedral's sides flood the church with tinted light providing luminous richness to the interior. Minor towers, with decorative pinnacles enriched with crockets, carved stone foliage, add accents to the main towers, and niches containing religious statuary are incorporated in the façade. The entire mass of the cathedral is decoratively treated for religious edification and visual enrichment through stained-glass windows and carved stone interwoven and laced across all surfaces.

In Rheims Cathedral subject matter is extensive; applied designs range from floral patterns carved in stone to a portrayal of Abraham securing bread in sacramental state from Melchizedek, King of Jerusalem. The kings of France are symbolized in the stained-glass windows, along with the baptism of Clovis, a great king of the Franks. The virtues of labor are even stressed through peasants, presented in bas-relief, threshing grain in the fields.

Far up in the towers of the cathedral exists a whimsical world of fantasy. Grotesque stone figures, half-man and half-beast, imaginary animals, birds, and a host of other strange forms are perched on the balustrades of the towers. Gargoyles, waterspouts carved to represent demons, also range over the upper surfaces of the cathedral. Far below this imaginative world a stone prophet, secure in the façade, seems to peer at the encircling French town.

The history of the church, the greatness of a nation, the toil of centuries, and the intellect, emotions, and fantasies of man are written in stone within the Rheims cathedral. It still stands as one of man's richest accomplishments in design.

The Romantic Influence in Nineteenth-Century America

Jean Jacques Rousseau is often called the father of the Romantic movement; for his impact on both Europeans and Americans during the past century was profound. This eighteenth-century Swiss philosopher was one of the most passionate, eloquent, and inspiring writers in the history of mankind. In strongly advocating a return to nature and naturalism on the part of man, he implied man was born free but at maturity is bound with chains. The bindings consist of the imposed unnatural restrictions of tradition. Comments by Rousseau, such as "Everything is good as it comes from the hands of the Author of things; everything degenerates between the hands of man," provided men with a belief in natural potential and a rebellious spirit which moved against the limitations of the classical tradition in art.

In addition to Rousseau's influence many factors stimulated interest in Romanticism in both Europe and America during the nineteenth century. The restraints of classicism, the sterility of art academies, an increased interest in nature — in part due to a desire for escape from the complexities of the Industrial Revolution, and also the challenge of the American wilderness contributed toward establishing the Romantic movement. New discoveries in the natural sciences, expanding historical studies of nonclassical lands, and exciting geographical explorations were other determining factors. Literary works and paintings relating to emotional fragments of life or the turbulence of nature heightened interest in the unusual, exotic, and romantic. The writings of George

[10] *Religious Art* (New York: Pantheon Books, Inc., 1949), p. 95.

Flying Buttresses of Chartres Cathedral, Gothic construction method, 1205–1270. (Courtesy Art History Department, University of Wisconsin)

110

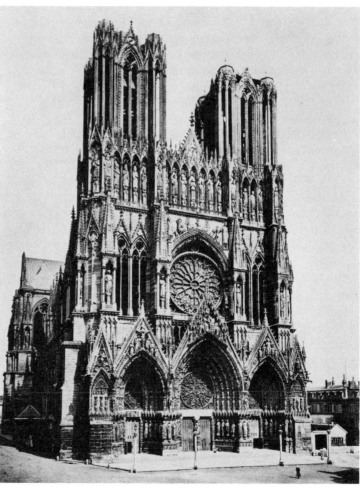

Rheims Cathedral, Rheims, France, 1211–1430. (Photographed by Ewing Galloway)

111

View on the Upper Missouri, George Catlin, painted approximately 1832. (Courtesy United States National Museum)

112

Gordon Byron, James Fenimore Cooper, Victor Hugo, Herman Melville, John Ruskin, Sir Walter Scott, Henry David Thoreau, and others germinated nonclassical interests. A tradition of American landscape painting, originated in the Hudson River School, was rapidly expanding and European painters, such as Eugène Delacroix and Caspar David Friedrich, were vividly communicating highly emotional themes.

Romantics naturally turned away from the currently popular classical revival in architecture in order to find new possibilities which would challenge and excite the emotions of man. Romantic architecture, however, also became revivalistic, with Gothic forms providing the earliest and most popular source for inspiration. The selection was logical, for many of the characteristic elements of Romanticism — interest in the picturesque, a concern with an nonclassical period, and nature, excitement, and superstition — are found in the Gothic cathedral. Victor Hugo's description[11] indicates the attitude of the nineteenth-century Romantics toward the Gothic cathedral:

> It is a vast symphony in stone, so to speak; the colossal work of man and of a nation, as united and as complex as the *Iliad* and the *romanceros* of which it is the sister; a prodigious production to which all the forces of an epoch contributed, and from every stone of which springs forth in a hundred ways the workman's fancy directed by the artist's genius, in one word, a kind of human creation, so strong and fecund as the divine creation from which it seems to have stolen the two-fold character; variety and eternity.

One of the first instances of Gothic-inspired architecture upon American soil was a private dwelling, near Philadelphia, designed by Henry Benjamin Latrobe in 1800. Within a few decades American Romantics such as Alexander J. Davis and Andrew Jackson Downing began to actively preach of the virtues of the Gothic style and its suitability for house design. Davis produced a Gothic residence in 1832, and Downing — implying that the classical style results in tasteless temples — stressed the Gothic style as fitting for the nation in an influential publication *Cottage Residences* in the year 1842. One may question the logic of these gentlemen in contending a house should resemble a Gothic cathedral rather than a Greek temple; however, the justification and acceptance of such reasoning in America becomes evident upon a consideration of the period.

During the presidential terms of Andrew Jackson, 1828 to 1836, the American dream began to materialize. The age of the common man had arrived, and many, tiring of the repetitious temple houses, believed the Romantic style more suitable to express the individualism inherent in a democracy. The time seemed suitable for a rebellion of taste against the formal qualities and restraint of classical designs, and the battle of styles commenced. The Gothic, in time, emerged victorious over the white temples advocated by Jefferson and other Founding Fathers.

[11] *Turrets, Towers, and Temples,*" edited by Esther Singleton (New York: Dodd, Mead & Co., 1898), p. 29.

Dreams Come True

The next sixty years marked a great age in America. The nation had already indicated its confidence in its strength in issuing the Monroe Doctrine and now looked toward the west (Figure 112). Man moved into the land of the buffalo and the Sioux, while American clipper ships roamed the seas. Reproductions of painting such as *View On the Upper Missouri* by George Catlin and Eastman Johnson's *Barefoot Boy* now became fashionable; for America had both a continent waiting for exploitation and the youth and vitality to fulfill its nineteenth-century destiny. Cities expanded rapidly; towns were brought into being; manufacturing and farming increased greatly; and inland waterways, roads, and rails began to pattern the landscape. The rigid symmetry and simplicity of the classical form was rapidly replaced by the exuberance of the Gothic revival as numerous Eastern and Midwestern houses (Figure 113) appeared patterned with lacy details and suggesting height through pointed roofs and elongated windows. In 1860, United States industrial production was about two-thirds that of England; within thirty-five years it was more than double. In the 1880s railroad transportation came of age, with the nation laying 65,000 miles of track, a record still unsurpassed. Supposedly inexhaustible sources of building materials existed in great forests or could be produced in expanding factories and easily transported. The Homestead Act spoke of the vastness of the land. The conservation of materials was not a consideration in design, nor was simplicity in building a virtue. Great wealth was amassed, and the Gothic design seemed appropriate to display the growing lushness and elegance of the nation. The American dream had become a reality during the second portion of the nineteenth century, and even waterworks (Figure 114) demanded enormous proportions and a Romantic treatment. Several decades earlier, waterworks in Philadelphia were constructed as Greek temples, but the Gothic style now reigned supreme. Public buildings, private dwellings, schools, and prisons, as well as waterworks, were made to look like medieval fortresses or Gothic cathedrals. Following the Civil War, the Romantic movement broke into full bloom; for in addition to neo-Gothic structures, Italian villas, Swiss chalets, Tudor cottages, Norman mansions, varied European fortresses and castles, and even Persian architectural forms began to blossom on American soil. Frequently, elements from various styles, such as the Italian, Queen Anne,

113   *Houston Homestead, Cambria, Wisc., Carpenters Gothic, mid-19th century. (Courtesy State Historical Society, Wisc.)*

114   *Water Tower, Chicago, Ill., 1869. (Courtesy Art History Department, University of Wisconsin)*

or Louis XIV, were combined with Gothic revival details to gain the greatest variation in windows, doors, and ornamental details. The results were often unfortunate and erratic, with the consistency of a particular style lost.

Glitter, Beads, and Fancy Scrolls

The term "Victorian design" is applied to the Gothic revival; for its development approximately corresponds with the reign, 1837 to 1901, of the English Queen Victoria. The Victorian age is also often referred to as the "gilded era" or the "gingerbread age." The contemporary artist scholar John Maass[12], author of the profusely illustrated and delightful book *The Gingerbread Age*, contends that the Victorian period through its boldness and vitality can teach a lesson to the present conformist. He states;

115   *Carson Mansion, Eureka, Calif., 1885. (Courtesy Eureka Chamber of Commerce)*

> Victorian architecture is distinguished by its pleasurable fancy and exuberant color. The "dark" Victorian house had more and larger windows than earlier American homes. It is true that these windows used to be barricaded with a five fold layer of shutters, blinds, muslin curtains, velvet draperies and tasseled valances, but most of these are gone and light is flooding in.
>
> These were the first houses to feature central heating . . . hot and cold running water, bathrooms, cooking ranges. . . . They also boast high rooms, a big kitchen, both a front and back yard, ample storage space in cellar and attic.

Many parallels link the Victorian house with the original Gothic cathedral. Both stressed great height and decorative details. Many Victorian houses of the latter portion of the past century possessed sharply pointed arches and peaks, towers with skyward-pointing pinnacles, balustrades nestled in roof areas, and clusters of decorative carvings on porches and framing doors and windows. An extensive variety of windows were evident in the design in addition to simulated arches and railings, and local craftsmen frequently provided distinctive character to the structure through personal solutions in the use of the jigsaw.

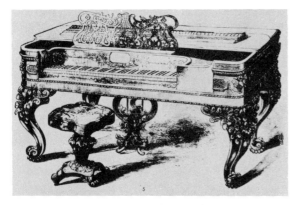

116   *Piano, late Victorian notion of furniture design.*

The Carson Mansion (Figure 115) in Eureka, California, is one of the finest examples of a fully matured Victorian design remaining in the nation. Located in one of the greatest stands of timber within the continent, in the heart of the redwood country, the Carson Mansion speaks both of the richness of the land and the elegance of its era. It was built in one

[12] *The Gingerbread Age* (New York: Rinehart & Co., Inc., 1957), pp. 10-12.

year, 1885, by William Carson, a lumber baron, from plans provided by Newsom and Company, an Oakland architectural firm. Local tradition relates that a hundred men were employed, at one time, during its construction. Such a claim seems reasonable when the intricacies of the house are considered. Cupolas, towers, and bay windows encrusted with inlaid and carved embellishment and carved flanking surfaces display a freedom and lushness in harmony with the design concepts of the time. A large porch, supported by decorative columns and topped with an ornate wrought-iron framework containing the builder's initials ornately arranged at various intervals, encloses a large portion of the front and one side of the house. The porch functions as shelter and provides an invigorating introduction to massive doorways leading into the interior. The huge entrance contains stained-glass panels which portray life-sized figures from a Shakespearean drama. Additional stained-glass windows located throughout the house provide colorful patterns representing figures from medieval legends.

The interior possesses a full basement and three stories containing eighteen rooms, including living rooms on the first and second floors and a vast ballroom and billiard room on the third floor. Mahoganies and primavera wood from South America, teakwoods from the Orient, and native redwood and oak add richness to the interior, while redwood and fir for timbering comprise the exterior. Immense fireplaces, constructed of onyx from Mexico, are scattered throughout the house. A spectacular stairway, enriched by patterns of tinted light cast by adjacent stained-glass windows, links the first and second floors. A rounded-arch hallway extends the entire length of the second floor, and at varied locales archways of plaster, stained to resemble wood, lead into sleeping quarters. Innumerable furnishings, imposing furniture, hangings, and miscellaneous objects contribute additional visual impact to the interior.

Why a Gingerbread Age Becomes Stale

Victorian interior design usually appeared to be a complete rebellion against restraint or simplicity. Parlors, in particular, reached extremes in ornate lushness; they were packed with furniture of every conceivable shape and form. Stuffed chairs, ottomans, marble-topped tables, and sideboards were surfaced with fluted or floral carvings or fringed with beads or shells. Fireplaces were often surrounded with plaster or marble frosting, while, directly above, a marble, gesso-surfaced, or carved wood mantel,

contained an inexhaustible number of objects ranging from wax flowers and bronze statuary to plaster casts, ornate clocks, silver candlesticks, leather boxes, and souvenirs of all sorts. Bold flower patterns covered rugs, drapes, and wallpaper. Chandeliers, dripping and drooping with bits of glass, were suspended from patterned ceilings framed by rich molding. Paintings with gilded frames, potted plants of all descriptions, beadwork curtains, fringed velvet cushions, Japanese fans, and often a precious teapot reeking with diversified surfaces served as frosting to enrich the main ingredients. Natural light was usually denied emergence into the parlor, because after filtering through layers of shutters, blinds, curtains, draperies, and valances, it no longer appeared to be in evidence.

A consideration of products of the period from houses or furniture to musical instruments readily indicate the notions of form and detail held by Victorian designers. The term "gingerbread" truly belongs to this age; for often every inch of surface was enriched with every imaginable device. Applied ornamentation and stress on miscellaneous shapes within form provided such a degree of visual excitement that usually enjoyment of the form itself, in its totality, was denied. The entire form frequently crawled with enrichment and pulsated with emphases; the result was a riot of nonessentials creating chaos. The Victorian era piano (Figure 116), suggesting a concert lacking a conductor, proves as fussy as many of our contemporary jewel-encrusted music boxes. (Juke boxes, which belch forth music and colored lights simultaneously and provide joy to young lovers but sadness to both serious musician and the sensitive contemporary designer.)

Proper detail is fine for enrichment, but when a molasses of detail, whether carving, sequins, beads, or chrome, pour over form, undue confusion and visual fatigue results. An overabundance of applied decoration and unnecessary structural modifications, whether evident in Victorian furniture or the modern juke box or automobile, merely places emphasis on nonessentials and misplaces impact. The Victorian age was marked at its best by grandeur and richness, at its worst by overindulgence, clutter, and confusion. It proved successful in fulfilling a demand for ornateness and regality to display the confidence and ego of a nation moving toward maturity. Its proper place, however, remained within the past century; for new social, manufacturing, and design notions, both logical and native to our land, were emerging at the turn of the century.

117   *National Farmers Bank, Owatonna, Minn., Romanesque revival, Louis Sullivan, 1908.*

118   *Typical Romantic Revival House Architecture of the 1920s, everywhere, U.S.A.*

The Romantic Revival in Our Century

While possibly ironic for the purist, contemporary architecture sprang, in part, from the Romantic revival. One Romantic style, the Romanesque, served as an inspirational bridge between past and present. New movements in art, though possibly appearing abrupt, upon examination seldom lack transitional roots. At the close of the last century, the designers Henry Hobson Richardson and Louis Sullivan were leading a rebellion against the existing confusion of styles in design through a rejuvenation of Romanesque architecture. Because of their interest in structural integrity and simplified monumentality, rather than the picturesque, the architects shared a mutual interest in Romanesque architecture. Both artists also stressed restraint in applied decoration and employed building materials in their natural state for character and enrichment. Rough block and brick buildings, with deep, arched entrances and semiround arched windows, now began to appear throughout the land. Richardson's architectural forms, as well as Sullivan's other than skyscrapers such as the National Farmer's Bank (Figure 117) in Owatonna, Minnesota, clearly illustrate the design tendencies of the Romanesque revival. Certain of Frank Lloyd Wright's early works, the Charnley House, in Chicago, and the Unity Temple, in Oak Park, Illinois, also possess a form in harmony with factors evident in the Romanesque revival. It should not be concluded, however, that the greatness of Sullivan and Wright are closely bound to a relationship with the rejuvenated Romanesque; for the scope of their contributions extends far beyond any linkage with traditional forms. Through their efforts man was to realize, in the light of his experiences and time, that he was to determine form rather than follow styles. Both contributed unique meaning to design and living patterns and caused great changes in the American landscape. Their stories remain to be related in terms of modern architecture; for both belong in the present rather than the past.

Concurrently with the Romanesque revival, numerous other architectural design streams patterned the first decades of this century. Classical buildings were still being produced, and Romantic design notions had expanded to include revived forms from every conceivable area and period. Terms such as Queen Anne, Provincial, and Empire, originally related to earlier European practices, served as a few of the descriptive means for indicating the profusion and often the confusion of styles; for styles were frequently blended to achieve eccentric and eclectic compositions. During the 1920s, Romantic "country houses" (Figure 118) became typical features in the residential districts of American cities; for they permitted man to visualize a role of feudal lord or country gentleman of old. Such practices continue into the present in the random cropping up of European country houses, French Provincial, Georgian, Norman, Spanish, and English timbered houses as well as Cape Cods, Southern colonials, and a host of others, in the suburbs ringing population centers throughout the land. It is unfortunate that revival tendencies are still prevalent in residential architecture, for such results anchored to practices of long ago, deny the blessings extended by the present.

Many examples of Gothic revival tendencies continued deep into this century to shelter a diversity of interests ranging from newspaper offices and university classrooms to motels and railroad stations. Often assuming the role of skyscrapers, Gothic-like structures are apparent in innumerable American cities; several of the more obvious are the Woolworth Building, erected in New York City in 1911; the *Chicago Tribune* Tower, designed in 1922; and The University of Pittsburgh's Cathedral of Learning, constructed in the mid-thirties. A pronounced neo-Gothic flair evident in the Woolworth Building resulted in the term "Woolworth Gothic" being applied to related architectural features in later large buildings such as the *Chicago Tribune* Tower. This skyscraper (Figure 119), with its flying buttresses, towers, and pinnacles piercing Midwestern air, resulted from a world-wide $100,000 competition conducted by the *Tribune* to acquire a future home. Raymond Hood, who later designed portions of Rockefeller Center in New York City, submitted the winning idea, and a modern communications empire assumed a guise of long ago.

119   CHICAGO TRIBUNE *Tower, Chicago, Ill., Gothic revival, 1922.*

A Question of Logic

A serious question of logic enters in any consideration of the suitability of constructing Gothic revival structures within this century. The use of flying buttresses, for example, while mandatory for supporting the walls of early Gothic cathedrals, function in skyscrapers such as the *Tribune* Tower only as pure ornamentation. As a radical departure from their original intent, such buttress treatments add needless weight, complexities, and expense to products of this century. Many engineering advances and building material developments of the past hundred years permit great building heights without the employment of buttresses. Those who would justify Gothic skyscraper design by the needs of great heights and a premium on ground space thus ignore the element of truth and the exciting potentials of structural steel, ferro-concrete, the curtain wall, and related contemporary architectural thinking. One must bear in mind that, within the very city of Chicago years before the *Tribune* Tower was conceived, huge structures having no relationship to Gothic forms were erected. These earlier skyscrapers also achieved great heights but were also original and functional.

The justification of twentieth-century Gothic-inspired skyscraper construction by associative implications, beyond religion, can also be seriously questioned. For example, the notion that a Gothic revival form is associated with a great tradition of learning and thus is fitting for a school building is questionable. Italian Renaissance man would most certainly question the validity of The University of Pittsburgh's Cathedral of Learning possessing a form in kinship with a period the scholars of the Renaissance considered to be primitive, barbaric, and devoid of intellect. Their judgment warrants consideration; for the Renaissance period of history proved to be a great era of intellectual achievement and attained much greater heights of scholarship than the earlier Gothic age, which made its greatest strides in religious architecture.

The idiosyncrasies of our time are such that in a major American city a university building patterned after a Gothic cathedral exists within several blocks of a Greek temple devoted to research and a church designed in the Gothic manner. All three were constructed in the 1930s. The surrounding landscape is dotted with skyscrapers and houses that are of a nineteenth-century revival style or are indicative of this century's organic or international architectural practices. Progress is marked with backward glances as well as forward momentum as man searches for significant forms for his time in history.

Many individuals may rightly reason that, since the deeply religious Gothic age made its greatest contribution in church architecture, the Gothic style is more appropriate for church construction than for newspaper offices, university buildings, or restaurants. Though the Gothic age represented a period of religious fervor and great architectural achievement, the suitability of its form for present church architecture is also certainly not above reproach. Its time-consuming and expensive construction, ignorance of current technology and materials, denial of original thinking to men of this century, and lack of harmony with the social attributes of this era are but a few of the major shortcomings of an imitative continuation of the style. The Roman Catholic Bishop Robert J. Dwyer[13] contends that the Gothic style, which began in the twelfth century, has

> lost its reference and validity for the age we live in. The Cathedral symbol is dead and should be buried. The sooner we get it out of the system the better it will be for the ultimate development of living art and architecture in the service of religion.

Many non-traditional religious buildings now appear in the American environment and more than justify their existence and continuation. In addition to appearing visually pleasing, they are frequently economically feasible and enjoy full advantage of the building possibilities offered by their time. Rather than being dictated to by a frozen style with predetermined results, modern designers seek new means of offering unique, suitable, and stimulating architecture to congregations. It would be impossible to adequately list more than a few of the innumerable religious structures recently constructed which are indicative of interesting and contemporary practices in design. Such churches and synagogues as the Kneses Tifereth Israel Temple, designed by Philip C. Johnson and located in Port Chester, New York; The Beth Sholom Synagogue in Elkins Park, Pennsylvania, created by Frank Lloyd Wright; the First Methodist Church of Midland, Michigan, by Alden B. Dow; The Roman Catholic Chapel of the Holy Cross, by Anshen and Allen, in Sedona, Arizona; or Pietro Belluschi's First Presbyterian Church in Cot-

[13] *Time Magazine*, Vol. LXXII, No. 9 (Chicago: Time, Inc., Sept. 1, 1958), p. 46.

120　　*Crystal Chapel and Student Religious Center, model of structure proposed for the University of Oklahoma, Norman, Okla., Bruce Goff. (Courtesy the Architect)*

tage Grove, Oregon are several religious structures which are indicative of contemporary inventive approaches and foretell of things to come.

Aluminum-sprayed muslin, irregular chunks of glass embedded in masonry, and transparent plastic sheathing supported by steel grids are several of the unusual combinations of materials which Bruce Goff employs in many of his highly imaginative architectural solutions. This modern Romantic designer seeks new creative answers for each specific design undertaking and employs no formula beyond that which appears while he is actively engaged in imaginatively and experimentally pursuing an architectural solution. His model (Figure 120) of a proposed Chapel and Student Religious Center for the University of Oklahoma refutes many who claim that utmost directness and extreme austerity must mark contemporary

design. Goff's design incorporates a somewhat Gothic pattern as regards surface fluctuations within a form composed of contemporary materials and structured in a direct manner. Devoid of traditional restrictions, the design indicates one ingenious solution to contemporary religious architecture arrived at through the creative spirit of man. Regarding the chapel, Bruce Goff says:

> It is non-denominational, to be constructed of stainless steel frames and "sandwich" panels of hail proof plate glass enclosing translucent pink fiber glass insulation, vacuum sealed. The masonry piers and spire base are of light pink Oklahoma granite with large quartz crystals. All previous religious symbolism has been eliminated because of the non-denominational use of the structure and it is my aim for the building itself to contain within its design spiritual qualities which I hope will transcend materials, structure, and function.

121 *The Wayfarer's Chapel, bell tower and formal garden, Portuguese Bend, Calif., Lloyd Wright, 1957. (Courtesy Independent-Press Telegram, Long Beach, Calif.)*

122 *Interior of Wayfarer's Chapel. (Courtesy* INDEPENDENT-PRESS TELEGRAM, *Long Beach, Calif.)*

Contemporary church architecture ranges from bold, conspicuous ventures to tranquil solutions in harmoniously relating form to landscape.

The rugged grandeur of the California coast serves as the setting for The Wayfarer's Chapel (Figure 121). Designed by Lloyd Wright, the son of Frank Lloyd Wright, the chapel is visually related through material, similarity of shapes, and placement to an adjacent fifty-nine foot campanile and attached cloister. Serving as a sheltered passageway to other areas of the grounds, the cloister tends to link surrounding plantings of trees and flowers to both the bell tower and chapel. The total design harmonizes with both the contour and climatic conditions of the area and sensitively fulfills a major obligation of good architecture. The prime responsibility of architecture, an inspirational and functional interior which determines exterior form, is sensitively solved by Lloyd Wright (Figure 122). Through the use of local materials — a foundation of native stone and laminated redwood arches to encase large expanses of glass—the chapel has a natural and direct quality in providing shelter. The interplays of somber-grained semidark redwood, rough light-valued stone, and the slick transparancy of glass create pleasing passages of texture, color, and pattern. The repetition of identical materials in interior and exterior and the use of large areas of glass unify interior with exterior surfaces and extend the suggestion of space far beyond the inner walls of the chapel. This logical extension of structure with environment, the direct use of building members for both constructional and visual attainment, and the interdependency of all parts of the structure result in organic harmony and imply truth, qualities in sympathy with religion. The extensive use of glass, in addition to assuring an abundance of natural light and creating interesting space relationships, offers a natural and personal means of spiritual communication. The mind is not artificially retained within sheltering walls but is encouraged to speculate; for as the outer eyes sweep the distant sky, the inner eye, the soul of man, seeks his reason for being and the truths of the universe. Freedom from the imposed edicts of traditional architecture and a fusion of strength and dignity are strong attributes of this chapel by the sea.

TOPICS FOR CONSIDERATION

1. Identify the following terms: applied order, basilica, buttress, Byzantium, finial, frieze, leading, nave, pediment, post and lintel construction, rib, Romanesque, spire, thrust, tracery, vault and vault web. Dictionary, encyclopedia, and suitable art publications are appropriate for consultation.

2. Why did Greek, Roman, and Gothic builders incorporate painting and sculpture within their temples and cathedrals?

3. Why was American architecture during the past century based primarily on ancient design practices?

4. Indicate the differences between 19th century neoclassic and Romantic attitudes.

5. What are the strong and weak features inherent in architectural revivals?

6. Do you think late 19th and 20th century scientific advances pertaining to mechanical aids, building technology, and the development of new materials influence architecture? Cite specific examples.

7. Should contemporary man still appreciate the Greek temple and the Gothic cathedral? Should they be ignored or continued to be duplicated?

SUGGESTED ACTIVITIES

1. List notable examples of classical and Gothic revival architecture in your state. Consider governmental and religious structures as well as private dwellings.

2. Locate several houses within your community which are richly embellished with gingerbread. Sketch on paper, with pencil or ink, their intriguing features.

3. If possible, visit a museum and analyze exhibits relating to architectural detailings and practices from the distant past.

4. Collect suitable pictures from magazines and refer to any publication in your local library that contain illustrations of the revivals which patterned the last century. Consider how building practices from Spain and Norway, as well as England and China, were followed upon our soil. If feasible, display your collection and speak of your favorites.

APPROPRIATE REFERENCES AND READINGS

Bowra, C. M. *The Greek Experience*, New York: The World Publishing Co., 1957.

Hamlin, Talbot. *Greek Revival Architecture in America*, New York: Oxford University Press, 1944.

Lethaby, W. R., and Rice, Talbot D. *Medieval Art*, New York: Philosophical Library, 1950.

Lynes, Russell. *The Tastemakers*, New York: Harper & Brothers, 1954.

Maass, John. *The Gingerbread Age, a View of Victorian America*, New York: Rinehart & Co., Inc., 1957.

Pevsner, Nikolaus. *High Victorian Design*, London: Architectural Press, 1951.

Upjohn, Wingert, and Mahler. *History of World Art*, New York: Oxford University Press, 1949.

4 CONTEMPORARY ARCHITECTURE: NEW METHODS OF ENCLOSING SPACE

Glancing at our modern civilization we find on the surface crust essentially the same idea at work that has prevailed throughout the past. Yet if we search beneath the surface we discern a new power of the multitudes everywhere at work. It is the power of a changing dream, of a changing choice; of Life urging upward to the open the free spirit of man—so long self-suppressed under the dead weight of the 'consecrated wisdom of the ages' and its follies.

LOUIS H. SULLIVAN[1]
Early Modern Architect

123   *The Ted Liter House, panel exploration, James Dresser, Madison, Wisc. (Courtesy Ted Liter)*

[1] *The Autobiography of an Idea* (New York: Dover Publications, Inc., 1956), p. 274.

124 *The F. J. Smart House, inverted form, James Dresser, Madison, Wisc. (Courtesy F. J. Smart)*

Houses Now Assume Many Forms

Architects may work with civic planners, traffic engineers, and a host of others in solving the complicated problems confronting large urban areas or operate alone in developing groupings or single buildings for metropolitan or rural locales. Meeting the responsibility of providing inspirational shelter, skyscrapers, and churches as well as elaborate or economical houses falls within their realm. Owing to their constant and personal search for significant structures, an obvious diversity in solutions now exists within these forms. Even houses in a single community assume a variety of forms. They may have great expanses of glass and a variety of roof solutions; they may be recessed into the earth, perched on concrete slabs above the soil, placed at sharp angles on the lot, or even faced completely away from the street. Such a range in architectural solutions results not from a borrowing from specific historical styles, but rather from present stress on experimentation and originality of concept.

Both the Ted Liter and the F. J. Smart homes (Figures 123 and 124) were created by James Dresser as explorative undertakings in providing direct and economical means in building. The Ted Liter house, secured through the incorporation of preformed wall, floor and roof panels, makes use of new building methodology currently exerting a noticeable and logical influence in architecture. Such a method of prefabrication takes advantage of the construction procedures available in a factory containing power equipment for cutting, joining, and constructing large segments of a house. Flooring and roofing rafters are precut indoors; walls are assembled in sections; cabinets are constructed and windows formed so that more immediate and direct erection may be obtained upon the site. Thus standardization of materials and predetermined sizes in building units contribute simplicity and economy to building. James Dresser, as well as many other designers, considers such factors in advocating preformed-panel construction systems.

The long, low, overhanging roof of the Liter house encloses the house proper and also creates an organically related carport and shelter to an entrance leading into living room or directly into kitchen. The roof projection also emphasizes the rectangular form of the house and, along with the repetition of windows, visually unifies the structure. The elongated mass of the house tends to hug the ground and securely relate itself to the surrounding environment. The exterior primarily consists of preformed window units and concrete-block walls surfaced with a smooth coating of cement. The smaller windows afford privacy and additional interior wall space in the sleeping quarters, while large windows in living area provide natural light and invigorating view. Cost-saving techniques are apparent in a directness of construction: flat roof, simplicity of form, concrete slab for flooring which eliminates undue excavation, the use of concrete blocks, and stock windows and beams.

The F. J. Smart house, built upon a circular concrete slab recessed into the earth, provides a most economical means of creating shelter; for a circular form requires a minimum of wall to enclose a given area. While possibly appearing strange to many, such a form is not unique to this century; ages ago, Romans built circular structures, and in the past century many circular houses and farm buildings were constructed in our own land. The F. J. Smart house employs berm-type insulation secured by heaping mounds of soil around the base of the

The Merle Curti House, precut and partial prefabricated form, Marshall Erdman, Madison, Wisc. (Courtesy Merle Curti)

125

structure. This procedure provides excellent insulation and proves economical in eliminating a large portion of the exterior finish. While the home has been titled *The Sunflower House* in association with its form, a reversal of usual organic practices is apparent in that the design tends to ignore its surrounding environment. Owing to this inverted plan, which functions as a tight, self-contained unit, the experimental house is intended for locales, such as certain small city lots, where great privacy is desired and invigorating views are not available.

Identical prefabricated structures such as the Merle Curti and John Hurlbut homes (Figures 125 and 126) can offer, in addition to savings in building costs, a certain degree of individuality through personal selection in interior and exterior finishes and detailing, placement, and landscaping. Notice the large glass areas and spaciousness in the living areas of these homes. Within these spaces the ceiling reaches to the roof line, thereby exposing a great amount of overhead space in the interiors. Large windows in portions of the basements assure natural light and pleasantness in areas frequently ignored as unusable by conventional builders. Stained wood siding on the exterior of the Curti home harmoniously relates the structure to surrounding trees. Located on the edge of a gentle slope, the design incorporates a balcony to gain entrance into the raised living room, and the entire form in perching above a paralleling street suggests dignity and warmth. The John Hurlbut house is

orientated within the environment in more of an informal manner, being placed at a sharp angle to an adjacent street. The lot is banked and landscaped in a consistent and logical manner to provide ease of entrance to the living area, which faces the most exciting view offered by surrounding nature.

The Charles Thompson house (Figure 127), designed by William Kaeser, functions perfectly within its environment. Located on a hilltop lot which rolls southward, the house faces away from a street located to the north and opens to the south through a large expanse of windows overlooking a rich landscape far below. Privacy is assured by the lack of large windows on the north, or street, side of the house, which in conventional building usually contains a picture window facing the street and rows of other houses each of which contains a picture window. Economy of heating is also gained by a minimum of glass on the northern side, exposed as it is to chilling winter winds. The garage at street level is easily accessible, while the house takes full advantage of its hillside locale through levels which step downward to follow the contour of the land. A large roof overhang provides shelter and shade to the windows overlooking the valley below, and a windowless west wall offers protection from the late afternoon summer sun. The exterior building materials, brick and redwood bleached by the sun, add rich surfaces which complement the uncluttered exterior form.

126   *The John Hurlbut House, variation in setting, Marshall Erdman, Madison, Wisc. (Courtesy John Hurlbut)*

127   *The Charles Thompson House, the front becomes the back, William Kaeser, Madison, Wisc. (Courtesy Charles Thompson)*

Shattering the Chains of the Past

How did the present variety and freedom in architecture come about? What factors contributed toward breaking the traditional bindings and making man free? Certainly the development of new materials and building techniques, new engineering findings and accomplishments, and the unique needs of this era, but most importantly the creative contributions and concepts advanced by architects such as Louis Sullivan, Frank Lloyd Wright, Le Corbusier, and Walter Gropius. The roots of mid-twentieth century architecture have been nourished in various soils both native and foreign; for the fruits of this tree are now extensive and varied.

Chicago; The Beginning of the Modern Period

The Eastern states lay claim to being the cradle of democracy, but from Midwestern soil sprang a unique American style in architectural design. Separated by almost a thousand miles of prairies, forests, and mountain chains from the eastern seaboard, Chicago, during the last decades of the nineteenth century, was turning from a thriving frontier town into a huge metropolitan transportation, business, and manufacturing center for the mid-continent. It was within this city that the first seeds of a contemporary American architecture burst forth, with large office buildings, warehouses, department stores, and hotels being erected in a manner which proved unique and nonrelated to either classical or Gothic styles. Designers such as William Le Baron Jenney, the firms of Holabird and Roche, Burnham & Root, and Adler and Sullivan produced buildings which were direct and functional and wisely employed the products of their age: iron, structural steel, and glass.

This remarkable building spurt was centered in Chicago, in great part, as a result of a disastrous fire which destroyed 17,450 buildings valued at 192 million dollars. One-third of the city disappeared in flames during an October night in 1871, and the citizens, confronted with a huge rebuilding task, promptly undertook an extensive amount of new construction. Chicago designers viewed the opportunity as a challenge to develop new methods of obtaining more permanent and practical structures, and the period was one of extensive research and testing of architectural designs. Many new building materials and techniques were introduced, such as methods of fireproofing structures by the use of hollow tile, the introduction of the hydraulic elevator which made rapid movement possible in multifloored buildings, concrete caissons for sturdy foundations, and the use of steel skeletons in framing large buildings. The use of steel, as well as the elevator, made skyscrapers possible. Steel offered numerous advantages; steel beams and framing members provided great strength with comparatively little weight, ease of fabrication in the scaling of great heights, fire-resistant qualities, and precision of form through the use of predetermined and exact structural members produced in a factory. The first all-metal-framed building in the world was erected in Chicago in 1885. Designed by William Le Baron Jenney, the ten-story Home Insurance Building was a highly unique yet logical accomplishment and served as a model for skyscrapers which followed. Jenney's approach was to let a metal framework of iron and steel carry the entire weight of the building; the outside walls merely hung from this frame and thus were released from bearing the building load. The true skyscraper was thus born, free from the limitations of Grecian columns, Roman domes, and Gothic buttresses.

Until the 1800s, American architecture was produced somewhat in the manner in which children build when playing with wooden blocks; blocks of material were stacked to enclose space. The Chicago School of architecture's notions of building were more in harmony with the methods employed by children when creating forms with an Erector Set, which permit large areas of space to be defined with a limited use of materials. In addition to building with cage-like construction methods permitting the iron skeleton to suggest the form, the Chicago School advanced new notions of floating foundations to compensate for unstable soil and developed the Chicago window, a horizontal elongated expanse of glass. Large areas of walls could now be enclosed with glass panels, owing to skeleton construction. Therefore windows no longer were thought of as pierced holes in walls instead, they were conceived of as sheathing and as a wall itself, thus simplifying building methods and assuring natural lighting in an effective manner. Structural iron and steel and a great use of glass permitted extensive heights to be scaled and interiors flooded with light without massive stone walls or flying buttresses for support. Thus the Chicago School of architecture employed materials and constructional opportunities available in its age and considered the needs of the era as a determining factor in design.

A Man Named Sullivan

The Carson, Pirie, Scott and Company department store, constructed at the turn of the century, serves as an excellent example of the attitude of the Chicago School toward design (Figure 128). The interior of the building possesses great spaciousness, with the skeleton construction providing unrestricted floor areas while the exterior of the structure contains huge areas of glass which act as a transparent curtain wall. The rectangular windows, with their stress on the horizontal, provide a massive dignity suggesting both strength and lightness. Simplicity in construction is evident, and unity of parts is achieved by the repetition of the window forms and also by the use of a continuous thin band of inscribed ornamentation flanking the windows and flowing the length of the lower exterior portion of the building.

The following comment by Louis H. Sullivan,[2] designer of the Carson, Pirie, Scott building, illustrates his reaction toward classical design.

> The Roman temple was a part of Roman life, not of American life; that it beat with Roman pulse, was in touch with Roman activities, and that it waned with Roman glory — it died a Roman death. The Roman temple can no more exist in fact on Monroe Street, Chicago, U.S.A., than can Roman civilization exist there. Such a structure must of necessity be a simulacrum, a ghost.

Sullivan, a great architect and a leading member of the Chicago School, played a key role in the development of an American style in architecture and is frequently thought of as the father of contemporary American architecture. While many of his architectural solutions were derived from the Romantic revival of Romanesque forms, many others, such as his Wainwright Building in St. Louis and the Carson, Pirie, Scott building in Chicago, were free of revivalistic influences and stood as original monuments of their age. Sullivan advanced the notion that form follows function, which implies that a building's style grows out of the purpose or role the building is to serve. Since commercial skyscrapers were a late-nineteenth-century architectural achievement, they demanded a new and unique form; for a previous style or tradition in this area did not exist. Sullivan's concept of "form follows function" did not, however, exclude visual richness

of form as a function of good design; for he was not a purist who would strip form until it stood naked and devoid of interplays of ornamentation. He frequently provided areas of detailing to give pleasure to the eye and attempted to maintain a point between sterility and chaos, between an egg and an ornate wedding cake, as regards surface detailing.

Louis H. Sullivan's views provided designers who followed him with insight into simplicity and logic in building. His contention that "the true work of an architect is to organize, integrate and glorify utility" provided a sensible approach toward design. Function and beauty, he felt, were inseparable in that pleasing form emerged from the effective solution of the practical. This attitude is widely held in this century, but during Sullivan's period, designers felt that both machine and handmade products should be made beautiful through the application of needless details and mimicry of some historical style, frequently without concern for function or intended purpose. In his *The Autobiography of an Idea* Sullivan[3] says regarding himself:

> As buildings varying in character came under his hand, he extended to them his system of form and function, and as he did so his conviction increased that architectural manipulation, as a homely art or a fine art must be rendered completely plastic to the mind and the hand of the designer; that materials and forms must yield to the mastery of his imagination and his will; through this alone could modern conditions be met and faithfully expressed.

Sullivan placed great importance on will and imagination. He contended that systems, styles, and machines should not dictate to man. However, he insisted, man should consider the processes, machines, and building products of his age. The spirit of man thus remains free to invent and dictate, to exist as a controller and manipulator of machine possibilities, rather than be under machine suppression.

While the influence of the Chicago School is now apparent both in America and abroad, its views, unfortunately, were generally ignored in America for several decades following its decline at the turn of the century. Its loss of immediate impact can be attributed in great part to the Chicago World's Fair

---

[2] *Kindergarten Chats and Other Writings* (New York: Wittenborn, Schultz, Inc., 1947), p. 39.

[3] *The Autobiography of an Idea* (New York: Dover Publications, Inc., 1956), p. 258.

128 *Carson, Pirie, Scott Building, Chicago, Ill., Louis Sullivan, 1899.*

buildings of 1893, which were patterned after Roman architecture by way of French academic interpretations. This outside influence, representing the approved taste, the noble manner, of Europe and the American eastern seaboard, was generally accepted in the Midwest following the Fair, and for several decades Romantic and classical revival forms were greatly stressed. Thus is explained the reasoning behind the acceptance of the Gothic-like *Tribune* Tower for a newspaper's offices and plant, several decades later in the very heart of Chicago. The prophecies of the members of the Chicago School, however, have now been fulfilled manyfold in commercial buildings; for they clearly foretold of the construction methods and form of the structures which currently are rising in our age (Figure 129). The Inland Steel Company's nineteen-story structure recently completed in Chicago's Loop serves as a prime example of the Chicago School's continued influence. Designed by the architectural firm of Skidmore, Owings and Merrill, it explicitly incorporates the notion of skeleton construction and the curtain wall. Consisting primarily of a transparent surface unhindered by interior columns, the skyscraper contains the widest unhampered span of any tall building ever built. Fourteen steel columns sheathed in stainless steel support the floors and permit a total freedom in arranging interior space; for facilities such as elevators, fire stairs, and heating and air conditioning are housed in a service tower adjacent to the main structure.

Sullivan, as well as others, indicated the way, but it remained for a youth who had come under his influence to create a twentieth century movement which encompasses the entire range of architecture from economical houses to skyscrapers, from churches to museums. The youth, Frank Lloyd Wright, who in the twilight of his life still referred to Louis H. Sullivan as "Lieber Meister," developed an attitude toward design which possesses comprehensive possibilities for contemporary man. Wright termed his architectural design beliefs organic architecture and spoke with vision, eloquence, and logic to our age.

Organic Architecture: Design Attuned with Nature

Building methods and growth processes in nature unfold their structural secrets in innumerable manners. The endless shapes assumed by shells (Figure 130), a daffodil supported by its stem, a spider's web or beaver's dam, nests high overhead or burrowed deep in the earth are organic relationships found in forest and stream. As a bird extends its wings or the chameleon takes on the color of its surroundings, so an ancient system repeats its scheme to remain a reality of today. As complicated as the universe and as simple as the amoeba, such is the organic procedure; for it is the evolution and continuation of life. Its realm encompasses all the engineering principles and the logic of growing organisms. Its process is as functional as the universe and as natural as the blinking of the eye, the opening and closing of the hand, or breathing in rhythm with the pulsations of a growing organism.

Frank Lloyd Wright

Many artists have long advocated the gaining of design inspiration and insight through observing nature, but one in particular strongly advocated such a practice and directly related natural or organic principles to architecture. His early heritage was broad expanses of earth and sky and nineteenth-century American society, but his architecture bridges the centuries to penetrate deep into our era. His name was Frank Lloyd Wright.

Considered by many to be one of the greatest architects the world has known, Frank Lloyd Wright was born in Richland Center, Wisconsin, four years following the close of the Civil War. Though he died April 8, 1959, in the American southwest, his work continues through former students and followers who share his belief. Wright joins the select few who imprint a civilization with their power of vision and determination of purpose; for he originated many of the architectural principles of modern building and created highly influential architecture throughout the breadth of our land and beyond the seas. In addition to providing man with an awareness of nature and the art of creating contemporary and universal forms, Wright initiated such building techniques as precast concrete blocks and introduced air conditioning, indirect lighting, and panel heating. His engineering feats are remarkable; as one example, his unique designing skill enabled the huge Imperial Hotel in

129   *Contemporary Cage Construction, the growth of The Inland Steel Company Skyscraper, Chicago, Ill., 1958. (Courtesy Inland Steel Company)*

130   *Structure in Nature, radiograph of chambered nautilus sea shell. (Courtesy Eastman Kodak Company)*

131　　*Interior of Massachusetts Bay Colony House, 17th century. (Courtesy United States National Museum, Division of Cultural History)*

Tokyo to remain standing during a severe earthquake which leveled large portions of the city in 1923. He presented a new notion of naturalism in a mechanical era through the employment of space and building materials which create harmony between dwelling and surrounding nature.

Several factors were acknowledged by Wright as determining influences in his development as a designer. As a youngster his interest was stimulated toward architecture by his mother, who exposed him to numerous reproductions of great architectural designs of the past. His early schooling fostered confidence which Wright attributed to the teaching method devised by Friedrich Froebel, founder of the kindergarten method of schooling, which introduces children to problem solving and encourages creativity. Experiences as a youth on a Wisconsin farm provided Wright with an interest in nature and its pattern of growth and organic organization. As a young practicing architect during the period of the extensive building activity in Chicago, his contacts with Louis Sullivan provided insight into architectural possibilities. These influences, combined with a naturally endowed sensitivity and great intellect, assured his success, and a romantic spirit stimulated by the natural philosophies of Whitman,

Emerson, and Thoreau provided courage to rebel against prevailing sterile design practices.

Several Organic Relationships of the Past

"Organic" is the term which Wright employed in reference to his architectural beliefs. A standard dictionary defines organic as "characterized by correlation and cooperation of parts; organized . . . by laws like those of life; not mechanical; . . . depending on structure; fundamental." Thus organic architecture is design which places emphasis on the direct use of materials and the exposure of their surfaces and on an interdependence of all parts of the structure with one another, as well as the sum total of parts and its relationship to the environmental setting. "Organic" therefore implies logical and natural growth, a harmony within the structure, and a sense of belonging evident in the relationship of the building to its site.

Certain historical styles possessed organic qualities as regards use of materials, the relationship of parts to the entire structure, or the harmony of form and surroundings. Regarding a dependence of parts to achieve the whole, the Gothic cathedral may be thought of as containing organic elements. Flying buttresses perform a prime function in supporting the walls; for without their support or thrust

132 *Troxell-Steckel House, Lehigh County, Pa., late 18th century. (Courtesy* CALL-CHRONICLE, *Allentown, Pa.)*

the cathedral could not grow. In addition, buttresses tend to wed the structure to its environment by suggesting ribs emerging from the earth. It would be highly improbable that a Gothic cathedral would remain standing if buttresses were removed; however, many columns might be removed and walls and roof remain standing in various classical temples, because a structural interdependency would not be apparent. Romanesque architecture contained organic evidences in retaining the natural surface qualities of building materials for visual enrichment. Much Japanese architecture possesses strong organic features in construction method; the employment of materials with emphasis on natural surfaces and transparency and the incorporation of surrounding nature within the form.

Over a century ago, during the classical revival, the term "organic" was employed by the American sculptor Horatio Greenough, who mentioned it as pertaining to the logic of designing architecture from the inside outward. Rather than having a prescribed traditional style determine the form of a building, Greenough contended that the design should be originally conceived through a consideration of the purpose for which the interior is to serve and thereby naturally unfold. During the earlier, prerevolutionary period, Colonial architecture con-

tained certain organic relationships, but the form was usually based on traditional styles carried from the mother countries of the various settlers.

The style of New England Colonial architecture, for instance, was mainly derived from seventeenth- and eighteenth-century English forms. New York was influenced by Dutch designs, while in Pennsylvania and Delaware, Welsh, German, and Swedish designs flourished. In Virginia and the Carolinas, English influence was also in evidence; however, often brick rather than wood and a more open plan were used there than in the more frigid north. Italian and Spanish baroque styles were carried into Florida, the Southwest, and California by Jesuit missionaries.

These transplanted styles possessed effective arrangements of interiors for living purposes. Treatments were frequently organic in the sense of a natural unfolding of these interiors, with exposed structural members and inherent surfaces contributing fundamental visual relationships (Figure 131). The use of local materials to provide shelter, such as stone in certain locales, with a correlation of exterior and interior through a consistent and sequential use of the material also provided natural or organic relationships in many Colonial structures (Figure 132).

133 *Taliesin West, the desert, near Phoenix, Ariz., Frank Lloyd Wright, 1938. (Courtesy Samuel C. Sabean)*

134 *The Mountains Below the Kaufmann House, Bear Run, Pa., Frank Lloyd Wright, 1936. (Photographed by Bill Hedrich, Hedrich-Blessing)*

The Style of the Master in Desert and Mountain

Timeless architectural tendencies were retained by Frank Lloyd Wright and reinterpreted in terms of contemporary engineering, personal sensitivity, and inventiveness to formulate the basis of his architecture (Figure 133). Designed to hug the desert floor, exposing little surface to warm winds, Taliesin West was constructed by Wright and his students with common materials: canvas, redwood boards, and rough masonry. Visually in tune with its surroundings, the winter camp housed living quarters, workshops, and studios of both teacher and apprentices. Conceived as a great, tent-like structure, it both grasps and releases interior and exterior space with exciting vitality. Large redwood trusses support partial walls and roof panels of translucent canvas which filter natural light and provide shade during the heat of the day. Certain areas of the roof are hinged, enabling sections to be thrown open to admit cooling evening breezes and a view of the star-studded Arizona sky. Thus a spatial penetration was secured between nature and man-made form, with climatic and environmental conditions affecting its style.

The rugged grandeur of a mountain setting demands a vastly different architectural solution than does the drifting-sand and warm-wind environment of the American Southwest. Wright, in creating the Kaufmann house, beautifully and effectively solved the problem of building in a challenging mountainous site, encompassing a series of rocky ledges, creek, and waterfalls. Called *Falling Water*, the house, (Figure 134), completed in 1936 at Bear Run, Pennsylvania, clearly illustrates that a level lot is not a prime requisite for building, and its form, highly influential on numerous architects, serves as an excellent example of organic principles incorporated within architecture. The house is fully integrated within its locale, suggesting a belonging between itself and the surrounding environment, through utilizing the contour of the land, employing local stone, and cantilevering portions of the form. Wright compared cantilever construction to a waiter balancing a tray upon his fingers and frequently incorporated it in his architectural ventures. Secured through balancing and anchoring steel beams into surrounding rock, the Kaufmann house is cantilevered beyond the limits of surrounding rocky ledges. Great portions of the structure thus soar outward, grasping and enclosing areas of outlying nature through projected movements of steel and concrete slabs (Figure 135). Wright also harmoniously related the house to an adjacent stream in providing suspended steps which permitted descent to the water below. Surrounding retaining walls wed house and stream by enlarging the frame of reference of concrete and stone. Textural interplays between rough masonry, concrete, and glass within the design complement one another while providing contrasting surfaces, and during the day an ever-changing pattern of shadows denies a static mood through joyful fluctuations in light and shade. Strong segment penetrations and thrusts with a major emphasis on horizontal movements give sensations of fused, retained, and liberated space and a comprehensive yet consistent unity of form. Can you imagine peering over the lower porch to view the mountain brook or feeling that surrounding mountain laurel, ferns, and pines harmonize with your man-made shelter?

A semirough stone floor carries the rocky environment indoors and joins masonry walls and glass in unifying exterior with interior (Figure 136). Changing ceiling levels and deviations in wall areas add exciting space relationships and release the interior from a conventional rectangular treatment. Built-in furniture also offers ease of maintenance and economizes space, while large expanses of glass suggest an extension of space and provide natural light and invigorating view.

Frank Lloyd Wright[4] enclosed space in manners which provide stimulation and excitement as well as refuge and privacy. In addition to fulfilling the needs of the occupants, the interior determined exterior relationships. Wright did not, however, rigidly differentiate between interior and exterior, but rather conceived both as being inseparable and free to intermingle and naturally unfold. He made his attitude explicit when he said,

> We have no longer an outside and an inside as two separate things. Now the outside may come inside and the inside may and does go outside. They are of each other.

Proving to be a great Romantic in handling space and material, he freely took advantage of machine technology and frequently developed new processes in order to express his notions of architecture. Though fully aware of the unique possibilities obtainable through the use of steel, concrete, glass, plastics, stone, wood, and innumerable other materials, he went far beyond being dictated to by these substances, or by contemporary machines and processes. His beliefs were based on life and limited only by the bounds of man's ability to conceive of new architectural solutions. His design ability is apparent in all areas of architecture ranging from private housing to religious, civic, educational, and industrial structures; his creations are evident in New York City in the form of a great circular museum housing paintings as well as across the continent in San Francisco in a downtown business establishment selling china, glass, and silver. A consideration of several of his major design undertakings reveals his skill and imaginative powers and provides one with an awareness of the extensive possibilities of enclosing space, providing natural light, using materials in exciting manners, and developing unique forms.

[4] *The Natural House* (New York: Horizon Press, Inc., 1954), p. 50.

135   *Above the Kaufmann House. (Photographed by Bill Hedrich, Hedrich-Blessing)*

136   *Interior of the Kaufmann House. (Photographed by Bill Hedrich, Hedrich-Blessing)*

Museum, Library, Factory: Form, Light, Structure

Rather than follow the conventional solution of stacking floor upon floor, which involves climbing numerous steps in moving from floor to floor, would it be possible to produce a museum which permits spectators a more pleasant means of viewing a multitude of paintings? Frank Lloyd Wright certainly thought so in designing the Solomon R. Guggenheim Museum in New York City. He solved the problem by creating the means which enable spectators to take elevators high into the structure and reverse the common procedure by walking from the top downward. A continuous ascending ramp, subtly sloped to go unnoticed, permits a gradual descent as individuals move from painting to painting (Figure 137). Clustered in groupings or separately hung upon unpierced walls, the paintings are keenly visible for a great amount of natural light is admitted through a huge overhead glass dome which acts as a portion of the roof. Additional natural light is provided through continuous bands of overhead glassed panels which circle the sides of the entire structure. The gently unwinding ramp hugs the enclosing wall and permits the central core of the building to consist of a huge expanse of unoccupied space. Thus observers are enabled to sense innu-

137   *Main Gallery and Exhibition Bays, Solomon R. Guggenheim Museum, New York, N. Y., Frank Lloyd Wright, 1959. (Courtesy The Solomon R. Guggenheim Museum and Ezra Stoller, Photographer)*

merable paintings arranged on distant encircling walls. On the ground level, areas are available for displaying huge sculptures. The interior solution, conceived and treated as a huge, gently unwinding spiral, determined the exterior relationships of glass and reinforced concrete (Figure 138).

Wright frequently employed unusual and exciting means of obtaining natural light in an interior without depending on conventional window treatments which offer distractions and deny essential wall space and privacy. Somewhat as the Roman Pantheon admits light from an overhead source, natural light livens the E. T. Roux Library (Figure 139). Wright's solution effectively illustrates how light may sensitively define relationships, suggest naturalism, extend space, and cast invigorating patterns of dark and light within an interior. Students in the library retain a sensation of linkage with the outside world while contemplating the written word. An easily accessible service desk enables ease of inquiry and assistance, and structural detailing provides both serenity and charm. Organic architecture is not frigidly contained within itself, but permits visual excursions through variations in light and space.

The treatment for housing the S. C. Johnson and Son Company, a large manufacturing concern, is acclaimed by many as a great contribution to business shelter and one of the high watermarks of twentieth century architecture (Figure 140). In addition to containing rich visual relationships and a great work practicality, the buildings were among the first to have offices completely air conditioned and to use radiant floor heating. Wright's unified plan elegantly groups and relates a variety of structures devoted to research, production, advertising, purchasing, administration, and allied activities essential to a leading industrial firm.

An administration building, located to the right of a giant globe indicating the company's worldwide operations, and a research tower are major structures within the grouping. The administration building possesses circular portions which blend and flow into one another to provide a united composite of parts. The top circular structure, related to the main structure through surface and shape, houses a "nostril" through which air is drawn for air conditioning equipment. A driveway to the left of the administration building leads to a carport and main entrance. A Plexiglass bridge and

138 *Exterior of Solomon R. Guggenheim Museum. (Courtesy The Solomon R. Guggenheim Museum and Ezra Stoller, Photographer)*

139 *E. T. Roux Library, Florida Southern College, Lakeland, Fla., Frank Lloyd Wright, 1936. (Courtesy the President, Florida Southern College)*

various covered passageways provide shelter and easy access to various portions of the company, while to one side a garden, partially enclosed by surrounding buildings, display plants and flowers to the employees, thus serving as a focalpoint of natural richness.

The lobby of the administration building and a huge work area beyond contain cast reinforced concrete "golf-tee" pillars only nine inches at the base, thereby saving a great amount of floor space (Figure 141). The pillars flare outward high overhead and appear to soar amidst shimmering expanses of light. This pattern of solidity against the transparency of the skylights provides great emotional impact in addition to wide areas of support for the ceiling composed of tubular lighting. The circular upper masses of the columns in repeating the external circular forms of the structure also tend to unify the interior with curved exterior masses.

An interesting episode occurred when Frank Lloyd Wright first proposed employing the golf-tee columns. Several building inspectors and engineers suspicious of anything new scoffed and protested that such a shaft was not capable of bearing weight of any sort. Wright, not limited by formulas or proven forms but rather possessive of keen engineering insight and creative ingenuity, proposed a test of the columns before they were used in the building. A golf-tee shaft was set up in a field and a crane placed ton after ton of bagged cement upon the top of the column. It remained erect under a load far exceeding what it was intended to bear, and the test was terminated only when no space on its top surface in which to stack additional weight remained. Wright, now fully vindicated, was free to use his columns.

The Research Tower also illustrates an original system of support employed by Wright (Figure 142). The tower, completed in 1950, is supported by a narrow hollow shaft exposed at the bottom of the structure. Rising 153 feet in height, the tower, owing to this small base, appears suspended in space and proves to be the tallest building ever constructed without foundations directly under the side walls. Each of the fifteen floors is cantilevered from the central shaft, which is anchored in a concrete foundation that penetrates fifty-four feet into the earth (Figure 143). Support is secured in a manner similar to that by which a taproot, deeply embedded in the ground, supports a giant oak which above the earth flares outward with branches and foliage.

Within the supporting shaft are housed supply and exhaust chambers for air conditioning plus utility services. An elevator and a circular stairway are located on opposite sides of the shaft. The reinforced concrete walls of the shaft, which are seven to ten inches in thickness, prove more than adequate to support the projected floors which thrust into space.

A conventional window functions only in providing light during the daylight hours, but Frank Lloyd Wright devised a means of extending the role of a window in the Research Tower. Can you conceive of a means of creating windows which provide light both day and night and also serves as walls?

If fluorescent lights, possessing long tubular relationships, were used to build a wall, the entire wall surface could be lit during the evening, and in daytime the semitransparent wall would permit the passage of natural light as well as assuring privacy. Wright originated such a means for sheathing the Research Tower by employing seventeen miles of glass tubing to present artificial light in the evening, permit the filtration of natural light during the day, and encircle the tower to serve as outer walls. Bands of brick also comprise a portion of the walls and provide interest through contrast with the glass surfaces. The glass walls of tubing and plate glass are secured by stainless-steel wire which binds them to aluminum supports in the interior of the Research Tower (Figure 144).

Floors consist of reinforced concrete slabs suspended outward through cantilevered construction from the inner supporting shaft. They alternate between circular areas which do not project completely to the outer wall and square floors which do. The curved undersides of mezzanine, or balcony, floors provide a partial ceiling for alternating square floors, and in terminating before reaching the outer walls they create interesting space relationships and also assure an overhead source of natural light for the level below.

Frank Lloyd Wright's organic style is an influential factor in contemporary design. A Romantic blessed with great creative vitality and building logic, his architecture also proves in tune with the great design compositions of all time. His ability to create new methods of handling space and light and material for emotional impact as well as shelter, his development of original means of suspending and supporting forms, and his ability to unify structure and site assure him a rightful and dominant position in the history of architecture.

140   S. C. Johnson and Son Company, Racine, Wisc., Frank Lloyd Wright, 1938. (Courtesy S. C. Johnson and Son Company)

141   Administration Building, S. C. Johnson and Son Company, Racine, Wisc., lobby with golf-tee pillars, Frank Lloyd Wright, 1938. (Courtesy S. C. Johnson and Son Company)

142   *The Research Tower, S. C. Johnson and Son Company, Racine, Wisc., evening view, Frank Lloyd Wright, 1950. (Courtesy S. C. Johnson and Son Company)*

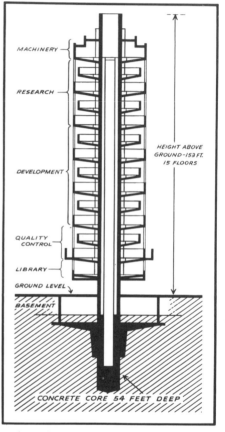

143   *Construction Details, The Research Tower, S. C. Johnson and Son Company, Racine, Wisc., Frank Lloyd Wright, 1950. (Courtesy S. C. Johnson and Son Company)*

144   *Working Space and Wall Treatment, The Research Tower, S. C. Johnson and Son Company, Racine, Wisc., Frank Lloyd Wright, 1950. (Courtesy S. C. Johnson and Son Company)*

145   *Front View, Arvid Molitor House, Elgin, Ill., sketch, 1952. (Courtesy the Designer, Herb Fritz)*

Two Organic Designers and Their Homes

In order to meet the varying needs of individuals and relate the structure to its particular environment, each house presents an individual and specific design problem which demands a unique solution. Thus organic architecture remains a series of creative challenges with a wide range of potential solutions which can be arrived at only upon consideration of the physical and social needs of the intended occupants and the characteristics of the site.

The Midwest prairie presents a challenge in relating structures to vast expanses of level land. Herb Fritz, organic architect, solved this problem by accenting strong horizontal movements in his design of the Arvid Molitor home in Elgin, Illinois (Figure 145). The house appears wedded to the landscape through long low walls and a broad horizontal roof which harmonize with their environment of fertile prairie and boundless sky. A continuous exchange of mass results in exciting extensions and penetrations of space and material repetition within the form. Interior and exterior become one; rich surface contrasts occur as wood and concrete intermingle indoors and outdoors; and create broad passages of light and shadow to enchant the viewer. A dramatic structural sequence also permits a cantilevered porch to extend the livability of the home (Figure 146).

Through consistency and inventive variety Herb Fritz permitted the form to naturally unfold and elegantly shelter the occupants.

An oriental philosopher once said that it is the hollow that makes the bowl. Architecture should be considered in a somewhat similar manner; for enclosed space, not roof and walls, is the true reality of architecture. One should consider the three-dimensional aspects of house design as a flexible mass with the enclosed area comprised of plastic space which can be defined, controlled, restricted, and released in manners which provide delight and impact. Interior space should not be visualized as a large square or rectangular box containing numerous smaller boxes, or rooms, which is the concept apparent in conventional housing, but rather as an enclosure which, through exciting divisions, sensations of additional space can be achieved by elimination and suggestion. Organic architects frequently eliminate basements, attics, and interior partitions except those essential for privacy in order to secure spaciousness and freedom of floor space. Ceilings are often formed by the roof itself and lowered or raised to produce interesting masses and fluctuations in overhead space. Partial walls and variations in room

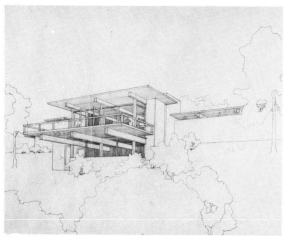

146 *Rear View, Arvid Molitor House, Elgin, Ill., sketch, 1952. (Courtesy the Designer, Herb Fritz)*

147 *Interior Living Area, John L. Haughwout Home, Milroy, Pa., 1959. (Courtesy the Architect, John L. Haughwout)*

levels are also manipulated for interesting and continuous spatial flow. Space is also retained and released by glass areas which provide sequence between the exterior and the outdoors, and overhanging roofs and walls projecting outward from the interior also tend to suggest, when viewed from the interior, additional space. Ceilings and portions of walls are often produced of an identical material, thereby becoming part of each other and presenting a coherent movement. Wood, stone, and plantings provide an organic or natural effect within interiors, and built-in furniture and lighting fixtures provide simplicity and unity. Feeling that natural light is the beautifier of the building, organic designers frequently employ skylights and large window expanses. They do not ignore decorative possibilities, but rather, at times, arrange building materials to provide decorative pattern or employ small areas of inscribed or applied decoration in key locales. This tends to provide contrast and richness to the interior, but the element of control or restraint is always evident.

In describing his organic home, the architect John L. Haughwout speaks of many important factors:

A change of floor elevation can often suggest a change of space use. In my home, the Living Room is only partially separated from the Dining Area on the level above, and the eye is allowed to travel to areas beyond. (Figure 147)

Natural light, admitted by the use of clerestory windows, can often enhance an interior room, as a Kitchen Work Area, by lending a cheerfulness while adding a refreshing change of ceiling height. (Figure 148)

If architecture is not to be over-stated, it must simply be a functional shelter, a cultural expression and a compliment to its environment.

A structure intended for human occupancy should reflect human scale through the use of materials and dimensions proportioned to their intended use, so that one feels directly related to his environment and thus becomes an inherent part of it.

Romanticism with a suggestion of classicism sometimes can touch the human soul more intimately than abstract purity or skeletal honesty.

If a site is naturally informal, it would seem sheer folly to attempt to formalize the environment. Maintaining an informal character can effect an indigenous quality so that the structure becomes part of the landscape. (Figure 149)

Perhaps more important to architecture than any other single aspect is its environment, here expressed intimately with nature on a hillside site commanding an outlook of the valley below. Such environment not only fosters good design, but fairly cries out for recognition. (Figure 150)

Kitchen Work Area, John L. Haughwout Home, Milroy, Pa., 1959. (Courtesy the Architect, John L. Haughwout)

148

149 *Details of Suspended and Integrated Masses Housing the Living, Dining, and Kitchen Areas, John L. Haughwout Home, Milroy, Pa., 1959. (Courtesy the Architect, John L. Haughwout)*

Roof, Window, and Wall Details, a strong suggestion of shelter while admitting nature, John L. Haughwout Home, Milroy, Pa., 1959. (Courtesy the Architect, John L. Haughwout)

150

International Architecture: Harmony With the Machine Age

151   *The Castel Henriette, Belgium, Art Nouveau architecture, designed by H. Guimard, 1903. (Courtesy Museum of Modern Art)*

Radical changes in architectural design became apparent in Europe, as well as America, during the first quarter of this century. Designs such as Castel Henriette, indicative of the Art Nouveau Movement, were accepted in Europe, especially in France and Belgium, at the turn of the century (Figure 151). Henry F. Lenning[5], an authority on the movement, contended that houses such as Castel Henriette were "built for effect alone, to astonish the eye with incredible architectural manipulations." Stressing extensive variations in details and segments, ornate complexities, and usually lacking compactness or unity, Art Nouveau was frequently representative of visual exhibitionism and structural chaos. Common traits link it with many American late-Victorian forms through a mutual sharing of overindulgent practices. Though lacking evidences of economy of means or logical sequence, Art Nouveau served as a transitional link between the artificiality of European revival forms and contemporary architectural expression. It tended to use materials in an honest manner by retaining natural surfaces rather than attempting to cover them with foreign substances so that iron would appear to be stone, or wood marble. Alas, however, the Art Nouveau designer was still reluctant to treat materials in uncomplicated manners, but rather preferred to beautify through bending, twisting, and organizing toward structural ornateness.

Although separated by only twenty-five years in time, a world of differences exists between H. Guimard's Castel Henriette and The Savoye House designed by Le Corbusier (Figure 152). The latter is representative of the international style of architecture which emerged in Europe during the 1920s. This design movement, led by Le Corbusier, Walter Gropius (the founder of the Bauhaus), Ludwig Mies van der Rohe, and others, stands in complete opposition to practices evident in Art Nouveau. The international designer considered this century as a machine age and contended that contemporary technology should assist architecture in providing explicit means toward achieving logical and direct forms. In addition to the influence of the machine, the visual imagery composed by the painter Piet Mondrian and the Dutch de stijl group were stimulating factors to international designers. A shared admiration of direct construction methods and simple rectangular shapes led to uncomplicated geometric arrangements.

152   *Savoye House, Poissy-sur-Seine, France, designed by Le Corbusier, 1929. (Courtesy Museum of Modern Art and Le Corbusier)*

[5] *The Art Nouveau*, (The Hague, Netherlands: Martinus Nijhoff, 1951), p. 89.

Living Room and Terrace, Savoye House, Poissy-sur-Seine, France, designed by Le Corbusier, 1929. (Courtesy Museum of Modern Art and Le Corbusier)

153

Le Corbusier

The designs of Le Corbusier[6] are clear, crisp solutions to enclosing space with classical undertones.

> . . . there has been nothing like it anywhere or at any period . . . pure forms in precise relationships

His opinion of the Parthenon indicates an awareness and appreciation of Grecian proportion and visual harmonies. But Le Corbusier's designs are not linked to the past; for he takes full advantage of the materials of his age, develops highly personal solutions to identify architectural space, and provides man with a belief in his period of history. His creative ingenuity is apparent when one considers forms such as the Savoye House, a hallmark of early, yet mature, international architecture. Raised on pillars, acting as stilts, with inclined ramps leading from the ground level to living quarters and terrace on the second level and topped with a roof garden, the ferro-concrete house possesses dignity through extreme simplification and precise arrangements. The use of slender pillars, uncluttered surfaces, and large areas of glass contribute a buoyant quality which tends to refute the massiveness of the form. An examination of the interior indicates the justification of the term *les heures claires*, the bright hours, employed by former occupants in describing this home (Figure 153). The interior, based on an open plan, permits rooms to be easily enclosed or opened. Such an interior modification of space is obtainable by the use of non-bearing interior walls which can be rearranged to suit the desires of the tenants. Large sliding glass panels form one wall, from floor to ceiling, in the living quarters and assure an abundance of natural light and easy accessibility to an adjacent terrace. The entire house, supported as it is above the surface of the earth, has a commanding view of the surrounding French landscape.

Though he is sympathetic toward nature, Le Corbusiers' attitude[7] toward design is in complete harmony with modern technology and machine production for he says,

> If we eliminate from our hearts and minds all dead concepts in regard to houses and look at the question from a critical and objective point of view, we shall arrive at the House Machine, the mass-production house, healthy (and morally so too) and beautiful in the same way that the working tools and instruments which accompany our existence are beautiful.

Individuals may tend to question the implication of mechanization, the lack of the human element in the above notion; however, its practicality is in opposition to the abuses of Art Nouveau. Le Corbusier, one of the great architects of this century, has contributed much to raise the living standards of large segments of society by creating designs ranging from single houses to huge public buildings in France, as well as Russia, Brazil, and elsewhere. He has even devised an entire city plan for the new capital of East Punjab in Asia.

[6] *Towards a New Architecture* (New York: Brewer, Warren and Putnam, Inc., 1926), p. 219.

[7] *Ibid.*, p. 227.

Walter Gropius

Walter Gropius[8], another founder of the international style and a leading designer of our century, views the international movement as design which,

> instead of anchoring buildings ponderously into the ground with massive foundations . . . poises them lightly, yet firmly upon the face of the earth; and bodies itself forth not in stylistic imitation or ornamental frippery but in those simple and sharply modelled designs in which every part merges naturally into the comprehensive volume of the whole.

Walter Gropius strongly advocates standardization in building as a means on increasing quality while decreasing costs, contending that doors, staircases, portions of walls, floors, and fittings can now be machine produced and a range of design possibilities will still exist because modifications in assembling and unifying parts will permit varied solutions. Furthermore, through technical proficiency and power equipment — saws, joiners, presses, and lathes — materials and segments can be rapidly produced and thus provide decent housing to a larger portion of society. Gropius created excellent factories and public buildings in Germany during the first quarter of the century; he employed structural steel and a cage method of building which permitted the incorporation of huge areas of glass in the form.

During the turbulent 1930s, various architects of the international movement settled in the United States. Their influence soon became evident in the American landscape, and their roles as teachers served to assure that their views would be assimilated in our society. Houses composed of rectangular and square arrangements of concrete surfaces, painted white and topped with flat roofs, now began to appear in our nation. Flat roofs permitted uncomplicated interior planning, economical construction and ease of future expansion, safety through the elimination of timber rafters (frequently a cause of fire), a usable roof area for a sun deck, and the elimination of unnecessary surfaces presented to wind and weather. The John Hicks home (Figure 154), designed by John J. Flad, clearly indicates form growing out of the European internationalists' design attitude. Such a severe logical form, exact and formal in execution, was a popular

architectural expression during the second quarter of our century; several may possibly be found within your immediate neighborhood.

Following their arrival in America, Walter Gropius served as Chairman of the Department of Architecture, Harvard University, and Ludwig Mies van der Rohe journeyed inland to teach in Chicago. Both have designed numerous exciting and unusual structures such as Walter Gropius's Harvard Graduate Center and his tentative Civic Center for Tallahassee, Florida, and Mies van der Rohe's Farnsworth House and Seagram Building.

The proposed Tallahassee Civic Auditorium illustrates the engineering skill and originality of concept of Walter Gropius in providing a suitable structure for sheltering numerous occupants (Figure 155). A pillar-free interior that offers an unhampered view is achieved through use of a reinforced concrete tubular roof composed of segments supported at one end by struts and held in suspension at the other extremity by the action of a huge arch bowing above the roof mass. This solution for overhead shelter gains a solidity through sequence of mass; for each tubular roof segment tends to exert pressure against neighboring members. Though the poured-concrete shells must be reinforced with steel mesh or rod arrangements — for concrete is not possessive of strength in compression or tension — the material retains a molded form when dry and proves relatively inexpensive, maintenance-free, and permanent. Such a reinforced concrete roof is readily obtainable by pouring one segment at a time. Following a short drying process, underlying supports are removed and employed for adjacent pourings.

The main floor of the auditorium is to be partially supported by pillars, which enable the form to perch above its surroundings. The use of these pillars, as well as a huge pierced screen flanking a portion of the building, permits a sweeping circulation of air, thus assuring natural air conditioning as well as suggesting space penetration and subsequent lightness to the form. The white surface of the auditorium, in addition to refuting a notion of massiveness and great weight, acts to reflect rather than retain heat cast by the warm southern sun.

[8] *The New Architecture and the Bauhaus* (Boston: Charles T. Branford Co., 1937), p. 43.

154   *The John Hicks Home, Village of Shorewood, Wisc., international design prac-*
tices as transplanted during the 1930s in America, designed by John J. Flad.
(Courtesy John Hicks)

155   *Auditorium, Tallahassee, Fla., model of proposed design by The Architects Collaborative,*
Partner in Charge: Walter Gropius. (Courtesy Walter Gropius)

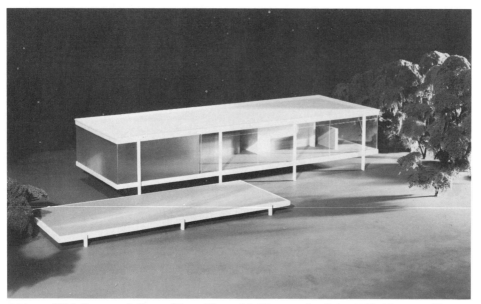

156 *Edith Farnsworth House, Plano, Ill., model, Mies van der Rohe, 1950. (Courtesy Museum of Modern Art and Mies van der Rohe)*

Ludwig Mies van der Rohe

The Edith Farnsworth house is indicative of the contemporary practices of Mies van der Rohe in creating shelter through a minimum of detail (Figure 156). The house consists of floor and roof suspended between eight steel columns with kitchen, bathroom, heating unit, and fireplace centrally housed in a wood-paneled utility core. This solution presents a surrounding free expanse of interior space that offers innumerable furniture arrangements. The steel frame and the floors of Italian travertine, a marblelike substance, provide great durability to the structure, while the liberal use of glass adds charm and sparkle to the uncomplicated rectangular design. An adjacent raised platform, serving as a patio, extends the living area of the house.

Absolutely no superficialities are evident in Mies van der Rohe's solutions; for he believes that the most direct and practical solution leads toward the greatest result. Many of his constructions make demands on industry to provide new materials, large sheets of nonglare and tinted glass, lightweight concrete, new metal alloys, and precise structural members. Thus the frontiers of research are extended through these unique requirements essential to fulfilling his intentions. Bronze sheathing 158,000 square feet in area and weighing over 3 million pounds, subjected to a hurricane test of 120–miles per hour winds, and 3676 nonglare glass panels, tinted pinkish gray to blend with the bronze as it ages and weathers, were used in Mies van der Rohe's Seagram Building (Figure 157). Steel weighing 25 million pounds and secured by 190,000 high-tensile bolts was used to frame the approximately twelve acres of floor space in the 520–foot-high, 38–story skyscraper. The dramatic skeleton construction skinned with bronze and glass expresses the sensitivity of selection, proportion, and scale as well as the integrity possessed by Mies van der Rohe. Blending the precision and accomplishments of our technological age with echoes of Jenney and Sullivan as well as international design practices, the skyscraper's crispness of form enriches the New York skyline. Twentieth century skyscraper design has now come of age and appears as an honest expression of its era. Flying buttresses and pediments have gone the way of the crossbow and the kerosene lamp; for the words of contemporary organic and international architects now ring true as their prophecies are fulfilled.

A New York City building ordinance limits the tower of any skyscraper to twenty-five per cent of the building site. The restriction serves to permit light and air to sweep through the city's man-made canyons and, in part, combat the exhaust fumes of vehicles. Rather than follow the usual practice of designing a skyscraper in several stages so that step-backs occur as the height increases, Mies van der Rohe set the entire form back from the street so that an unbroken mass soars toward the clouds. This solution also made possible a plaza with fountains, trees, various plantings, and benches that offers city dwellers a moment of contemplation amid the chaos of traffic and the hectic pace of the city. The sacrificed building space devoted to plaza, in addition to providing an area of enchantment, serves to set off and accent the monumentality and dignity of the Seagram skyscarper. Beneath the paved plaza and surrounding sidewalks and entrances an underground heating system, capable of melting five hundred tons of ice a day, is available for the season of slush and snow. Also beneath the earth is a subbasement garage with space for parking 150 cars. Directly above, on street level, a recessed lobby gives shelter to man and the sensation that the massive overhead skyscraper is delicately yet firmly balanced upon the adjacent slender columns.

What makes this skyscraper a great architectural accomplishment while innumerable others warrant consideration only as engineering feats? Simplicity; for Mies van der Rohe handles the best engineering practices of our age with originality and purity. He fulfills his objective in creating a unified form with the directness of concise poetry; for proportion and truth provide the dressing. Ordering space, vertical and horizontal planes, and structure into harmonious relationship, his design stresses an apparent logical and effortless ease of construction. The concise clear form, seemingly almost transparent and with surfaces free of indentures or protrusions, implies a discipline in tune with the maximum values obtainable from a machine age. Such values are strictly controlled and manipulated as expressive and effective elements by Mies van der Rohe to produce highly functional architecture.

157   *Seagram Skyscraper, New York, N. Y., Mies van der Rohe, 1958. (Courtesy A. A. Schechter Associates)*

Organic and International Style
Comparisons: Differences in Opinion

The particular advantage in considering factors which separate organic and international architects is the resulting awareness of a diversity in attitudes which may broaden and enhance design understanding. However, in contrasting the styles it becomes obvious that, while major differences exist, many factors bond them to common design practices. Any evaluation of conceptional differences should not be viewed as derogatory of either or imply the suitability of one at the expense of the other. Both movements and tentative offshoots have made and will continue to make major contributions to the landscape of man in offering spiritual and physical warmth. Neither group has a monopoly on ingenuity and creative action, and both groups share a common cause; the creation and continuation of great architecture to serve and inspire man. Even the terms which identify both styles can be viewed as false barriers; for organic qualities such as an interdependency of segments and a logical sequence in structure are frequently strongly apparent in international architecture. Also, the term "organic" may be viewed as international if used to imply an influence not bound to a specific region; for the impact of Frank Lloyd Wright is not restricted to our shores. Furthermore, contemporary architectural practices are not limited to either or both movements; for numerous architects combine features of both styles as well as bring to bear their unique personalities, beliefs, and particular experiences independently of both styles.

Both international and organic architects stress the importance of the machine and its products as a determining influence on design and employ current engineering practices. The internationalist remains closer to machine determinates, while the organic designer frequently tends to incorporate organic materials — field stones, for instance — rather than preformed panels or concrete to serve as walls. This leads to more romantic and less formal results and tends somewhat to counter our machine age. It should not be concluded, however, that a primitive quality is sought for; rather the concept is that, when feasible, structure and nature are one. An emphasis on nature is prevalent throughout the organic designer's thinking. For instance, consider the use of color. Internationalists and followers tend to employ primary colors, bright reds, yellows, or blues, to present striking contrasts and imme-

diate impact, while organic designers are sympathetic toward Wright's attitude:[9]

> Go to the woods and fields for color schemes. Use the soft, warm, optimistic tones of earths and autumn leaves in preference to the pessimistic blues, purples or cold greens and grays of the ribbon counters; they are more wholesome and better adapted in most cases to good decoration.

The organic architect sets the house into an environment and, through roof and wall projections, retains and releases the form in tune with its surroundings. The contour and natural features of the earth in part determine the solution, and horizontal masses frequently are employed to relate the structure to its earthen base. The international designer often isn't concerned with maintaining such a relationship but rather, at times, with stilts, even projects the house above its environment. Man thus tends to rule nature. Confined to roof gardens and enclosed terraces, nature is both controlled and retained in international solutions such as the Savoye House by Le Corbusier. While organic architecture unfolds and extends beyond its form, an international form usually tends to be confined within itself and thus be self-contained. Interior space is usually handled in a more explicit and concise manner in international solutions. Nonsupporting interior walls permit a number of rearrangements within the enclosed rectangular mass. Spatial flow is more complex and plastic in organic architecture through frequent fluctuations in floor, wall, and ceiling levels. Both styles admit a wealth of natural light, but more variety in admittance, through skylights and clerestory as well as window walls, is probably evident in organic solutions.

An apparent difference exists in degree of directness in achieving intended form. Internationalists strongly stress conciseness and simplicity and the avoidance of applied decoration. Visual richness is sought for in the structural memberships and their straightforward arrangements as well as in the surface properties of manufactured materials, such as transparency, color qualities, reflective tendencies, and textural characteristics. The over-all mass is treated as a functional form with emphasis on economy and utility.

[9] *Seven Arts*, edited by Fernando Puma (Garden City, N. Y.: Doubleday & Co., 1953), p. 73.

It should not be concluded, however, that in meeting the utilitarian requirements of architecture in the most effective manner function is completely fulfilled and good design automatically results. Such a simplification would deny architecture its rightful place as an art form; for the creative spirit of man would not be permitted to fully operate. At its extreme, directness or simplification leads toward sterility and form devoid of personality. An emphasis on simplicity, however, has an economic value and is a natural reaction to, as well as at times overcompensation for, the abuses of applied decoration and absurd complexities of Art Nouveau and late Victorian design.

Two notions of function are currently widely accepted, and many practitioners fluctuate between the two as extremes. Mies van der Rohe tends to operate at one end of the range, while Frank Lloyd Wright was active at the other. The greatness of both is found in their effective interpretations within their particular positions; for their architectural productions fully reach their intended purposes and logically operate in conjunction with their beliefs. Louis Sullivan's famous and frequently misinterpreted view that "form follows function" may act to clarify the cleavage between international and organic practices while serving to indicate the visual practicality of both. Sullivan advanced his notion as a means of breaking away from the classical and Romantic limitations of the past century and intended his comment to imply that style or form grows out of purpose or role the form is to play. A skyscraper should look like a skyscraper and not a church, an office building should solve the problems to be carried on within its interior, and the outside should convey these intentions rather than speak of the glories of Greece. Sullivan, however, viewed function as involvement with visual satisfaction as well as physical shelter. Architecture involved more than permitting one to remain warm and dry in adequate shelter; for it also included the visual qualities of such shelter, exciting, stirring. Sullivan therefore did not exclude decorative detailing as a prime requisite of architecture, and he viewed function and form as inseparable. Frank Lloyd Wright[10] also echoed this attitude:

Decoration is intended to make use more charming and comfort more appropriate, or else a privilege has been abused.

Many followers of the international style would refute such contentions regarding decoration. They tend to view visual richness as an inherent component achieved automatically through direct architectural execution devoid of any decoration either applied or emerging through deliberate manipulations in building. Therefore, views differ greatly; they range from extreme purist notions to thoughts advanced by more ornate-minded practitioners. Divergent attitudes are healthy signs in contemporary architectural expression; for architecture is thus related to other ventures in the visual arts and functions as a creative activity. The problem of creating practical and exciting enclosures of space has many solutions, but one factor is obvious: The function of architecture is not fulfilled if both aspects, practical shelter and exciting organization of enclosed space, are not treated as one in a consistent and coherent manner. Walter Gropius[11] clearly pointed out this obligation when he said,

The aesthetic satisfaction of the human soul is just as important as the material. . . . For whereas building is merely a matter of methods and materials architecture implies the mastery of space.

The Problems of House Design

Since design views vary and many solutions are apparent in the field of architecture, one may wonder which path leads toward effective results. The answer, of course, is found in considering the intended purpose of the proposed plan. Residential architectural design, for instance, is dependent on fulfilling several prime requirements which share equal billing. The solution of a family's needs is the first and prime step in house design. These needs naturally vary with each family and are dependent on such factors as size and age of family, income, and social and recreational inclinations. Following the designing of a floor plan, the interior layout of space which functions properly for a particular family, the exterior of the house may take form. Compensation for climatic conditions, taking advantage of the contour of the land and the possibilities for viewing the surroundings, southern

[10] *The Natural House* (New York: Horizon Press, Inc., 1954), p. 44.

[11] *The New Architecture and the Bauhaus* (Boston: Charles T. Branford Co., 1937), p. 24.

158   *Entry Side with Garage and Sheltered Walkway, Techbuilt House, Devon 360 model, Cambridge, Mass. (Courtesy Techbuilt Incorporated)*

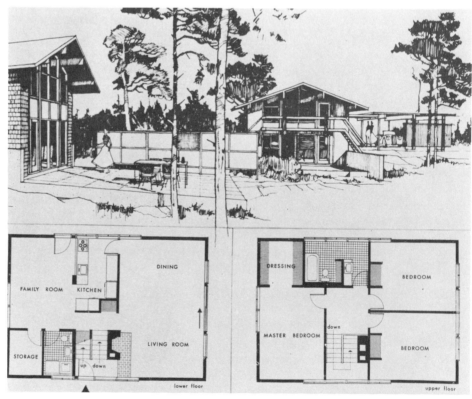

159   *Floor Plan, Techbuilt House, Devon 360 model. (Courtesy Techbuilt Incorporated)*

160   *Two-Story Living Area, View Toward Patio, Techbuilt House, Devon 480 model, Northboro, Mass. (Courtesy Techbuilt Incorporated)*

orientation when feasible, and the use of logical building methods and materials which prove sympathetic to the natural environment are now problems to be solved through wise selection and arrangement. The interior plan may be modified in conjunction with the preceding factors and a series of compromises may be made to attain a consistency between the various design considerations. Cost is also usually a determining factor in form realization, and thus economical practices and an emphasis on compactness are usually mandatory components of the design process. As a form expands, costs naturally increase; therefore, interior space is at a premium and must be ingeniously treated for maximum effect.

The Techbuilt house, acclaimed by many as an economical and pleasing solution to contemporary housing, contains a number of practical and exciting solutions (Figure 158). Designed by the architectural firm of Carl Koch and Associates, the direct and coherent plan offers a number of modifications within the confines of a particular structure. Conceived as a two-story structure with lower level set partially into the ground, the design permits entry

between floors, resulting in a minimum of stairs being encountered in moving to either level. The floor plan indicates a simplicity of arrangement and structure with specific spaces arranged for separation of work, recreation, and rest (Figure 159). A floor plan can be visualized as a map, usually drawn to a scale of one-fourth inch representing one foot, which illustrates the interior arrangement of floor space. In the case of a two-level house the levels are drawn adjacent to one another, though in building, of course, the second or upper floor would be above the lower floor. Lines indicating the outline of the house are thick and dark in certain areas to indicate solid walls and light elsewhere to represent window locations. Exterior and interior doors are symbolized by adjacent arcs which indicate the direction in which the door swings to open. Storage areas are represented by gray masses and stairs by a series of small rectangular shapes, each representing one step. The floor plan of the Techbuilt house, Devon 360 model, encloses 1728 square feet of floor space in a two-level rectangular form measuring 24 by 36 feet. Designed to be built within a gently sloping environment, the entrance side containing interior stairs is to be nestled into the slope. This recession of house into earth offers several unique advantages: ease of entry and construction, a minimum of excavation, natural insulation, and a harmonious mass which relates to the horizontal qualities of the surroundings. Both attic and basement are eliminated, and the post and beam construction affords utilization of all enclosed space below its broad, gently sloping roof.

A number of solutions are available in the Techbuilt plan through manipulation of building units; for the building method of this precut structure is based on a system of predetermined modular components. Thus flexibility in interior planning is possible through various arrangements of these sectional units. Adjacent garage or carport is obtainable, depending on desires of the occupants. Joist and beam construction, panel units, partial walls, two floor levels to minimize excavation and roof area and curtain windows, contribute toward great savings in construction. Predetermined and precut units and procedures take full advantage of the benefits of standardization in building and the products and processes of an industrial age. Determined architectural ratios such as units of two or four feet secure full advantage of building material; for sheets of siding, insulation, wallboard, and lumber are produced in specific sizes related to such measurements.

If interior space is at a premium, the second floor may extend the full length of the Techbuilt house. Such a plan offers additional sleeping quarters above the living room; however, certain plans eliminate a portion of the upper level to enable great space fluctuations to occur on the first level (Figure 160). In such a living area a huge floor-to-ceiling expanse of glass provides sparkling natural light and visually strongly links exterior and interior. An unhampered panoramic view of the outdoors extends spaciousness and offers a large ever-changing natural backdrop. A durable flagstone floor also provides naturalism and, through its continuation outdoors, unites man with nature through an organic sequence. At the opposite end of the living room a soaring mass of brick masonry houses fireplace and stairwell (Figure 161). The large fireplace suggests warmth and hospitality, and the raised position of the hearth gives unhampered and practical viewing of a fire by being at eye level to seated spectators. In addition, the raised hearth simplifies the stacking and arrangement of kindling and logs and facilitates cleaning.

161   *Fireplace, Materials and Space Details, Living Area, Techbuilt House, Devon 480 model, Northboro, Mass. (Courtesy Techbuilt Incorporated)*

Exciting variations in enclosed space occur in a number of manners which refute rectangular implications and add exciting dimensions to the interior. For instance, differences in height are obtained through sections of overhead space liberated to follow the pitch of the roof, while adjacent low ceiling passages emphasize a retention of overhead space. Additional spatial movements occur as horizontal masses of space flow into adjacent areas beyond the living room, thereby producing interest through vertical and horizontal spatial projections. Fluctuations in textural and color properties of brick, wood, and stone also add impact to the living room and provide invigorating patterns. The vertical arrangement of wood paneling serves to enhance the sensation of height and contrasts with the interlocking arrangement of bricks that surfaces the fireplace mass. Plants, interestingly placed, add an element of naturalism through patches of greenery. A kitchen, with well-organized work and storage features, and dining, utility, general storage, and recreational areas are located beyond the living room on the first level.

The upper floor of the Techbuilt plan offers a number of solutions ranging from four bedroom areas and bath to plans with fewer sleeping quarters and more space devoted to family or general-purpose activities (Figure 162). This flexibility offers opportunity to fulfill individual needs and is adaptable to constant change as a family expands through births and growth or contracts through marriages and the subsequent departure of various members of the household. Thus the design can properly function in numerous ways. A sensation of spaciousness can be achieved on the second level by employing partial walls and large passways which can be effectively blocked by sliding doors. Thus expanses of space can be divided or extended. The exposure of structural members — horizontal beams and vertical posts — also extends space and identifies areas.

The continued movement of the horizontal beams beyond the interior provides structural integrity and sequence to the outer form (Figure 163). Glass curtain walls, located in both ends of the structure, facilitate construction as well as simplify form. Such a window treatment conveys consistency in erection by functioning as a sheathing member rather than appearing to be a glassed hole punched into a wall to admit light. This latter quality, unfortunately, is too frequently evident in numerous house designs. An outside cantilevered balcony and stairs permitting a direct exit or entrance to the second level is also incorporated in the Techbuilt house.

162   *Living Area, Second Level, Techbuilt House, Devon 360 model, full two-level plan. (Courtesy Techbuilt Incorporated)*

163   *Structural Details, Exterior End Wall and Roof Sheltering Living Areas in Two-Level Plan, Techbuilt House, Devon 360 model. (Courtesy Techbuilt Incorporated)*

164   *Assembly Hall and Sports Arena, University of Illinois, Urbana, Ill., model, designed by Harrison and Abramovitz, Architects, 1959. (Courtesy Department of Art, University of Illinois)*

165   *Interior, David S. Ingalls Hockey Rink, Yale University, New Haven, Conn., 1958. (Courtesy the Architect, Eero Saarinen; photographed by Joseph W. Molitor)*

The Present Situation

Experiments are currently underway to harness solar energy to heat and cool houses which pivot to follow the sun. Prefabricated units of aluminum and plastic are being used to produce portable structures, from houses to schools, which can be easily expanded or dismantled and reassembled elsewhere. Great geodesic domes, simply assembled from panels and tubes, serve as houses, theaters, and railroad repair shops. These domes, with their sphere forms comprised of equilateral triangles, offer innumerable solutions for industrial as well as residential shelter through manipulation of determined units. Huge shells of concrete now emerging from the earth are to function as airports or civic centers. The massive Assembly Hall designed by Harrison and Abramovitz for the University of Illinois, also convertible to a basketball arena, serves a duality of purposes (Figure 164). Architecture now spans huge areas and encloses great masses of space in spectacular displays of engineering (Figure 165). A plasticity of form obtainable through recent engineering and architectural accomplishments appears to be a dominant factor of contemporary architecture, and the fulfillment of interior requirements are clearly foretold in the exterior solutions (Figure 166).

166 *Entrance, David S. Ingalls Hockey Rink, Yale University, New Haven, Conn., 1958. (Courtesy the Architect, Eero Saarinen; photographed by Joseph W. Molitor)*

An Excellent Representative: Eero Saarinen

A consideration of several achitectural solutions by Eero Saarinen, one of America's contemporary architects, illustrates structural practices which are currently influencing the art of building. Saarinen's belief that there are many ways of getting different solutions seems to summarize the present condition; for diverse architectural expressions are presently being formulated throughout the land. The influences of the organic and international styles, while still profound, are modified by a pertinent factor, the force exerted by independent designers such as Saarinen. It would be a great misconception to think that future architecture will be built primarily upon the foundations of organic or international beliefs. They served as, and continue to be, major movements, but innumerable designers conceive forms through personal intuitive processes and, while possibly influenced by organic and international solutions, create outside the scope of both movements.

Eero Saarinen's ingenuity and creative sensitivity are apparent in numerous ventures from airports and hockey rinks to civic buildings and industrial plants. Having mastered the major building processes of our period, ferro-concrete as well as grid construction with its curtain wall, he follows no rigid formula or particular style, but rather fulfills the needs of a building with an inventive and unique form balanced between austerity and ornateness. Engineering knowledge is tempered with a keenness of proportion and detail, and the resulting architectural imagery is poetic yet monumental, powerful yet visually pleasing and refined. His Hockey Rink at Yale University, composed of sweeping curves and slopes, contains an organic interdependency of structural relationships. Handled with a clearness of concept, the rhythmical architectural form offers a column-free interior with an exuberant sensation of spaciousness through the actions of a huge arch. Suspension cables supported by the arch and cradled in concrete side walls support the sheltering, slightly concave board roof covered on the exterior with black plastic sheeting. Saarinen's solution can be conceived somewhat as a large, inverted Viking ship, with the arch serving as a keel supporting an overhead hull that shelters numerous spectators. A broad sheltered expanse of playing surface on which hockey players can freely move and battle for the puck is also provided.

167   *Milwaukee County War Memorial Building, Milwaukee, Wisc., view which faces the city, Eero Saarinen, 1957. (Courtesy* THE MILWAUKEE JOURNAL)

Saarinen's problem in Milwaukee, to design a County War Memorial Center to "honor the dead and serve the living," entailed certain restrictions and complications. The selected site, atop the slope of a hill overlooking Lake Michigan, involved a restriction in that the view of adjacent city and lake were not to be eliminated by the structure. In addition, two distinct needs were to be fulfilled: interior space for veteran and civic affairs and quarters for an art center (Figure 167). Saarinen solved these problems through cantilevered construction which houses offices and auditoriums for veteran and civic activities in lightweight reinforced concrete units. Pillars were used as structural members, not to mimic the international style, but rather to raise sections to provide a view of lake and also divide activities in the building. A glassed lobby and open court located on the street level provide easy access to offices and auditoriums above or art galleries below.

An honor roll with the names of the World War II and Korean War dead inscribed on black granite encircles a pool in the open court area of the lobby level. Interior space in the two upper floors is saved by locating stairways outside the main structure.

The open courtyard, ringed by surrounding overhead masses, permits natural light to pierce inner walls and also contributes spaciousness to the form (Figure 168). Huge expanses of glass in end walls of the cantilevered wings relate interior and exterior through visual penetration and deny bulkiness to the projected masses (Figure 169). The area housing art galleries, by being partially embedded in the earth beneath the lobby and open court, considers the natural contour of the site and provides stability to the design in counteracting the strong horizontal thrusts exerted by the overhead cantilevered masses. Vertical banding in these masses, secured through inscribed lines in the projected reinforced concrete, also tends to retain interest within these segments and deny an overemphasis on horizontal movements (Figure 170). Exciting engineering, sensitivity in proportions, and integrity in use of material and detailing contribute both monumentality and dignity to the original form of the War Memorial Center. These factors, combined with the exposure of structural segments and large uncomplicated masses, assure a contemporary quality to the functional form.

168   *Open Court and Inner Walls of Milwaukee County War Memorial Building, Milwaukee, Wisc., Eero Saarinen, 1957. (Photographed by Ezra
Stoller)*

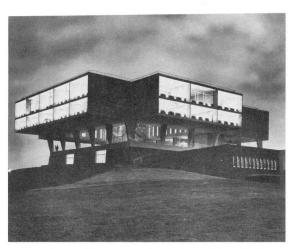

169   *Large Glass Areas Overlooking Lake Michigan,
Milwaukee County War Memorial Building, Mil-
waukee, Wisc., Eero Saarinen, 1957. (Courtesy* THE
MILWAUKEE JOURNAL)

170   *Details of Engineering and Surface Treatment, Milwaukee County War Memorial Building, Eero Saarinen; Ezra Stoller, Photographer.*

171   *Water Curtain and Artificial Lake, Administration and Studio Buildings, General Motors Technical Center, Detroit, Mich., designed by Eero Saarinen, 1956. (Courtesy General Motors Corporation; photographed by Ezra Stoller)*

172   *Metal Screen, Entrance to Central Restaurant, General Motors Technical Center, Detroit, Mich., sculptured by Harry Bertoia. (Courtesy General Motors Corporation; photographed by Ezra Stoller)*

Eero Saarinen's design and layout of the General Motors Technical Center indicate an excellent solution for contemporary industrial housing. The entire complex of twenty-five buildings, arranged in practical groupings, was carried out with explicit precision in harmony with the purpose of an industrial technical center. Saarinen enriched his design through a deliberate and logical fusion of the arts; he incorporated the works of leading landscape artists, sculptors, and painters into the architectural environment (Figure 171). Landscaping includes a twenty-two-acre artificial lake with huge fountains, one of which was created by Alexander Calder. Using water as a mobile-like fountain sculpture, Calder produced a water ballet with twenty-one jets of water crossing, rising, and falling to create melodies of sight and sound. Paintings and sculptures, such as a decorative thirty-six feet long and ten feet high screen of steel and allied metals applied in a molten state, created by Harry Bertoia, are located in interiors of various buildings of the Technical Center (Figure 172). Such a venture illustrates how a combining of the arts can culminate in an integrated form and act as an inspirational and purposeful environment to shelter man and industry.

The buldings are composed in the latest manner of skeleton construction, with north and south curtain walls of steel ribbing sheathed with glass and

173   *Details of Glass and Enamel Panel Side Walls Forming the Styling Administration Building and the Steel-sheathed Dome of the Styling Auditorium, General Motors Technical Center, Detroit, Mich., designed by Eero Saarinen, 1956. (Courtesy General Motors Corporation; photographed by Ezra Stoller)*

enamel panels framed in aluminum (Figure 173). The panels are standardized and constructed so that they may be easily interchanged within the wall plane. This versatile feature enables transparent or opaque panels to be manipulated within the curtain wall to modify the use of interior space. The enameled steel panels, only two inches thick, possess heat-insulating qualities comparable to a fourteen-inch masonry wall. This high insulating factor is due to sandwich construction with the exterior enameled steel plates bonded to a sturdy kraft paper honeycomb core filled with granular insulation.

The end walls of each building are composed of bright-colored glazed bricks which provide gay notes to the architectural composition. Saarinen's concern with color as well as the benefits obtainable from modern technology is apparent in the information released by General Motors regarding the Technical Center's end walls.

> Not since the fabulous palaces of the Assyrian Kings of the 9th century, B.C., have brilliantly colored glazed brick walls been used for architectural effect as they are at Technical Center.
>
> The intense colors of deep crimson, scarlet, tangerine-orange, lemon yellow, chartreuse, royal blue, sky blue, tobacco grey, brown, black and white cover endwalls of drafting-office-laboratory buildings and all the solid walls required for shop, special use and utility core spaces.
>
> Development of this gleaming chromatic material within 20th century technology was undertaken especially at the architect's behest. It began with a few experimental bricks baked in a ceramist's kiln and ended in a large kiln financed by General Motors. These bricks are now standard products on the market and may revolutionize American architecture in terms of color.

Many of the structural processes as well as materials specified by Saarinen in the construction of the Technical Center, such as the steel-domed auditorium, were unobtainable until recently. The auditorium, built on a pressure-vessel construction system, is composed of steel sheets three-eighth of an inch thick, as thin in relationship to their area of coverage as one-thirtieth of an eggshell to its area. These steel sheets, covered with insulation and thin aluminum plates, enclose an interior space possessing a width of 185 feet and a height of 65 feet at the highest point. Such precise engineering feats, deriving from contemporary machine production, are consistent with the scientific endeavors of our age and serve as a major and current influence on architecture. Roman domed-structures had main walls up to twenty feet in thickness; today, but an insignificant fraction of that mass can function as shelter. Who can conceive of what tomorrow may hold?

174 *Proposed Civic Center for Tallahassee, Fla., designed by The Architects Collaborative, Partner in Charge: Walter Gropius. (Courtesy Walter Gropius)*

Tomorrow and the Day After

Many generations ago, when civilization was young, huge smooth horizontal surfaces of marble reflected the glories of the Grecian world; centuries later, man stacked stone upon stone to create religious monuments to pierce the heavens. Each epoch searches and finds its particular means and forms. Man still continues this constant quest for significant architectural imagery and, assisted by mechanical means undreamed of until recently, even plans changes in the very pattern of the land. Imagine a mass of earth two miles in length, one hundred yards wide, and fifty feet in height. Detroit planners have requested the sculptor Isamu Noguchi to give shape to such a bulk resulting from sixty million cubic yards of soil excavated in new road constructions. His earthen creations, with appropriate plantings are intended as intriguing contours adjacent to these new highways. Even sculptural form can now be given to great surfaces of the earth.

Soft music, multicolored paving beneath leisurely strolling feet, the shelter of trees, and the pleasures of flowers and fountains hardly bring to mind the features evident in the centers of the majority of our towns and cities. Rather, horns, gasoline fumes, trucks, flashing lights, and innumerable chrome bumpers seem to convey the sights and sounds of a metropolitan downtown area. From Alliance, Ohio, to Dallas, from Kalamazoo to Toledo, from Memphis to San Francisco plans however are now underway to transform sections of the hearts of these cities into pleasant malls and parkways bright with greenery. By banning trucks and cars in stretches of downtown streets, planners in Kalamazoo and Toledo no longer permit motor vehicles to disrupt pedestrian flow.

Fountains, sculpture, and flowers bloom in the streets to greet shoppers now free from the blur of passing cars, while play areas complete with slides, swings, and sandboxes amuse their children. Kalamazoo's mall consists of over three hundred yards of former street now surfaced with gardens, benches, play spaces, and colorful paved walks. Other cities have also closed blocks to downtown vehicle traffic to offer pedestrians relaxing areas of fountains, plantings, and soft music. Many merchants adjacent to the malls strongly back the undertakings, and many community members no longer greatly fear the effects of a flight to the suburbs. Such ventures, only the beginning, are warm with the promise of things to come in man's constant and universal endeavor to improve his environment through creative action.

The direction is clearly indicated, and current efforts in city planning incorporate the efforts of architects and landscape designers as well as traffic planners and allied specialists. A Renaissance or reawakening, the dawn of a new age, is in the making to rejuvenate our architectural landscape. New York City is transforming a twelve-block West Side slum neighborhood into an organization of exciting buildings, malls, and plantings. Termed Lincoln Center for The Performing Arts, this cultural development is to contain a new home for the Metropolitan Opera, a concert hall for the New York Philharmonic Orchestra, theaters for drama and dance, quarters for the Julliard School of Music, and a library-museum. Innumerable cities, north, south, east, and west, have similar plans, although usually on a smaller scale, for providing grandeur to their environment. The Civic Center proposed by Walter Gropius for Tallahassee, Florida, would add much to that southern city. Such a serene grouping, with flanking structures complimenting an imposing auditorium, can assist in fulfilling both the physical and aesthetic requirements of the citizens of any community (Figure 174). Shortly before his death, Frank Lloyd Wright submitted a proposal which indicated his interest in civic planning (Figure 175). Intended for Madison, Wisconsin, a Midwestern city blessed with surrounding lakes, the Civic Center was conceived to project beyond the shore line, uniting an area of Madison with adjacent Lake Monona (Figure 176). The upper portion of the plan, located at street level, was to contain fountains utilizing lake water, interesting arrangements of plantings, passages offering exciting views of lake and shore, and adjacent parking spaces for automobiles. A theater-auditorium, a smaller theater, an art gallery, and the office space needed for a civic center were proposed for the intermediate level. Boathouses and mooring facilities were to be contained in the lower level. Endeavors such as Lincoln Center, Tallahassee's proposed Civic Center, and the Monona Terrace Plan for Madison formulate a portion of men's dreams and strivings for beautiful and beneficial settings for society in the latter portion of this century.

In this age of science, while man probes space and considers movement beyond the moon somewhere between the stars, reasons for being and controlling, reasons for joy and breathing, remain to be fulfilled. The purpose of earth surely goes far beyond serving as a launching pad for hissing missiles intent upon escape beyond the bounds of our atmosphere. This is not to imply that many eyes should not sweep the sky and ponder what lies beyond distant clouds, but rather that they should also peer about the tangled architectural growths of our cities and towns and wonder what new architectural forms and concepts are to spring forth from the soil. The answers are for the future; for new challenges and opportunities inconceivable in the present remain to unfold. One answer, however, is apparent: the architectural giants of tomorrow will raise their ideas with steel, concrete, plastic and substances yet to be found and employ methods now unknown. The seeds of these future solutions now exist, dormant in the minds of youth, for this has always been and will always be so. One question still remains. As the years move toward the coming century, who will match or surpass the contributions of the architects of past and present? Could it be you?

175 *Monona Terrace Plan, Madison, Wisc., model, designed by Frank Lloyd Wright and Associates. (Courtesy* THE CAPITAL TIMES, *Madison, Wisc.)*

176 *Monona Terrace Plan, Madison, Wisc., detail, designed by Frank Lloyd Wright and Associates. (Courtesy* THE CAPITAL TIMES, *Madison, Wisc.)*

TOPICS FOR CONSIDERATION

1. What qualities in modern architecture distinguish it from the solutions of the past?
2. Do you think public buildings and houses will assume new forms in the coming decades? If so, what type of solutions do you guess lie ahead?
3. What are the strong factors of the international style of architecture?
4. List the beliefs of the organic practitioners.
5. Considering both the international and the organic styles, which point of view do you most favor? Why?
6. How would an effective modern house differ from a conventional dwelling? Consider such factors as economy of means, materials, and treatment of space.
7. How can houses be related to their environment?

SUGGESTED ACTIVITIES

1. Consider the latest buildings erected in your community and note structural methods. Do they appear modern? Visualize other possibilities which could be incorporated into their forms.
2. With the consent of your teacher, contact a local architect and request permission to visit his office. Or possibly, he would appreciate the opportunity of visiting your school and speaking to the class.
3. Refer to various magazines and study many contemporary house plans. Notice cost-saving factors, ingenuity in admitting natural light, interior and exterior proportions, and landscaping features.
4. Work up sketches, both floor plans and elevational views, of a mountain cabin, beach house, or dwelling for city or suburb. Use a scale of $\frac{1}{4}$ inch per foot and attempt to keep costs within reason. Attempt to dramatize interior space, create adequate storage space, and provide logical traffic flow. Relate your design to a specific locale in considering terrain, view, and total environment. However, primarily consider the interior and make certain it meets your anticipated needs.
5. Design several features which you think would increase the effectiveness of your own home and lot.
6. Select a block in your neighborhood and sketch creative modifications that could enrich the area. Within your redevelopment plan, incorporate garden spots, sculpture, play areas, parking facilities, etc. Emphasize decorative and practical spacial divisions through fencing and plantings.

APPROPRIATE REFERENCES AND READINGS

Periodicals

Architectural Record, New York: F. W. Dodge Corporation.

House and Home, New York: Time, Inc.

Interiors, New York: Whitney Publications.

Progressive Architecture, New York: Reinhold Publishing Corporation.

Texts

Built in U.S.A.: Post War Architecture, edited by H. R. Hitchcock and A. Drexler, New York: The Museum of Modern Art, 1952.

DREXLER, ARTHUR. *Mies Van Der Rohe*, New York: George Braziller, Inc., 1960.

FAULKNER, RAY. *Inside Today's Home*, New York: Henry Holt & Co., Inc., 1954.

FORD, K. M., and CREIGHTON, T. H. *The American House Today*, New York: Reinhold Publishing Corporation, 1954.

GIEDION, SIGFRIED. *Space, Time, and Architecture*, Cambridge, Mass.: Harvard University Press, 1956.

GROPIUS, WALTER. *The New Architecture and the Bauhaus*, Boston: Charles T. Branford Co., 1937.

KAUFMANN, EDGAR, JR. *What Is Modern Interior Design*, New York: The Museum of Modern Art, 1953.

LE CORBUSIER. *The Marseilles Block*, London: The Harvill Press, 1953.

————. *Toward a New Architecture*, New York: Brewer, Warren, and Putnam, Inc., 1926.

LENNING, HENRY F. *The Art Nouveau*, The Hague, Netherlands: Martinus Nijhoff, 1951.

Living Spaces, edited by George Nelson, New York: Whitney Publications, 1952.

SULLIVAN, LOUIS H. *Kindergarten Chats and Other Writings*, New York: Wittenborn Schultz, Inc., 1947.

WRIGHT, FRANK L. *The Living City*, New York: Horizon Press, Inc., 1958.

————. *The Natural House*, New York: Horizon Press, Inc., 1954.

To draw does not mean simply to reproduce contours; drawing does not consist merely of line, drawing is also expression, the inner form, the plane, modeling. See what remains after that. Drawing includes three and a half quarters of the content of painting. If I were asked to put up a sign over my door I should inscribe it: SCHOOL FOR DRAWING, and I am sure that I would bring forth painters.

Drawing contains everything, except the hue (color).

One must keep right on drawing; draw with your eyes when you can not draw with a pencil.

JEAN AUGUSTE DOMINIQUE INGRES[1]
19th Century French Artist

Before the Woolly Rhinoceros Lost Its Coat

This is how it began long ago. Cro-Magnon men in western Europe traced outlines on cave walls, and our knowledge of drawing was born. It, the Aurignacian period of twenty-two thousand years ago, was an age of stone tools, damp cave shelters, huge bears, wild horses, magnificent stags, ferocious boars, and the woolly rhinoceros. Assisted by flickering light cast by burning fat in crude stone lamps which threw harsh patterns of light upon surrounding rock walls, men of this age created vital images through line (Figure 177). Through the application of mineral ores with finger tips, sticks, or possibly other implements, concise and beautiful renderings were brought into being. These explicit and keen drawings, originally produced to gain a magic-like control over the objects represented, served as a guiding spirit to the warrior hunters. It was believed that animals made visible upon cave walls would later be obtainable during the hunt and the hunter, through mental osmosis, could absorb the strength and cunning of the subject portrayed. Such an attitude should not appear unduly strange; for even now

177   HORSE, *Fonte de Gaume Cavern, Dordogne, France, cave drawing. (Courtesy American Museum of Natural History)*

[1] *Artists on Art*, edited by Robert Goldwater and Marco Treves (New York: Pantheon Books, Inc., 1947), p. 216.

178   Hero, *oil brushed on linen, Morris Graves, 1953. (Courtesy Willard Gallery)*

football teams are termed the Colts, Rams, Mustangs, and Panthers in somewhat the same hopes.

Prehistoric drawings also functioned, ages before writing was developed, as the only means of conveying ideas through visual communication. Drawings served somewhat as the first alphabet and were a major foundation upon which our present alphabet evolved. Many of the letters on this very page find their roots in ancient line drawings of various birds and animals, bowls, lassoes, and hands. Our alphabet — based on the Roman, which traces back to Greek, Phoenician, and Egyptian endeavors — finds its backbone in hieroglyphics which consisted of drawings. Originally quite factual in details, such drawings, through time, were simplified and abstracted until today letters such as A, I, and L bear no resemblance to drawings of eagle, hand, or lioness from which they originally developed.

From Caves to Graves

While comprehensive alphabets have come into operation, drawing still remains the keystone of visual language and a universally understood expression. Manners and reasons for drawing may fluctuate and themes expand in the light of each age; for angels appeared in Renaissance drawings of the fifteenth century, while astronauts are available for treatment in this century. Certain factors, however, are constant; elements retain a sameness and much subject matter remains appropriate. The same art elements manipulated in antiquity to freeze a moment of action are carried unchanged throughout the centuries, and man still treats creatures that were once of the forest.

Line, shape, texture, and value are the means by which Morris Graves shares his idea of the attributes of a *Hero* (Figure 178). Call is obstinacy, arrogance, courage, or stubbornness, the determination of the hero is obvious in its proud bearing and firm stance. Alert and free of fear, the animal conveys spirit; whatever its purpose, one feels sympathy and tends to wish it well. Graves gives his subject a strong personality with a sure rendering balanced between simplicity and great detail. Notations of physical features and surface qualities are presented through variation in lines and detailing, which results in a dynamic form. One senses in many drawings by Graves the implication that certain characteristics are shared by man and beast; for his renderings go beyond mere factual recordings in stressing specific virtues while underplaying superficial relationships.

179   LANDSCAPE WITH BARN, *pen and ink, Rembrandt van Rijn, 1606–1669 [Dutch]. (Courtesy Metropolitan Museum of Art, Bequest of Mrs. H. O. Havemeyer, 1929)*

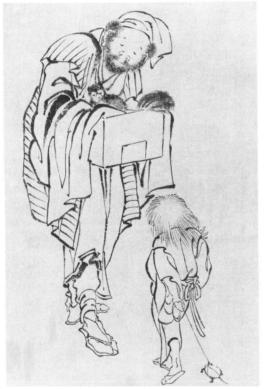

180   MEETING, *brush and ink, Katsushika Hokusai, 1760–1849 [Japanese]. (Courtesy Freer Gallery of Art, Washington, D. C.)*

Visual Comments About Life, Living, and Joy

Whatever one has experienced or imagined, tranquil scenes, happy childhood episodes, violent adventures, or even fantasies can be rapidly delineated through line. Long before combines, huge barns, and tractors, Rembrandt van Rijn, through a flutter of lines, told of life in the fields in his drawing *Landscape with Barn* (Figure 179). The vitality of pen strokes denies the static in capturing characteristics of growth and movement associated with foliage, while accents of dark identifying the barn contribute both solidity and impact to the ink sketch. The Dutch master frequently treated the most common of subjects but transcended the conventional through creative power and intensity of treatment. His visual messages were devoid of the superficial and composed in bold passages of dark and light, and his use of line implied both freedom and boldness.

A definite line quality, positive, concise, is apparent in Katsushika Hokusai's drawing (Figure 180).

ARAB ON HORSEBACK ATTACKED BY LION, *pencil,*
Eugène Delacroix, 1798–1863 [French]. (Courtesy
Fogg Art Museum, Harvard)

181

Rhythmical movements and abrupt changes in the sweeping curves indicating garment folds add deftness and zestfulness to the rendering, while deviations in line thickness provide both subtle and bold dark and light interplays. The drawing, suggesting a thrilling moment as a boy and his pet turtle confront a man with a monkey, relates the joys and surprises of childhood. The child, appearing to peer upward, leads to the monumental figure of the man, resulting in unity and an emphasis on height through vertical movement. Turtle, child, and bulk of man interestingly contrast in both size and placement in space. Notice how contour differences achieved in breaking and varying line by an active handling of the drawing instrument present a sense of life and atmosphere to the lyrical rendering.

Spears and Tears

Eugène Delacroix's pencil drawing *Arab on Horseback Attacked by Lion* (Figure 181), complex in movement, detail, and linear deviations, results in a comprehensive organization of form. His lines search, find, and denote through multiplicity, thereby creating a complex interweaving of movements and a complete unity of mass. Diagonal treatments of horse, rider, lion, and implied thrust of spear express force and action consistent with the theme. While other great Romantics of the past century, Scott and Cooper, to mention but two, wrote of exciting adventures, Delacroix kept a massive journal of his travels and recorded dramatic happenings with drawings and paintings as well as words. To his dying day Delacroix, aided by the drawing through which his North African travel experiences could be relived and intensified, could undoubtedly recall the lion's roar and visualize the violence of combat — clawing, rearing, and jabbing. This encounter of man and beast also came to be shared with all who view this terror and fury of a moment captured through line.

182   Croak's House, *pencil, John Wilde, 1955. (Courtesy Museum of Modern Art)*

Beyond Appearances:
A Little of the Supernatural

Beyond the actual — barns, children and pets, lions — exists another world, at times very real, for it deals with the imagination. It unfolds in strange manners from the subconscious and may long be dormant or often grip us fiercely. Episodes transpire in the mind, free from the realm of what is known and perceivable, linked to the world of twilight, night or day fantasies, and dreams. Drawing, as all other areas of art, is not restricted to what has been or can be, nor is it limited by experiences which vividly appear and suddenly dissipate beyond the mind's eye. Occurrences deep in the recesses of the imagination zone can be captured and crystalized through creative action. Great adventures can even be created; for the magnificence of Edgar Allen Poe rests not on cold logic or the breath of reason. The powers and suitability of imaginative themes has long been recognized and engaged in by those who create with pen and brush as well as the written word. Five hundred years ago, Leonardo da Vinci[2] wrote that the artist

> Has the universe in his mind and hands ... If he wishes to see monstrosities, whether terrifying, ludicrous and laughable, or pitiful, he has the

power and authority to create them. . . . Indeed whatever exists in the universe, whether in essence, in act, or in the imagination . . .

Robert Browning[3], an English poet of the past century, indicated a somewhat similar view when speaking of an artist, he said,

> I can do with my pencil what I know, what I see, what at bottom of my heart I wish for, if I ever wish so deep . . .

John Wilde frequently makes little or no differentiation between reality and fantasy within his drawings. Regarding his intentions in producing *Croak's House* (Figure 182), he speaks of imaginative reality and indicates that drawings can capture qualities beyond the merely conventional.

> I hope each of my drawings indicates that the only reality is reality, for through the close examination of the object I hope to search out something

[2] Jean Paul Richter, *The Literary Works of Leonardo daVinci* (London: Oxford University Press, Inc., 1939), vol. 1, p. 54.
[3] *Browning's Complete Works*, edited by Horace E. Scudder (New York: Houghton Mifflin Co., 1895), p. 346.

of its hidden total meaning: the more found the closer the approach to truth or order.

The drawing "Croak's House" is one of a series which I continue even now, which examines as precisely as I am able natural forms (whether it be a figure, a made object, or a found object). These drawings attempt to bring to forms certain psychological and literal overtones whether direct or implied.

I was interested in this old lime-stone house for a long time and finally sat down to draw it. While drawing the owner of the land stopped by and told me the stone had been hand-shaped during the course of two years by his grandparents (or great-grandparents in the 1830s). The original cabin was used as a chicken-shed when the stone house was built. It (even in its tumbling condition) was well built — but has since been bulldozed into its cellar so I'm glad I recorded it.

The subject of course was qualified by the fact that as I drew it I felt it filled with ghosts — all crying and yelling the terror of their temporary stay in this world. I first made the drawing in pen and ink and then did the pencil drawing in the studio. That's about all I can say about it except that the idea expressed here is what I feel about all reality — that the physical universe is pregnant with meaning beyond itself and can express all shades of human feeling.

The shrieking ghosts which Wilde conceived as inhabitants of the supposedly deserted dwelling are indeed strange. Their gigantic heads suggest the unusual and in comparison with the size of their home clearly imply the complete occupancy of the house. Strong and serene uses of dark and light masses join textural and shape notations to contribute an invigorating and highly controlled pattern in the drawing. Though the theme suggests haunted houses and goblins, even witches' brew may come to mind. While one may imagine the latter as being a mysterious concoction, there is little mystery as to the recipe of the drawing. It's composed of observation, imagination, and perseverance, seasoned with a mastery of technique akin to the old masters' and a pinch of surrealism, all sensitively stirred and served in an original manner. Such a procedure results in a highly flavorful drawing, especially if the placement is keen.

Drawing Can Serve Many Purposes

While drawing is an end in itself and exists as a separate identity in the art field, it can also fulfill additional functions. Drawings can serve the architect, craftsman, painter, printmaker, and sculptor as the means of securing preliminary views of what

can later emerge in these areas. Acting as a bridge for creative action in bringing to bear immediate thinking, drawings permit early visualizations of anticipated problems and can stimulate subsequent action. Frequently the transition of drawings into another form results in slight change, as in lithography. In other areas such as sculpture, modifications may be extensive, with the final product bearing little resemblance to the original drawings.

Käthe Kollwitz's lithographic print *Mother and Child by a Wayside Shrine* (Figure 183) directly emerged from an initial crayon drawing. One of the great expressionists of the century, this German woman produced innumerable drawings pungent with feeling and frequently highly charged with social commentary. Her drawing of mother and child contains a full range in value gradation and detail definitions which compliment one another, emphasizing and subordinating desired relationships. The rendering goes beyond the factual or the sentimental in appearing to penetrate the borders of melancholia. Possibly Henry Wadsworth Longfellow's poem relating to weariness seems appropriate to describe the thoughts of the mother sheltering her awe-stricken child.

> O little feet! that such long years
> Must wander on through hopes and fears,
>   Must ache and bleed beneath your load;
> I, nearer to the wayside inn
> Where toil shall cease and rest begin,
>   Am weary, thinking of your road!

Numerous artists, no matter what their area of concentration, involve themselves with drawing as the first step in undertaking a problem. Consider the *Sheet of Sketches* (Figure 184) by the sculptor Henry Moore. Though the final sculpture emerging from such studies may differ greatly from the drawings, an initial direction is clearly indicated.

What do you notice in closely examining Moore's drawings? While each is dependent on line, do they vary in treatment? How are shapes emphasized? Does each drawing contain strong evidences of texture? Are surfaces of equal intensity and similar in character? What qualities do you think contribute to effective drawings?

Have you noticed how background can identify form and also how form can bleed into background? Is solidity suggested through intense contrasts?

Learning to Draw

One may wonder, why learn to draw? Many obvious reasons exist for the development of drawing skill. It should provide pleasure through increasing

183 Mother and Child by a Wayside Shrine, *crayon drawing, lithograph, Käthe Kollwitz, 1867–1945 [German]. (Courtesy Philadelphia Museum of Art)*

an awareness of one's unique abilities and extend the capacity to reveal and share experiences in a visual form. Insight into the qualities of man and nature, gained from observation or recall in the search for subject matter, and knowledge of media and materials, secured through experimentation, combine to contribute information, courage, and a sense of accomplishment. While practice and perseverance are essential, drawing skill depends not on an elaborate technical display, but rather on relating the actions of your hand with eye, heart and mind. Looking and analyzing, personally discovering the effects achievable with particular media and methods, thinking, feeling, doing — not necessarily in that order — culminate in attainment.

Only one individual really knows which drawing style can most effectively suit you, and that person is obviously you. The technique, or drawing method, must emerge from self; however, it can be greatly assisted through personal experimentation. Such searching is highly dependent on personal resourcefulness in finding and selecting the means to delineate with feeling and directness. Simple investigations with tools, media, and materials can reveal innumerable possibilities which increase sensitivity and fulfill potential. Tools (pencils, brushes, blunt and fine pointed pens, Flo-master pens, sharp sticks, or even small twigs) and media (inks — full strength or diluted, crayon, graphite, charcoal, or chalk) employed on smooth or rough paper offer a number of exciting possibilities. The paper, light or dark in value, can even be dampened, and unique qualities can then be obtained through partial absorption. Each tool, medium, and material offers certain possibilities as well as contains limitations, but all provide a diversity in execution within their limitations. Even a pencil offers many opportunities for obtaining a diversity of means (Figure 185). The side of the exposed lead, as well as the point, can be employed by holding the pencil at a sharp angle. Dragging and pushing the drawing instrument, varying the applied pressure by pressing firmly when producing portions of the line, and breaking the contour by randomly lifting the tool from the surface for a moment add variation and vitality to line. Jagged, curved, straight, rough passages offering smooth or abrupt transitions through serene or active lines can thus be created. Strong value ranges and even effects suggesting transparency may soon follow.

Conducting a personal search to find what line can do should prove exciting and revealing. Many implications can become evident, and frequently the discoveries can be directly related to future drawings.

SHEET OF SKETCHES, *studies for sculpture, pencil, Henry Moore, 1939. (Courtesy Philadelphia Museum of Art)*

184

PENCIL INVESTIGATION, *line, texture, and value, James A. Schinneller.*

185

186   THE BRIDGE, *pen and ink, High school student. (Courtesy Pittsburgh Public Schools)*

Line, Gesture, and Contour Drawing

A line may be defined as a mark possessing length — a streak produced by pencil, pen, or any other drawing tool. Often the tool used in rendering determines in great part the most effective sorts of lines to incorporate in the endeavor. Some drawings possess a limited number of lines similar in character, while others contain a variety of lines: long, short, thick, thin, continuous, broken, angular, and straight. Lines may be abundantly used, appearing to be actively searching to define shapes and form, or deliberately used, with each line responsible for outlining an essential portion of the drawing. While many avenues exist in drawings, two distinct approaches in the use of line, gesture, and contour can be clearly ascertained. Both contain lucrative qualities and can complement one another, though tending to stand in opposition pertaining to line treatment. A natural manner of drawing can frequently emerge through experiences with either or both of these methods.

Gesture drawing — evident in the style of the high school student's interpretation of *The Bridge* (Figure 186) — is rapidly executed, and many lines serve to identify the subject. Such drawings do not have exact or accurate edges but appear to suggest movement in space by line repetition. The approach conveys the spirit or essence of things rather than accurate aspects of appearances. Since action is strongly apparent, the procedure may be thought of as somewhat of a controlled scribbling method; for the artist, rapidly capturing an impression of the entire form without a great stress on particular details, reveals instantaneous reaction rather than indications of involved observation.

187 THE TEMPTATION OF SAINT ANTHONY, *pen and ink, Salvator Rosa, 1615–1673 [Italian]. (Courtesy Metropolitan Museum of Art, Rogers Fund, 1912)*

A continuum and permanency often appear evident in drawings by past masters and closely relate their styles to current expressive endeavors. Possessive of gesture undertones, *The Temptation of Saint Anthony,* (Figure 187) by Salvator Rosa, illustrates such a continuum relationship. Bordering on the abstract through many areas which enhance interest while denying the obvious, the style is firmly linked to contemporary expressionism. Have you noticed how the decisive and faint lines repeated adjacent to and over one another suggests turbulence and action consistent with the passions and anguish inherent in the theme?

A comparison of *The Bridge* and *The Temptation of Saint Anthony* with *Self Portrait* (Figure 188) illustrates the difference between gesture and contour drawing. The latter may be thought of as a method which employs a single deliberate line to indicate outline. Secured through the assistance of a mirror which permitted a personal facial examination, *Self Portrait* is both economical and explicit in line. The drawing achieves charm through exaggerations and scale, and these attributes combine with its conciseness of style to warmly communicate the personality of the performer.

Contour drawing should depend not on constant reference to the drawing while in progress, but rather on a coordination of hand and eye. The procedure involves placing the point of the drawing tool on a paper surface and relating the movement of the drawing tool to the movement of the eyes as they slowly roam over the object to be drawn. Contour drawing encompasses deliberation, coordination, and keen observation and offers sensitive and simplified renderings.

Both contour and gesture drawing share a mutual relationship in being dependent only on line. While contour emerges from a deliberate and concise line treatment and gesture is the reverse — appearing as it does through numerous lines culminating in form, each method can assist the development of a personal manner of drawing. The mastery of line drawing lies in seeing and reacting, each in his own manner, to the distinctive qualities of familiar subjects — their shapes, proportions, and form — and emphasizing such traits. Liberties and directness plus a distinctiveness of concept are united in Ben Shahn's version of *Two Men* (Figure 189). The images imply wonderment and contemplation as well as anticipated action and mark Shahn's statement as effective and revealing. Simplicity of execution, enhanced through fluctuations in line, combine with an imposing placement to provide a monumentality to the brush and ink contour drawing. Inexhaustible possibilities exist for the expression of ideas through line alone.

The Structure of Drawing

Drawing, as the French artist Ingres contended, is concerned with all the elements of art with the exception of color. It is of course possible to have color in drawing by employing colored pencils, chalk, crayons or the like; however, the majority of drawings do not possess color, nor is it usually associated with drawing. Line is the major component, with shape, texture, value, and form growing out of it. A separate consideration of each element can simplify an understanding of the qualities and characteristics in drawing, but such a division should not imply that each element rigidly operates independently of the others. For

188   SELF PORTRAIT, *pencil, High school student.* *(Courtesy Pittsburgh Public Schools)*

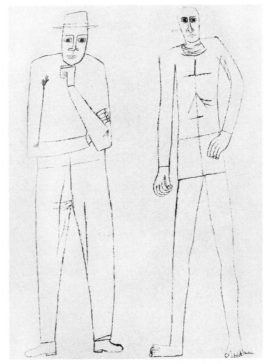

189   TWO MEN, *brush and ink, Ben Shahn, 1951.* *(Courtesy Wright Art Center, Beloit College)*

190   RACE TRACK, *pencil, William Glackens, 1909. (Courtesy Philadelphia Museum of Art)*

example, line may produce texture, and value may suggest form.

Form, the culmination of the elements and the totality of drawing, can be achieved in innumerable manners. While obtainable through contour identification alone, the use of the elements of texture and value in conjunction with line can frequently sensitize form and increase the comprehensiveness of the visual statement. In numerous drawings, lines, texture, and value are united in manners which make it exceedingly difficult, even impossible, to divorce them and conceive of each as a unique characteristic. This should not be thought unusual, because many drawings have an interdependency and fusion of parts which are not open to dissection and picayunish examination.

Form: Solidity and Unity

Form may be conceived as the total composition resulting from the unity of all parts. As one example of form, consider your body; for it is a unity of parts — head, shoulders, chest, hips, legs, feet, toes, arms, fingers, hair, eyes, and so on. Each part contributes a shape to your form or figure, as well as texture — slick, smooth, semirough—and a range of values— dark and light relationships dependent on flesh, eyes, hair. A drawing may contain a portion of a form, a full form, or many forms or figures, with several or numerous shapes organized within the drawing. The sum total, no matter the number, can still be identified as form; for while form possesses distinct parts, all parts share a common purpose in contributing toward the theme and achieving its final and total form.

Composing a number of parts into a unified form and securing full advantage of the value range obtainable from a pencil enabled William Glackens to interestingly portray a *Race Track* (Figure 190). The changes in solidity, from intense indications of bulk to minimized suggestions, provide an active atmosphere to the somewhat serene mood as horses and riders journey toward their starting position. Bystanders tend to frame the scene and serve to inject and retain interest within the framework of the drawing. A directness of presentment, containing the attributes of both a concise and comprehensive treatment, marks Glackens' style.

Form can achieve solidity and imply dimensions in space through notations of shadow as well as substance. A vigorous handling of pen and ink by Pablo Picasso soon resulted in the sketch titled *Head* (Figure 191). The form bears a semblance of modeling through value distribution obtained by proximity of line indicating curvatures and planes of a facial mass. Abrupt and blending transitions imply bulk, substance, and volume and convey a sense of existence in space.

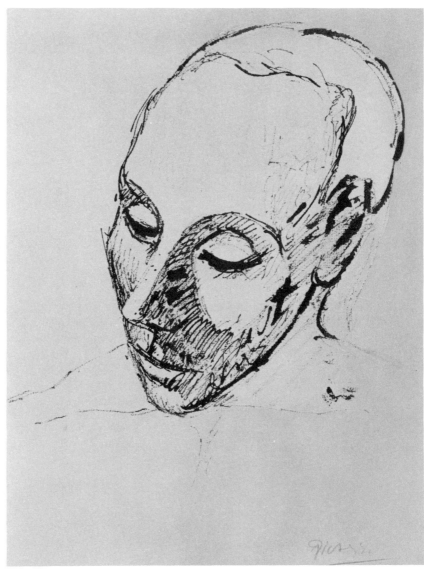

191   HEAD, *pen and ink, Pablo Picasso, 1906. (Courtesy Philadelphia Museum of Art)*

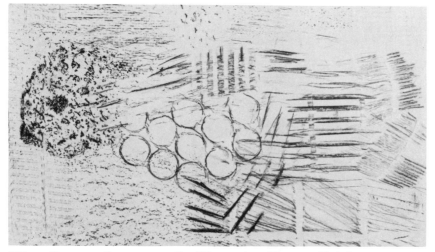

192   FANTASTIC CREATURE, *pencil rubbing, student, Wisconsin High School, Madison, Wisc.*

193   STUDY FOR THE CYPRESSES, *pen and ink over pencil, Vincent Van Gogh, 1853–1890 [Dutch]. (Courtesy Brooklyn Museum)*

Texture: The Surface of Things

Run your hand through the hair on your head or over a polished piece of furniture. Imagine how sandpaper and velvet would feel to the touch of the finger tips. Does the stem of a leaf have a surface similar to the bark of a tree trunk? Can you imagine how all things might appear if as slick as glass or as rough as gravel? If so, the endless variety of surfaces or textures which enrich our universe would be no more, contrast would be lost, and man's sensations would be both limited and monotonous.

The unusual image *Fantastic Creature* (Figure 192) might suggest the bird which missed the ark, if Noah could possibly have overlooked one creature. Or such a strange form could exist only in the imagination. Or is yet to come through the long line of evolution?

Can you guess how the student solved the problem of composing the creature through textural exploration?

Concrete, coarse sandpaper, burlap, rubber mats, cane, wire screening, and innumerable other materials can transfer exciting surface impressions and indicate textural potentials through rubbings. The

194   STREET SCENE, *pen and ink, High school student. (Courtesy Pittsburgh Public Schools)*

image emerged from placing paper upon a number of these rough and semirough materials and rubbing with a soft lead pencil.

Many artists indicate a great concern with surface qualities in explicitly denoting the textural details of matter. Vincent Van Gogh, a great expressionist, strongly stressed such surface characteristics in his powerful renderings. His interpretations such as *Study for the Cypresses* (Figure 193) appear to intensify and structure nature in tune with the qualities associated with actively growing surfaces. Great exaggerations in his drawings portrayed a textural sequence that expressed the vitality of soil, sun, wind, and growing matter. Van Gogh simplified or cast aside details in order to advance the particular qualities which disclosed his reactions toward nature. Foliage and grass, for instance, were treated in manners that caused the viewer to experience a strong tactile sensation from common matter. The Dutchman's style often unified surfaces and shapes in that textural definitions assisted in the delineation of matter, and texture and form tended to become one.

Knowing what and when to simplify and where to strongly emphasize is an important attribute in art. Thus, nonessentials do not conflict or deny the full emergence of what the heart deems important. Possibly this was a portion of Van Gogh's secret which enabled clear and moving communication with pen and pencil as well as brush.

The City's Coating

Street Scene (Figure 194) indicates a young artist's concern with the distinctive surfaces which comprise a portion of his environment. The drawing richly describes textures through a mosaic of black and white. A multitude of detail, captured through line and the use of minute shapes, deposits areas of surface interest throughout the composition. The arrangement enables the eye to rest in large serene areas, devoid of detail, scattered throughout the layout. Clarity and order sensitively blended with an awareness of rough and smooth textures enabled the high school student to portray his version of the coat that shells matter.

OLD SHIPS OF THE LINE, *scratchboard and ink,
Student, Oak Park and River Forest High
School, Ill.*

195

Simulated and Actual Texture

Manners of suggesting texture in drawing can be related to simulated or actual endeavors in creating surfaces. The former implies textural properties through a rendering of details, while the latter actually secures texture through building up or digging into the drawing surface. If the finger tips were moved across simulated textures, as in *Study for the Cypresses* or *Street Scene*, the surfaces would be smooth and the transition unbroken. The same procedure with an actual surface, of course, would indicate areas of roughness to the touch. Textures in paintings are often actual, built up through the plasticity of paint, the addition of foreign matter, or even the cutting and piercing of thickly applied paint with an instrument such as a palette knife; drawings, owing to their media, are more limited. Though graphite, charcoal, crayon, ink, do not possess the body or substance of paint, actual textures can be incorporated into drawings. Various devices — drawing upon rough materials, linens, sandpaper or coarse papers, using string for building line, pasting scraps of paper to a larger sheet and rendering upon the fluctuating surface—can add contrast and excitement to drawing through the introduction of actual textures. While often-novel effects can be obtained, care should be taken that such endeavors do not unduly focus interest on material and deny lucid comment. Effective manners of obtaining actual transitions of roughness and smoothness in drawing can also be easily secured through piercing and scratching processes such as crayon etching or scratchboard.

Digging In for an Idea

Crayon etching is achieved through drawing with a sharp tool upon a coating of dark crayon, ink, or tempera paint which covers a surface of thickly applied crayon. By removing portions of the top surface, through a combination of drawing and scratching with a knife, compass point, needle, razor blade, or similar sharp instrument, underlying crayon areas of contrasting values and colors can be rapidly exposed. Thus, intriguing surfaces can be easily secured, provided inquisitiveness is evident in discovering a variety of manners of removing the overlying surface. Two factors may assist success in the preparation of the surface: a random scattering of bright and dull, light and dark colors, thickly applied, and a small amount of soap rubbed upon the brush if tempera paint or ink is used to cover the wax crayons; for soap facilitates coverage of the wax surface. Scratchboard is a light cardboard with a commercially prepared white surface which can be drawn upon with ink or crayon or even painted. Portions of the surface can then be scratched out to achieve additional relationships in value and actual texture.

Through cutting into a scratchboard, a high school student once again permits proud *Old Ships of the Line* to parade upon a choppy sea (Figure 195).

Value: Light and Dark Pattern

A simple investigation will readily indicate qualities of value; merely squint your eyes until almost closed and look around your immediate surroundings. You will notice that lines, shapes, colors, and details will not be extremely distinct, but large light, medium, and dark patches will be evident. These areas usually combine into interesting patterns of value. If reference is made to the outdoors, value seems to lose impact as distance increases; objects in the far distance appear much lighter than they would if closer.

In painting, value is associated with all colors in conjunction with their degrees of lightness and darkness; in drawing, value is usually linked with white, grays, and black. Obtainable in numerous manners from white chalk on dark paper, diluted inks, rubbings, and damp paper to a host of other media and procedures, value can easily provide exciting relationships to drawing.

The eighteenth-century Italian master Gian Battista Tiepolo often captured keen and lyrical qualities in mass and space through a fluid treatment of value. His depiction of a Biblical episode *Rest on the Flight into Egypt* (Figure 196) contains an underlying proximity of value in harmony with the implications of rest and inactivity inherent in the theme. Any indications of monotony in value relationships are shattered, however, by evident dark values which emphasize and solidify the composition. Though predominantly registered through the application of washes of diluted ink, the figures are further articulated through line. Tiepolo's use of washes, easily varied in value with a reduction or increase of water mixed with the pigment, provides rich contrasts, diffused masses, and flowing transitions to his drawing.

A manner of indicating value vastly different than Tiepolo's method was employed by Charles Sheeler in his *Barn Abstraction* (Figure 197). His arrangement of specific shapes with abrupt value changes produces definite and strong value contrasts and precise interplays of space within the drawing's surface. Horizontal and vertical movements, as well as depth recession, are apparent in the reactions of the eye as it views the value discords, proportions, and construction of the total form. Sheeler's drawing clearly indicates that the most conventional of themes contains exciting possibilities for drawing; for even the commonplace has fruitfulness when seen with a creative eye.

196   REST ON THE FLIGHT INTO EGYPT, *pen and wash, Gian Battista Tiepolo, 1696–1770 [Italian]. (Courtesy Fogg Art Museum, Harvard)*

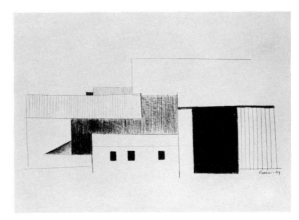

197   BARN ABSTRACTION, *Conte crayon, Charles Sheeler, 1917. (Courtesy Philadelphia Museum of Art)*

198 STUDY FOR THE PORTRAIT OF LOUIS FRANCOIS BERTIN, *charcoal, Jean Auguste Dominique Ingres, 1780–1867 [French]. (Courtesy Metropolitan Museum of Art, Bequest of Grace Rainey Rogers, 1943)*

199 THE LISTENER, *ink rubbing, Siegfried Rinehardt, 1954. (Courtesy Wright Art Center, Beloit College)*

Capturing the True Light

While value handling need not be marked by rigidity or be highly intellectualized, such tendencies were evident in many drawings of the past. Involved studies of the action of natural light as it struck substances, and the resulting highlights, diffused light, and cast shadows, were undertaken in order to capture the particular and restate actual appearances in drawing. Innumerable studies illustrating close value examination, such as *Study for the Portrait of Louis François Bertin* (Figure 198) rendered by the great nineteenth-century draftsman Jean Auguste Dominique Ingres, were often the order of the day. Academicians studied, pondered, and depicted with a sureness of hand qualities which seemed apparent to their scrutinizing eye in attempts to suggest the actual existence of light and matter. These elaborate studies involved value compositions tied to technical skill and close observation and often were presentments as close to fact as humanly possible. Surface modelings, supposedly three-dimensional, were thus achieved, and while light and darkness were identified, other values unfortunately remained cloaked or ignored in the shadows.

200   CLIFF AND FOLIAGE, *charcoal, University student.*

More Important Values

The ultimate in drawing is not reached through a restating of the obvious or actual; instead, it must be individually nurtured and attained by a personal use of the elements in the expression of ideas. Rather than follow scientific formulas and past art practices or adhere to the findings of factual examinations, the artist must originate his own means of using light and dark as well as line and texture.

Siegfried Rinehardt brought impact and strength to his ink drawing *The Listener* (Figure 199) by handling value in an original, decorative, and semirealistic manner. Obtained by rubbing, rather than by wash or directly by tool, medium-dark passages activate the background and provide changes of pace, tone, and unity to the expression. The design is highly structured, with distortions and foreshortening acting to focus interest on facial features and projecting hand. Notice how the grasped string assists entry into the foreground and the triangular treatment of the form extends security to the organization through a firm planting of shapes. What other qualities do you notice?

The suggestion of listening is intensified by the look of contemplation on the part of *The Listener*. The characterization appears to portray a somber mood, possibly an individual deep in conversation, enthralled by an inspiring musical score or even intent upon ascertaining the meaning of a mysterious echo.

Cliff and Foliage (Figure 200), a university student's charcoal rendering, functions somewhat as shallow pattern rather than a grouping of three-dimensionally executed forms distinctly organized to convey a deep recession in space. While recessions in space occur, indicated by overlapping of shapes and value differences with light areas receding and dark masses advancing, the distribution of value is in keeping with the flat two-dimensional paper surface. Thus the over-all surface is stressed in this treatment of a minute portion of nature's wonderland. The liberty taken in the delineation of shapes and value placement implies human involvement in the activity of drawing, and the rapid execution in a direct and declarative style indicates a current emphasis on freedom and spontaneity in drawing.

201   Classmate, *pen and ink, damp paper, High school student. (Courtesy Pittsburgh Public Schools)*

Damp Paper and Vivid Line

Faint line and wash passages intermingle with strong linear notions to create a vibrant surface in the high school student's sketch *Classmate* (Figure 201). The bleeding and absorption of ink, achieved by drawing upon damp areas of paper, bring forth strong value contrasts between hair mass and face and shoulder contours. The sensitive rendering may be linked to a simple and coherent song; for its expressive style appears as an invigorating melody of line and value.

202   JORG, *pen and ink and watercolor, Paul Klee, 1879–1940* [*Swiss*]. *(Courtesy Philadelphia Museum of Art)*

Close Values and Distant Fantasy

Paul Klee's drawings, strongly tempered by his active imagination, usually featured the familiar in fantastic guise. *Jorg* (Figure 202), a watercolor and ink drawing, is indicative of his direct and inventive style. While it may be possible to consider *Jorg* as a mixed-media painting, its classification as drawing appears more appropriate owing to its dependency on line produced by a drawing tool and the lack of color masses serving to identify the form. The large scale of the partial figure dominates the entire space, demanding and assuring attention; however, value is keenly subordinated. A minimum of value contrasts due to rendering upon a medium-dark background with a dark medium denies great value variation and serves to permit other qualities to more firmly emerge. Thus close value control can subdue line, assure unity, and spread interest throughout a drawing.

Klee's strange semiabstract style was as basic as a young child's expression, yet highly sophisticated. *Jorg*, seeming to suggest "see my pretty flower," appears warm with wit yet not funny, humorous but with a touch of pathos. Notice how line continuum unifies and emphasizes the exaggerated facial features in an extremely economical and somewhat whimsical manner. A translation of the inscription, applied in German by Klee and located in the lower corner of the drawing, relates that it is "after an old peasant painting." It would be revealing to compare Klee's drawing with its original counterpart, if possible; for in its reinterpretation a world of difference would most certainly exist. A skilled artist, Klee developed a unique style, and in his prolific lifetime he produced innumerable drawings with themes, usually charming, ranging from treatments of buildings and figures to animals and strange plants. This Swiss artist is very influential on modern art in that he is one of the great contributors to this century's visual imagery. Stating a desire to make memories abstract, he undoubtedly saw with more than merely his eyes and, handling drawing in the tradition of great art, always transmitted strong visual evidences of his creative personality.

TOPICS FOR CONSIDERATION

1. What types of lines are contained in drawings and what qualities can they convey?
2. In reference to drawing, what is meant by balance, emphasis, subordination, form, movement, simulated texture, value, and wash?
3. List a number of tools and media that can be used to produce drawings.
4. How can movements be implied and a range of values secured in drawing?
5. What practices should one follow in learning to draw?
6. What qualities comprise an effective and original drawing?
7. Select three drawings in this text which you favor, and indicate reasons for your choices.

SUGGESTED ACTIVITIES

1. Create ten gesture drawings relating to objects which surround you. Use a soft, dark drawing pencil and rapidly draw anything from chairs, cups, and figures to hands, tables, or trees. Following their completion, substitute pen and ink for the pencil and redraw the same subjects, but this time employ a contour approach. Observe closely and render with singular, precise lines.
2. Request a friend to pose while you make several ink drawings of the figure in different positions. Emphasize balance, bulk, and action, and employ both pen and brush.
3. Feel several rough objects and exaggerate their surface qualities in a pencil or ink drawing. Rough sensations can easily be conceived by lightly rubbing the finger tips over an orange, a thistle, sandpaper, rough wood, or innumerable other obviously textured objects. Do not attempt to be factual when engaged in this drawing, but rather distort freely to increase implications of roughness.
4. Draw an impression of a landscape or interior scene with chalk on dark construction paper. Present a number of values from light to dark, and stress a rhythmical pattern, through repetition, in the drawing. Exhibit this venture, if possible, in conjunction with the works of your classmates, then display it in your home.
5. Try rubbings with crayons, randomly investigating different surfaces and subsequent patterns upon a single sheet of paper. Cut out suitable shapes and compose a fantastic creature. Adhere with paste to a background sheet of paper.
6. Sketch an episode derived from an athletic or social event. Employ pen and ink, charcoal, or drawing pencil on an 18 by 24 inch sheet of drawing paper. Stress fluid linear relationships by keeping the drawing tool in constant contact with the paper, and do not erase but rather correlate all lines into a unified composition.
7. Select a subject of your choice and render a drawing with brush and diluted black ink upon a large sheet of paper, rough if possible. Emphasize value gradations and occupy the entire space with linear or mass notations.

APPROPRIATE REFERENCES AND READINGS

Artists on Art, Writings from the XIV to the XX Century, edited by Robert Goldwater, New York: Pantheon Books, Inc., 1945.

Modern Drawings, edited by Monroe Wheeler, New York: The Museum of Modern Art, 1947.

NICHOLAIDES, KIMON. *The Natural Way to Draw*, Boston: Houghton Mifflin Co., 1941.

One Hundred Master Drawings, edited by Agnes Mougan, Cambridge, Mass.: Harvard University Press, 1949.

SACHS, PAUL J. *The Pocket Book of Great Drawings*, New York: Pocket Books, Inc., 1951.

WATROUS, JAMES. *The Craft of Old-Master Drawings*, Madison, Wisc.: University of Wisconsin Press, 1957.

WHEELER, MONROE. *Modern Painters and Sculptors As Illustrators*, New York: The Museum of Modern Art, 1947.

6 | VISUAL REALITIES AND IMAGERY

However impressive the artist's notes or colours, the beholder sees and hears in them only himself, and if he can not do so, the work is for him meaningless.

OSWALD SPENGLER[1]
German Philosopher and Art Critic

203   CHILD'S BURIAL, *woodcut print, Ernst Barlach, 1919. (Courtesy Wright Art Center, Beloit College)*

205   VIEW OF BENJAMIN REBER'S FARM, *oil painting, Charles Hoffmann, 1872. (Courtesy National Gallery of Art, Collection of American Primitive Painting)*

204   ANIMALS, *oil painting, Rufino Tamayo, 1941. (Courtesy Museum of Modern Art)*

[1] *The Decline of The West* (New York: Alfred A. Knopf, Inc., 1929), vol. 2, p. 56.

Subjects and Moods:
Sources Unlimited

Themes for art are concerned with the whole of man's experiences; for subjects are secured from the entire theater of life. Themes may range from a *Child's Burial* (Figure 203) or the ferociousness of *Animals* (Figure 204) to a serene *View of Benjamin Reber's Farm* (Figure 205) or an imaginary *Bird from Outer Space* (Figure 206). Whatever man has encountered or imagined, be it terrifying, tranquil, or fantastic, proves appropriate for statements in art; for the artist may cry out against injustice, reveal the beauties of environment, or even treat ideas emerging through flights of fantasy.

Subject matter in sculpture, drawing, or painting can be completely abstract or figurative; that is, it may have no representative relationship with manmade or natural forms, or it may portray recognizable objects or episodes such as a mountain meadow, a figure, or the city. Fluctuations may even exist between abstract and figurative presentments, with certain works being dependent upon title to present meaning.

The *Painting* (Figure 207), by Ben Nicholson, consisting of a geometric pattern of square and rectangular segments of color, exists for itself. It represents a complete abstraction, with no indication of portraying or representing objects or themes outside the painting. Milton Avery's *Clear Cut Landscape* (Figure 208) contains a simplicity of space and value distribution similar to Nicholson's painting, but it differs in having associative relationships beyond the painting. Shapes representing trees, meadow, and mountains are identifiable in Avery's composition; therefore, it can be classified as a figurative painting. Its theme can be readily identified without reference to title, while Nicholson's intentions were completely abstract. Between the two exist many degrees of abstraction. In certain works attributes of both completely abstract and figurative art are fused. Hans Arp's painting *Birth of the Rock* (Figure 209) illustrates such a tendency; for without insight provided by title the idea expressed would hardly be recognizable. The title in Arp's painting serves to assist the spectator in recognizing and interpreting the theme of rock achieving a formative state. Notice how black, implying weight, tends to compress the white core to suggest a process of force which solidifies matter to form rock. Or could the white mass represent molten magma intruding into a bed of limestone, which, through contact metamorphosis, gives birth to marble?

206 BIRD FROM OUTER SPACE, *scrap cloth and paper, student, Wisconsin High School, Madison, Wisc.*

207 PAINTING, *oil painting, Ben Nicholson, 1936. (Courtesy Philadelphia Museum of Art)*

208   Clear Cut Landscape, *oil painting, Milton Avery, 1951. (Courtesy San Francisco Museum of Art)*

Towards the Abstract

While figurative painting has existed for innumerable centuries, abstract painting developed in this century through the efforts of individuals such as Wassily Kandinsky. This artist received musical training as a youth and later a formal education in economics and law before turning to painting at the age of thirty. Following a period of working in a representative manner, he began to strongly advocate nonobjective art, another term for completely abstract art. Figurative art was denied by Kandinsky, for he believed representative subject matter reminded man of contact with his environment and thereby risked the recall of the frustrations and failures of life. The Russian artist constructed elaborate theories to justify nonobjective art as a means of escaping worldly concerns, contending it offered a new reality of spiritual harmony and a pure art.

Oriental mysticism and an interest in music were factors which influenced Kandinsky in formulating his attitude toward subject matter and visual reality. He was particularly interested in aspects of Hinduism; for beliefs held by the Hindu, especially his attitude toward life, proved in harmony with Kandinsky's notions of the role of subject matter. The Hindu believes the individual must control his inner being, his spirit, in order to acquire calmness and inner satisfaction and through meditation deny unsatisfac-

tory factors such as physical discomfort and worldly conflicts. Kandinsky looked upon nonobjective art as a somewhat similar means of projecting beyond worldly concerns through a visual escape from recognizable forms. Such an attitude offered both a release from conventional subject matter and a new world of possibilities for art.

Experiences with music as a youth, the other factor strongly influencing Kandinsky's attitude[2] towards subject matter, later encouraged him to devise parallels between music and painting. He frequently spoke of correlating the senses of sight and sound, contending that various colors are allied with certain sounds:

> Keen lemon-yellow hurts the eye in time as a prolonged and shrill trumpet-note the ear, and the gazer turns away to seek relief in blue or green.
>
> Color is the key-board, the eyes are the hammers, the soul is the piano with many strings. The artist is the hand which plays, touching one key or another, to cause vibrations in the soul.

Kandinsky also stressed that colors are capable of generating associative emotional responses through

[2] *The Art of Spiritual Harmony*, translated by M. T. H. Sadler (London: Constable and Company Limited, 1914), pp. 48, 52.

the impact of their physical characteristics. Warm colors, such as yellow, are suggestive of energy and restlessness, while cool colors — for instance, blue — are associative with peacefulness or somberness. Serene and vivid color relationships providing both harmonious and discordant passages were a major element in his compositions. With shapes and notions of placement secured from his imagination Kandinsky composed rhythmical symphonics through colors, and unusual arrangements which contributed sensations of great space and movement. Paintings such as *Composition 8, No. 260* (Figure 210) are indicative of his matured style which provided great impact to art of this century.

Much music possesses the quality of nonobjectivity in presenting melodies lacking reference to recognizable topics such as tree, house, or man. Painters and sculptors now often produce abstract visual imagery to entertain the sense of sight in somewhat the manner a musician composes melodies through sounds. While the musician employs notes and scales in building compositions, the painter and sculptor work with line, shape, color, and texture to create rich forms to provide pleasing visual sensations. Such is the case in Isamu Noguchi's sculptural wood *Structure* (Figure 211). By incorporating highly inventive shapes with a personal sensitivity of proportion, Noguchi created an exciting abstract form which both encloses and releases three-dimensional space. The pierced and interlocking segments, united through surface and placement and varied through contour deviations and shadow pattern, assure visual interest through an organic continuum.

Nonobjective art has become a dominate force in areas of industrial, architectural, and advertising design. For instance, sculptural forms such as Noguchi's now suggest new solutions in furniture design by extending possibilities beyond conventional angularity.

In its separation from the great majority of painting, which employs subjects drawn from direct and recognizable physical and social experiences, nonobjective art contains apparent shortcomings as well as attributes. It has both the challenge of a new formal language and the dangers of sterility owing to its lack of consideration for the extensive activities of man which are dependent on recognizable imagery for adequate communication. Combined with figurative subject matter, however, nonobjective art removes all subject restraints and extends opportunities for themes from the most basic of experiences to beyond the stars.

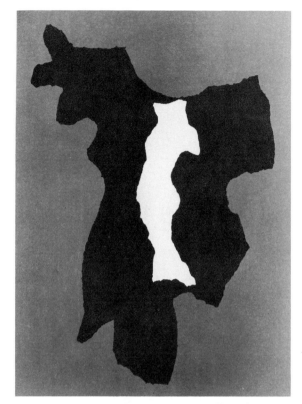

209   BIRTH OF THE ROCK, *oil on paper, Hans Arp, 1958*. *(Courtesy Carnegie Institute)*

210   COMPOSITION 8, No. 260, *oil painting, Wassily Kandinsky, 1923 (Courtesy The Solomon R. Guggenheim Museum)*

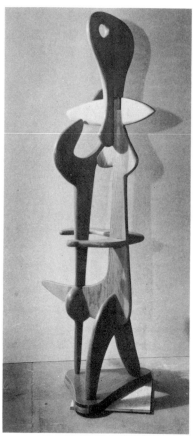

211   STRUCTURE, *wood sculpture,*
Isamu Noguchi, 1955. (Courtesy
Carnegie Institute)

212   MAJESTIC TENEMENT, *oil painting, Arthur Osver,*
1946. (Courtesy Pennsylvania Academy of The Fine
Arts)

213   SINGER BUILDING, *watercolor, John Marin, 1921.*
(Courtesy Philadelphia Museum of Art)

PIGEONS, *oil painting, John Sloan, 1910.*
(Courtesy Museum of Fine Arts, Boston)

214

Variations in Expression:
It All Depends on Your Point of View

Inexhaustible opportunities exist for personal interpretations within the bounds of even a single subject. There can be as many manners of producing nonobjective compositions or painting a rural or city theme, for example, as there are individuals exposed to such themes. A consideration of several paintings dealing with a city environment reveals the possibilities for a diversity of views. Presentments range from examinations of minute portions of the forms comprising the city to comprehensive panoramic surveys. The city is portrayed as both a busy mass and a tranquil area, with moods ranging from a suggestion of intense motion to serenity. Since individuals are unique beings, each artist reacts in a personal manner stressing the aspects deemed important in an individualized style.

Arthur Osver featured a small serene portion of an urban region in his painting *Majestic Tenement* (Figure 212). He created an interesting pattern through the suggestion of light cast upon façades surrounded by dark contrasts. The strong value deviations provide impact to the quiet mood obtained through the uncomplicated structure and a shallow recession in depth. Height and dignity are implied through narrow vertical movements, and interest is gained through the rectangular masses offset by lines and masses and pierced by dark shapes denoting windows. The repetition of similar shapes and values unifies the composition and provides a quality of rhythm, through sequence, to the tenement theme.

John Marin portrayed the rapid tempo of the city in the watercolor painting *Singer Building* (Figure 213). Full advantage of the fluidity and transparency of watercolor was taken by the artist, resulting in an extensive fusion of intermingling lines and shapes within his interpretation. The apparently instantaneous technique, combined with the undertones of bombastic movement in foreground, implies the vitality apparent in sections of a city. The diversity of window treatment through emphasis and subordination denies monotony to the dominant form of the building. Adjacent diagonals in surrounding space suggest movement and tend to focus interest into the center portion of the composition.

John Sloan presented an activity familiar to many city dwellers in his painting *Pigeons* (Figure 214). A human element is incorporated within the composition through the portrayal of a gazing youngster and a man involved with birds on a roof top. Notice how the pigeons are stressed through key areas of white and how passages of thick paint provide rich textural surfaces. Strong horizontal as well as vertical movements of dark values give a dominant, yet not overpowering, structure to Sloan's urban interpretation. Such devices provide stability to the design and through contrast permit the small fluttering symbols of pigeons to assume additional attention.

215   Night Hawks, *oil painting, Edward Hopper, 1942. (Courtesy Art Institute of Chicago)*

A tranquil mood recognizable to those who wander the deserted canyons of towns or metropolitan centers long after the dissipation of day is apparent in *Night Hawks* (Figure 215). Edward Hopper, in the painting, advanced his concept of several inhabitants possibly waiting for coffee, even a hamburger, before scurrying homeward. Attention is directed into the interior by the impact of a light segment ringed by dark masses. Various areas are subdivided into uncomplicated segments which add interest to the theme while playing a subordinate role. Subtle interplays of shadows emphasize lighter areas as well as contribute to the painting's pattern. The arrangement of the figures creates counterplays of direction which imply a variety of thrusts in space and diversified movement. Edward Hopper frequently treats segments of the city in a highly personal style and secures ideas from common experiences often ignored by less observant eyes.

John Hultberg titled his painting *Panorama* (Figure 216); it presents a continuous scene complete in all directions. Imaginative shapes stretch far into the background, with interplays of active and restful areas bleeding into a unified whole. Visualizing the urban environment as a compartmentalized mass, with cubbyholes housing man, the artist probes beneath and beyond concrete, wood, steel, and stone which coat the city. Interiors of randomly arranged segments, exposed through surface penetration,

reveal activities which offer insight into the theme. A deep recession in space implying a never-ending structure and the repetition of basic rectangular shapes suggest the vastness and similarity of existence in huge metropolitan areas. Frequently, men stand shoulder to shoulder yet are strangers, with each existing in a self imposed shell, a restrictive boxed environment.

One ascends far above roof tops to find the city sprawled out below when viewing the painting *Madison from the Air* (Figure 217). The artist, Warrington Colescott, contends that in his mind's eye he went up about two miles when creating his unique presentment of Wisconsin's capital city. Such a view is becoming common as plane travel above American cities increases. The composition retains interest through a diversity of lines, shapes, and surfaces. Entire city blocks assume impact through imaginative roof treatments and contrasting dark bisecting bands representing city streets patterned with automobiles. An overhead view of the State capitol incorporated into one corner of the exciting interpretation permits a rich segment contrast to occur, offsetting the uniformity of the cityscape.

Unlimited views and styles exist, and more are to come as painters search for personal ways of commenting about metropolitan centers, an important aspect of American life. How would you interpret the city?

216 PANORAMA, *oil painting, John Hultberg, 1957. (Courtesy Martha Jackson Gallery)*

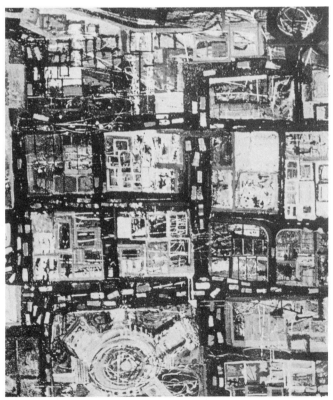

217 MADISON FROM THE AIR, *oil painting, Warrington Colescott, 1952. (Courtesy the Artist)*

Misconceptions That Block Understanding

Much misunderstanding regarding imagery in drawing, painting, and sculpture may be traced to limited notions of beauty and reality in association with art. When viewing a painting, for example, many individuals often exclaim, "The painting can't be good for it isn't beautiful!" or "It's poor; for it isn't real, lacks likeness to the model, or differs from past masterpieces of art!" Such attitudes too often are based on false relationships and a misunderstanding of beauty as well as art and reality.

The belief that a painting can be beautiful only if concerned with a visually beautiful subject or theme imposes undue restrictions on the role of art. Such an attitude, prevalent during the past, was usually associated with morality. Many authorities went so far as to fuse beauty with truth or the ideal, contending that painting must concern itself only with those qualities. Shortcomings and confusion became extremely apparent owing to such notions as "beauty is truth" and "truth is beautiful." A moral quality such as truth can not be identical to nor identified completely with an aesthetic characteristic such as beauty. One can readily see that many truths are not beautiful. The lack of tolerance within society, disease, famine, slums, accidents — all are truth in the sense of actualities but certainly could not be advanced as qualities or themes possessing beauty. Universal agreement as regards beauty is also an impossibility, because notions regarding beauty would vary with the society, the race, and even the individual. If general agreement could be reached on a topic that all individuals would consider beautiful, probably a subject concerned with a young child or a grand view of nature would be selected. The choice of these particular topics for treatment in painting would not, however, assure success. Many poor paintings of children and nature have been produced in a restrictive and unoriginal manner lacking the warmth or grandeur inherent in the themes. The treatment of a particular subject or topic, therefore, whether beautiful or morbid, guarantees neither success nor failure within the arts. Subject matter provides little, if any, merit in art judgment.

A consideration of literature may illustrate the relationship of subject matter and beauty. Much literature of the past century dealt with the whaling industry; factual and often terrifying accounts were written of the voyages of the men of New Bedford and the adjacent areas of the New England coast. Neither the subject "whales" nor the theme dealing with the whaling industry could be considered a topic usually associated with beauty. However, there emerged in the latter portion of the nineteenth century a book dealing with a great white whale which many consider one of the finest works of art produced by man. The adjective "beautiful" fittingly belongs to *Moby Dick,* the heroic story by Herman Melville. Why? The story did not deal with beauty; much literature with an identical theme proved longer, or shorter, more factual, even more imaginative. The success of Melville's work was due to its structure, the organization of the material and its presentment in an original, consistent, and revealing manner. The work possessed the qualities essential to all art, and the result was a beautiful form.

In drawing, painting, and sculpture, as in literature, many artists produce beautiful works dealing with themes other than those concerned with the usual notion of beauty. Rembrandt van Rijn drew and painted beggars, haggard and disillusioned. The subjects, while certainly not pleasant or beautiful, were presented in beautiful drawings and paintings. The themes were revealed in penetrating, sensitive manners, with the elements of art and principles of design handled in a most effective manner. Francisco Goya, a Spanish artist active during the French campaigns in his homeland, often employed his skill in producing strong protests against the invasion and man's inhumanity towards man. His themes are often morbid, haunting, terrifying accounts portraying subjects far from beautiful (Figure 218). Goya's concern was to deal not with the beauties of life, but rather with the harshness, brutality and difficulty of living; yet many contend his treatment of line and form seem to beautifully express a soul in turmoil. The term "beauty" may possess many meanings in art other than association with a pleasing theme. The term "reality," in relationship with art, may also have many implications.

Touching the Heart of the Matter: Reality and Art

Reality is that which is genuine, has actual existence; in this sense paintings, drawings, and sculpture are realities existing as substances for their own sake. However, art should not be confused with reality; for while artists are concerned with exposing aspects of reality through symbols, they are not imitators but interpreters of reality, reacting with feelings as well as thoughts. Often judgments of art based on likeness to a model, a factual photographic rendering, deny many features of both reality and art. Such attitudes ignore visual inventiveness and deny increased awareness and resulting enjoyment because of assumptions based on limited knowledge or false conclusions. Contemporary evaluations of art should be made in terms of factors such as originality, organization, consistency, and revelation rather than imitation. Revelation may be thought of as providing insight or advancing consciousness of the real; it consists not in duplicating what exists, but rather in visually exposing personal reactions derived from experiences with reality.

Notice how Graham Sutherland reveals the prickly quality evident in the theme *Thorn Heads* (Figure 219). The painting does not attempt to duplicate a particular group of thorns, but rather consists of an arrangement of shapes which seem to pierce, are thornlike. A universal quality characteristic of all thorned growth is stressed, with its basis in reality and its form tempered, for effect, by the sensitivity of the artist. Sutherland organized line, shapes, and value to imply textures and form which reveal the nature of the theme in an original and consistent manner. Consistency is apparent in the boldness of technique, which provides the painting with a direct vitality and harshness, in kinship with the grasping and turbulence of such an organic theme. The artist invents the means of providing unique insight into themes by revealing aspects of both self and reality.

Attitudes toward both reality and art fluctuate; for notions vary with what one knows, the society in which he lives, and his age. A South Sea islander's sense of reality would differ greatly from yours. A great difference of opinion regarding reality, what is real, may even be evident between members of a modern society. Particular experiences may determine attitudes. Would a doctor's concept of reality be in harmony with a soldier's? Would the concept of flight be more of a reality to a jet pilot or a building contractor? Reality can be what one knows but also extends far beyond those bounds. Would an artist who is interested in new manners of seeing and is engaged in developing original visual presentments hold the same attitude toward visual reality as the layman would hold?

Each age creates its own notions of reality, and artists living within their time are aware of visual forms and knowledge emerging from other fields.

218   WRECKAGE OF WAR, *plate 30 of Disasters of War Series, etching, Francisco Goya, 1813. (Courtesy Metropolitan Museum of Art, Rogers Fund, 1922)*

219   THORN HEADS, *oil painting, Graham Sutherland, 1946. (Courtesy Museum of Modern Art)*

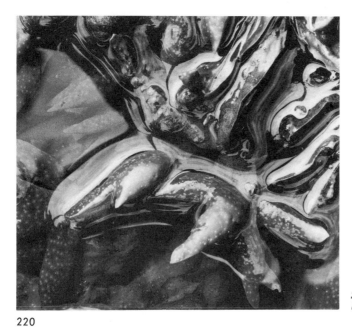

Sea Weed, photograph. (Photographed by Bill Hanson)

220

221   *Insect Nest, photograph. (Photographed by Ed Leos)*

222   *Television Set, Interior Workings, photograph.*

Man's experience with and concept of reality in our present age differs greatly from man's experience with and concepts of reality in the past. Man now probes beneath surfaces with X-ray machines, closely examines matter with microscopes, explores distant stars with telescopes, records the contour of earth and studies the atmosphere with cameras housed in rockets hurtling through space, and even searches beneath the sea with sonometers and beyond the horizon with radar. He now sees in many ways, with charts and graphs, microscope, and telescope, far into the heavens, deep into the sea. Photographic images of the products of sea (Figure 220) and earth (Figure 221) as well as the gadgetry of man (Figure 222) can now be minutely examined and even retained for further visual study. A trip to distant planets now seems probable. The atom has been split, rain has been artificially produced, high-speed cameras have captured objects in flight, art from all areas and all times is on view — all these are realities yet often prove difficult to comprehend. Possibly there can be as many visual realities as men with imagination; for it seems that what man has imagined he has created, resulting in a constant flow of new visual experiences.

Images and theories deriving from current undertakings in psychology, sociology, mathematics, physics, archaeology, even physical geography frequently suggest to artists means of contributing new dimensions to visual language (Figure 223). Studies captured on film and chart of the functioning of the mind, changing social patterns of society, higher mathematics, solar energy, the unearthing of lost civilizations, and the examination of a galaxy of natural forces, tides, erosion, hail, and wind present new manners of portraying and charting the strength and pattern of the universe. Men of science and many of their brothers in art view this imagery as a prime segment of the basic language of life. Meteorologists now photograph the hurricane eye and the atmospheric violence of the tornado, while geophysicists measure great disturbances beneath the earth (Figure 224). What can be more real than the visible recording of a seismometer which captures, in linear pattern, the erratic trembling of the very earth we stand upon?

Many artists, such as George Zoretich, are deeply interested in the new images of their age as well as the timeless happenings of nature. Concepts as logical as the torrential movements of natural forces and as basic as the scientific formulas of life, tempered with the imaginative and sensitive powers of man,

hold his interest. Regarding his manner of creating, and the painting *Torrent* (Figure 225), Zoretich contends:

> Through man's observation and through scientific discovery happenings in nature's complex pattern of change and development become evident. Yet in spite of all achievement and knowledge gained, the finding is never complete: something beyond the discovered is yet to be discovered. And so it is in the activity of most creative people. I feel that I approach my work with a similar neverending curiosity and investigation.

> I am concerned with the unknown energies that exist somewhere in the body of creation. I am interested in the forces that act upon any visual statement that I choose to make, and I am interested in the changes that these forces can promote. In every sense of the word painting becomes a living thing. When life is truly breathed into a work of art it takes on a meaningful existence. I paint in terms of making a statement somewhere on the canvas, an initial commitment, attempting to relate it to other parts that follow. These parts are energized; some are broken down to give way to a new organization and others accumulate complexities in an organic sense. In the final statement there is an overall development that makes for a new creative whole.

> Though I refer to nature as a means of explaining my approach to painting I would like to further credit man for his uniqueness on the thinking creative level plus the additional ingredient of the spiritual. The artist must possess something of eternal invention, and eternal hope, and creation will continue unending.

> In the painting "Torrent" the idea grew out of an initial commitment in color and form along the general lines already stated. It found its relationship to nature in its later form. The whole idea was activated physically and spiritually until it grew into its own existence.

Scientific Reality and Art; Past and Present

Many artists of this century feel mankind's discovery of the existence of a fourth dimension resulted in new meanings for art as well as science. Art is certainly not science, nor is it scientific; however, it is possible to understand various relationships often evident in modern drawings, paintings, and sculpture in terms of science. A consideration of the previous century's scientific viewpoint indicates a search for a static world, definite terms, clear-cut divisions. Individuals felt there existed an absolute reality, a final truth. A clear distinction was evident between matter and space. Both the artist and scientist thought in terms of rules governing motion, gravity, and matter. The camera was the norm. This tended toward a mechanical concept; for qualities could be

Segment of Our Earth, aerial photograph

223

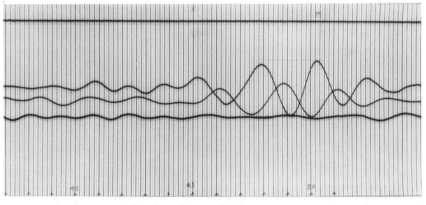

224 *Charting an Earthquake, photograph of seismometer recording. (Courtesy of Geo-Physics Department, The Pennsylvania State University)*

Torrent, *oil painting, George Zoretich, 1958. (Courtesy the Artist)*

225

broken down into clear thought and definable values. The age may be termed antipoetic as regards expressing or experimenting with color, form, or space. The great majority of nineteenth-century paintings were definite and contained absolute standards; time, space, and motion were separated. Frequently, the painter devoted himself to the mastery of technique, with skill in observation and execution playing prime roles.

Paintings such as *Old Models* (Figure 226) by William Harnett, which stresses the natural characteristics of light, surface, and form as perceived by the eye, are generally indicative of the nineteenth-century attitude toward reality and art. Harnett's painting, a rich display of technical proficiency, possesses a likeness to the original models in kinship with the imagery produced through skillful conventional photography. In addition to being in harmony with traditional scientific reality and displaying great skill, does the painting contain evidences of imagination, feeling, or originality?

Twentieth-century science broke with traditional scientific truth in combining and fusing matter, space, and time (Figure 227). Contemporary scientists now contend that it is impossible to tell whether something is in motion or static, because there exists no absolute. Man also no longer needs to visualize or imagine a definite division between matter and space; for, occupied or unoccupied, positive and negative space can be one and the same. As Albert Einstein[3] said,

> The idea that there exist two structures of space independent of each other, the metric-gravitational and the electromagnetic, was intolerable to the theoretical spirit. We are prompted to the belief that both sorts of field must correspond to a unified structure of space.

Modern science demonstrates that long-accepted ideas are not in any manner sacred. Contentions of our age such as "space is curved," "parallel lines eventually meet," "the shortest distance between two points is not a straight line" and the addition of time as the fourth dimension refute much that had been held valid.

Both the modern scientist and the modern artist often see relationships fused, dynamic, not static, constantly merging. Matter, energy, time, space, and motion combine to form a new reality.

[3] *Ideas and Opinions* (New York: Crown Publishers, Inc., 1954), p. 285.

226   OLD MODELS, *oil painting, William Harnett, 1892. (Courtesy Museum of Fine Arts, Boston)*

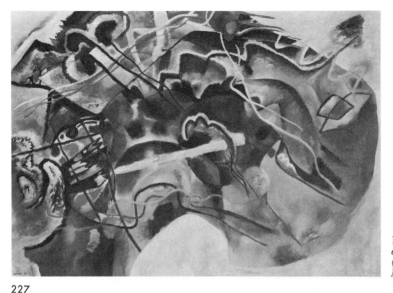

PICTURE WITH WHITE EDGE, No. 173, *oil painting, Wassily Kandinsky, 1913.* *(Courtesy Solomon R. Guggenheim Museum)*

227

Cubism, an important art movement of this century, can be approached in terms of science. Cubism attempts to make matter less and less recognizable with blendings into space. It seems to be a dematerialization, an abstraction of matter, with rearrangements to create both unusual and original images.

The inventive atmosphere of the age with its great strides in art and science, African sculpture with its angularity of mass, and the thoughts of the late-nineteenth-century French painter Paul Cézanne were prime influences on the formation of cubism. Contending that all forms could be understood in terms of the basic volumes and contours of cylinders, cones, and spheres, Cézanne's notion suggested an emphasis on planes and solidity with geometric implications to many artists at the turn of the century. While its beginnings may be understood in terms of Cézanne, science, and African sculpture, the concept and growth of cubism however were due to the creative vision and inventiveness of three men, Pablo Picasso, Georges Braque and Juan Gris. Their investigations during the first decades of this century ignored the restraints of existing styles of painting and led to methods of advancing previously unapprehended aspects of visual reality. By rearranging segments, employing sumptuous colors and strong and subtle values, structuring space for pleasing effects, painting bold simulated textures such as wood grain for warmth, building up segments through the addition of foreign materials such as sand, plaster, and scraps of printed paper patterns to paint, they sought to bring forth sensitive and new pictorial designs.

Georges Braque's painting *Still Life with Grapes* (Figure 228) is indicative of the fully matured cubistic style. Interweaving shapes and overlapping planes obtained through transparency of color and wedding of masses provide rich visual areas as well as give unity and consistency to the painting. The style is architectonic, owing to implied solidity, and highly decorative, with interplays of rich textures and colors, a shallow treatment of space, exciting proportions, and distorted shapes contributing to a poetic pattern.

William Harnett's painting *Old Models*, while separated by only a short passage of time from *Still Life with Grapes*, differs immensely as to both intentions and final form. Each exists within its century. Harnett attempted to capture existing reality and brought forth factual imagery. Cubism brought forth a new formalism, a pictorial reality as unique as the unusual images of twentieth-century science and as full of promise.

Many of the aims of science and art are similar in seeking economical treatments and developing compact theories which do not necessarily have to fit into a pattern as long as they function within the area under consideration. Painters must be granted the same latitude to experiment that we accord the scientist; for they must have the freedom to distort forms and relationships in order to develop new visual possibilities.

Modern Methods and New Visions

Through distortions which modify form, artists of this century have created new realities which extend and deepen the potentials of expression. It is now possible to tell more in painting and sculpture than usually meets the eye, to indicate rapid movement, to suggest the passage of time, peer beneath surfaces, present a totality of experience, imply sound, even assist the blind to see. Such accomplishments, secured through creative exaggerations, offer liberation from many limitations and conventions of the past.

MOVEMENT

Captured momentarily in space through photography, an Atlas missile suggests rapid movement as, climbing skyward, it thrusts a flaming trail (Figure 229). To suggest motion, painters frequently use multi-imagery secured through a concurrent repetition of shapes. Such distortions are effective devices for providing insight into many themes. A consideration of the exaggerated features of the painting *Nude Descending a Staircase* (Figure 230), by Marcel Duchamp, indicates how aspects of movement can be fulfilled through distortion. A sequence of similar relationships in the painting, united through overlaps and a fusion of lines and masses, resulted in a pattern flow associated with motion. The artist maintained a consistency between organization, technique and theme which, combined with his creative imagination, marked this painting as one of the early and influential masterpieces of this century.

Distortions in art, as in other areas, can reveal logical aspects which are an integrated segment of man's experiences. For instance, theater and television films transmit huge distortions in scale through the projection of multi-images derived from time and form sequence.

THE PASSAGE OF TIME

Marc Chagall incorporated a number of activities, engaged in at various times, in his painting *I and My Village* (Figure 231). The painting, concerned with the reminiscences of childhood, captured not a moment, nor a season, but rather the years of growing up. Toil, joy, and inquisitiveness are implied in the composite painting. Chagall even ignored the law of gravity when portraying the small figure appearing to hang upside down in one corner of the composition. This tends to add directional contrast, diverting and retaining interest within the painting. Qualities of transparency and superimposition permit several themes to occupy one area of the painting, which gives compactness as well as diversity to the design. Chagall clearly indicated that many experiences and many seasons may be included in a single painting to present a multitude of experiences divorced from the limitations of one moment or a single episode. Within our era paintings can sweep the horizons of memory, capture the flow of time, and even penetrate beyond the veil of surface.

228   STILL LIFE WITH GRAPES, *oil painting, Georges Braque, 1927. (Courtesy Phillips Gallery, Washington, D. C.)*

229   *Atlas Intercontinental Ballistic Missile in Flight, photograph. (Courtesy U.S. Department of Defense)*

230   NUDE DESCENDING A STAIRCASE, *oil painting, Marcel Duchamp, 1912. (Courtesy Philadelphia Museum of Art)*

231   I AND MY VILLAGE, *oil painting, Marc Chagall, 1911. (Courtesy Museum of Modern Art)*

232   CHIPMUNKS AT WORK, *tempera, student, University Elementary School, Iowa City, Iowa.*

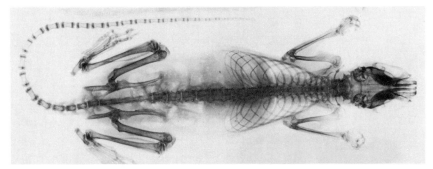

233   *X-Ray Photograph of Rodent, nutrition study in Bio-Chemistry Department. (Courtesy of The Pennsylvania State University)*

BEYOND THE SURFACE OF THINGS

Distortions in art, while possibly appearing strange to various individuals, are often based on natural tendencies. The painting *Chipmunks at Work* (Figure 232) indicates how a nine-year-old child visualized how rodents live beneath the surface of the earth. The view, made possible by an imaginative penetrating vision, pierces soil to present the activities of the small creatures. In an X-ray-like fashion the youngster indicates a cross section of earth, channeled with passageways containing chipmunks busily storing food in anticipation of winter. Views, both above and below the earth, have been expressed by the child to clearly indicate the locale. Similar ventures in the penetration of surfaces and forms are found in the art of many periods. Prehistoric men, as well as primitive men of the present, often include the skeleton, or portions of the bone structure, in their renderings of fish, birds, animals, and humans. Such simultaneous recordings of both interior and exterior, unhampered by restrictive notions of what can not be done, expose a wide range of exciting and basic realities.

If surfaces, usually linked with reality, provide only one level of meaning, many degrees and levels of reality must exist (Figure 233). Much in the manner that scientists expose interior structures to discover new truths, artists use creative visual penetrations to increase the comprehensiveness of their presentments. What thoughts come to mind when viewing Pavel Tchelitchew's painting *Hide-and-Seek (Cache-Cache)* (Figure 234)? It certainly indicates relationships beyond association with a child's game, but who can really tell? Can one precisely read the

mind of man? Many factors become apparent and others remain clouded when one contemplates the mysteries of human action, hidden, discovered, lost, emerging from a mystical ground. The painting seems to imply that consciousness and unconsciousness make up pulsating human life, with inner mysteries comprising a large portion of the external world. The surface of the painting, appearing as a transparent veneer, a tissue glaze, permits underlying substances to clearly appear or dissolve through linear and mass transformations as the eye plays hide and seek searching out shadowed substances. If man understood all, existence would be devoid of many challenges, and wonderment would be no more.

The duty of the artist, as he searches for the ultimate, is to expose to the world a vision that is revealing and original. Notice how Pablo Picasso employs the principle of penetration as well as multi-imagery in his painting *Seated Woman* (Figure 235). The constant state of flux between occupied and unoccupied space uniting foreground and background, broad simple sweeps of lines, and an interweaving of shapes reveal a unique version of a human form. Strong value contrasts, decorative textures, and an interplay of segments contribute to an active pattern in the painting. Picasso's concern was not to advance a factual recording of a woman, but rather to reveal new means of using the elements of art to produce imagery. The stress was on invention rather than recording. Examine the area implying a head and note the inclusion of several distorted views of front and profile. What else do you notice about the painting?

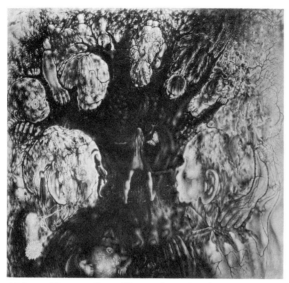

234 HIDE-AND-SEEK (CACHE-CACHE), *oil painting, Pavel Tchelitchew, 1940. (Courtesy Museum of Modern Art)*

236 CARNIVAL, *oil painting, Walter Quirt, 1942. (Courtesy Addison Gallery, Phillips Academy, Andover, Mass.)*

235 SEATED WOMAN, *oil painting, Pablo Picasso, 1926. (Courtesy Museum of Modern Art)*

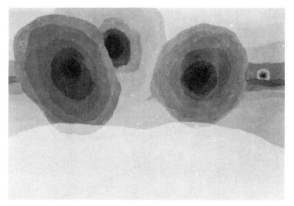

237 FOG HORNS, *oil painting, Arthur Dove, approximately 1921. (Courtesy Colorado Springs Fine Arts Center)*

238   SCULPTURE FOR THE BLIND, *carved marble, Constantin Brancusi, 1924. (Courtesy Philadelphia Museum of Art)*

TOTALITY OF EXPERIENCE
THROUGH DISTORTED PATTERN

Spun candy, ferris wheels, merry-go-rounds, barkers and the midway, a wealth of sights, bright lights, sounds and movements, penny pitching, waving banners, popcorn, colored balloons, and an abundance of bobbing faces combine to suggest *Carnival* (Figure 236). Walter Quirt distorted shapes and movements in the painting and organized fluttering textures and a diversity of values and colors to convey the carnival atmosphere. The painting doesn't relate to a particular scene or specific carnival, but rather implies all carnivals in capturing the tempo, vivid passages, and strong accents inherent in the theme. The abstract pattern reveals a totality of experiences unified to create an impression rather than relate a specific experience. Such an approach, achieved through the breaking up and rearrangement of shapes, is employed by many contemporary artists to encourage comprehensive sensations which intensify feelings and extend the scope of visual awareness.

SEEING WHAT IS HEARD

How would you create the sensation of sound in a painting? Arthur Dove, one of America's earliest abstract painters, revealed his notion by relating imaginative imagery to sound in the painting *Fog Horns* (Figure 237). Bellowing shapes radiating out from a serene background and bleeding into foreground through transparency suggest fog banks pierced by the emergence of sound. The distortion should be easily perceived by those who have heard the gloomy blasts from fog horns. The sounds are mandatory in coast areas where fog, depositing its curtain of mist, blots out dangers of rocky shoal or approaching vessel. Transformation takes place, the ears become the eyes as man listens to see what lies ahead. Such experiences were often encountered by Dove during years of cruising the eastern seaboard exposed to sounds and action of sea, wind and fog.

TOUCHING TO SEE

Constantin Brancusi presented an opportunity for the blind to conceive of a simplified form in creating *Sculpture for the Blind* (Figure 238). The sculpture, sympathetic to handling, could assist the blind to see through the action of hand and consciousness of mind. Physical contact with the marble surface through touch and caress would offer knowledge of existence, properties of surface, and curvature of mass resulting in a mental image approximating the visual form of the sculpture. The slick, hard surface and the gentle transitions in mass could give tactile sensations which would convey evidences of simplicity, solidity, and consistency and arouse corresponding fluent pleasures.

There are many manners of experiencing art and many methods of interpreting reality.

239 SNAP THE WHIP, *oil painting, Winslow Homer, 1872. (Courtesy Butler Institute of American Art, Youngstown, Ohio)*

240 THE CHILDREN, *oil painting, Pablo Picasso, 1956. (Courtesy Saidenberg Gallery)*

Directness, Experimentation, and Contemporary Imagery

Simplification of form and explorative tendencies are prime factors which often determine outcomes in modern art. When judging paintings of the last century with the present in terms of such factors, it should not be concluded, however, that the more recent are necessarily superior. Each fulfills its purpose in terms of the aesthetic beliefs of the day and frequently serves different purposes that are often decided by the circumstances of the era. It would be ridiculous to criticize Galileo in light of what is now scientifically known or belittle the achievement of Lindbergh by comparing his flight with current ocean flights. Man builds on past revelations, but epic accomplishments, past or present, are not tarnished by time. The heroics of Michelangelo or Shakespeare are certainly not dimmed when judged by present actions.

A comparison of Winslow Homer's painting *Snap the Whip* (Figure 239) with Pablo Picasso's *The Children* (Figure 240) illustrates the great difference in detail between similar themes produced at different times. Both paintings are valid, one in kinship with the past century's notions of detail, perspective, and reality, the other allied with a current view regarding directness, distortion, and reality. The great difference in detail between the two paintings is due to the current premium placed on an economy of means which provides direct impact to much contemporary art.

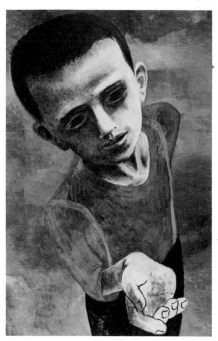

We Want Peace, *tempera, Ben Shahn, 1945. (Courtesy U.S. Department of State)*

241

Under a scrutinizing eye an abundance of detail and a concern with conventional perspective become obvious in Homer's work. The painting appears visually neutral and as accurate as technical proficiency and close observation can determine an outcome. A factual recording of details in all areas of the painting indicates a faithful recording of an environment which contained joyful children, of long ago, at play.

The harsh directness of Picasso's painting opposes the softer harmonies of Homer's portrayal. The lack of an abundance of detail in *The Children* provides an economical quality which germinates austere and powerful undertones. Deliberate distortions with stress on foreground give variation and vitality to the design, and the boldly emphasized facial features of the foreground figure cause immediate contact. The permeation of background into middle ground and foreground through the linear penetration of shapes rigidly unifies the composition. Notice the unusual treatment of foliage. Picasso invents his own pictorial realities which permit the expression of concepts in a powerful and unique visual language.

Through creative deviations in the treatment of form, the emotional content of a theme can be intensified and more directly transmitted to the spectator. Notice how Ben Shahn in his tempera painting *We Want Peace* (Figure 241) both emphasizes and subdues certain aspects of the form of a youth. The head and hand gain impact through exaggerated size and forward projection as well as value contrast and a surrounding economy of detail. Shahn's treatment of the composition elicits an immediate and personal response to the youth's plea, thereby effectively fulfilling the intentions of the painting. Study the painting closely for other evidences of creative ingenuity on the part of the artist. What additional qualities do you observe?

Experimental attitudes toward materials and organization, as well as directness, characterize much art of this century. Unusual as well as traditional materials employed in various combinations to achieve particular effects now mark many paintings. Factors such as scraps of paper, gravel, sand, and string added to paint, corrugated cardboard or burlap serving as painting surfaces, sticks and miscellaneous implements employed to render imagery contribute unusual relationships and, in part, determine the resulting form. *Battle of Fishes* (Figure 242), by André Masson, clearly indicates such an undertaking. It contains strong evidences of both an experimental process and a rapid method of organization which assisted in the formation of imagery. A great portion of modern art differs in execution and intention from art of the past, because the final form is derived from a rapid and explorative working procedure. Differences in organizational method, working process, and even intention cause a cleavage between present and past.

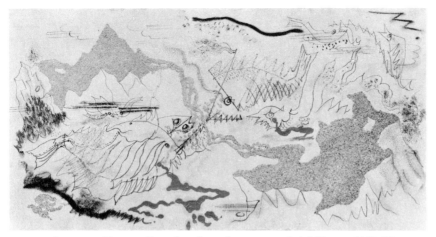

242   BATTLE OF FISHES, *oil, sand, and pencil on canvas, André Masson, 1927. (Courtesy Museum of Modern Art)*

Changing Songs, Different Tunes

Long before the development of photography, a young man, buckskin clad and armed with sheath knife and tomahawk, ventured into the American wilderness. His intention was to portray the forms which comprised the life of a continent; for he wished to accurately portray and preserve for posterity the creatures of forest, plain, and shore. He explored the land from Labrador to Florida and northwestward to the tributaries of the Missouri. Capturing the images of the snowy owl of the north, the scrub jay of the south, as well as prairie creatures, he painted approximately five hundred species of birds and over one hundred and fifty different animals. His accurate studies permitted man to examine the markings of the wild turkey as well as marvel at the daintiness of the *Towhee Bunting* (Figure 243). Once again one may see the Key West quail-dove and the passenger pigeon, now extinct, recalling life that once inhabited the land and sky. The painter's name, Audubon, has become synonymous with birds. Both as naturalist and artist he proved to be one of the great American figures of the past century. John James Audubon fulfilled his intentions completely in portraying his subjects with authenticity in detail, appearance, and habitat.

Currently, subject matter often appears while artists are actively engaged in painting, with the appearance of such forms bearing little resemblance to any counterparts in nature. Such a tendency is evident in the implied birds in Hans Hofmann's painting *Elegy* (Figure 244). The bird symbols emerged directly from an experimental process of painting rather than develop as a result of close observation and subsequent recording. They appear to have rapidly crystalized from a minimum of lines boldly superimposed over fused passages of paint. An instantaneous quality indicating agility in technique and organization seems apparent in the painting. The title provides insight into the artist's intentions; for a dictionary identifies the word "elegy" as a funeral song, a sad farewell, implying a sorrowful theme. The activity of painting, with resulting passages of color and form, subsequently told of the coming of the song. The muted bird symbols permit little examination, nor do they commit themselves to species. Rather they act to convey the theme, a pessimistic tune in comparison with the imaginable chirp of *Towhee Bunting*, yet representative of the melancholy which comprises an aspect of life. Hofmann's painting fulfills its purpose in advancing its theme of sorrow and chaos, possibly symbolizing the condition of man as he reaches for understanding in a world complicated with contradictions and in conflict with long-established standards.

Both Audubon and Hofmann ably achieved their desires, though their paintings exist for different ends. One possesses accurate imagery of specific species, the other but a general impression of birds to serve as a means of commenting on man in a world of turmoil.

In this age of photographic marvels, with competent cameras and a wide range of lenses, flash attachments, and miscellaneous aids, one may question the logic of painters following Audubon's trail. The camera now provides the most simple and effective means for securing factual visual statements, if so desired. Just as the passenger pigeon winged across the sky to disappear, it seemed an age fluttered away as new attitudes and methods brought forth great changes in painting.

243　　Towhee Bunting, *watercolor and pastel, John James Audubon, 1812. (Courtesy Smithsonian Institution, National Collection of Fine Arts)*

244　　Elegy, *oil and plaster on composition board, Hans Hofmann, 1950. (Courtesy Walker Art Center, Minneapolis, Minn.)*

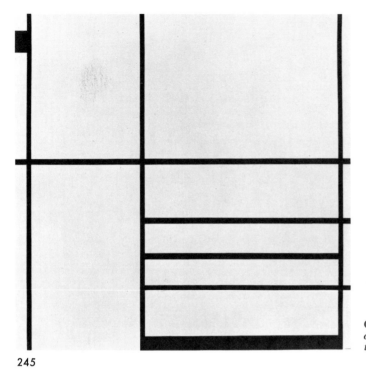

COMPOSITION IN WHITE, BLACK AND RED,
oil painting, Piet Mondrian, 1936. (Courtesy Museum of Modern Art)

Deliberate and Spontaneous Organization

In the early part of this century many artists undertook intense searches for new methods of organizing compositions. A Russian, following deep thought regarding the effects of color, value, and economy, composed *White on White*. Frenchmen intellectualized while reorganizing form. Italians attempted to organize dynamic movement through paint. Germans intuitively arranged themes intense with emotions, while certain Americans considered the virtues of simplification in rendering and arrangement. Two distinct manners of organizing paintings were now becoming apparent, one deliberate and the other spontaneous.

The paintings of Piet Mondrian such as his late creation *Composition in White, Black and Red* (Figure 245), which is also indicative of his earlier style, clearly indicate a deliberately controlled and highly intellectual approach toward organizing a work of art. Intense concentration and deliberation were essential to his process of dividing two-dimensional space with line.

Mondrian's desire was to create harmonious compositions possessing both serene and dynamic visual relationships. His work often echoed a much earlier Grecian concern with space divisions and ideal proportions to obtain dynamic symmetry. He organized many of his paintings by meticulously arranging and rearranging black tape upon the canvas surface until pleasing rectilinear relationships became apparent. The tape was then removed and lines were painted to correspond to the previously achieved layout. Though he conveyed sensations of control and simplicity, a considerable expenditure of intellect and time were essential to produce the deliberately contrived abstract patterns.

Hans Arp's *Automatic Drawing* (Figure 246) resulted from a method which was the opposite of Mondrian's approach. Its organization was dependent on chance or the circumstances of the moment and derived from spontaneous means. Random and haphazard qualities, rather than intellectual deliberation were brought to bear. Arp's effort was of a semicontrolled or automatic nature in sympathy with the automatic reflexes of man and denied any implications of thought, serenity, or predetermined form.

The works of both Mondrian and Arp have a considerable effect on current ventures in art. Mondrian's forms have greatly influenced concepts of design and imagery in architectural, industrial, and commercial design such as book jackets and poster layouts. Arp's manner of automatic drawing can be directly linked with present abstract expressionism and action painting and partially germinated views such as those advanced by Knud Merrild.

Regarding his attitude toward tradition and organizational procedures in art this contemporary artist says that,[4]

> Everything seems to depend on the whim or law of chance, accidental judgment by accidental authority and forced cause. And by chance and accident we live and die. To reflect this, I attempt a personal intuitive expression where 'laws' of aesthetic evalution becomes meaningless. Therefore I do not subscribe to any former concepts.

The existence of spontaneous and deliberate behavior, a great dualism of this age, plus the comprehensiveness of past art forms, suggests innumerable organizational methods. Such a situation enables artists to completely reject tradition or to accept the past and justify their achievements through relationships with previous styles. The physiological fact that heart and mind do not operate independently prohibits a rigid categorical division of art periods or particular artists on a strict intellectual or emotional basis. However, a consideration of the history of art indicates that specific movements and styles usually stressed organizational methods based on intellectual control or intuitive and emotional means.

Contemporary painters or sculptors favoring an intellectual or deliberate approach toward organization often lean toward close observation, traditional craftsmanship, and planned layout. They usually align themselves with the classical style, represented by Greek art of the Golden Age, beginning about 470 B.C., or its derivatives which continue into the present. The majority of western European and subsequent American art has been in harmony with this tradition, with paintings such as Raphaelle Peale's *After the Bath* (Figure 247) representing its early American roots.

Modern artists in sympathy with intuitive or spontaneous arrangement may also stand in kinship with art of the past. They tend to favor Oriental and primitive art, as well as the liberal effects achieved by past expressionists, contending such art is direct and intense and contains both evidence of personal involvement and emotional content. The American painter Albert P. Ryder, in a painting such as *Moonlight* (Figure 248), is typical of the nineteenth-century expressionist. His imaginative style emerged from self rather than being prescribed by the limits of traditional craftsmanship or derived from faithfulness to close observation.

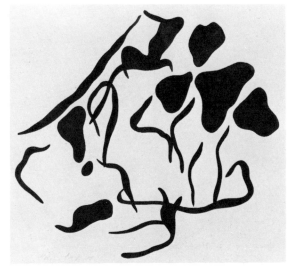

246   Automatic Drawing, *brush and ink on light brown paper, Hans Arp, 1916. (Courtesy Museum of Modern Art)*

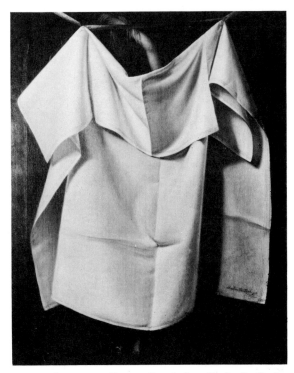

247   After the Bath, *oil painting, Raphaelle Peale, 1823. (Courtesy William Rockhill Nelson Gallery of Art, Kansas City)*

[4] *Contemporary American Painting* (Catalogue of University of Illinois Exhibition, 1952), p. 214.

248 MOONLIGHT, *oil painting, Albert P. Ryder, 1880–1890. (Courtesy Smithsonian Institution)*

249 PORTRAIT OF JESPER DIBBLE, *oil painting, John Wilde, 1956. (Courtesy the Artist)*

Present Styles in Organizing Painting

John Wilde, the creator of the *Portrait of Jesper Dibble* (Figure 249), is a traditionalist or classicist; for he would build on the past, interpreting the present in light of what has been proved valid. A consideration of his painting indicates an individual deeply interested in the richness of natural surfaces and forms. John Wilde contends that painting need not have scientific or rational limitations, but only those limitations, if any, found in the realm of poetry. This view, not unusual, could be considered traditional; for such an attitude was in evidence before the decline of the Greek civilization. "Painting is silent poetry; poetry, speaking painting" is attributed to the poet Simonides, 500 B.C.

"Need I state that I venerate the masters and nature and that I close my eyes to as many nature debasing contemporaries as possible," a recent statement by John Wilde affirms his relationship with the traditional intellectual approach in painting. His portrayal of moods and substances indicates highly competent craftsmanship, close observation, keen awareness, traditional organizational methods, and controlled emotion.

Many who are currently active within the arts would seriously question the importance of tradition, especially the understanding of past methods. Their contention would be that only by constant discoveries through experimentation can art exist, and man should not repeat what has been done. Their cultural heritage is of this century, often in kinship with current scientific, psychological, or philosophical thought. However, such efforts can also become traditional as styles crystalize and followers emerge.

Willem de Kooning possesses a point of view in opposition to John Wilde's attitude. During a symposium, at The Museum of Modern Art, de Kooning said that;

> Art never seems to make me peaceful or pure . . .
> Some painters, including myself . . . do not want
> to sit in style.

A comparison of *Woman VI* (Figure 250), a painting by Willem de Kooning, with John Wilde's *Portrait of Jesper Dibble* indicates a variation in approach which is evident within current painting. Willem de Kooning's spontaneous expression possesses an intense display of feeling stressing an emotional rather than an intellectual approach. Violent movement, rapid transitions of forms and colors, bold brush technique, and great abstraction of natural form marks *Woman VI* as a highly expressive interpretation. An uninhibited technique with a rapid application of paint caused the emergence of vibrating and merging colors, lines, and shapes which played a great part in the presentment of the subject matter.

While actively engaged, the contemporary painter often developes content as well as form through intuitive or spontaneous manipulations of paint; however, this is not always the case. Painters now freely move away from recognizable or figurative subject matter, return to it, or ignore it completely depending on their beliefs and desires. Directions in contemporary painting appear to be limited only by man's inability to conceive of additional means of presenting human experiences or handling materials and media. One must keep in mind that the breadth, logic, and uncertainties of an age are not specifically determined by the artist; rather they are portrayed.

"Speed, intuition, excitement: that is my method of creation," so says Georges Mathieu, the producer of *Painting* (Figure 251). Termed "action painting," its instantaneous application of paint emerged from an energetic and uncontrolled outburst of technique. Reminiscent of Arp's organizational methods through laws of chance and automatic drawing, action painting does not attempt to bring to the surface preconceived notions of form; instead, its intentions are to imply kinesthetic action and the spirit of painting as an end in itself. Such unchecked paintings contain a completely subjective approach toward organization beginning and terminating with self. The approach, completely automatic, is comprised of a series of unrelated responses without deliberation or conceived imagery. Action painting is somewhat akin to Persian or Far Eastern calligraphy as regards line quality or suggestive of the linear movement of electronic impulses. It is as natural as the uncontrolled crayon and paint movements of the very young child who exists in the presymbolic stage, and it contains somewhat the same beauties and limitations.

Two major and effective manners, each with a number of degrees, exist for organizing figurative painting. It is possible to start with specific subject matter and work away from a literal interpretation; it is also possible to move toward figurative painting without an original concept of a particular subject. Each process is concerned with a fusion of the intellect and the emotions and demands both thought and sensitive feeling. Both may also draw upon intuition

250   WOMAN VI, *oil painting, Willem de Kooning, 1955. (Courtesy Carnegie Institute)*

251   PAINTING, *oil painting, Georges Mathieu, 1957. (Courtesy Carnegie Institute)*

252 LANDSCAPE WITH ROCKS, *oil painting, George Pappas, 1959. (Courtesy the Artist)*

sensitized through previous experiences of organizing paintings in automatic or completely controlled manners.

Landscape with Rocks (Figure 252), by George Pappas, is indicative of a current emphasis in painting of a spontaneous and experimental style with movement toward subject matter. The painting provides an impression which reveals a quality of landscape rather than a particular scene. Beginning without preconceived imagery, Pappas intuitively created interesting passages of color, lines, shapes, and textures which grew toward fulfilling a visual impression. As interesting color relationships and form appeared, a suggestion of meaning became evident and content began to crystalize to produce a realization of theme. The approach is related in method to the musical composer who first experiments with sounds secured from an instrument and then begins to compose. The original sounds suggest aspects relatable to a subject and, instead of any preconceived notions of specific imagery held by the composer, provide mood and theme ideas.

Speaking of both his manner of working and his painting *Landscape with Rocks*, George Pappas says,

At this particular period in the development of my work, ideas evolve through countless visual and emotional experiences with nature. Although I prefer the spring and summer seasons on the New England seashore, there is no direct relationship in my work to specific locales or situations.

The act of beginning the painting is always swift, direct, and at times almost uncontrolled. From within this strong initial statement the painting is "discovered" and developed. It is during this period of discovery that a vague and mystic relationship with nature is established. The work begins as paint and arrives at nature in its broadest sense.

Observe the painting closely and sense the mood portrayed. Notice how the bold brush technique created strong value and textural passages consistent with a rocky environmental theme. Can you imaginatively sense the appearance of great vertical strata of rocks with intermingling bands of organic matter? Your visualization may not be constant or specific, and, like nature, it may be prone to great change. As the sun moves across the heavens, fluctuating highlights and shadows are cast upon the earth. During the hours of dawn and dusk appearances are markedly modified; moods vary as patterns appear as well as dissipate. Great visual differences register with the changing seasons; for the movements, both predictable and unpredictable, of nature, like art and man, are never static.

Many artists, employing a traditional approach, begin their paintings with a particular subject definitely in mind and engage in considerable planning before creating a final form. Bringing sensitivity to bear, they move away from a factual recording by structuring their painting in their most inventive

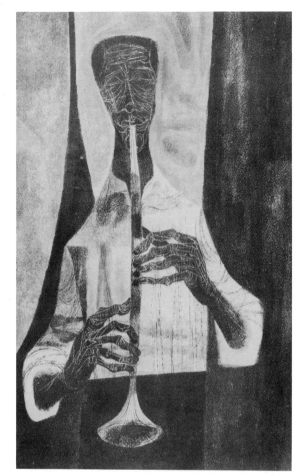

253   PRACTICE, *mixed media, ink, crayon and watercolor, Donald M. Anderson, 1954. (Courtesy the Artist)*

manner. Such a procedure was used by Donald M. Anderson in organizing his painting *Practice* (Figure 253). An interest in music and admiration for musicians frequently determine his choice of subject matter. Modifying such a preconceived theme through keen deliberation, he arranged his composition in a fully controlled and deliberate state. A consideration of his thoughts regarding the organization of *Practice* provides insight in his plan for gaining interest through uniting basic shapes, arranging dark and light contrasts, and using line in certain areas for emphasis. Of his painting *Practice*, Anderson states:

This picture evolved from a series of drawings of clarinet players. The picture was planned to have several very large areas to serve as a foil for some shapes of intermediate size. These smaller areas contain the areas of more intense decoration, face and fingers, which prove to be the most animated parts of such a performer. The element of coincidence can be seen at the performer's left shoulder where the shape in back of the head runs into the shape forming the left arm. This device can be used to obtain an interplay between shapes which are in foreground and background. Obvious repetition occurs in the dark shape to the left, the bell of the horn, nose and the right shoulder where it is inverted. In general, by using strong light and dark contrasts and simple shapes I tried to give the picture a feeling of dignity.

Art: A Natural Manner

The existence of many styles and manners of working within art should encourage students; for such a situation provides great freedom in personal interpretation and expression. A natural manner in harmony with personality and desire is fully justified; therefore, each individual must bear the responsibility of developing a personal style which most effectively expresses intentions. Only in this manner may the realization of oneself result and a proper balance of intelligence and feeling be evident within the art produced. Long ago Eugène Delacroix,[5] the nineteenth-century French artist, advanced excellent advice which is still pertinent and not necessarily limited to drawing when he said,

> One should draw according to one's own temperment—inspiration is preferable to everything else—

In addition to inspiration, other factors can assist in formulating and increasing art ability. Certainly, active participation in producng art, intense experiences in the observation of nature and society, an experimental attitude, and inquisitiveness regarding art of the past and present should prove rewarding. One should attempt to increase knowledge through keen observation and a sensitivity toward all experiences in order to gain insight into the nature of things. Such knowledge develops awareness, often appreciation, and results in more comprehensive feelings. An experimental attitude, a willingness to try, is also essential to both mature artist and student for experimentation with media, and materials of art provides an understanding of their characteristics and potentials. Also, viewing and reading about art develops an awareness of new possibilities for creative adventures. Thus extensive experiences in art production, as well as studying, increases creative ability, develops confidence, and enriches the imagination; for an individual can imagine only in relation to possessed experiences.

Had not man possessed an inquisitive experimental attitude and the ability to imagine, he would have remained at the entrance of a cave fearful of the stars.

[5] Linonello Venturi, *Modern Painters* (New York: Charles Scribner's Sons, 1947), p. 103.

TOPICS FOR CONSIDERATION

1. How has science changed our notion of reality and what effects has this had on painting?
2. How does the painter's experimental process both differ and relate to investigations conducted by the scientist?
3. Can subjects grow directly from the manipulation of paint? Explain.
4. Are subjects and themes limited in painting?
5. Explain how the artist reveals his reaction toward nature and social environment rather than imitating or copying either of the experiences.
6. What are the obvious differences between nineteenth-century and modern painting? Consider economy, directness, inventiveness, and general approach toward developing imagery.
7. What are the common relationships and differences between figurative and non-objective painting?

SUGGESTED ACTIVITIES

1. Select from Chapter 6 three reproductions of paintings, which you favor. Analyze them closely and determine the specific features which influenced your choices. Discuss these qualities with your friends.
2. Produce a tempera painting entitled "The Forces of Nature — Winds and Water." Employ large brushes, and paint on a large sheet of colored construction paper.
3. Select several small organic items, such as seed pods, weeds, leaves, pebbles, and a bit of bark, and work up a few rapid, preliminary sketches. Stress two-dimensional pattern and both strong and subtle contrasts. Select your favorite sketch and have it serve as the basis for a large mixed-media painting. You may combine watercolor paint, chalk, crayon, ink, and even scraps of torn paper. Upon completion, exhibit your work in conjunction with the paintings of a similar theme executed by others. Notice the wide range of solutions and various effective discoveries.
4. Paint a landscape derived from the imagination or from life using watercolor and ink.
5. Develop a nonobjective composition with the assistance of scissors, paste, and construction paper.

APPROPRIATE REFERENCES AND READINGS

BARR, ALFRED H., JR. *What Is Modern Painting*, New York: The Museum of Modern Art, 1956.

BAUR, JOHN I. H. *Nature in Abstraction*, New York: Whitney Museum of American Art, 1958.

Dictionary of Modern Painting, edited by C. Lake and R. Maillard, New York: Tudor Publishing Co., 1956.

ELIOT, ALEXANDER. *Three Hundred Years of American Painting*, New York: Time, Inc., 1957.

RATHBUN, M. C., and HAYES, B. H., JR. *Layman's Guide to Modern Art, Painting for a Scientific Age*, New York: Oxford University Press, 1949.

RODMAN, SELDEN. *Conversations with Artists*, New York: The Devin-Adair Co., 1957.

SEUPHOR, MICHEL. *Dictionary of Abstract Painting*, New York: Tudor Publishing Co., 1957.

7 PAINTING—THE ADDITION OF COLOR

More and more the artist of the future will be driven into the recesses of his own subjectivity, there to find, not a country nor a class, but the unknown self. The American artist might well be the pioneer in this new frontier of consciousness.

SIR HERBERT READ[1]
British Art Critic and Philosopher

The Passing Parade: Different Banners from Neoclassicism to Abstract Expressionism

Painting as an art form offers a greater creative range than other areas of the visual arts offer. It does not have the technical limitations of many printing processes, nor does it suffer from the form limitations of various crafts. The inclusion of color extends creative opportunities in painting beyond drawing. Because it is free of the engineering restrictions associated with architecture and less costly in money and time than either architecture or sculpture, painting enjoys distinct advantages over those arts. Innumerable painters are also free of any restrictions imposed by the demands of donors or building committees. In summing these distinctions, the total is a set of conditions highly conducive to intense and experimental manipulation. Contemporary painters have taken full advantage of this factor of free inquiry to research distant frontiers in pursuing visual potentials. To the casual onlooker, it may now seem that opportunities appear to be exhausted. Though additional movements and new styles are difficult to conceive, come they will; for progress, in any of man's activities, is not a prerogative of the past. Extensive modifications and often abrupt changes similar to those marking painting within the last and present century will most certainly penetrate into the future. Exciting new methods, forms, and meanings are yet to unfold.

A rapid consideration of the major painting movements of the recent past indicates that worthy attributes are not limited to any specific manner, nor are they exclusive to a particular style. Visualize a number of paintings hanging in a gallery. If each represented a particular movement popular during the past one hundred and sixty years, every painting would bear distinctive imagery. Each would differ from its neighbor. Extensive treatments and varied solutions would be obvious. Some would be highly decorative, bright in color, bold in form; others would be serene, indicating close observation and calculated technique. All, however, would warrant close examination; for their sum total would convey many of the historical currents and moods of painting. Manners would be Expressionistic or Cubistic, Impressionistic or Surrealistic. Look, hung on that distant wall are indeed fascinating paintings. One portrays a lonely figure adjacent to a huge sea; another merely consists of a geometric pattern. A third contains representations of armored members of an ancient Roman legion. The main figure, a proud centurion, appears to be addressing several of his foot soldiers. A close scrutiny yields a faint French signature followed by a date: 1805.

[1] Herbert Read, *The Philosophy of Modern Art* (New York: Meridian Books, Inc., 1955), p. 288.

THE NEOCLASSIC MOVEMENT —
HOMER TRANSPLANTED

For somewhat the same reasons as in architecture and sculpture, classical forms and themes were introduced into painting at the beginning of the nineteenth century. Influential thought dictated the need for the rejuvenation of ancient Greco-Roman visual and literary forms. Through such means, greatness could reign once again and serve to motivate the populace toward noble heights beneficial to the welfare of the state. Episodes relating to ancient Athens, Rome, and Troy were therefore introduced into the period of Napoleon. At the time of Austerlitz, Cadiz, and Waterloo, during the adolescent puffs of the Steam Age — actually, the dawn of our modern era — Jupiter and Thetis, Paris and Helen, and Venus were reborn in the painter's studio. Mount Olympus was scaled in the imagination and even Socrates died, once again, on French canvas.

Originally emerging in France, the Neoclassic attitude stressed traditional values in painting. Proficiency and precise technical skill were held to be of prime importance. Idealized themes, strongly based on drawings and containing intellectual rather than passionate implications, served as the foundation for painting. Lines were singular and positive, color was usually flat, and composition was static. Imagery was sentimentalized, somewhat factual, and less frivolous than treatments evident in the earlier baroque or rococo manners.

With few exceptions, the Neoclassic movement in painting represented the official doctrine of the art academies of the past century. Its influence reached throughout the Western World and permeated innumerable schools. Only one other style, Romanticism, offered a major challenge. Several of the more prominent Neoclassic painters were the Frenchmen, Jacques Louis David, Jean Auguste Dominique Ingres, and Adolphe William Bouguerau; the English painter, Frederick, Lord Leighton; and the American, Maxfield Parrish. Their slick and skillful paintings served as moral edification in communicating the glorious episodes of long ago. Their aim was to visually bridge their present with a selected past. Supposedly, the ideal existed in classical antiquity, though the life span of the average Athenian during the Golden Age was but eighteen years.

THE ROMANTIC REBELLION —
ONE STEP FORWARD

Painting characteristics that were unlike Neoclassic tendencies — in being less restrained in subject selection and treatment of color and form — made their appearance in France during the second decade of the past century. The followers of this freer, more lyrical manner were classified as Romantics. The impact of Jean Jacques Rousseau, the increasing belief in the validity of original thought, and the cry of "liberty, equality, and fraternity" issuing from the French Revolution, plus expanding historical and geographical explorations of nonclassical areas, were dominant features in the development of Romantic painting. The painter was now conceived to be not a guardian or interpreter of the past, but rather a commentator of the present. Contemporary costume, rather than ancient drapery, clothed painted figures now placed in exotic, mysterious, and conventional locales. The movement stressed inquiry into the actions of man and the forces of nature without the bindings of prescribed themes or predetermined technique.

Romantic beliefs and practices were rapidly assimilated in Germany; for, in many respects, the qualities of Romanticism are highly Germanic. The movement also spread to England and America, and in the latter portion of the last century it was highly popular throughout northern Europe and the United States. *Lion Devouring Hare, Mad House, Race at Epsom, Two Men Viewing the Moon,* and numerous related subjects now made their appearance. Practitioners included the painters Théodore Géricault and Eugène Delacroix in France; the Germans, Casper David Friedrich and Arnold Bocklin; and the Americans, Thomas Cole, George Inness, and Albert Ryder.

NATURALISM AND REALISM —
PHOTOGRAPHIC REPRESENTATION
AND BEYOND

In addition to Neoclassicism and Romanticism, two other painting movements were in evidence midway through the nineteenth century. However, unlike the former movements, neither of the latter styles, Naturalism and Realism, attracted numerous followers. Rather, both consisted of independent painters who shared common qualities in rendering imagery.

Clear differentiation between Naturalism and Realism can at times be difficult to ascertain; for many artists have fluctuated between the two manners of painting. Therefore, various artists — Gustave Courbet, for one — have been classified in either or both categories. However, though overlaps occur, an examination of Naturalism and Realism illustrates two distinct styles.

The development of the first practical method of photography by the Frenchman, Louis Jacques Mandé Daguerre, in 1839, and its immediate popularity played an influential role in shaping nineteenth-century Naturalistic painting. Daguerre's findings made possible the rapid capture and retention of exact shape, detail, and texture notations through the action of light, chemical substances, and subsequent processing. With the advent of the camera it can be assumed that many painters cursed while others rejoiced. The new photographic process was in harmony with the painters who followed the creed of Naturalism; for they also pursued factual and literal effects. Beyond evidence of patience and skill, their results denied any participation of the painter in the painting activity. Personality and temperament were ignored. The artist functioned as a neutral recorder of objects observed. Transcriptions were indicative of photographic duplication. Thus materialistic and impersonal rather than spiritual or imaginative qualities were presented through smooth paint application, factual color, and exactitude in suggesting shape and textural details. However, while no emotional reaction is evident on the part of the painter (beyond subject selection) and skill replaces inventiveness, Naturalistic paintings frequently prove highly intriguing owing to the painter's display of technical versatility. The painting *Stone-Breakers*, produced in 1849 by Courbet, is indicative of the magnificent technique and abundant and precise detailing contained within a Naturalistic painting. Portraying a youth and a man tediously laboring, the painting speaks of an explicit and particular occurrence in a direct and fluent manner. Referring to this painting, in a letter to a friend, Courbet writes, "All this takes place in broad daylight, beside the embankment of a roadway. The men stand out against the green slope of a great mountain which fills the canvas and over which cloud shadows pass; only in the right-hand corner does the slope of the mountain allow a little blue sky to be seen. I invented nothing, dear friend; every day, going out for a drive, I saw these men."[2]

Another French Naturalist, Ernest Meissonier,

proved one of the most successful artists, as measured by financial rewards, of any period in the history of art. Specializing in battle themes composed of a multitude of minute details, Meissonier sold his paintings for sums up to $10,000 per square inch of treated canvas. Unfortunately, his paintings, especially when judged by present standards, were somewhat small. The early works of Edgar Degas, Édouard Manet, and Auguste Renoir were also Naturalistic in treatment.

One of the obvious differences between Naturalism and Realism is that the latter imaginatively distorts for emotional emphasis. Poetic license, therefore, marks Realistic interpretations; for creative manipulation accents essentials. Realism, in permitting evidences of personal involvement and exaggeration, correlates both the actual and hidden through fusing what is seen and what is felt into unified imagery. It exposes the essence of matter and experience. Therefore, the term "Realism" warrants usage in identifying any expression which probes beyond the obvious and is not theatrically inclined. Treatments may be harsh and brutal or highly poetic in the application of paint and the use of color, shape, and texture in determining form.

One of the great Realists of all time, Honoré Daumier, was active in France during the middle of the past century. His social consciousness and passionate nature were evident in numerous drawings, lithographs, and paintings. Universality and timeliness are revealed within his works; for even his political cartoons are appropriate for striking at problems which currently beseech our society. The commentaries of this prolific Realist ranged from humorous, yet caustic, interpretations to sympathetic and serene presentments. At times, all four qualities were blended within one powerful display. Paintings such as Daumier's *The Third-Class Carriage*, produced in 1865, and *Washerwoman with Child* relate the common lives and common episodes of a nation in uncommon terms. A personal and monumental style, with dramatic clashes of dark and light and earthy colors, enables this Realist's comments to continue to stir the hearts of generations beyond his time.

Realism is a more comprehensive term than "Naturalism"; for in providing a more extensive scope to creative activities, it encourages and encompasses more diverse solutions. In addition to

[2] Lionello Venturi, *Modern Painters* (New York: Charles Scribner's Sons, 1947), p. 210.

Daumier, Jean François Millet was a French Realist during the mid-century. The earlier Spaniard, Francisco Goya, the Dutchman, Rembrandt van Rijn, and a host of other artists, past and present, can also be classified as Realists. Certain features in Expressionism, Cubism, and contemporary Abstractionism may also be linked with aspects of Realism; for movements in tune with current scientific and aesthetic knowledge comprise the beliefs and determine in part the realities of any era. Therefore, Realism is an apt description in reference to various paintings, regardless of time of production. Certain paintings, some ages old and others modern as tomorrow, can be conceived as being within the movement; for the movement appears to involve the painter's continuing divergent quest to discover the most effective means of visually conveying a reaction to an ever-changing environment.

It should not be supposed that Naturalistic as well as Realistic tendencies are limited to painting or restricted to any particular period of time. For instance, much Hellenistic and Roman sculptures were Naturalistic in treatment. Such statuary involved the specific in emphasizing a magnitude of exact and trifling details. Muscular structure, facial peculiarities, and costume delineations were treated to convey a singular and particular human form. These carvings remained bound in space and time to one moment in history, resulting in a static rather than a universal quality. Earlier Hellenic and Athenian sculpture of the Golden Age differed from the later Hellenistic and Roman works. Sculptors of the Hellenic and Golden Age tended to denote the human form with restraint. By the suggestion of only those qualities essential to convey an impression, idealized or universal form was attained. Simplicity in detailing permitted a more comprehensive implication; for in denying explicit or singular identification, a more extensive interpretation came into being. Such works could move beyond their time to represent the ideal of generations to come. Their appropriateness was thus extended and their timelessness assured.

IMPRESSIONISM — SUNLIGHT AND PAINT

Under the influence of Naturalism, which encouraged close observation and thought, painters in the 1870s became intrigued with the effects of brilliant sunlight striking the fields, orchards, and woodlots of France. To suggest this natural phenomenon, Claude Monet, Camille Pissarro, Alfred Sisley, and others devised a distinctive manner of painting.

They composed painted surfaces from numerous tiny patches of bright colors rapidly deposited by short brush strokes. Their paintings achieved mosaic-like qualities as regards shape and color distribution. When viewed from a distance, a fusion of these differing color passages occurred, resulting in a shimmering color field. Owing to the eye's inability to perceive each tiny area of contrasting color, optical sensations activated physical responses which automatically suggested color mixture and provided vibrant and lush painted surfaces.

By expounding theories and formulas in opposition to attitudes held by Neoclassic or Romantic painters, the Impressionists contributed a new and exciting chapter which furthered possibilities in painting. Capturing a splendid moment in time, suggestive of bright sunlight caressing a rich earth's surface, they provided colorful vitality to the art of painting. Seeking only momentary occurrences, they froze seconds of time for eternity within paintings which still speak of sparkling landscapes.

THE POST-IMPRESSIONISTS — EARLY BUT MODERN PIONEERS

The classification Post-Impressionist is applied to Paul Cézanne, Paul Gauguin, Georges Seurat, Henri de Toulouse-Lautrec and Vincent van Gogh. Active in the latter portion of the last century, each evolved a unique and influential style within the modern development of painting. In part growing out of, yet going beyond, the mandates of Impressionism, these artists brought forth profound changes in notions of artistic reality and the nature of painting. Their placement of importance on personal inventiveness in handling color and form enabled keen eyes, at the start of this century, to view the diverse but firm foundations upon which a great portion of modern art has been built. Cézanne's stress on solidity, structure, form, and a sensitive rearrangement of pictorial elements, and Seurat's pursuit of pointillism and systematic design provided strong analytical influences to twentieth-century painting. As one example, a major movement within modern art, Cubism, with its new visual language of decorative and contrived form, owed much to the findings of Cézanne. In great part, the Expressionistic movements of the present century also find champions in members of the Post-Impression group. Gauguin, Toulouse-Lautrec, and, especially, van Gogh had profound impact on later individuals who also saw through their hearts and distorted accordingly.

EXPRESSIONISM AND CUBISM —
EMOTIONS AND INTELLECT

Expressionism is highly subjective. It demands the inclusion of evidence of the emotional participation and reaction of the artist within his painting. Form is personally distorted, and in most instances the color is possessive of symbolic associations. Paintings are executed as rapid, bold, and simplified statements. Strong evidences of the action of painting are often apparent through visible indications of brush application and thick passages of paint. Both French and German painters were the originators of the Expressionistic movement at the beginning of this century. While their painting techniques were similar, the German's attitude toward subject matter generally differed from his southern neighbor's, with the possible exception of Georges Rouault. Violent and tragic implications, derived from brutal or melancholy themes, were usually in kinship with German Expressionism. The French were more neutral regarding subject matter, but possibly more involved with the problems and actions of painting as an end in itself.

Several Expressionists were the Germans, Ernst Barlach, Käthe Kollwitz, and Karl Schmidt-Rottluff; the Norwegian, Edvard Munch; and the French painters, Raoul Dufy, Henri Matisse, Georges Rouault, and Maurice de Vlaminck.

Cubism, in addition to Expressionism, was a major and influential painting movement during the first decades of this century. Unlike Expressionism, Cubism, owing to its rational, formal, and constructive manner of composing imagery, contained profound intellectual rather than emotional characteristics. The movement involved the disintegration of matter and its creative reorganization into colorful, highly textured, and decorative compositions. A multiplicity of viewpoints, shallow depth recession, rich color contrasts, exaggerated and often applied foreign substances for textural effects, and emphasis on the transparency of material marked Cubist paintings. The Frenchman, Georges Braque, and the Spaniards, Juan Gris and Pablo Picasso, were major exponents of this movement. Of these three artists, Braque has proved to be the most consistent Cubist; for Gris died at rather an early age and Picasso devised further styles and manners beyond the range of Cubism. In a broad sense, Cubism is classical in concept, while Expressionism is closer to Romanticism.

FUTURISM: THE ACTION OF AN AGE

In 1909, several Italian artists banded together to inaugurate the Futuristic movement in literature and painting. Contending that speed, excitement, and movement were major components of their mechanized age, these artists undertook to vitalize painting through compositions based on dynamic arrangements of active themes. *Dynamism of an Auto, Train at Full Speed, The Life of the Street Enters the House,* and *Unique Forms of Continuity in Space* now became typical themes for their paintings. Twentieth-century technology—in particular, aspects of the machine age — and, to a lesser degree, the findings of the Cubists active in Paris influenced the paintings of the Futurists. The works of the Italians, Gracomo Balla, Luigi Russolo, Carlo Carra, and the Frenchman, Marcel Duchamp, are indicative of this early modern movement.

MOVEMENTS IN ABSTRACTION:
NONOBJECTIVE ART

During the second and third decades of the twentieth century, both Russian and Dutch artists were deeply involved in devising abstract art. The development of new subject fields exposing unusual shape and space relationships were their major concern. Russian sculptors, Naum Gabo for one, created fully abstract three-dimensional constructions while other Russian artists, such as Wassily Kandinsky, painted imagery unique to this century. While Kandinsky's works implied active tempos, the Dutchman, Piet Mondrian, painted severe and serene geometric arrangements. It soon became apparent, through the efforts of the Abstractionists, that artists were now completely free to devise and improvise from the depths of their imagination and the recesses of their inventive powers. Subjects and themes now no longer needed to be limited to nature or man and his activities. The nonobjective movement removed such frames of reference. Many barriers were no more.

DADA AND SURREALISM —
CHAOS AND DREAMS

Midway through World War I, a small group of writers and painters assembled in Zurich, Switzerland, and organized Dadaism. Somewhat as the Romantics had protested against neoclassic edicts one hundred years before, the members of the Dada movement now preached complete rebellion. Violently opposed to any and all existing canons of beauty or the employment of logic in aestetic undertakings, Dadaism advocated automatic and unrelated organization. The members, Hans Arp, André Breton, Max Ernst, Kurt Schwitters, Tristan Tzara, and others, were dedicated to a simple, yet profound, proposition: the use of the intellect, when engaged in creative activities, arouses sterile ideas. The Dadaists pursued deliberate chaos and contrived disorder as organizational methods. Thus, all barriers were removed, enabling complete freedom and possibly anarchy to reign within a segment of the arts. Touches of humor and gleeful nonsensical inventions now became fashionable in certain circles. Only a single century now separated the execution of paintings bearing the titles of *Birth of Venus* and *Reading from Homer* from those which spoke of *Infant Carburetor* and *The Little Tear Gland That Says Tic Tac*. The prime importance of Dadaism remained for the future; for in advancing automatic and intuitive expression it served as a rib in the growth of contemporary Abstract Expressionism.

Surrealism emerged in the mid-twenties, partly because of the findings of Freudian psychology. This painting movement implied the existence of a super-reality derived from the subconscious. Advocating a universal visual language, the Surrealistic practitioner believed that all peoples perceived particular symbols which represented specific things. Frequently occurring in dream sequences, these symbols conveyed identical meanings to all, regardless of race or creed. Therefore, the duty of the painter was to communicate through such visual symbols. To bring to the awareness of the spectator previously buried but now recognizable imagery was his final goal. To strike through a new level of consciousness was his means.

Paintings developed in the Surrealistic manner are often classical in execution in that they possess precise delineation of form and slick paint application. While arrangement in these paintings is supposedly spontaneous, emerging from pure intuition, technique remains highly disciplined. For instance, traditional manners of glazing and underpainting are often incorporated into Surrealistic painting. Unlike the Dadaist, the Surrealist usually employed great care to present imagery in a well-established and positive style of rendering to assure direct communication. Space was presented as infinite, never ending. In many Surrealistic works, weird foilage and strange creatures inhabit moody dreamlike landscapes with frequently terrifying implications.

Eugene Berman, Salvador Dali, Kurt Seligmann, Yves Tanguy, and Pavel Tchelitchew are several followers of Surrealism. Their paintings bear titles ranging from *Heredity of Acquired Characteristics* to *The Persistence of Memory*. While such works appear highly imaginative, the Surrealist would resent the implication of imagination. He would surely contend his sources exist beyond the obvious, somewhere deep in the subconscious. In attempting to activate this submerged consciousness, the Surrealist assumes that all individuals share similar reactions toward certain pictorial elements indicative of dream imagery. Possibly one is confronted with several questions. Do individuals have feelings and visions which they don't fully comprehend? If so, can the painter bring these to a level of awareness through visual representations? Many believe he can.

REGIONALISM — THE PRECIOUS PROVINCES

During the 1930s, in America, there arose a reaction on the part of many artists against foreign art influences. While Americans such as Arthur Dove and Georgia O'Keeffe were followers of the modern manner, other voices rose against the new styles. Citing their path as one of sanity and tradition, painters such as Thomas Hart Benton, John Curry, and Grant Wood recorded the American scene in conventional pictorial terms. Views of Kansas and Iowa, labor in the fields, tornados, and even folk tales such as *The Jealous Lover of Lone Green Valley* issued from their easels. Literal and at times lyrical forms were captured on canvas as the painters gazed at broad level expanses or viewed hamlets nestled in hills or valleys. Neither invention nor uniqueness was their cry; rather, it was the fluent visual presentment of a land and the folks they knew. Sharing a philosophy somewhat like the earlier Hudson River School, the regionalists' influence permeated the mid-continent. Their impact was especially pronounced in the Midwest; for the majority of the regionalists called the Plains their home. Ignoring the findings of the Cubists, Abstractionists, Surrealists, they brought forth imagery blended with touches of photographic illusionism and Romantic sentiment.

With the advent of World War II, America was to realize the absurdity of closing its eyes to what was happening in all other portions of the world. Advances in science, as well as art, in the world community made such an attitude impractical. Alas, shrinking distances and expanding communications soon involved commitments beyond one's home, thereby refuting an age of isolation.

ABSTRACT EXPRESSIONISM:
INTUITIVE ACTION

Following World War II, many painting styles and divergent attitudes patterned the American scene. Various painters were intrigued with expressionism; others held to classical tendencies. Some engaged in Cubistic ventures or dealt with Surrealistic imagery; abstractions were also coming to the fore. Within this hodgepodge of conflicting styles, stress and strain were obvious. Academic Illusionism, Contemporary Romanticism, Realism, Surrealistic Formalism, Abstract Expressionism, and many more terms were now employed to classify painting movements. Sunday painters and students, calandar artists and beatniks, as well as dedicated professionals, advanced definite views that were frequently derived from self-prescribed merits. One fact, not unique to this age, appeared obvious. The great majority of painters, professional as well as amateur, leaned toward a particular style after it was conceived and well developed by a few inquisitive originators. Many also fluctuated from one style to another. Such a situation is natural, however, for geniuses are few, no matter what the profession.

While many artists still took their cue from classicists of the past century — the less-adventurous Romantics, even the regionalists, innumerable others were less conventional. Many of the latter are now Abstract Expressionists. Initially centering in New York City in the late 1940s, Abstract Expressionism has now spread throughout the land, even beyond our shores. At times the movement has been termed Action Painting. Opponents, considering the style incoherent, have even sneeringly referred to it as the Smear Abstractionists School. Naturally, its champions disagree with such pronouncements. Those actively engaged in the movement view it as a vital style which resolves many of the shortcomings of preceding manners of painting.

Neither traditional craftsmanship nor conventional visions are their goals; for Abstract Expressionists conceive of painting as intuitive activity demanding automatic responses. Therefore, painters within the movement function not as spectator recorders, but rather as participants embodied in the act of painting. Initial applications of paint, resulting in mass and color notations, demand the placement of adjacent relationships which are to be immediately devised and presented. Direction and subsequent applications, therefore, automatically emerge through sensitive responses relating to visual rhythms established moments before. Following intuitively upon such sequences, painters actually build upon impulses. Reactions are sensitized and keenness is expanded through a number of painting experiences; therefore, in time, responses are conditioned. However, answers remain embodied within the painter's being, to be released only when he is intensely involved in applying paint.

Though Abstract Expressionism was derived in great part through the ingenuity and determination of early practitioners, as all other art movements are, it has traditional roots. More Romantic than classical, the movement is in kinship with Expressionism in its rejection of established aesthetic norms, its use of color for mood or symbolic purposes, and its dynamic and generous paint application. Abstract Expressionism is also linked with earlier abstract movements owing to its rejection of traditional figurative imagery. Dadaism, with its emphasis on automatic response, and Surrealism, with its stress on intuitive organization, can also be considered as influential on the formation of this modern Expressionistic movement.

The painters Arshile Gorky, Hans Hofmann, Franz Kline, Willem de Kooning, Robert Motherwell, and Jackson Pollock, among others, contributed toward establishing styles within the field of Abstract Expressionism. Bold in appearance and indicative of rapid execution, their work expresses the artist's never-ending quest for absolute inventiveness. Rather than record phenomena outside their borders, many of their paintings exist as ends in themselves, for brushwork can convey its own meaning. Ignoring historical linear perspective with its implied third dimension, these expressionists suggest deep recessions through mass and color. Structure usually appears as a violent staccato composed of intense thrusts and counterthrusts, though in certain creations tranquillity seems to reign.

Several Directions in Contemporary Painting

Currently divergent and often unharmonious attitudes exist regarding the styles and directions that modern painting should assume. At times it appears that each artist, as well as influential layman, advances definite and conflicting viewpoints. Such a tendency is only natural in an age which advocates personal search and self-discovery and further holds to the democratic principle of original pursuit. Therefore, to attempt to resolve painting into an approved style or categorize in specific and inclusive manners would involve dangers and difficulties. However, general tendencies do exist. In addition, means of evaluation also exist; for there can be excellent or poor paintings in any style based on judgments consistent with the limits and intentions of the particular movements. To recognize these fluid and broad movements, based as they are on varying performances by members, transmits an understanding of modern

254   Young America, *oil painting, Andrew Wyeth, 1950. (Courtesy Pennsylvania Academy of the Fine Arts)*

painting. Several questions should be kept in mind. How do certain painters react when confronting blank canvas, tautly stretched? Why, after grasping brush, do some gently squeeze oil paint from tubes while others squirt profusely? Possibly even the color selection and general order of their palettes could provide an insight into future form. What are their intentions?

CAPTURING WHAT SEEMS TO BE — REALISTIC REPRESENTATION

As applied to painting, the explicit meaning of the elusive term "Realism" is highly dependent on one's particular experiences and personal judgment. Academic illusionism, primitive ventures, Abstract Expressionism, and many other terms may be compounded into a broad movement involved with current Realism. Certainly, the intentions of painters such as Andrew Wyeth are to portray ideas and environment as viewed with a keen eye and recorded with a deft hand. Extreme technical proficiency and

traditional aesthetic values are evident in Wyeth's *Young America* (Figure 254). Physical properties from flesh to handle bars, a G.I. jacket reminiscent of journeys now accomplished, and even shoe eyelets and a waving fox tail are rendered with care and exactitude. Owing to the lack of surrounding landscape details, distractions are averted, permitting attention to be focused on bicycle and rider surveying his world. The diverted gaze of the cyclist demands that the viewer ponder. What lies beyond the scanned horizon is dependent on the onlooker. Is it frustration or promise?

Some consider Andrew Wyeth to be one of the last of the classicists; others view him as a Naturalist or Realist. One factor, however, is certain: he is a representative of the few who remain with objective reality, as perceived by the eye, and masterfully illustrate its natural qualities. Commercially highly successful, he appears as a champion of popular taste. Such recordings of pictorial reality may be highly polished or, at the other end of the spectrum, somewhat naïve.

255   END OF WAR, STARTING HOME, 1918, *oil painting, Horace Pippin, 1931. (Courtesy Philadelphia Museum of Art)*

Displaying high degrees of intensity and vigor, the modern primitive or unschooled artist also seeks reality. Works by Grandma Moses or Horace Pippin are indicative of such a quest. Horace Pippin's *End of War, Starting Home, 1918* (Figure 255) displays a total involvement with the theme. Though technically raw, the painting forcefully and directly communicates sincerity and deep emotional involvement on the part of the painter. Refusing to confine his experience to only the canvas surface, Pippin forces his message to overflow into the frame itself. Upon the wooden border, fragments of battle — grenades, helmets, bombs, tanks, guns, and even knives — appear to have been randomly deposited by the tides of war. These objects, treated in relief, surround a vigorously suggested field of battle. As flaming planes and bursting shells clutter the sky, doughboys move forward into and beyond the barbed wire. Opponents fall or raise their arms in defeat. The Hun is done, the frontiers of Germany are pierced. What does the dramatic painting signify? Possibly many things to its creator: the conclusion of trench warfare; the end of a mixture of mud and boredom, violence, and death. Probably also the grand moment when the warrior-artist realized the means of returning home —home to Philadelphia, Penn's city of brotherly love, far from the fury of Flanders.

Pippin's painting is certainly involved with reality; for his intentions were undoubtedly to present a vivid visual account derived from actual occurrences. He focused his entire ability on attaining that end. Paint was merely the means to inform and relate; yet its handling called upon the entire resources of the painter. Many contemporary artists now employ less deliberation than Wyeth and Pippin employ when presenting their notions of reality. By fusing subject with the action of painting, they paint commentaries that are stark and bold.

Adolph Gottlieb reveals the brutality of one aspect of contemporary reality in the painting *Blast II* (Figure 256). Gottlieb conceived of the moments of atomic blast and cloud and no more; for what can exist following it? In step with contemporary realism in painting, the visual imagery brings much to mind with a minimum of means. It speaks of concentrated power, terrifying as the A-Bomb and becoming more ominous when H is reached. Torn and burnt desert flats, as well as tests which eradicated South Pacific isles, are recalled. The rubble of Hiroshima and Nagasaki also move into the mind's eye. What does the painting represent? In part, the answer may involve a counterquestion: What does the bomb itself represent? The strength of science? The threat of annihilation? The shield of freedom? Defense or conquest? The bomb means many things to many people.

In comparison with more traditionally orientated styles, Gottlieb's manner is vigorous and harshly simplified. The blast symbol emerges from an explosive-like brush application composing strong, intermingling, spontaneous lines. This vigorous effect is achieved with noncalculated rhythms based on automatic and passionate reflexes. Suspended overhead, a large static mass symbolizing the mushroom-like cloud associated with atomic blasts serves through contrast to increase the action below. Great contrasts in value, black against white, also serve to emphasize force. In addition, impact is provided to the imagery through the use of a scale which dominates space. In many respects, the painting heightens reality in bringing into being a new realism depicting a form unique to our century.

256   Blast II, *oil painting, Adolph Gottlieb, 1957. (Courtesy Joseph E. Seagram and Sons, Inc.)*

THREE MUSICIANS, *oil painting, Pablo Picasso, 1921.*
(Courtesy Philadelphia Museum of Art)

257

A STRESS ON PICTURE MAKING — FORMALISM

Unlike Expressionists, Formalists view subject matter as but the means towards an aesthetic end. The final form, rather than content, is supreme. Their attention is focused on the manipulation of art elements and the subsequent development of effective organizational qualities. As they paint, they ponder many questions. Should more color and greater contrasts be employed? Is a textural passage now called for? Are the placements of shapes actively balanced? These and similar problems occupy their minds. Formalists, therefore, are not deeply involved with relating previous experiences through recall; instead, they seek orderly arrangements of neutral subject matter. As one example of their attitude, consider the artist who advanced the thought that he painted compositions dealing with bottles because he did not wish the subject matter to misdirect or get in the way of enjoying the painting. It should not be concluded that such passive attitudes toward subjects are due to a lack of emotions or experiences. Rather, such pronouncements may illustrate total dedication to the exclusive problems of painting. A consideration of Georges Braque's life clearly indicates such dedication.

During World War I service in the French Army, Braque encountered many horrid experiences

258   Lᴇssᴏɴ I, 1956, *oil painting, Stuart Davis. (Courtesy Downtown Gallery)*

while engaged in violent campaigns. He was twice wounded. From similar episodes, many artists drew themes for paintings containing bitterness and terror. Not Braque, however. Returning to his studio, even during short army leaves, he continued to arrange still-life material. Selecting items such as pears, grapes, bowls, and bottles, possibly a guitar and a bright checkered table cloth, he analyzed them closely. Following examination, he turned to his paints and brought forth Cubistic imagery of great charm. It appears, from a consideration of Braque's life, that war never occurred. Possibly he sensed beauties in his heart which proved stronger than any horrible experiences stored in the mind. Solutions to aesthetic problems were his major goal; for to Braque art was his life.

The majority of Pablo Picasso's art also indicates a formalistic point of view. His popular and influential *Three Musicians* (Figure 257) illustrates such a formal venture. This Cubistic painting has been rearranged beyond the laws or bounds of reality into the realm of plastic poetry. Examine it closely. Notice how depth is restricted and inventive shapes and textures are decoratively arranged. Note also how the general pattern is exaggerated and distributed. Creative ingenuity suggested those distortions. The mood

is gay, the tempo active. Overlaps and penetrations culminate to tightly wed the whimsical music makers. A blending occurs in keeping with the characteristics of music issuing from a small orchestra. For is it not impossible, at times, to discern the explicit sources of pleasant sounds, especially when several instruments are played simultaneously?

Picasso's belief that to search is more important than to find indicates his stress on never-ending inquiry. Such an attitude is in keeping with contemporary Formalism. Each painting remains a transitional step which, while resolving certain problems, also exposes new challenges. Discoveries, therefore, bring forth new problems. The end is never attained; for art, like science, demands constant search.

Paintings by Stuart Davis contain tendencies derived in part from Cubistic practices. Davis assembles simplified shapes into bold relationships. Composing with impact in mind, he gains the directness of a poster in his forceful communications (Figure 258). In his painted plea, *Lesson I, 1956,* he marks his ballot for freedom of speech. Such a cry is warranted when considering the large minority who forsake or are denied their voting right and obligation. Notice how the massive X provides visual relief from the activity contained in the more complex adjacent mass. In addition to balancing the vitality of the pictorial symbols, the X conveys the importance of the vote. Notice also how the placement of the artist's signature relates to other painted elements upon the canvas. Though applying paint in a flat manner and depending on only bare essentials in denoting shapes, Davis enlivens his compositions with bright color and active placements. He also always considers the total design.

Acrobats and Horse is an elegant and powerful statement. Both architectonic, in solidity and monumentality of masses, and atmospheric — for space appears as an actuality — this painting displays an excellent contemporary style (Figure 259). Created by Marino Marini, it defies a rigid classification. Featuring both classical and Romantic undertones, the painting contains aspects of Expressionism and contemporary Realism as well as implications of Formalism. All these divergent influences have been absorbed by Marini and resolved into a coherent and personal style. Active technique and vigorous form distortions provide an Expressionistic flavor. Suggested transparencies, the absorption of background and foreground, muted fusions and implied delineation contributed qualities akin to contemporary Realism. There are evidences of Formalism in Marini's consistent involvement with this specific theme. Both a sculptor and painter, the artist has produced a great number of studies relating to humans and horses. His sculptored horsemen are widely known and hailed, and many of his drawings and paintings are effectively resolved investigations dealing with those subjects. He appears fascinated with this topic and produces works which are highly structured with anatomical notations and keen exaggerations.

In considering the characteristics of contemporary painting, several important points should be kept in mind: A Formalistic point of view — deliberate construction to attain a maximum of visual effectiveness — guides innumerable artists in varying degrees. This is true regardless of movement. Abstract Expressionists, as well as Academic Realists, are guided in part by aesthetic principles, though they interpret such principles differently. Another point to retain is that many movements and styles are interwoven into the current fabric of painting. Specific threads may be difficult to pluck; therefore, many artists are beyond rigid classification. Man is a complexity made up of many influences and factors, and, like art, he is seldom static.

259   Acrobats and Horse, *oil painting, Marino Marini, 1951. (Courtesy Carnegie Institute)*

THE MEANS OF PROTEST—
SOCIAL COMMENTARY

While some contemporary artists advocate decorative pursuits, others have conceived of art as a weapon to strike at wrongdoings and injustices prevailing in their world. Their intentions are not to beautify or glorify, but to pronounce judgment. Verdicts are rendered in the most forceful of manners. Such paintings are not to entertain or please, but rather to sear the heart and fire the passions.

Though political satire has a long history, a major movement using art as social protest is unique to our century. Centered in Mexico during the turbulent 1920s and 1930s, this group composed bitter visual pronouncements which strongly denounced the existing social, economic, and political order. Armed with brushes, Orozco, Rivera, Siqueiros, and other followers attacked wealthy landowners and denounced the government. Strongly socially conscious, their imagery related the plight of the peasants and the lack of economic and social equality. During the American Depression, various artists within our land also undertook bitter satire and biting documentaries to denounce chaos and misery.

Extremely powerful paintings have also been produced to protest the brutality of the wars which have torn and defaced the twentieth-century environment. In particular, the Germans, Dix and Grosz, were extremely prolific in executing brutal visual pronouncements. Their Expressionistic paintings depicted the sordid aspects of war and a chaotic postwar society in the most bitter terms. Later, one of the great masterpieces of modern art, *Guernica*, was conceived as protest by Pablo Picasso. This monumental painting related the sufferings of the peoples of the Spanish town of Guernica. Exposed to a bombing raid during the civil war in Spain, the small town vanished in hellish chaos. The semiabstract painting tells in harsh blacks, grays, and whites of this moment of death. Grotesque and twisted figures, one a mother cradling her child, appear in fearful convulsions. The stark imagery remains branded in the consciousness of all those who view this immense painting. The taste is unpleasant; for art can not be pretty when it mirrors, in creative terms, the cruelty of men.

In *The Defaced Portrait*, Ben Shahn critically refuses recognition to a pompous warrior (Figure 260). Harsh smears eradicate the Iron Cross and miscellaneous merit badges bestowed by a grateful Third Reich. All these badges of service, from shining metals to campaign buttons, are struck down by the artist. It is apparent that Shahn feels the decorations

260   THE DEFACED PORTRAIT, *oil painting, Ben Shahn, 1955. (Courtesy Mr. and Mrs. Hoke Levin)*

signify the destructive features of a dark period. To fully comprehend the artist's protest, one must ask what these metals represent. How were they earned? Could one have been secured through directing crushing panzer units across the undefended tulip beds of Holland? Possibly another was received for sending Stukas northward to pierce the skies of Norway. Who is this bemedaled glutton? A specialist in gassing, hero of Auschwitz, friend of S.S. Captain Wirth, sadistic mass killer? Or might he have made a killing during the unprovoked invasion of Poland? Notice how smugness and arrogance mark the facial features of the hero. Indeed, the painting appears to imply that this warrior-hero wears his medals with vanity though his tunic may be stained with the blood of Rotterdam's children. Ben Shahn's contempt is obvious.

Many harsh affairs have rocked our century: the dead at Verdun, the rape of Nanking, Pearl Harbor, Buchenwald, and the crushing of the Hungarian revolt. These, as well as sunflowers and sunsets, are the concerns of artists. For instance, consider Buchenwald, site of a Nazi concentration camp. Inmates consisted of political prisoners, citizens of subjugated countries, and religious minorities, especially Jews. Floggings, starvation, atrocities beyond description, and mass executions were the order of the day. A crematory handling up to four hundred corpses daily was located on the grounds. Thousands upon thousands perished: the very, very young, the old, and all in between. It is not within the limits of mere paint to adequately suggest the horrors of this prison; for stench and screams, wailings, and death gasps are indeed beyond the realm of paint. Carts carrying human debris, now grotesque, forced deep ruts in spattered soil. Only the dead were offered escape. A pleasant picture, a pleasant theme? Most certainly not. But when sadistic affairs occur, gruesome beyond the conception of decent minds, some must protest in the strongest terms they can muster. Rico Lebrun, in his painting, *Buchenwald Cart*, has

done exactly that (Figure 261). Contemporary art is not restrictive in the selection of means or subject. Neither is the story of man.

History is full of horrid abysses. Open its pages. Count the walls scaled and cities plundered. Read of the Punic Wars. Recall that to retard a rival's growth, supposedly for one thousand years, Romans sowed salt upon Tunisian earth and plowed once-proud Carthage beneath layers of time. Flip a few more pages of this book of history. Consider the tragedy of Roland at the mercy of the Moors. Read of the Children's Crusade. Visualize thousands of these youngsters, not yet in their teens, trudging southward for points of embarkation. Faith led them onto Alpine slopes, soon to be pocked with their frozen bodies. Consider also the hatred and violence during Reformation and Counter Reformation. Though the volume of history is massive, read on into new chapters. Learn of the young drummer who was partially decapitated on Freeman's farm during the first battle of Saratoga. Who remembers his sacrifice? Consider later affairs, the desperation of Shiloh and the massacre at Sand Creek. Refer to the following chapter. Visualize the struggle for Verdun and fifteen years later an intense economic and social depression with its endless lines of hungry and poor. Imagine also, somewhat later on the other side of the world, heat, jungle rot, and explosions on Guadalcanal. Consider too the annihilation of Torpedo Squadron Eight; for but one of this squadron returned to his flight deck. A few more pages lead to Korea, danger at Pusan, flight from the Yalu, frozen feet and gangrene, and soon Heartbreak Ridge. Sadness marks a large portion of the occurrences of the past. Can these affairs be denied; should the drums of history be muffled? Are blood baths, massacres, and crematoriums inappropriate for recording by pen or brush? Will no one protest? If great numbers of the pages of history remain closed, will man be forced to repeat costly errors? Who decides? Who qualifies as the censor of life or art?

261   BUCHENWALD CART, *oil painting, Rico Lebrun, 1955. (Courtesy Pennsylvania Academy of the Fine Arts)*

262   VIEW IN PERSPECTIVE OF PERFECT SUNSET, *oil painting, Eugene Berman, 1941.* *(Courtesy Philadelphia Museum of Art)*

263   BLACK NIGHT, *oil painting, William Baziotes, 1954. (Courtesy Carnegie Institute)*

A PSYCHOLOGICAL POINT OF VIEW— SURREALISM AND MYSTICISM

Ego, id, superego, drive, inhibition, and frustration are now common terms. Innumerable books explaining the actions of child and adult have been rewritten, and influential playwrights weave these terms into dramatic stage productions. A portion of society, endeavoring to understand themselves more fully, visit specialists who probe for hidden meanings. Man now attempts to recognize himself in depth. Even dream imagery is closely viewed, through recall, for a pattern explaining the logic of thoughts and actions. Layers of consciousness are examined and meanings exposed, frequently in terms of the nonrecognized or socially unacceptable. Psychology has become a weapon of advertising and warfare, and its aspects have permeated into schooling, science, and art. "Freud" has become a household word. Many now contend the existence of a superreality veiled by a thin veneer which, applied by custom and society, shells the true self. This hidden universe now serves as an area of artistic investigation. Upon entrance, the curtains of the conventional world are drawn back and dreamlike imagery forms upon the stage of art.

View in Perspective of Perfect Sunset (Figure 262) portrays desolation and despair; for the sun has set upon a scene devoid of both joy and perfection. The title seems tinged with contradiction owing to melancholic and possibly sarcastic evidences. The figure in foreground, wrapped within self, indicates little concern for either day or the coming night. Time holds no promise, guarantees no rewards. Figures lacking purpose wander aimlessly or lounge without reason throughout the painting. The residue of existence lies scattered as if randomly flung about the moody landscape. Weird ornaments top strange and ravaged columns, which appear to continue far beyond the limits of the eye to see. Vast distances and multiple viewpoints are stressed through several implied and highly accented vanishing points. The onlooker's eye is thus moved about the landscape in pronounced directions terminating at distant horizons.

Eugene Berman's painting has all the qualities of conventional Surrealistic painting. Wishing to clearly communicate to the entire audience, the Surrealist usually employs traditional painting tendencies. His conventional methods in handling color, texture, and shape, however, unfold the unusual through a provoking theme selection. Both subject matter and compositional devices usually stress forlorn individuals, fantastic imagery, and infinite space. The Surrealist often implies the imprisonment of humans in a web of strange circumstances. Set within haunting, moody landscapes, such episodes arouse wonderment and, at times, an uneasiness on the viewer's part. Possibly one senses he has seen such imagery while recently deep in slumber. The problem of differentiation between realities and dreams, actualities and hallucinations, now confronts the onlooker. One must always wonder if the Surrealist is but a chronicler of the irrational. Or are his provocative themes addressed to an inner ear which determines the final truth?

William Baziotes creates personal symbols with challenging meanings. Flat monumental shapes exist within a hazy environment in his painting *Black Night* (Figure 263). What comes to mind in viewing this painting? Consider the title and peer at the imagery. Notice the fantastic beastlike mass that appears to be plucking at a heavier overhead shape. Can you now sense the spirit and mood of the painting?

The painter, in this surreal-like and unusual presentment, possibly tells of the coming of night. Its curtain of blackness appears about to descend to blot the landscape, with the occurrence but awaiting the actions of the creature with the jawlike pincers to drag darkness to the land. Thus, the spread of night is inevitable, for nature daily absorbs its day. Others may associate different meanings to the painting. Huge primeval matter may come to mind, for bulk and massiveness are greatly emphasized in the two major shapes. Notice how they contrast with the dainty thin lines suggesting an adjacent fluttering plant. Thus, monumental qualities of the two key elements were probably deliberately developed. Some viewers may even contend *Black Night* has mystical implications in signifying the spirit of night. For them the painting heralds the time of the hoot of the owl and the emergence of tiny furry creatures which hope to scamper undetected across distant dreamy forest floors. Or the painting may represent somber pageantry, as if dredged from deep in the subconscious of sleeping man. What do you think the artist intended? Contemporary painting can take many intriguing directions.

THE DISSOLVING IMAGE —
TOWARD NEW SENSATIONS

Contemporary painting often calls upon the viewer's personal sensitivity and imaginative powers to complete its meaning. One searches for suggested impressions and evaluates in terms of consistency between visual treatment and theme idea. Meanings are not exposed in a traditional illusionistic fashion, but rather are revealed in more direct and original, or individually centered terms. In such works, symbols tend to border on signs which are marks which possess no shape resemblance, or intend any counterparts, in nature. Great stress is frequently placed on color playing an associative role. Titles often provide the needed key to understanding the painter's intentions. Broad interpretations are brought into being. As the viewer discovers implications beyond the conventional, another level of visual consciousness, one beyond mere shape association, comes into being.

Consider the qualities which can be involved in a theme dealing with the season of spring. This period represents birth, the song of youth, soft greens and yellows and peeking reds, the flurry of growth following the dormancy of winter. Such a topic, expressed in paint, would involve a more active treatment of color, surface, and arrangement than demanded by *Black Night*. Hans Hofmann, a great Abstract Expressionist, captures the characteristics of spring in the painting, *Salute aux Printemps* (Figure 264). Alas, though the colorful painting is denied its original brilliance, owing to black and white reproduction, brilliant and colorful it most certainly is. The tempo of change, pulsating movements derived from thick paint application, the dance of relationships, the boisterousness of the season, all are captured in this painter's salute to spring. One must react to both theme and Hofmann's methods in paint treatment to fully sense the flavor and consistency of the painting. Its plasticity in surface treatment is slightly akin to the early Impressionist's manner of paint application; however, it conveys much more violence in displaying little, if any, contrived control in paint handling. Hofmann's presentment, in keeping with Abstract Expressionism, is both explosive and personal.

There are many effective manners of stating the qualities of spring in visual terms. Some painters would develop factual paintings displaying buttercups lolling upon a green hillside or young trees breaking into foliage. Hofmann, how-

264   SALUTE AUX PRINTEMPS *(Salute to Spring), oil painting, Hans Hofmann, 1958. (Courtesy Samuel M. Kootz Gallery Inc.)*

ever, is not dependent on such illusionistic, story-like approaches. He is interested in the qualities of the blush, rather than the literal reasons associated with it. He seeks for spirit and essence. For both his colorful discoveries and powerful achievements, he has long maintained an influential membership in the Modern movement.

A medieval German epic poem, dating from the twelfth century, relates the story of Siegfried. This prince, dweller of the lower Rhine, had legendary powers. A mighty warrior indeed, for Siegfried was dragon slayer, rescuer of damsels in distress, and hero to his people. He thus appeared somewhat equal to a composite of a part of Lancelot of Arthur's Court, a dash of Robin Hood, and a bit of William Tell. As his legend grew, musicians as well as painters paid Siegfried homage. Songs and musical scores, improvised and handed down from generation to generation, related the clashes and vitality of the ancient warrior prince. His battle ax, honed to perfection, therefore rang throughout the centuries.

During the past century, Wilhelm Richard Wagner devised a monumental musical composition which magnificently told, once again, of the ancient myths of the Rhineland. The third part of the four-part comprehensive work dealt with Siegfried. *Götterdämmerung* (The Twilight of the Gods) concluded the series. The Romantic Wagner, both expressionist and experimenter, developed his music into a dramatic and highly structured form. A sequential theme thread, as a heavy power-packed continuum of the leitmotiv, was interwoven into his compositions. Wagner's stirring *Siegfried* was first performed in the United States at the Metropolitan Opera House, New York, in 1889. Its sounds of power and sweeping grandeur immediately burrowed into and dominated the hearts of the listeners.

With broad brush and quick movements, Franz Kline recently presented his version of *Siegfried* (Figure 265). The swing and bite of Kline's brush fused paint into a violent pattern in keeping with Wagner's earlier interpretation of the ancient theme. The painter's visual orchestration of lines, values, and masses rejuvenates in strong abstract terms this tale from the lower Rhine. The mood conveys tension and strength, and the title assures the emergence of intended meanings. Though Kline provides a key to subject through title, many painters deny this assistance. Their concern is the surface alone.

265   Siegfried, *oil painting, Franz Kline, 1958. (Courtesy Sidney Janis Gallery)*

THE SURFACE ALONE —
THE ABSTRACT PAINTER

Only a slight distance separates Franz Kline's *Siegfried* from Jackson Pollock's painting *No. 4, 1950* (Figure 266). The step is crucial, however, for it leads into total abstraction. While through title substitutions it may not be too far fetched to read the spirit of *Siegfried* into Pollock's work — for instance, the warrior in battle with dragon — such an assumption would be totally false. Though Pollock had dealt with subject matter in various paintings, his intentions in *No. 4, 1950* were in terms of pure visual research. His purpose was to seek and expose new manners of handling paint upon canvas. Such ventures existed in complete freedom, because absolutely no subject or theme was consciously pursued. This is not to imply that in confronting totally abstract works the minds of viewers do not read into the paintings supposedly hidden meanings. Such wonderings may be the viewer's prerogative, but seldom do they encompass the artist's original intent. To the total Abstractionist, his painting exists as an end in itself and implications are confined within the frame. Means of handling color, devising new relationships of shapes and mass, textural passages, and the like demand his full attention.

Taught by a regionalist painter during his youth, Pollock later moved completely away from subject involvement. During the latter stages of a turbulent career, he pursued his new beliefs with both intensity and dedication to attain the ultimate in energetic inventiveness and action painting. Freedom, but also constant struggle, marked his efforts. The only restraints imposed on his style appeared to be the limitations of his endurance and ability in conceiving of new visual possibilities. His mature style demanded no preliminary drawings but unfolded through automatic procedures in brushing, dripping, and splashing paint upon a two-dimensional surface. Both highly controversial and eagerly collected, Pollock's paintings are now hallmarks in the Modern movement. While many of his paintings may appear effortless, they emerged through tedious trials which slowly led Pollock from treating figurative imagery to his later concern with the surface alone. Though his work meets with the full wrath of the layman, who often imagines a conspiracy, it represents one important and influential aspect of action painting. As always evident with innovators, his style has many followers. They must show care, however; for those who follow closely seldom cast their shadows.

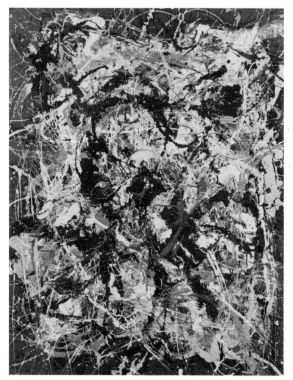

266   No. 4, 1950, *oil painting, Jackson Pollock. (Courtesy Carnegie Institute)*

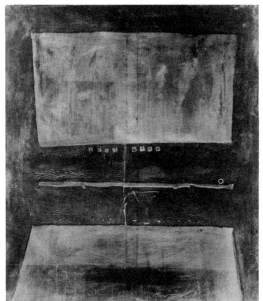

PAINTING, *oil and collage, Antoni Tapies, 1958.*
(Courtesy Carnegie Institute)

267

All abstract paintings, regardless of lack of subject matter, germinate certain physical and psychological response. Even an untreated canvas causes a reaction. The slightest mark upon its surface begins to develop tensions and mood; for visual relationships are becoming established. The complex relationships contained in Pollock's *No. 4, 1950* are beyond the physical limits of the vision to readily clarify and absorb. Therefore, there occurs a natural reaction that arouses turbulent sensations. Such sensations are then often associated with experiences in the viewer's background which have engendered similar response. Meanings are then read into the painting on the basis of the viewer's background. Pollock's swirling abstractions are thus frequently linked to a great variety of occurrences ranging from hectic traffic patterns to the Galaxy, or Milky Way.

One's immediate response to Antoni Tapies' *Painting* is usually passive, yet also apprehensive (Figure 267). Drab earthy colors and large austere masses create a somber mood. Various associations may register in the mind. Funeral boxes, dug from an ancient mound, or leathery sails, long exposed to arid winds, salt, and blistering sun, may cross the mind. Of course, vastly different ideas can also be visualized. Tapies style is both deliberate and experimental. Very large as well as tiny patches of cloth have been adhered to his canvas to obtain fluctuating heights. This procedure provided a subtle collage quality. In certain areas, the young Spaniard used liberal amounts of paint and modified portions of these applications through scraping. Other sections of the painting were merely stained with thin washes of diluted oil paint. The structure, in great part, was deliberately contrived. Tapies' organizational method is somewhat reminiscent of the procedures employed by Piet Mondrian when composing abstractions. Jackson Pollock's method, however, was more in kinship with the automatic drawing practices devised by Hans Arp.

The extensive nature of contemporary painting comes into focus when one realizes that Antoni Tapies' painting was awarded the first prize in a recent large International Exhibition and, within several months, one of the highest prices ever paid to an American for his painting was given to Andrew Wyeth. Both occurrences were in relationship to awards and purchases in major American museums. Competent authorities, therefore, extended both painters recognition. Painting, as it moves into the latter decades of this century, will continue to embrace varied styles and differing themes. Strange obscurities, colorful outbursts, and specific calculations in paint will surely be hung. Fads and novelties will appear and disappear, but the threads of significant painting will hold firm. Judgments will continue to be based on personal revelations and original attainments. These evaluation factors remain constant though movements and manners change; for, no matter the century, decade, or year, each painter fulfills his role only when developing his own distinctive manner.

268 ATELIER *(Studio), oil painting, Bernard Buffet, 1956. (Courtesy M. Knoedler and Company, Inc.)*

Paint; Technique and Media

The manner of performance in manipulating paint, or technique, is devised by artists in terms of personal sensitivity and desire. It grows from the evolving of particular means which are effective and natural for communicating ideas. Observation of the works of others, study, and deep thought can play roles in its formation; only through actual painting involvement, however, can technique be fully realized. Long and tedious sessions of trial and error, compromise, and satisfying discoveries brings forth its development. Resulting techniques are partially based on a variety of preferences regarding the proper manipulation of media. Even within a single medium, such as oil paint, attitudes relating to its handling vary widely. For instance, some painters prefer qualities of fluidity when applying oil paint and even seek transparencies through the use of thin washes and glazes of diluted paint. Others favor the characteristics of plasticity offered by untreated oil paint and are fully content with opaque surfaces.

Consider how Bernard Buffet, a young French artist, handles his oil medium (Figure 268). His technique, economical, vigorous, and direct, cultivates stark imagery. Painted surfaces appear as briskly brushed and stained through pronounced overpainting. Sensations of agitated expressiveness are thus strongly implied within his paint handling. As for pattern, it is structured in terms of value dissonances rather than color, and it is dependent on strong lines denoting shapes and details. Emerging from somewhat thin and flat applications, it is enlivened by dark and light linear and mass interminglings. While linear perspective is implied, depth is restricted by value distributions which convey a two-dimensional impression. Though architectonic and two-dimensional features are integrated within his technique, Buffet conceives of oil paint as a fluid medium.

Hans Jaenisch builds paint, in a cement-like fashion, into three-dimensional imagery akin to sculptural relief (Figure 269). This German artist conceives of paint not as a fluid medium, but as a plastic substance. His technique involves a great degree of actual rather than implied texture; for thick paint is spread about the surface of the painting probably with a palette knife — dug into, scratched, and also actually massed into projecting shapes. Jaenisch's technique is obviously heavy-handed and rigid owing to its extreme emphasis on the effects obtainable through the exploitation of the plastic qualities of paint. Examine Jaenisch's decorative and imaginative painting and note how an active balance is achieved. Though four related but distinct occurrences exist and great liberties are taken with scale, the painting is tightly unified. How is this unity achieved? A close examination should provide the key. Notice also that the large episode in the bottom field is prevented from dominating the painting. This control is due to the placement of flanking dark panels which greatly emphasize the smaller figures presented within their fields. However, above all else, sense throughout the total composition the thick and fluctuating application of paint.

Transparent watercolor paint is a remarkable medium for those who wish great degrees of fluidity and transparency. Somewhat instantaneous color mixtures can be easily obtained, especially when the paint is placed upon damp paper. Futhermore, owing to a short drying time, paintings can be rapidly completed. For such reasons, many painters tend to favor watercolor painting. A large number of the paintings of the modern master, Paul Klee, were executed in this medium (Figure 270). Klee's technique took full advantage of the actions of watercolor upon damp paper as well as the incorporation of the

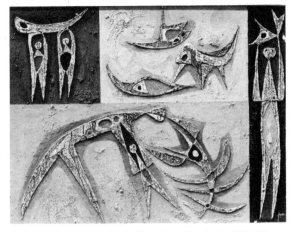

269   SCORPION, *oil painting, Hans Jaenisch, 1955. (Courtesy Carnegie Institute)*

270   LITTLE HOUSES WITH GARDENS, *watercolor and ink, Paul Klee, 1928. (Courtesy Philadelphia Museum of Art)*

271   The Curious Couple, *collage, glass, tile, cloth, and paint, Enrico Baj, 1956.*
(Courtesy Carnegie Institute)

paper itself as a tone or value factor. Advanced with childlike inventiveness, yet highly articulate, his charming transparencies were paintings usually full of joy. Writing ten years before the appearance of *Little Houses with Garden* he even then spoke of[3]

> Blobs of color. Stippling. Stippled and striped surfaces. . . . Broken, articulated movement. Counter-movement. Objects interlaced and interwoven. . . . Harmony with one voice. With several voices.

Klee's technique was designed to serve his purpose, and that it fully did. One can imagine he developed his means with a smile on his face.

Media used by contemporary painters range from oil paint and wax encaustic to opaque and transparent watercolors and even Duco, lacquer, and all sorts of synthetic resins. Innumerable miscellaneous materials — wood strips, string, gravel, glass, stones, and, yes, probably somewhere even pumpkin seeds — are now used with paint and incorporated into paintings. A variety of material forms *The Curious Couple* created by the Italian, Enrico Baj (Figure 271). The background, composed of bits of printed and textured cloth, contains a random scattering of

small stones and chunks of glass. A minimum of paint has also been nonchalantly brushed upon the surface. Chunks of felt, apparently torn, not cut, contribute ragged masses identifying portions of the figures. Scraps of white tile serve for eyes. Since various materials other than paint are predominant in this work, it is considered a collage rather than a painting. Baj indeed creates a curious couple indicative of a novel use of miscellaneous scraps of material.

The limits of contemporary painting seem to be constantly expanding. Few, if any, restrictions in the use or appropriateness of material, media, or method now exist. This great freedom extends many rewards in challenging man to the very borders of the imaginable. However, an apparent danger also exists in conjunction with complete or extremely extensive freedom. Such a situation can breed contempt of disciplined creations and unduly encourage a pursuit of pure novelty. Creativity involves more than rips and gouges and temper tantrums. Nor is experimentation alone the final end. One must always retain in mind that license need not imply the lack of obligation. Though in art there always emerge exceptions to the rule, the best of contemporary painting involves neither insignificant displays of dead technique nor brutal presentments of mutilated material. The best is always constructive even if, as protest, it is presented in a negative way.

[3] G. Di San Lazzaro, *Klee* (New York: Frederick A. Praeger, Inc., 1957), p. 108.

COLOR; PROPERTIES AND REACTIONS

Color is the most important element within painting, but owing to its high cost of reproduction, its exclusion from this text is necessary, if unfortunate. The decision was based on a desire for a very liberal sprinkling of photographs throughout each and every chapter, rather than a limited number of color plates. It is highly recommended, however, that the reader make many and frequent references to color in nature, its reproduction in various books and magazines, and its use in original works of art. One should search for evidences of both its subtlety and impact and constantly make note of its operation and effectiveness. Observant eyes will soon disclose that color is highly eventful in nature and that its use, as paint, assumes many directions.

Numerous painters employ color in a bold fashion, achieving bright decorative patterns. Great clashes of warm and cool, bright and dull, dark and light colors resound throughout their painted surfaces. Other painters favor subdued relationships with muted colors and strong evidences of gray. A monochromatic scheme involving the exclusive use of one color, with emphasis on differences in degrees of dullness and brightness and darkness and lightness, is a favorite device of many painters who wish to tightly unify a composition. Those who favor greater contrasts turn to all sorts of color combinations encompassing opposites and triads of color. Many painters also go beyond any contrived scheme. They base their selections on symbolic associations, personal appeal, or a variety of other factors.

A consideration of their physical properties can provide insight into how colors behave. All colors can be separated into two general classifications relating to their reactions upon the eye of the viewer. Yellow, orange, and red appear to expand and advance in space. They are termed warm colors. Positive and agressive, they are usually more stimulating than cool colors which appear more retiring or tranquil. Green, blue, and purple are considered cool colors; they tend to recede in space. Consider two blocks of equal size, both painted, one covered with a medium-value red, the other with a medium

blue. If the colored blocks were placed an equal distance from the eye of the viewer, they would cause opposite reactions. The warm-colored block would appear to be both larger and closer. If transferred, for instance, into a problem of home decoration, a room painted a medium-value red or yellow would tend to seem smaller than it would appear to be if coated with a blue or green; for the warm-colored walls would tend to move forward and restrict space. This physical characteristic of color enables painters to create striking climaxes with vivid movements and tensions and imply depth upon their canvas.

As you realize, yellow, red, and blue are primary colors. The secondary colors, in the six-color theory, are orange, green, and purple; they result from certain intermixings of the primary colors. Green, for example, results from mixing blue and yellow, and purple may be obtained by combining red and blue. Gray can be secured either by mixing opposites in the color wheel or by fusing black and white. Scientifically, white can be thought of as the sum total of all colors; for in the laboratory, as light, it is refracted by a prism into all the colors of the spectrum. Conversely, the colors of the spectrum can be focused on a second prism to produce white light. In the form of paint, of course, white cannot be attained by mixing colored pigments. Rather, it is acquired from various substances such as chalk. Black results in the laboratory from the total lack of light reflection. As paint, it is produced from mineral and synthetic compounds.

Three qualities, hue, value, and chroma, are contained in color. Each identifies a particular aspect. For instance, an examination of red indicates the hue or color as red, the value as light, medium, or dark, and the chroma as either bright or dull. In paint, the hue is colored pigment secured from mineral or synthetic substances. Initially usually in powder form, the dry pigment is subsequently mixed with a binder and a vehicle to obtain qualities of adherence and fluidity. The binder is frequently a glue- or paste-like substance that adheres the colored pigment to the painted surface. The vehicle, a liquid, carries the pigment and binder, permitting both to flow freely. Water is the vehicle for watercolors, and varnish is often the vehicle for oil paint. The binding agent in the former is water soluble, while the binder in oil paints is soluble only in certain liquids such as turpentine.

Colors can possess extensive degrees of value, from extremely light to very dark. The value can be regulated by the introduction of white or black. The addition of white is usually considered a tinting process, while black provides color shades. Chroma, the intensity or the brightness or dullness of color, can be controlled in several ways. Colors can be dulled with the addition of either gray or their opposites on the color wheel; thus, red may become less bright or less intense through the addition of either gray or green. Brightness is usually secured in pure color through subduing adjacent relationships and obtaining stress through contrast. The manipulation of surroundings can also greatly influence value as well as chroma. Painters, in handling color, usually think in terms of the surrounding relationships as well as the particular area of color being deposited. They realize that, when jointly used, colors greatly influence each other and relationships are never static. They also fully recognize that a color may appear brighter if placed adjacent to a dull gray or darker if employed in relationship with lighter colors. They further recognize that each viewer reacts to a specific color in his own peculiar way.

An individual's response to color is determined by several factors. Naturally, one reacts to the color's physical properties in becoming aware of its expanding or contracting characteristics or its suggestion of heaviness or lightness. Defensive mechanisms within the optic nerves will even react to relieve agitations derived from viewing extremely bright colors. Such reactions are automatically derived from visual contact, with results determined on the basis of the qualities inherent in the particular color. In addition to this physical reaction, the viewer often responds on the basis of symbolic and psychological associations. Within every society, various colors are representative of certain cultural aspects. Green is appreciated by certain Irishmen, though those coming from another region of Ireland may react unfavorably to it. The latter would advance orange as a favorite. Red within our society is often indicative of danger or implies "stop." To many, yellow symbolizes sacredness owing to its use in religious rituals; however, at times it may signify cowardice or treachery. Colors even symbolize certain seasons and events. In America, orange and black are linked with Halloween and Christmas is associated with green and red. Therefore, single colors and various combinations can bring to mind certain common meanings to members of a tribe, clan, state, or nation. These reactions are dependent on the color usage developed by the specific group or society. Color preference or reaction can also be traced, in many cases, to personal psychological responses. Colors may subconsciously become associated with either pleasant or unhappy experiences. Such early experiences can be recalled, with varying degrees of consciousness, when associative colors are later encountered. This response is unpredicatable and unique; for it fluctuates with the viewer. Red may germinate a negative response to a person who links it with a terrifying episode such as a fire. Another individual, not sharing such a background, may react highly favorably toward its use. A circus or even Santa's suit and Christmas may be recalled by the latter person. Thus, memories stored in each mind may, in great part, generate response and decide color preference. Psychologists even contend that individuals often react in a more intense manner toward color when it is allied with particular forms. Two identical greens may cause different reactions provided one green is related to a shape usually thought of as being green in color. For instance, a green placed on a leaf-like shape would appear to be more intense than an identical green coating a rectangle or other shape which possessed no implications of color association. Thus, it appears that, in some instances, the mind itself can enliven color.

High School Students Try Their Hand

UNRESTRICTED EXPLORATION —
COLORED INKS

Exciting findings which can be brought to bear in future undertakings can easily unfold through unrestrained color experiments in any medium possessive of color. Such endeavors should be conceived not as final forms, but rather as exposures revealing intriguing color interminglings, gradations, and mutations. Merely a *Color Splash*, composed of transparent and opaque inks, permitted one student to strike up an acquaintance with the characteristics of both color and the ink medium (Figure 272). From such probes, shades can loudly register while tints meekly disclose their existence. All sorts of nuances occur, as if by accident, through uninhibited spatterings and random brush trailings. Movements change, as if by magic, as color is deposited upon damp areas and spread into dry portions of the paper. The student soon discovers that spontaneous experimental ventures can gain an element of control if disciplined with a sharp eye and a keen hand.

CONTRIVED ORGANIZATION —
CUT AND TORN PAPER

Characteristics in opposition to the traits evident in *Color Splash* are involved in *Arrangement, Still Life* (Figure 273). Great control, economy of means, and deliberation mark this student's creation. The theme, derived from several bottles and fruit arranged upon a drawing table, was translated through observation, ingenuity, and construction paper into an actively balanced but placid design. Various shapes were cut, some were employed and others discarded, and positions were developed and redeveloped until the student's eye determined that the total organization seemed just right. Only then, following a number of choices, was paste used to retain the final form. A bit of newspaper and a segment of a colored sheet obtained from a magazine added a change of pace to the construction-paper imagery. The treatment of edges, both cut for sharpness and torn to delay visual flow, also contributed an element of contrast. Cut and torn paper ventures permit ease and dexterity in arrangement owing to the flexibility in placement during the pre-paste organizational stages. These endeavors can hone one's ability in handling organizational relationships and sensitize an awareness of divergent possibilities for pictorial layout.

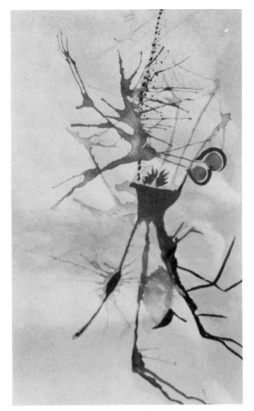

272   Color Splash, *exploration with colored inks, student, West High School, Madison, Wisc.*

273   Arrangement, Still Life, *cut and torn paper, student, Wisconsin High School, Madison, Wisc.*

274   DOWNTOWN, *watercolor, student, Wisconsin High School, Madison, Wisc.*

A SURFACE THAT SPARKLES — TRANSPARENT WATERCOLOR

Downtown, a transparent-watercolor painting, incorporates the actions of both wet and dry paper surfaces (Figure 274). Following a conventional procedure, the young painter dampened his grained watercolor paper and worked from light tints to dark shades. This sequence took into account the characteristics of transparency inherent in the medium, which offer a greater ease in darkening, rather than lightening, masses. Upon the drying of the washed surfaces, linear emphasis and details were secured through the actions of a brush tip recording black outlines. Both fleeting impressions and definite notations were derived from the difference in qualities of absorption when depositing paint upon wet and dry surfaces. Texture was gained through the use of somewhat rough paper as well as the employment of a semidry brush rubbing in several areas of the composition. Portions of the paper remained untreated, resulting in interspersed patches of white. This treatment tended to unify background and foreground and provided a rhythmical sequence to the scene. The mood is light and pleasant.

Frequently, ink or wax crayon is incorporated with transparent watercolor. Ink offers opportunities for fine opaque lines and a wealth of concise details. Crayon enables a resist process because a subsequent application of watercolor stains only adjacent unwaxed areas. Charming effects, pronounced contrasts with jewel-like sparkle, can easily be achieved with the use of crayon and watercolor particularly if light-value wax lines and masses are intermingled with dark somber shades of watercolor.

275   IN THE RAIN, *tempera, High school student, Pittsburgh Public Schools, Pa.*

THE MOOD CHANGES — TEMPERA

Tiny figures add a human element as they scurry about *In the Rain* (Figure 275). Several directions are indicated as the viewer's eyes glide about this student's tempera painting. Intersecting streets, implied pedestrian movement, overlapping, diminishing scale and atmospheric details suggest a depth and spatial complex. Notice how interest is retained within the setting by the large tree masses which deny a complete horizontal transition. Thin brush strokes impose light diagonal lines over previously painted shapes and details. This solution effectively captures sensations of pelting rain thundering from the heavens and spattering upon the shimmering cityscape. The mood is active and tinged with gloom, and the theme is common, at any season, to most any urban locale. In visual terms, how would you convey an impression of a dull damp day? What sort of colors would you select?

Though a watercolor, tempera, owing to its opaque nature, can be built up and lightened with more ease than a transparent-watercolor medium can be. It also permits more modifications through overpainting and generally involves a longer span of time for execution. Details and shapes can easily be sharpened or dimmed, and actual texture can be obtained for possessing a creamlike consistency, tempera also offers qualities of plasticity not available with its transparent kin. Many students achieve intriguing results through the use of dark construction paper as a painting surface upon which imagery is created with light- and medium-value tempera colors.

276   FIGURED PATTERN, *oil on burlap, student, Wisconsin High School, Madison, Wisc.*

A FIGURE IN OIL

Figured Pattern emerged from a number of preliminary charcoal sketches (Figure 276). Its producer, a young lady, was undoubtedly aware of
the achievements of the Cubists. The simplified geometric figure was effectively distorted to properly
relate to the space available upon the burlap surface.
Both figure and background are tightly linked by a
mutual sharing of light and dark accents. A quality
somewhat akin to a stained-glass window was
stressed through the use of broad black lines which
outlined and enhanced each flat area of color. A
decorative pattern came into being as light, bright
masses appeared to peek out amidst dark, somber
tones. The setting is imagination, and the color selection is personal. Such a painting could add a rich
note to most any setting.

Initially prepared by stretching and gluing inexpensive burlap to stiff cardboard backing, the painting surface was then sealed with shellac. Upon
drying, it was ready for the application of paint. The
student worked exclusively with a large broad brush
and enamel paints. Many possibilities exist in a high
school situation for the use of oil paints. In addition
to enamels, conventional tube oils, various household paints, and new synthetics are suitable for use.
Oil paint can also be easily obtained by mixing
powder tempera with varnish. Suitable surfaces
upon which to paint can range from traditional
primed canvas or Masonite to heavy drawing paper,
tagboard, or cardboard properly sealed.

MORE THAN A HEAD — MIXED MEDIA

A combination of chalk and tempera, deposited by an experimental hand, resulted in the *Imaginative Portrait* (Figure 277). Background is strongly united with foreground, yet both appear somewhat impulsive or spontaneous in indicating only an impression. A strong sense of contact is established as the eye of the rendered head sadly greets the onlooker. Harsh flickering lines radiating from the forehead — could they represent a crown of thorns? Sensations of compassion are transmitted in considering this student's theme. Though only a rapid expression, with but chalk and tempera, and treated as shallow space, the image conveys a great spiritual depth.

Effective painting demands the presentment of ideas, with feeling, in a revealing two-dimensional form. The means are readily available; they are merely paper, brush, and a box of paints. Anyone engaged in painting, regardless of medium, should mix colors with an explorative spirit rather than timidly limit himself to a direct use from tube, can, or cake. The resulting tints and shades should also be courageously applied with a broad brush, whenever feasible. Imagery should be directly painted, with the entire surface worked up as a unified whole rather than treated as isolated segments. A continuum is thus maintained and an organic unity is obtainable. Owing to its nature, painting confronts the participant with constant problems pertaining to the sensitive establishment of succeeding relationships. This factor must be fully recognized and personally resolved. In a school program, the function of painting is to arouse the inventiveness of the doer as well as to communicate when hung on walls. Singularly, or in various combinations, watercolors, inks, crayons, chalks, tempera, oils, and related substances can make specific demands and extend intriguing opportunities. They all can elicit pure discoveries and assist in exposing visions, which speak of one's own manner of looking at the universe.

277   IMAGINATIVE PORTRAIT, *mixed media, chalk and tempera, High school student, Williamsport Public Schools, Pa.*

TOPICS FOR CONSIDERATION

1. What are the differences between Naturalism and Realism?

2. Identify Surrealism, Cubism, Regionalism, Formalism, and Abstract Expressionism.

3. What is Action Painting? Is observation necessary to the modern painter?

4. How do painters develop their technique? Compare the probable approaches of Andrew Wyeth and Franz Kline.

5. List several examples of both symbolic use of color and psychological response towards color.

6. From the high school students' paintings contained in this chapter, select the reproduction which you consider the most expressive and explain your choice.

7. Select, from all the paintings contained in this chapter, the two paintings which most appeal to you and explain your reasons for these selections.

SUGGESTED ACTIVITIES

1. Build up a surface of paint on a 12 by 18 inch sheet of paper or cardboard. Do not concern yourself with subject, but stress color fusions and achievement of different textures by varying the brush application—swishing, patting, and so forth. Work toward unusual color mutations and gradations. Either tempera or oil is suitable for this explorative venture.

2. Employing the media used in the preceding undertaking, compose a painting relating to a musical score you prefer. Listen to the recording as you participate in this painting, and attempt to suggest the tempo and spirit of the music within your abstract visual pattern.

3. In oil or tempera, create an 18 by 24 inch painting of an actual or imaginary landscape. Limit this painting to the color green, but use many shades and tints of the single color.

4. Following several preliminary sketches, produce a mixed-media painting with a theme of protest.

5. Freely experiment with crayon and transparent watercolor upon several rather small segments of paper. Study the results and attempt to discover a direction for subject matter from these experiments. Possibly one may suggest a slight indication of a forest, a seascape, or countless other images. Have them, rather than you, suggest possibilities. Upon sensing a subject or theme, create a 12 by 18 inch crayon and watercolor composition with the implied meaning.

6. Using cut and torn construction paper, bits of newspaper, and a minimum of tempera paint, produce an impression of a city.

7. Select either the activity of producing a self portrait, in tempera or oil, assisted by a mirror, or an abstraction dealing with fear or fantasy. Paint on a large sheet of paper, cardboard, or burlap.

APPROPRIATE REFERENCES AND READINGS

Periodicals

Art in America, New York: Art in America Co., Inc., 605 Madison Ave.

Arts, New York: The Art Digest, Inc., 116 E. 59th St.

Texts

American Painting Today, edited by Nathaniel Pousette-Dart, New York: Hastings House, Publishers, Inc., 1956.

Fantastic Art, Dada, Surrealism, edited by Alfred H. Barr, Jr., New York: The Museum of Modern Art, 1947.

HESS, THOMAS B. *Willem De Kooning*, New York: George Braziller, Inc., 1959.

HUNTER, SAM. *Modern American Painting and Sculpture*, Laurel Edition, New York: Dell Publishing Co., Inc., 1959.

MAYER, RALPH. *The Painters' Craft: An Introduction to Artists' Materials*, New York: D. Van Nostrand Co., Inc., 1948.

NEWMEYER, SARAH. *Enjoying Modern Art*, A Mentor Book, New York: New American Library of World Literature, Inc., 1957.

O'HARA, FRANK. *Jackson Pollock*, New York: George Braziller, Inc., 1959.

READ, HERBERT. *A Concise History of Modern Painting*, New York: Frederick A. Praeger, Inc., 1959.

SEITZ, WILLIAM C. *Claude Monet: Seasons and Moments*, New York: The Museum of Modern Art, 1960.

The History of Modern Painting from Picasso to Surrealism, Geneva, Switzerland: Albert Skira Publication, 1950.

The New Decade, 35 American Painters and Sculptors, edited by John I. H. Baur, New York: The Whitney Museum of American Art, 1955.

8

GRAPHICS: IMPRESSIONS THROUGH PRESSURE AND INK

Beginners should at first practice on material that is familiar to them — students should not be overburdened with matters that are unsuitable to their age, comprehension, and present condition, since otherwise they will spend their time in wrestling with shadows.

JOHN AMOS COMENIUS[1]
17th Century Schoolmaster

278   FAÇADE, *woodcut print, student, Wisconsin High School, Madison, Wisc.*

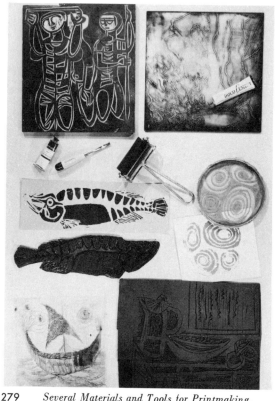

279   *Several Materials and Tools for Printmaking.*

[1] M. W. Keatinge, *The Great Didactic of John Amos Comenius* (London: A. and C. Black, Ltd., 1910), p. 197

The Graphic Method

Graphic methods can be either simple or complex; require a great amount of tools, materials, and equipment or but a few essentials; and demand comprehensive and technical or uncomplicated and concise explanations; for printmaking processes are widespread and fragmented into a variety of methods. While the term "graphic arts" at one time included all forms of representation on two-dimensional surfaces — drawing, painting, etching, engraving, and so forth, current usage tends to limit the term to activities which reproduce through impression. A typewriter key may illustrate a graphic process; for when struck, the key forces ink from the ribbon onto paper and thereby produces its image. Even a finger, if inked and pressed against paper, will leave a print. Most any conceivable material, from a block of wood or a portion of a sponge to a sheet of copper, if coated with ink and pressed against paper will transfer imagery composed of mass or line. If the surface of the material is scratched or portions are cut away, the resulting impression can be controlled to express a specific idea.

The print *Façade* (Figure 278) was transferred from a design originally cut into a wood block. While the student portrays but the front of a house, he has already entered the door leading to graphic understanding. Notice how suggestions extended by the wood grain are effectively combined with shapes, proportions, and value distributions to contribute a rich visual surface. The qualities of the cuts and extensive variation in the removal of portions of the original block which identify the form indicate inquisitiveness and inventiveness on the student's part. Such a print appropriately signifies the intriguing achievements of a fusion of imagination and skill in a printmaking activity.

Two great advantages of the graphic arts are that unique results and numerous reproductions are securable from one source. Thus a constant flow of duplications become available, permitting many individuals the acquisition of a work of art. For example, following the cutting of a single wood block, innumerable prints can be made merely by repeated inkings of the woodcut and the subsequent establishment of contact and pressure upon sheets of paper.

Materials, Processes, and Pressure

An examination of several materials and tools for printmaking (Figure 279) illustrates that many materials and processes are readily adaptable for simple graphic experiences. Prints may easily be obtained from a carved wood block, Duco-cement lines built upon a panel of glass, portions of inner tube glued to a cardboard backing, silk or organdy stretched within an embroidery hoop or wood frame, even through designs scratched into celluloid or cut into linoleum.

Ideas to be expressed through wood or linoleum are cut into these surfaces with sharp tools, knives, wood gouges, or linoleum cutters. Shapes can be cut with scissors for inner-tube printing, while lines emerge in the preparation of a Duco printing surface through the action of squirting out ridges of Duco cement directly from the tube. Printing ink is applied with a brayer (roller) onto the above surfaces, and imagery is transferred, through pressure, onto paper. Pressure can be applied in various ways: by rubbing the uncontacted side of the paper with the curved portion of a spoon, by running an uninked brayer over the paper, by gently but firmly applying one's full weight by stepping onto the reversed side of the printing material placed face down on paper, or through the action of a printing press. The nature of applied pressure would be determined, of course, by size of print and nature of process; for example, Duco cement on glass would not be sufficiently sturdy to accept excessive pressure exerted by a press.

Celluloid prints are obtained by first scratching and digging inscribed designs into the celluloid surface with a sharp pointed tool, such as a compass point or large sharp needle. Ink is not applied with a brayer, but rather is vigorously rubbed upon the surface with a tightly rolled section of paper toweling or newspaper. The entire surface of the celluloid is then wiped clean with a wad of cloth which results in ink being retained only in the inscribed or depressed portions of the surface. Paper is then placed upon the prepared celluloid, and pressure is applied by spoon rubbing or through the action of a printing press. A small commercial press or one improvised from a manual clothes wringer obtained from an old washing machine and fitted with a slab of oak for a printing bed usually offers the best

280   Tomah Rock, *lithograph, Santos Zingale, 1958. (Courtesy the Artist)*

results. Celluloid printing is dependent on a considerable amount of pressure; for the paper to be printed must be forced into contact with the ink located in the inscribed cavities of the celluloid.

While other printing processes are dependent on printing ink and share somewhat common relationships in transferring imagery, the silk screen process proves an exception. In the latter process thick paint, with properties of plasticity, is forced through unblocked mesh material, usually silk or organdy, through the action of a squeegee. Designs are registered on paper by open or unblocked sections of the screen permitting the passage of paint. Areas of the screen not contributing to the design are blocked, covered with a newsprint stencil or Pro-film (a commercial silk screen stencil paper), or coated with glue, varnish, or wax crayons. Thus portions of the screen are manipulated to deny or admit the transfer of paint.

Four Methods of Transfer

While innumerable materials, from Duco cement to inner tube and silk to celluloid, can be used in various graphic processes, there are but four major manners of printing: the planographic, stencil, relief, and intaglio methods. Their meanings are simple, they merely relate to the characteristics of the surface which imprints. "Planographic" refers to printing from a smooth surface such as a ground, inked slab of limestone used in the lithographic process. "Stencil" is self-explanatory and can be associated with a silk screen. "Relief," as the word implies, means the transfer of ink from the projecting or raised surfaces of a material, while "intaglio" is just the reverse, a method of creating impressions from indented or recessed surfaces which house ink. Each method offers unique opportunities to printmakers.

Rich patterns of dark and light are easily securable in the planographic process of lithography; for the process originates in a crayon drawing upon the printing surface and offers an accurate transfer of subtle value contrasts in subsequent printing. Notice how Santos Zingale secured full advantage of the value range obtainable in the use of a lithographic pencil — a greasy wax rather than graphite tool — in producing the invigorating interplays of dark and light which provide majesty to *Tomah Rock* (Figure 280). An outcropping of rock crowns the summit, while a curtain of trees in foreground contributes both a suggestion of transparency and grandeur through scale contrast to the towering rock formation which dominates the print.

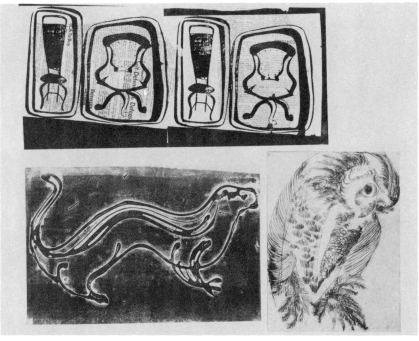

281   *Silk Screen, Duco, and Celluloid Prints.*

The stencil method of silk screen can also offer designs composed of bold masses as well as exciting color relationships. Color range, of course, depends on the number of stencils employed. A fluid and strong line quality can immediately emerge from a relief process such as Duco, while fine line and textural notations are readily obtainable from intaglio methods such as celluloid engraving (Figure 281).

Wood and linoleum cuts and inner tube, in addition to Duco, are relief processes; for their impressions result from the raised portions of their surfaces carrying ink onto paper. The intaglio process includes both etching and engraving; for each is dependent on indentations holding ink to create imagery when contacted with paper. The term "etching," derived from the Dutch term "etsen" which implies eating, relates to removing areas of copper through the use of acid. "Engraving," or "drypoint," refers to carving or inscribing a design upon a sheet of copper or celluloid with a sharp pointed instrument. The latter method results in linear rather than mass notations. Contemporary printmakers frequently combine both etching and engraving procedures upon a single copper plate to attain numerous interesting relationships within the intaglio process.

A Glance Toward the Past

All four methods, stencil, relief, intaglio, and planographic, have numerous roots in the past. The first three have long been practiced. A stencil-screen process was employed by ancient Chinese artists who wove an open mesh material from human hair and forced paint through its screen-like surface to decorate pottery and fabrics. Relief printing also had early roots in China; for the Chinese invention of paper, in A.D. 105, was soon followed by ink rubbings of inscriptions carved in stone. Incidentally, the earliest known use of type was found in Central Asia, and Orientals used movable type a full century before Gutenberg's discovery of typography.

Relief printing in the form of woodcuts has been used for many centuries, in both Europe and Asia, to express pictorial ideas. Many of these early prints, especially Japanese woodcuts, owing to their simplicity of form and bold use of color, greatly influenced European artists during the latter portion of the past century and continue to stimulate artists of the present.

Excellent examples of early intaglio printing are evident in the works of the fifteenth century German artist Martin Schongauer. A half century before Columbus beached a small boat on the shores of the Americas, Schongauer was producing rich and fascinating prints in nothern Europe. He lived in an age that greatly advanced the art of printing in Europe; for his period witnessed Johann Gutenberg developing movable type which, along with wood blocks and copper plates, provided great impetus to the communication of both word and pictorial imagery. His era viewed both the last act of an epoch, with its final curtain calls as the actors of the medieval drama were retiring deep into the wings, and the setting of the stage for the modern period.

Many now view Schongauer as one of the last performers of the medieval period; others consider him one of the first of a new age. Where would you place him? His copper engraving *The Temptation of Saint Anthony* is one example of the output of this prolific artist (Figure 282). Portraying Saint Anthony in a world of turmoil, beseeched and tempted by the evil demons of lust, greed, intolerance and a host of others, the print indicates that Schongauer was an imaginative and expressive artist with a full mastery of technique. His statement contains an extensive variety of textures secured through line engravings, great impact through dark and light

282 THE TEMPTATION OF SAINT ANTHONY, *engraving, Martin Schongauer, ca. 1445-1491. (Courtesy Metropolitan Museum of Art, Rogers Fund, 1920)*

SOL Y LUNA *(Sun and Moon), intaglio print, Mauricio Lasansky, 1945. (Courtesy the Artist)*

283

patterns, and rich and minute details which combine to form a pictorial design strong in line movement and emotional undertones.

The planographic method of transfer, featuring a perfectly level surface, is the most recent printing process to appear. In 1798 a Bavarian dramatist, Aloys Senefelder, found that areas of grease located upon flat limestone would retain ink, whereas other portions of the stone surface, if wet, would resist ink coverage. Thus lithography was born, and the Greek term "lithos," meaning stone, was aptly employed to partially describe the procedure. Though other materials such as zinc and aluminum are now often substituted, a slab of limestone, smoothly ground, is still favored by numerous printmarkers. The lithographic process consists in drawing with a greasy crayon upon a smooth surface followed by chemical treatments with gum arabic and nitric acid and subsequent inking which adheres only to the areas containing grease deposits originating from the initial drawing. Prints are secured through the actions of a lithographic press which forces, through a scraping pressure, ink from stone onto paper.

An Ancient Theme on a Copper Plate

The actions of sun and moon have provided artists of all periods and locales with meaningful symbols and themes for art. Mauricio Lasansky, one of the great printmakers of our century, employs such a theme in his intaglio print titled *Sol y Luna* (Sun and Moon) (Figure 283). Subjects, technique, and execution fuse as one to dramatically cry out of the eternal conflict of these natural adversaries. Lasansky's illuminating concept is strengthened and enhanced by complex interplays of imagery, suggestive of the intense forces of the sun and moon. Each

symbol counteracts the other and gains emphasis through contrast with adjacent areas of serenity. Further tensions are implied through great variations in line direction and the relationships of shapes and values in space. The complete potential of the copper plate as a printing surface is attained in the expressions of Mauricio Lasansky; for his prints reveal a link with the great print tradition of the past while in harmony with and extending the possibilities of contemporary expression.

Close observation of *Sol y Luna* indicates many unusual treatments of surface and space achieved through both engraving and etching. What qualities do you notice upon an examination of this print? How would you portray the conflict between sun and moon? Such a struggle of natural forces has long been a concern of individuals, tribes, and empires. Men have always questioned their world and, when peering skyward, naturally wondered about the objects which fill the sky. History tells us that societies worshiped and feared the passage of clouds; moon, sun, and even the distant stars. For instance, long ago inhabitants of North America chanted and danced for rain from the clouds and made human sacrifices to the sun. Far to the south along the dry coastal sands of Peru a society honored the moon as the giver of dew and pictured the sun as a demon who scorched their arid lands. Their inland brothers, the Incas, were called the "people of the sun." Living high in the Andes, they reversed the procedure of the coastal Indians by worshiping the sun as the provider of warmth to their environment of bitter cold and frigid winds. In southern Africa the Hottentot tribe worshiped the moon, while far to the north the Egyptians also honored the moon as well as the sun

god Ra. To the east Assyrians represented the sun as the mighty god Assur, and Persian, Babylonian, and Hindu also paid homage to the sun. Appolo and Helios were Greek sun deities, while the birthday of the unconquered sun, Dies Natalis Invicti Solis, was a sacred day throughout the Roman Empire. Inscriptions upon rock in Denmark indicate early sun worship even in northern Europe. In the far east the Chinese believed in Yang and Yin, terms which represented negative and positive forces in nature. This duality of force was evident in passive earth and active sun, seasons of sowing and harvesting, winter and summer, light and darkness. Mauricio Lasansky's *Sol y Luna* indeed voices an ageless theme.

Crayon, Stone, Humor, and Pathos

Alfred Sessler employs the lithographic process in a highly personal manner, thereby creating sensitive prints frequently warm with wit. His crayon drawings, which are subsequently printed, communicate the actions and characteristics of man in intriguing arrangements of dark and light. Born and raised in an urban environment and keenly interested in people who inhabit the city, his social commentaries, in the tradition of Rembrandt and Daumier, reveal the effects and contradictions of life. An artist with complete mastery of his craft, Sessler's lithographic prints illustrate man's powers of expression with crayon upon stone. Referring to his lithographic print *Clown Head* (Figure 284) he speaks of both the subject and his working procedure:

284   CLOWN HEAD, *lithograph, Alfred Sessler, 1956. (Courtesy the Artist)*

In order of their importance the elements that add up to form my visual statement are content, manipulative potential in the materials worked with and upon, and traditional and current experiments in the area of visual expression.

I have always held a sympathetic feeling towards the expressions of the masters of satire in art and literature.

The clown as used in my work is a personal symbol. He can be a multitude of things, noble, mean, humble, egocentric. Through him I release various statements reflecting the relationship between myself and the human environment surrounding me. More often than not the resultant image is satire in its fullest sense.

An important element is the medium or the material I work with. In this case the lithograph with its particular characteristics determines the character of the image to a great extent. Also, although not immediately apparent, contemporary experimentation has been influential in the development of the form I use in my work.

Silk Screen, Thistles, and a Word About Botany

Through knowledge of the silk screen process, design sensitivity, and experimental attitudes, artists such as Dean Meeker achieve colorful and vigorous prints. Regarding his *Thermotropic Thistle* (Figure 285) he says,

> The subject is a thistle pod and various associated forms. The subject is of course magnified. In several preliminary drawings the various aspects of the thistle organism were developed. These characteristics, or aspects, were then formalized in an organization of implied space-balance, with careful attention given to value and tactile qualities.
>
> This serigraph print was made with six separate stencils, one for each color; the colors being transparent developed additional colors. The stencils were made on silk screens, first drawn with a resist (toosh) then covered with glue. When the resist was washed out the stencil was then ready for printing since the remaining glue blocked out areas not to be printed. Paint was then pressed through the stencil openings with a squeegee resulting in a transfer onto paper.

Additional insight into theme hinges on an understanding of the meaning of "thermotropic" as used in the title. Botanists tell us that it relates to movement in growing plant organs brought about by the influence of heat or cold. Curvature in plants may be either positive thermotropic, that is, toward a source of heat, or negative, away from the source. Meeker frequently prints such subjects as underwater vegetation, bones, and weeds as strong sensuous symbols in tune with the laws of nature; for a keenness of concept enables him to sense pictorial possibilities in objects and concepts overlooked by less observant eyes.

285   Thermotropic Thistle, *silk screen print, Dean Meeker, 1957. (Courtesy the Artist)*

JAZZ SERIES, No. II, *woodcut print, Bruce Sho-baken, 1958. (Courtesy the Artist)*

286

287   THE JUGGLER, *linoleum print, Robert Marx, 1955. (Courtesy the Artist)*

Sounds of Our Century Conveyed Through Wood

Numerous artists capture the spirit and vitality of twentieth-century life in expressions incorporating various printing methods. Highly charged designs — activated, portraying rhythmic and energized moods, suggesting a feeling or comprehensive impression rather than visual particulars—are apparent features of much contemporary printmaking. Bruce Shobaken clearly indicates such intentions in correlating sensations of sound and sight in his woodcut *Jazz Series No. II* (Figure 286) when he says:

Jazz Series No. II is one of a series of woodcuts in which I attempted to evoke the "look" and "feel" of jazz music. Using forms that were suggested to me by jazz sounds, I tried to convey some of the excitement, spontaneity and drive inherent to jazz. In conceiving of the series, I decided at the outset that purely representational forms would be ill-suited to my intent; what I wanted was not the picture of jazz being played by musicians, but rather the look of how jazz sounds.

The qualities characteristic of the woodcut seemed most compatible to my idea. While cutting the blocks I worked directly, looking for concise and clear forms, striving for a fluidity and boldness which would carry the rhythm and pulse of the music. Mine was a commitment to creating a vibrancy; to expressing a feeling.

Activities in Space Cut into Linoleum

Have you ever imagined what juggling feels like with its rapid movements in space and blurring forms? Robert Marx uses linoleum rather than wood to reveal his version of this activity and, referring to his print *The Juggler* (Figure 287), explains:

> The Juggler is an idea abstracted from the naturalistic way of seeing nature. Any idea, in order to be visualized, needs a variety of forms and actions which are ordered by an artist so that a rightness happens in the picture.

Subjects that involve rapid action hold his interest as exciting means of providing intriguing organization and impact to works of art. Vivid movements suggesting rapid projections in space are therefore often integrated into highly creative forms by this artist. His topics grow out of a great variety of experiences, from observing the actions of flying insects to considering episodes dealing with flight which reach back to antiquity. In searching for appropriate themes for prints, Marx makes no distinction between fact and fantasy, reality and myth, or present and past. He has even related, in contemporary pictorial terms, the ancient Greek myth of Icarus, the first youth to fly. Possibly you recall the story. Fitted with wings constructed by his father Daedalus, Icarus soared high into the sky to flee from Minos, the King of Crete. Venturing too close to the sun proved his undoing; for the intense heat from the sun melted the wax fastening his wings. The youth, so the Greeks relate, fluttered for a moment, then fell, crashing into the sea.

Easily Obtained Materials and Simple Processes

While a few schools have large presses and a wealth of equipment enabling processes such as lithography and copper intaglio, these circumstances are unfortunately rare. Excellent prints, however, need not be dependent on elaborate equipment or expensive materials; for through ingenuity many exciting experiences are readily available. Simple facilities and modifications which can easily be made enable an extensive range of printing. Several possibilities are substituting celluloid for copper, improvising a washing machine wringer as a press, securing planks for wood cuts from lumber yard or carpenter shop waste bins, adding soap to tempera for silk screen paint, using organdy rather than silk, and employing cardboard and discarded inner tubes. Good prints depend not on specific equipment, tools, and materials, but rather on originality and sensitivity in expressing ideas in visually appealing forms.

Difficulties in printing usually arise from technical aspects and can soon be remedied through actual experience in pulling or registering prints. Two factors which at times cause beginners undue difficulty are improper inking and insufficient printing pressure. Several comments relating to these two matters may prove pertinent. Oil-based ink usually provides better results than water-based inks, though it necessitates turpentine in cleaning equipment and a longer drying period for prints. Printing ink should be placed upon relief surfaces with an even coverage. The brayer or roller has been designed for this purpose, and its correct use assures the proper deposit. To coat the brayer with ink involves placing a small amount of ink on a hard nonporous material — a small sheet of glass, block of plastic tile, or cookie sheet — which serves to transfer ink onto the brayer. This can be accomplished by rolling the brayer over the surface containing the ink until the ink is spread smooth on the original surface and completely covers the surface of the brayer. The inked brayer is then rolled over the relief surface — wood cut, linoleum, Duco, or whatever — in a manner which assures an even and complete coverage. The inked relief surface when then contacted with paper must have an equal amount of pressure applied throughout the entire surface. The first print, called a proof, should be studied; if modifications in design are desired, the relief surface can be further treated by the addition or removal of details. If the proof appears thick and blurred, it probably is due to an excessive amount of ink originally applied to the relief, while a faint print indicates insufficient ink or inadequate pressure. If slightly dampened with water before printed upon, paper will often assure clearer and more satisfactory prints. Enough about particulars, let's examine several specific possibilities for graphic explorations.

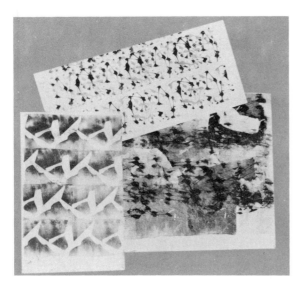

288   BRAYER INVESTIGATIONS, *student, Oak Park and River Forest High School, Ill.*

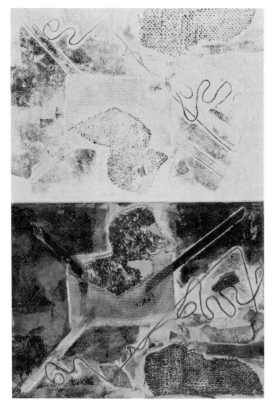

289   EXPLORING MAN MADE MATERIALS, *burlap, sandpaper, screen, and string print, student, Williamsport High School, Pa.*

Most Anything Goes

Consider Figures 288 to 291. Can you guess how and why these ventures were undertaken? *Brayer Investigations* (Figure 288) indicates a high school student's search for interesting effects obtainable through the use of the brayer directly upon paper. Such explorative ventures unearth intriguing fusions of colors and unfold abstract patterns which can provide insight into numerous effects usable in printmaking. The resulting awareness can also be incorporated into activities beyond the making of prints in possibly suggesting backgrounds for posters and even ideas for textiles, wall hanging, scarfs, or drapery. Diversified brayer movements — short and long, overlapping, patting sequences — and the use of paper stencils, string wrapped around rollers, rough-surfaced materials placed beneath paper before brayer contacts paper, and many other means can serve to expand one's knowledge of unusual printing potentials. Often a tin can can even be substituted for the brayer and foreign material — felt, burlap, or rubber bands — applied to the can, inked, and rolled across paper.

Exploring Man Made Materials (Figure 289) consists of both a number of materials such as string, screen, burlap, and sandpaper glued to a cardboard surface and the printed patterns emerging from the arrangement following its inking and contact with paper. The result indicates the personal acquisition of several answers on the part of the high school student undertaking the activity. Such studies can lead toward explicit and expressive textural designs and figurative or abstract prints depending on the intentions of the doer. Can you think of five or six other materials which could be employed in a printing investigation on your part? How about bottle caps, bits of cork, sponge, or cardboard? Now you add three. Which would suggest rough and which smooth surfaces in the final print? What sorts of patterns could emerge from such an activity?

A decision to study the printed characteristics of natural surfaces encouraged a university student to

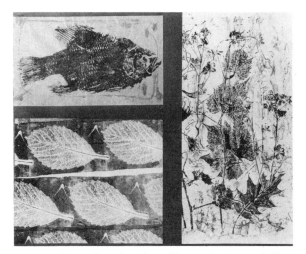

290   *Direct Transfers from Nature, Leaves, and Fish, University student.*

produce direct transfers from nature (Figure 290). Such studies, evolving from coating substances with ink and pressing tissue paper against their surfaces or inking and braying or pressing in various related ways, disclose basic value patterns and various form notations. In such undertakings a soft brayer made of gelatine, rather than a hard rubber brayer, permits crisper transfers. Printing directly from natural forms has long been practiced by Oriental artists, and such experiences undoubtedly sensitized their keenness of concept. The validity of direct transfers from nature lie in their power of initial stimulation; however, personal improvisations and original constructions must follow to carry results beyond mere factual investigations. Such explorations are thus a means to an end rather than the end itself. One must keep in mind that art is not a mirror held to nature, though such was advocated in the past; rather, art is the creative interpretation and original rearrangement of the mirrored image.

Notice the evidences of invention and ingenuity in *Multi-Experimental Abstraction* (Figure 291). The print grew out of previous inquiries into printing characteristics of various surfaces on the part of a university student. Segments of contrasting colored paper pasted upon a printed surface enriched from contact with inked string and cardboard shapes, provides variation and impact to the design. Areas of transparencies and active placements in space further enhance the experimental print. Such ventures can be joyfully pursued as abstract patterns or, with a few deft additions or modifications, transformed into statements with figurative implications. Study the print for a moment. What can you imagine in association with the design? Moving traffic, a beach theme? Or does it remain an intriguing complete abstraction?

The field of graphic inquiry is vast, because many explorative directions may be taken to attain elegant prints. When treated with a creative hand, most anything goes.

291   Multi-Experimental Abstraction, *brayer, string, and applied paper, University student.*

292 FACES, *inner-tube print, University student.*

293 ROOMMATES, *woodcut print, University student.*

The Tube from an Auto

Faces (Figure 292), composed of simple shapes organized in an ornate but concise arrangement, harmonizes with the characteristics of the material employed. The university student considered the nature of inner tube, its cutting features and ease of large shape transfer, in conceiving of the design treatment. The execution of the print involved the preparation of two separate plates, one section of cardboard containing the inner-tube segments relating to the white masses of the print and the other plate contributing the dark areas. The incorporation of two plates permitted the acquisition of a three-color print in that medium-brown paper provided background color and each of the two plates contributed a color. The print possesses a touch of the whimsical in the implied facial expressions.

The process employed by the student to obtain *Faces* was both direct and uncomplicated. Following sketching and planning with cut paper, suitable imagery was determined and segments of inner tube were cut with scissors to correspond to the idea. The inner-tube shapes were then glued to firm cardboard; however, wood or Masonite could also serve as backing. Following the application of glue, several books were placed upon the relief surface to prevent curling and loss of contact between inner-tube pieces and cardboard during the drying period. The relief surface was subsequently inked with a brayer and pressed against dampened construction paper. While pressure to transfer ink onto paper may be applied by rubbing the uncontacted side of the paper with the rounded portion of a spoon, *Faces* was printed through the application of body weight. This procedure entailed placing a pad of newspaper on a floor and arranging upon the soft bed a sheet of slightly damp construction paper. The inked inner-tube design was then placed face down upon the construction paper and pressure was applied by stepping onto the cardboard backing and exerting full body weight. The foot was gently shifted several times to distribute pressure over the entire area of the print; for owing to size, the surface to be printed warranted such a treatment. The cardboard containing the tube relief was then lifted from the construction paper to expose the transferred design.

Consider Grain, Cut, Attain

Woods such as pine or fir, owing to the ease of cutting into and removing portions of their surface, offer excellent opportunities for printmaking. In woodcuts the surface removed permits the color of the paper printed upon to emerge as an inherent portion of the design, while the remaining wood surface carries ink onto the paper. An examination of *Roommates* (Figure 293) indicates that the light areas of the print relate to areas on the original wood surface which were cut away by gouges or wood chisels. Note the various ways the wood was removed and how each method contributed distinctive effects to the design. Large masses interestingly contrast with minute areas, evidently removed through a flicking action in handling the tool, and both intermingle with thick and thin lines to simulate textures and define form.

Personally conducted investigations with knife, gouge, or chisel and scraps of wood can soon disclose many avenues of treating wood surfaces. A word of caution is warranted, however. Keep in mind that the cutting tools are sharp instruments, and never place the hand restraining the wood block forward of the direction in which the tool is cutting. Grasp the wood surface to the rear so that tool movements are away from rather than toward hand and body; then if the tool slips, it will not contact flesh. Undesired wood areas should be removed with a number of shallow cuts, slowly and thoughtfully. Additional wood can be removed at any time; however, once gone, it can not be replaced. Whenever possible, cut in the same direction as the wood grain, and when feasible, incorporate the grain of the wood, if sufficiently pronounced to print, into the design of the imagery to be printed. Grain may provide vigorous and exciting relationships, especially if a rough piece of wood with an obvious grain pattern is employed. Many printmakers run an inked brayer over the wood and print upon paper to study the resulting grain pattern before cutting into the wood. This permits preliminary planning and may even suggest a subject or theme if viewed with an active imagination.

Wood cuts can be inked and printed in the same manners employed in inner-tube printing. Following the pulling of a proof, more detailing can be achieved by additional cutting or added emphasis can be gained by varying the paper background. Creative action, in printmaking, as well as all other areas of art, is a fluid process in that constant choices and alternate courses are always open for exploration. For instance, many means are available for adding color in woodcut prints beyond the usual means of employing more than one wood block. Several colors of ink can be placed on a single woodcut, with each color located upon a particular area of the wood surface, or the paper to be printed upon may receive various preliminary treatments. It may be stained before being printed upon or directly treated with a brayer, even enriched through contrasting colored paper segments glued to its surface. Limitations are defined merely by the experience and inventive power of the printmaker.

Squeezing Out a Form

Squirting Duco cement directly from a tube upon a sheet of glass and subsequent printing enabled high school students to create simple and intriguing images of *Horses and Duck* (Figure 294). This unique process permits drawings to be rapidly transformed into printed forms which, while not possessive of subtle details, are strong and bold in the treatment.

While Masonite, wood, or any firm surface can be employed as a base for the Duco cement, glass, owing to its transparency, has a particular advantage. A pencil sketch placed beneath the glass can easily be recorded by squirting a continuous thick line of Duco, corresponding to the underlying drawing, upon the glass surface. A liberal amount of cement should be used in building lines, and the Duco must be permitted to dry thoroughly before undertaking subsequent steps. Printing may be accomplished in either of two manners. Slightly damp paper placed on an uninked Duco surface can be printed by rolling an inked brayer over the paper surface. The other method of registering the design consists in inking the Duco surface with a brayer, placing paper upon the inked surface, and applying pressure by rubbing with the palm of the hand or a spoon or running an uninked brayer over the paper surface. Through experimental color-mingling, either method offers the means of obtaining gay results which convey their intentions through energetic lines. Duco printing is highly suited for many purposes ranging from creating large wall prints to adding accents to greeting cards.

Scratching Out an Image

A sharp pointed tool, sheet of celluloid, ink, and paper combined with skill, design sensitivity, knowledge, and imagination can result in intense involvement and provide a true sense of accomplishment. Such was the case for the producers of *The Strutter* and *Cat 'n Kittens* (Figures 295, 296). Intricate details, richly implied textures, and intriguing themes held their concern and, when expressed in printed form, increased their possessions. Although separated by age, the two students share several traits: a lightness of hand, courage, and a common experience in an intaglio process. Notice how the junior high school student treated the surface of his bird with unusual and decorative feathery notations which complement the proud stance of the bird. The university student reversed the procedure in *Cat 'n*

294 HORSES AND DUCK, *Duco prints, students, Wisconsin High School, Madison, Wisc.*

Kittens by emphasizing the main form through surrounding details rather than numerous and explicit detailing within the form itself. Thus the animals are mainly implied through definite background identification which provides sensations of serenity and contentment to the theme. Is this consistent with the subject? How do the treatments of space differ in the two prints?

A few words about material and printing process will give insight into the technical aspects of celluloid engraving, also called dry point. Suitable celluloid may be obtained through art supply houses or possibly locally from auto supply or hobby shops; 25/000 gauge or thicker provides satisfying results. A center punch, single-edge razor blade, large needle, compass point, portion of welding rod sharpened to a point on a grinding wheel, or similar sharp-pointed instrument can be used to incise or scratch a design into the celluloid. Placing the celluloid over a preliminary pencil or ink drawing and tracing the main lines serves as an effective means of getting underway; later, a sheet of dark paper inserted beneath the celluloid permits a clear examination of the scratched lines and assists further modifications. Since ink is to be retained in the material, the inscribed lines should vary in thickness for contrast, and if large passages of dark are desired, a number of cross-hatched lines or closely paralleling lines should be cut into the celluloid surface. Following the engraving, a dab of ink can be spread upon the celluloid and forced into the inscribed cavities by vigorously rubbing with a dabber constructed from tightly rolled paper towels or newspaper firmly tied or taped into a short column-like form which can easily be grasped in the hand. The plate can then be wiped clean with a wad of cheesecloth or tarlatan, thus permitting ink to be retained only in the indentations. Proper transfer demands a considerable amount of pressure, and while the spoon-rubbing method of printing can be employed, the most satisfactory results are obtained through the use of a commercial press or a washing machine wringer fitted with an oak bed and padding. The printing paper should be damp; newsprint may be used for proofs, and heavier drawing paper, provided a press is available, can serve for final prints. The distribution of values can be modified somewhat through a controlled wiping of the inked celluloid before printing.

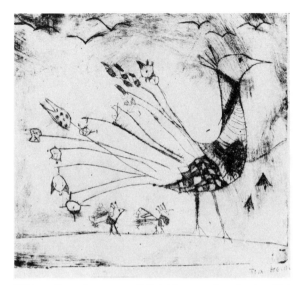

295   THE STRUTTER, *Celluloid engraving. Junior high school student, Wisconsin High School, Madison, Wisconsin.*

296   CAT 'N KITTENS, *Celluloid engraving, University student.*

Screening Ideas

An intermingling of shapes, values, and colors contributes energetic movements to the semiabstract pattern comprising the *Musician* (Figure 297). This high school student's silk screen print is organized through rhythmical changes which achieve a fluctuating tempo in keeping with the musical theme. The performer, gayly costumed as a harlequin, is closely united with background, resulting in a complete dependency of parts as background and foreground tend to become one. Gold, black, red, and white play throughout the composition and join both figurative implications and design qualities in richly conveying impressions of invention and song.

The print involved the registering of three impressions, one for each color, and also took advantage of the white paper in using its light relationship as an inherent feature of the design. The process did not necessitate construction of three different frames and screens, but rather depended upon modifications in the screen surface of a single frame. Different Profilm or Water Sol stencils blocked portions of the screen during various phases of the process, with one stencil serving to transfer each color. A number of identical impressions were made, the stencil was changed, and additional impressions were recorded. Thus, through succeeding printing stages, the imagery evolved and a number of prints were made.

Silk screen prints can be secured in a number of manners involving rather simple procedures. Frames may be constructed from one- by two-inch fir lumber or even secured by removing the bottom and using the sides of a cigar box. Inexpensive organdy, rather than silk, may then be tightly stretched and secured to the bottom of the frame with staples or drawn up along the outside and tacked. Gummed kraft tape should be applied along inside areas where frame and organdy meet and then be sealed with shellac. While commercial silk screen paint is desirable, paint can be improvised by mixing powdered or liquid tempera with soap powder, such as Ivory Snow, until a liquid with a thick cream-like consistency is achieved. If not obtainable, the usual rubber squeegee employed in dragging the paint across the screen may be replaced by a section of stiff cardboard. The screen may be blocked with a wax paper or newsprint stencil rather than a commercial film. Sections of the screen not intended to pass paint can also be blocked with wax crayons, LePage's glue diluted with water, varnish, or shellac. Newsprint or waxpaper stencils are adhered to the screen by merely pulling one print; for the paint itself will bind the stencil to the organdy

297   MUSICIAN, *silk screen print, student, Oak Park and River Forest High School, Ill.*

298   *Each Process Has Distinct Qualities.*

surface. If newsprint is employed, it should be coated with shellac immediately following its application to the screen to prevent paint absorption and bleeding. Prints are secured by placing paint inside the frame and moving the paint, with pressure applied with squeegee, across the inner surface of the screen. The unblocked areas of the screen permit the passage of paint to an underlying paper surface which registers the impression. Several actual experiences in printing familiarize one with the process and provide the feel of creating silk screen imagery.

Suspense and Surprise

From the preciseness of etching to the line spontaneity of Duco, each printmaking method offers particular possibilities and unique achievements (Figure 298). Determining in part whether line or mass, flat pattern or deeply implied depth, great detail or simplicity should be brought to bear, each process actually assists in shaping subject matter. Anticipating these results frequently builds suspense, and upon attainment the sought-after results can fulfill pleasant expectations or keenly surprise. Unexpected transformations as lines, shapes, textures, values, and colors assume new relationships in transfer — at times even the paper appears to sparkle — can point toward new potentials and challenges. Sensing these discoveries, as the proof is peeled from a woodcut or an intaglio print is closely examined, exposes many avenues of rearranging, and reproducing ideas. Even in registering a leaf, suddenly it can be spring if, as the form repeats, ensuing imagery happenings instill feelings of growth and awareness which permeate beyond the paper's border. Think for a moment of the intended meaning of the preceding sentence.

TOPICS FOR CONSIDERATION

1. What unique advantage does the graphic arts extend which no other art area can offer?
2. Explain the differences between the planographic, stencil, relief, and intaglio printing methods.
3. What are the differences in imagery secured through the silk screen process, wood cuts, and copper engravings? Consider treatment of both line and mass as well as textural implications.
4. How does an engraving differ from an etching?
5. List various means by which additional colors can be secured in wood-cut prints.
6. How can scrap materials be used in various printing undertakings?
7. While knowledge of process is essential, why is an experimental attitude also important in printmaking?

SUGGESTED ACTIVITIES

1. Produce a print, at least 6 by 12 inches in size, with a religious theme. Use pine or battleship linoleum and stress a variety of line treatments within the imagery. Mat and display your print.
2. With scrap materials, such as bits of sponge or screen, sandpaper, string, and burlap, print an abstraction. You may also incorporate the actions of a brayer into the background; however, emphasize the transference of divergent textural impressions.
3. With ducco or celluloid, create a print revealing an imaginary insect. If the former process is selected, exaggerate linear relationships. However, if celluloid is chosen, place the emphasis on distorted and fantastic textural surfaces. Several bold pencil sketches may assist in conceiving suitable possibilities in either venture. If you prefer, you may substitute your favorite character from literature for subject matter.

4. Print a cityscape or sports endeavor with inner tube or cardboard. Preliminary studies with cut construction paper can rapidly indicate how several simple shapes may be combined to relate the theme. Major stress should be placed on discovering a pattern involving large basic shapes and a minimum of small details.

5. Create a design suitable for either a greeting card or a drapery. The solution can be nonobjective or figurative and the process dependent on personal preference. Print on appropriate paper or cloth. Following any desired modifications and refinements, repeat the printing process and use the results for the proper holiday or enrichment for your home.

APPROPRIATE REFERENCES AND READINGS

Periodical

Journal of Commercial Art, Palo Alto, Calif.: Coyne and Blanchard, Inc., 809 San Antonio Rd.

Texts

HELLER, JULES. *Printmaking Today*, New York: Henry Holt & Co., 1958.

IVINS, WILLIAM M., JR. *How Prints Look*, Beacon Paperback, Boston: Beacon Press, 1958.

PETERDI, GABOR, *Printing Methods Old and New*, New York: The Macmillan Co., 1959.

SACHS, PAUL J. *Modern Prints and Drawings*, New York: Alfred A. Knopf, Inc., 1954.

9

SCULPTURE, DISCOVERIES IN THREE-DIMENSIONAL FORM

Artists have come to realize that, like life itself, art is not a direction in which there may be progress, as if it were a road or railway line, but rather an area of limitless imaginative possibilities that extends in every conceivable direction as far as the heart and hand may reach. They do not expect to explain things or to find a single truth that will uncover the entire nature of reality. Neither do the scientists. They do, however, hope to enlarge our relationship with the world, to open our eyes to new aspects of the living mystery of creation and to offer certain large and small truths of human experience for our sharing.

GORDON BAILEY WASHBURN[1]

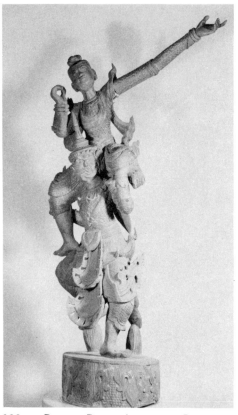

299   DEMON BILAN ABDUCTING PRINCESS, *carved wood (38 inches high), Cambodia. (Courtesy Wright Art Center, Beloit College)*

Traditional Implications

Sculptors have found it possible, no matter what their environment, from the barren far north to the rain-soaked jungles of the Equator, to locate suitable materials to express their experiences and beliefs. The Eskimo carved walrus bone, while South Sea islanders shaped fibers and wood. The African carved segments of ivory from elephant tusks, cast forms in bronze, and used a variety of woods. The Oriental artist also employed bronze and often carved jade. The American Indian composed bits of wood, fur, and feathers, while the Greeks dragged massive blocks of marble from their quarries. Indeed the only limitations in the use of materials were due to their availability, the amassed knowledge and skills developed by the particular societies, and the inherent potentials of the specific materials.

[1] Mr. Washburn is Director, Department of Fine Arts, Carnegie Institute, and Chairman, Pittsburgh International Exhibition of Contemporary Painting and Sculpture. Quotation is from the Introduction to the 1958 Catalogue of the Pittsburgh International Exhibition of Contemporary Painting and Sculpture.

It would be a great misconception to consider ancient or primitive sculpture as naïve or crude; for such works were often indicative of well-organized and somewhat sophisticated societies and were keenly expressed and elegantly executed. Frequently, exaggerations were due not to any supposed lack of ability, but to a deliberate intention to arouse and intensify feelings on the viewer's part. Sometimes the forms resulted from the prescribed imagery developed over a long period of time within the society. Photograph-like illusions were seldom desired.

Sculptural form solutions have ranged from the idealized features chiseled into stone by Greeks, active during the Golden Age, to the elongated treatments obtained by Gothic carvers. Results have been excessively treated with comprehensive and precise detailing or highly economical and devoid of details. Cambodian carvers exemplify the former relationships in tediously carving an abundance of minute and specific notations within their ornate wood sculptures (Figure 299). Mexican carvers of long ago tended to favor stone and concise and compact solutions in their three-dimensional forms (Figure 300). While the shaping characteristics of wood and stone differ greatly, and in part determine form possibilities, such diverse solutions go beyond any material difference; for imagery is also greatly determined by visual and social customs in different periods and societies. Thus divergent views and desires affecting form treatments are prevalent features in the history of sculpture. This assures a vast diversity in the area of historical sculpture, enabling specific examples to be plucked to justify or refute most any aesthetic notion or judgment value. Those who favor virtuosity, displays of technical skill, and refined factual sculpture can feel secure in viewing the past. Others, convinced of the validity of great distortion, strong evidences of human involvement, and imaginative imagery, look elsewhere and find examples to back their claims. One of the great wonders and blessings of art is the existence of this fertile field covered with innumerable epic achievements in shallow and deep relief, as well as freestanding sculpture. Great civilizations planted the crop and others continue the seeding. Great areas of the field have now been transplanted in museums or, transformed into pictorial images, captured on film or inserted into books. The intriguing characteristics of this sculptural field, whether actual or transposed, seem to guarantee a bit of most anything if one searches to find or reinforce his way.

300   WOMAN, *carved stone, Southwestern Mexico, 15th century. (Courtesy Philadelphia Museum of Art)*

301   IMAGES OUTSIDE CRATER OF RANO RARAKU, *carved tufa, Easter Islands. (Courtesy American Museum of Natural History)*

302   THE PRESIDENTS, *Mount Rushmore National Memorial, carved granite, Gutzon Borglum and Son, 1927-1941. (Courtesy Publicity Division, South Dakota Dept. of Highways)*

The Many Roles of Sculpture: From Easter Island to the Lands of Daniel Boone

Think of a gentle sea lolling against a small island. As dawn breaks, great stone heads, perched on bluffs, slowly appear. Repeating an occurrence centuries old, they stare seaward, beyond their island home, beyond the lapping edges of the South Pacific (Figure 301). Measuring from three to thirty-six feet in height, a total of 550 of these sculptures cover the forty-six square mile island; therefore, their number averages to slightly more than twelve for each square mile. Carved from tufa, a stone of compressed volcanic ash, all are similar in consisting of huge elongated forms sharply and concisely featured. What purposes did they fulfill? One can only guess. Authorities conclude that many lined ancient roadways to represent certain clans, while others were placed on large stone burial platforms to honor ancestors. More specific reasons regarding their uses remain clouded in mystery; for the monumental stone heads stand mute. Even Polynesian inhabitants, who once knew, have long vanished.

Imagine a Dakota mountain far inland from the Pacific, its locale not distant from where, but yesterday, tribal chieftains held their councils and the Seventh Cavalry rode into a circle of death. The land is peaceful now, and Great White Fathers survey the Western domain (Figure 302). The very face of nature was transformed through dynamite and power tools to attain their features. The sculptor, Gutzon Borglum, directed the feat, and its purpose is readily apparent: to portray, for posterity, through monumental carvings, the compassion and strength of America's most illustrious sons. Visible from a distance of 60 miles and estimated to last for 100,000 years, these great stone faces far surpass in size and permanency the Polynesians' efforts. The words and actions of Washington, Jefferson, Lincoln, and Theodore Roosevelt are thus assured for the minds and hearts of innumerable generations yet to come. And who knows which future greats will also be imprinted upon this granite mountain wall? There is room for more.

In another segment of the world, somewhat midway between Easter Island and Mount Rushmore, in both time and space, many sculptural columns once pierced a coastal skyline (Figure 303). Towering over sprawling Indian villages of hunters and fishermen, they were covered with stylized and expressive imagery. The poles were attained through the efforts of Indian sculptors who cut and stripped native trees. The sculptors then carved and added projections, then painted and erected their imaginative trees. What purpose did they serve? They asked the blessings of spirit gods and identified the clans. Each clan, composed of several families, possessed its own pole brightly painted and carved with symbols of humans, animals, or birds. Certain clans called on the bear or beaver for protection, while others sought the cunning of the raven. It was felt the spirits of these creatures would hover over and guide the fortunes of the clan, provided their images were carved on the column. While the majority of these great totem poles have decayed owing to the ravages of weather, a few remain. Planted in museums or located outdoors as tourist attractions, they now stand for a different purpose in the twentieth-century landscape.

Though few now call upon the raven or look toward the beaver, such was not always the case. Symbols of creatures of sky and forest have prominently and universally been presented in sculptural forms. While some have measured as high as trees and others were but a mere inch or two, all have played a major role in the drama of man's past. In great part the very history of man is modeled in clay or preserved in wood, stone, or metal. Even fragments can tell a story; archeologists have unearthed in a French cavern clay segments of what was once a cave man's sculpture representing a bear nearly four feet in length. The fragments had been

303   *Totem Poles of the Northwest Carvers. (Courtesy Washington State Museum)*

304 Bird Amulet, *carved stone, Mound Builders, Ohio Territory. (Courtesy Ohio* **Historical Society)**

305 Tiger, *bronze container, China, Chou Dynasty, 1122-255* B.C. *(Courtesy Freer Gallery of Art, Washington, D. C.)*

mutilated by dart thrusts vigorously delivered by early man. Through destroying this image, the cave dweller reasoned, the threat of his actual adversaries, the huge cave bears, would be eliminated. This destructive act served to provide man with confidence in future encounters with his ferocious enemy. After all, in contesting living quarters with a snarling half-ton creature capable of shattering the sturdiest man with one blow, courage was an essential asset. Thus sculpture of animals gave man one means of beginning his long and hazardous journey toward mastering his world.

One can only ponder on the qualities and sizes of many sculptures which, now decomposed in the earth, escape the eyes of man. Many, however, remain to tell of ageless rituals and superstitions and illustrate the skills and ingenuity of ancient peoples. Not so long ago, American Indians silently moving through Eastern woodlands dangled tiny sculptures from their necks (Figure 304). Shaped to represent animals or birds, the forms were pierced and laced with rawhide to function as necklaces. Precisely carved and inscribed, they served to guard against accidents or witchcraft. This practice should not be surprising to many moderns, who often carry or associate a rabbit's foot with luck or good fortune. Often, animal and bird sculptures were viewed as amulets or fetishes and were thought able to transfer the powers of the creature portrayed to the producer, viewer, or clan. Fetishes were considered more powerful than amulets in actually being the dwelling place of spirits. Therefore, they were cut into or totally destroyed to release or eliminate the imprisoned spirit. Sculpture has a long and complex tradition in being used in involved mystical rituals of all sorts. Purposes were also often extended in producing sculpture to act as receptacles, thereby advancing utilitarian aspects. Many examples of clay, wood, and metal modeled as animal or bird sculptural containers exist in all regions of the world (Figure 305). Some are highly pot-like, while others remain quite close to sculpture. Their intentions were in part to assure the safety of the stored contents in calling upon the protection of the tiger, owl, or dragon who represented various deities or spirits.

Animals and their symbolic two- and three-dimensional representations are interwoven into the fabric of history. For instance, consider the writings of the Macedonian historian, Polyaenus. Writing about the strategy of war, during the second century, he relates a fascinating episode which indicates the high esteem held by ancient people for animals. Polyaenus states that, in 525 B.C., the Persian leader Cambyses conquered Egypt by taking into account the Egyptians' reverence for animals. The Persians merely drove cats, dogs, and sheep in front of their advancing troops, and the Egyptians refused to release their arrows for fear of injuring the supposedly sacred creatures. Animals, particularly cats, were often portrayed in stone by Egyptian carvers of long ago. These little, cunning creatures were thought to be representatives of the goddess Bastet, the protectress of women.

Far from the eastern basin of the Mediterranean, Mexican Indians created innumerable clay sculptures of dogs. Attitudes toward their use varied even within the land. The Tarascan culture of western Mexico felt the dog represented certain virtues. However, their eastern neighbors, the Aztecs, looked upon the dog as symbolizing Mictlautecuhti, the lord of the region of death, and indicative of evil. At approximately the same time but across the Atlantic, Richard the Lion Hearted rallied decorated troops to embark on a great crusade. The enthusiastic armored warriors stood with battle-axes and lances amid a field of pagentry. Symbols of lions, bears, bulls, falcons, as well as the cross patterned their shields and banners.

Later, in America, Benjamin Franklin preached the virtues of the native turkey, but the eagle became the national bird and artists hurried to produce its form to decorate the paraphernalia of government. Through succeeding decades Americans marched into many campaigns beneath fierce and determined bronze eagles; their claws firmly grasped the mastheads of regimental banners and flags carried throughout the land and beyond the seas. It was not too long ago that American pilots even flew planes decorated with fierce animal imagery. Terming themselves the Flying Tigers, these armed warriors swept Far Eastern skies. Even now, in autumn, football teams, the Panthers, Mustangs, Bears, and Badgers, represent their schools. As seasons change, professional teams, the Cardinals and Orioles, Cubs and Tigers, select gloves and take the field. Symbols of the creatures of nature are with us still, and in both two- and three-dimensional forms continue to fulfill a multitude of purposes. At this very moment, possibly, an American submariner, pinned with a small metal dolphin, is boarding a soon-to-be-submerged deck. Elsewhere, a tiny cast eagle perches on a colonel's shoulders.

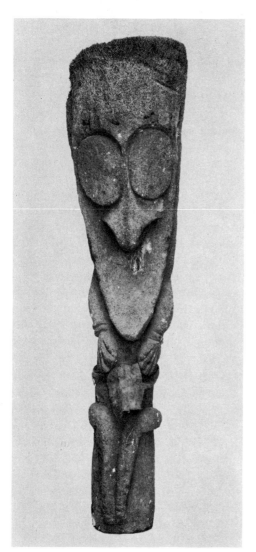

306 ANCESTRAL FIGURE, *carved fern tree (90 inches high), New Hebrides. (Courtesy Chicago Natural History Museum)*

Sculpture has been produced to serve purposes as diverse as controlling nature to speaking of the greatness of empire. In a land where violent earthquakes, immense tidal waves, and furious hurricanes are frequent happenings, carvers produced tall narrow imageries to serve as salvation columns (Figure 306). Their intentions were to seek the aid of ancestors in escaping the constant wrath of nature. The carvings were even covered with clay — to eradicate the roughness of the underlying material — and boldly painted with pinks, reds, greens, whites, and blacks to increase the effectiveness of their call. Other peoples, intent upon aggression, employed sculpture as a means of relating the nobility of the warrior class and the fruits of conquest. Attached to appropriate walls, reliefs such as the Benin plaque informed the society of tribal customs and glories (Figure 307).

An examination of the *Warrior and Attendants* brings to mind the words of Andre Malraux,[2] the contemporary art philosopher, who said,

> So long as the artist pays no heed to him, a conqueror is a mere victorious soldier; Caesar's relatively small conquests mean more to us than all Genghiz Khan's far-flung triumphs. It is not the historian who confers immortality; it is the artist with his power over men's dreams. For it is art whose forms suggest those of a history which, though not the true one, yet is the one men take to their hearts.

Scale differences accent the warrior, astride a tiny steed and catered to by less-dominant figures. Resplendent in hand-crafted fineries, the proud horseman has every need met as attendants provide shade from a fierce sun and transport his implements of battle. While the deep cast relief has a charming scale and possibly a touch of the whimsical, let no one be fooled. The Benins were determined warriors intent upon conquest, and like the Aztecs, they practiced human sacrifice during ceremonial orgies. These warriors controlled a great portion of Africa for five hundred years; from the fifteenth to late in the nineteenth century, they ruled territory reaching from the Congo River to the upper Nile. Through the work of their sculptors, Benin beliefs and customs, skills and concerns appear once again in the minds of men. Their dress, artifacts, weapons, design sense, physical features, and other aspects

[2] *The Voices of Silence* (Garden City, N.Y.: Doubleday & Co., Inc., 1953), p. 620.

WARRIOR AND ATTENDANTS, *bronze plaque, Nigeria, 16th-18th century. (Courtesy Museum of Primitive Art)*

307

suggested in bronze thus live far beyond their territorial conquests.

The doings of kings and goddesses, nobility and empire have long been captured in sculpture. Near-Eastern civilizations such as the Assyrian created relief sculpture to enrich palaces and temples long before the birth of Christ. These shallow reliefs both related amusements such as the hunting of lions from speeding chariots and portrayed rulers and affairs of state. The Egyptians continued these procedures and also erected great sculptures to honor their pharaohs. Sculpture served both Greece and Rome well. Artists now sought the likeness of gods and goddesses, noble athletes, and statesmen of the era. Pericles and a discus thrower, Jupiter, Athena, and many Caesars now made their appearance in marble. Ornate slabs of relief were incorporated into many buildings, and in several instances even the very columns of temples were carved in the form of maidens. Sculpture gave life to the centuries and in the case of Rome actually lined the Appian Way to delight the traveler. Chisels striking stone were prevalent sounds throughout the land and diminished only with the roar of invading northern hordes as they marched across the soil.

Sculpture was rejuvenated during the twelfth century by Christians to decorate their emerging cathedrals. A new God replaced ancient myths, and figures from the gospels were now the concerns of stone and wood carvers. Christian attitudes and beliefs were greatly assisted through the extensive production of imagery consistent with the teachings of the Church. In a relatively short period of time, in terms of history, the Renaissance appeared to encompass sections of northern and southern Europe. The age of the giants had now arrived; for sculptors such as Ghiberti, Donatello, and Michelangelo carved stone and cast metal. Once again the sound of sculpture echoed throughout the landscape and new forms patterned churches and public squares. Huge bronze doors spoke through relief sculpture of the Sacrifice of Isaac and portrayed Christ driving the money-changers from the temple. Mighty bronze figures astride sturdy bronze horses were also now issuing from foundries. Tremendous marble carvings symbolizing the vitality of the youth David and heroic tomb sculptures joined numerous other forms to serve the Church and wealthy nobility, in particular the Medici family.

Following the Renaissance, sculpture continued to perform religious services and public functions of all sorts. It immortalized notable public figures and recorded the grand moments and daily routine of Western man. It served to decorate fountains, add enrichment to architecture, and both delight and inspire throughout the cities and towns of Europe. Not long after the birth pains of a new republic subsided, the three-dimensional art was transported from Europe to assist in grandly proclaiming the promise of a new frontier, America.

ARMED LIBERTY *(Freedom), original plaster model for bronze sculpture atop the Capitol dome, Thomas Crawford, 1855. (Courtesy Smithsonian Institution)*

308

The Spirit of a Land

Various means are available to explain or transmit the promise, purpose, and glorious episodes of a nation. Words, written with clarity and truth, can explain and inspire. Stirring music and three-dimensional form can also deeply inspire and germinate intense feelings. All three, words, music, and sculpture, are mandatory to adequately suggest national purpose and assure a nation's destiny. Possibly the latter of the three at times can more quickly grasp the heartstrings firmly. This assumption can be imaginatively resolved somewhat by conceiving three distinct experiences and then personally deciding which demands the greatest response.

First, consider viewing the Declaration of Independence encased in a glass housing within somber surroundings. While we read slowly and thoughtfully, meanings suddenly flow. ". . . when, in the course of human events . . . . We hold these truths to be self-evident . . . . And for the support of this Declaration, with a firm reliance on the protection of Divine Providence, we mutually pledge to each other our lives, our fortunes, and our sacred honor." The experience concludes as the eyes rove over the signatures: John Hancock, Samuel Adams, Benjamin Franklin, Thomas Jefferson, and fifty-two other patriots.

Next, you must imagine a different situation. It is a bright day as you suddenly hear music. Yes, listen, for it's the Star Spangled Banner. The melody is familiar, "the rockets red glare, the bombs bursting in air, . . . our flag is still there." The pace is rapid and harmonious; however, bear one factor in mind. Disassociate any implications of viewing or participating in a parade; for you are only listening to music, receiving auditory but not visual stimulation. There are no waving banners or marching men within the environment, and any images conceived are purely mental and isolated in the mind.

The next situation depends on the eyes but not the ears. It is also a bright day and, skyward, clouds slowly drift by. You are standing adjacent to a huge stone pedestal. Slowly peering upward, and upward, and upward, you view an immense metal figure. She holds a huge torch well over three hundred feet about your eyes. It almost appears to pierce the clouds. You now recognize this maiden; for her name is Liberty.

The Statue of Liberty resulted from the enlargement of a nine-foot scale model by a Frenchman, Frédéric Auguste Bartholdi, in 1875. Alexandre Gustave Eiffel, the creator of the Eiffel Tower in Paris, designed the supporting metal construction upon which are riveted the copper sheets which compose the 152-foot figure. As you realize, it was a gift extended by the people of France to America on its hundredth birthday. Transported in sections, by battleship, to the new world, it was erected upon a small island in New York Harbor. Opened to the public in October, 1886, the colossal statue measured over one hundred yards from the base of its pedestal to the top of the torch. Elevators and staircases enable movement within its spacious interior. Forty people, for instance, can stand in the head of the goddess. There have been many instances of tears trickling down the cheeks of grown men and prayers of thanks whispered by women even upon viewing her at a great distance. She radiates both positive and mystical qualities — hope, aspiration, protection, shelter — as she greets the traveler at our shores. Her meaning may even vary with the viewer; for — representing, as she does, a versatile land — she signifies opportunities for meeting various pressing needs. Somehow a major role of sculpture and the purpose of a nation are wrapped within the form.

Even our nation's Capitol is topped with a metal goddess (Figure 308). Christened Armed Liberty, the nineteen-foot statue also portrays Liberty as a woman clad in flowing robes. Rather than raising a torch, however, her right hand rests upon the hilt of a sheathed sword, while her left clasps the shield of our nation. Originally produced in clay, transferred to plaster, and then cast in bronze, she stands high above the Washington scene. Beneath her, stretching across vast areas, are innumerable other sculptures which speak of our land. A solemn Lincoln in stone, George Washington portrayed in Roman toga (Figure 309), and even a great equestrian statue of General Andrew Jackson, cast from British cannons captured by Old Hickory during the Battle of New Orleans, are found within the shadow of our Capitol. One sees Sheridan in sculptured form and again recalls his dusty ride from Winchester. Great bronze relief doors add somber and subtle coloring to the entrance of the Congressional Library. And shadow patterns seem to play as they move about the shallow spaces of sculptured pediments above the columns of many government buildings. In the distance a towering, four-sided, column-like sculpture shaft stands alone. This, the tallest masonry monument in the world, pays tribute to the Virginian considered the Father of the Republic and from whom the Capitol derives its name.

309   GEORGE WASHINGTON, *carved marble, Horatio Greenough, 1843. (Courtesy Smithsonian Institution, the National Collection of Fine Art)*

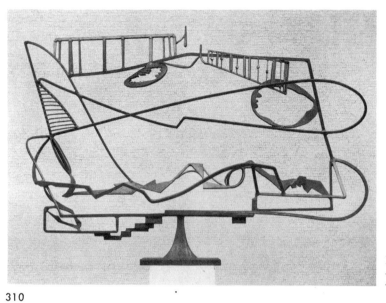

HUDSON RIVER LANDSCAPE, *welded steel, David Smith, 1951. (Courtesy Whitney Museum of American Art)*

310

Relief, poured concrete slabs obtained from clay molds, Peter Recker, 1960. Designed as decorative building members for the Goldendale Elementary School, Germantown, Wisc. (Courtesy the Architect, William P. Wenzler)

311

EAGLE, *aluminum (35 ft. span), perched upon New United States Embassy, London, Theodore Roszak, 1960. (Courtesy U. S. Department of State)*

312

It is highly probable that a sculptured Grecian goddess perches upon your own state capitol building and monumental figures flank the grounds. Such statuary, created in the nineteenth-century illusionistic manner, also exists in numerous public squares and parks throughout the land. These sculptures, frequently in the form of lions resting outside public libraries or local dignitaries placed throughout the town, attempt to duplicate factual features in bronze or stone. As relief sculpture usually depicting floral or ancient themes, the factual style also serves to embellish architecture. Neptune and his friends frolic in heroic allegorical fountain compositions in most every large city. Joan of Arc, a dancer and gazelles, pioneer women, and Admiral Farragut, indeed most any appropriate theme or conceivable figure can be found in traditional American sculpture. Yes, even Stephen Foster and, somewhere surely, bronze or stone Spanish conquistidors and French explorers still stand upon our soil. Though themes and subjects differed vastly within the style, surface and form treatments remained basically the same.

Many sculptors have displayed technical proficiency, patience, and factual inclinations in producing nineteenth-century three-dimensional imagery. Their attainments, inspirational and historically important, served to portray the grandeur of antiquity, the nobility of public figures or the glories of the republic. If size, inspirational purpose, or even permanency were the only virtues, it is obvious that few, if any, opportunities still remain to even equal, let alone surpass, these achievements in the Neo-Classic style. For instance, the immense scale of the Statue of Liberty would indeed be difficult to surpass. How many other sculptured figures could hope to possess relationships such as an index finger measuring eight feet in length or meet their purpose in serving as a major gateway to America? Even consider the possibilities of equaling the feat attained at Mount Rushmore. Each head represented in this carving reaches a length of approximately seventy feet and is located five hundred feet up a sheer granite mountainside. The life expectancy of each has been judged at 100,000 years. Such achievements representing the academic illusionistic manner join an endless number of smaller sculptures in indicating heroic form in the service of man.

If democracy is to survive, however, freedom to pursue procedures other than the following of, or mimicry of, traditional classical thought must be cherished. Free inquiry, self-development, and inquisitiveness must reign if men and sculpture are to properly serve and uniquely mark the latter portion of this century. Thus many American artists no longer follow the footsteps of the makers of the past, regardless of their immense and noble achievements. Rather, contemporary sculptors, in kinships with many architects, painters, and allied artists, have broken from the safety of the proven style. Handling material, interpreting space and form, and expressing personal themes in new manners they spread a fervent and original spirit across the land. Sculptors now seek new Neptunes in the age of the atom or twist and bend to weld new landscapes fitting to an age of steel and an age of search (Figure 310).

While sculptured forms have greatly changed, purposes remain basically the same. As always, sculpture serves to lift the spirits in gardens and parkways, as fountains or architectural reliefs, indoors or outdoors. Whether expressed in plastics or stone, it aims to fill the spectator with wonder, to inspire and serve to counter the void of life. To reveal beauty or enlighten beyond the restrictions of any prescribed norm is its noblest goal. For sculpture is young again, free to seek and discover, full of vitality and promise. If this were not the case, new visual pleasures and suspense would be no more. Like science, it is no longer dependent on ancient ways as it researches intriguing combinations and probes for different forms. This very moment, in conjunction with the architect, the sculptor assists in erecting the pillars of the future (Figure 311).

Unconcerned with rejuvenating the monuments of the past, sculptors now recognize a major truth. It may be simply stated as an obligation. For sculptors now realize it is the responsibility of each era, indeed every participating member of each generation, to pursue solutions which can mark their period as distinctive. A particular and notable link can be forged only in the light of the present. Thus many contemporary sculptors confidently shape the present while viewing the future with a challenging eye; for they well realize their final goal, that elusive relationship, that universal aim and common term: significant form. Mighty symbols still retain their meanings but are now feathered with new shapes and materials. Viewing an ever changing world, even our eagle assumes a new form; for it no longer perches in the past century. Its flight is forward toward new skies (Figure 312).

313 FLIGHT INTO EGYPT, *bronze cast, Ernst Barlach, 1921. (Courtesy Wright Air Center, Beloit College)*

314 HEAD, *stone, Amedeo Modigliani, approx. 1910. (Courtesy Philadelphia Museum of Art)*

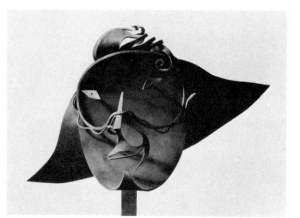

315 HEAD OF HARLEQUIN, *copper, Pablo Gargallo, 1928. (Courtesy Philadelphia Museum of Art)*

New Meanings in Sculpture

The early decades of this century witnessed several new and distinct tendencies in sculpture. Using plastic, wire and thin metals, Naum Gabo, Antoine Pevsner, and others, constructed three-dimensional forms which spoke of a mechanical and scientific age in poetic terms. Their investigations in space tended to refute bulk and mass through transparency and line contributing important components to their geometric nonobjective structures. In kinship with Auguste Rodin's earlier findings, other sculptors such as Ernst Barlach continued investigations into simplicity and plasticity of mass. Strong light and dark modulations, economy of detail, and fluidity marked their results (Figure 313). Under the influence of nonclassical sculpture and an expressive social environment, other artists, Amedeo Modigliani for instance, also began to freely exaggerate features (Figure 314). Elegant and unusual distortions with strong evidences of personal invention now made their appearance. Umberto Boccioni conveyed sensations of activity in mass with themes which implied great speed in space. Alexander Calder conceived the mobile and created sculpture that actually moved. No longer were solidity and bulk the prime qualities of sculpture; for it was found that space itself could be sculptured. Even a symbol of a head was now identifiable through combining convex and concave shapes which through restricted and released spatial play implied form (Figure 315). Thus, both occupied and unoccupied space became valid means for the sculptor.

As the century matured, accelerating deep into the age of atoms and rockets, new meanings, tools, and processes revealed new ideas and opportunities for three-dimensional form. Creations such as *Hydro-Gyro* now appeared in man-made landscapes (Figure 316). Towering forty feet high, the sculpture is subject to constant change. Composed of revolvable aluminum abstract shapes, highly susceptible to movement through subtle breezes, the creative construction appears even to reflect the changing state of sculpture; for, no longer limited to static mass or solidity, man can organize visual pageantry in extensive manners. Even sound can now be considered an element. Various sculptors construct mobile forms which, through vibration or more pronounced movement, cause the meeting of segments and resulting sounds. Such concepts, while novel, are also reminiscent of ancient Oriental wind harps. Contemporary sculptors freely combine traditional and new materials and findings and transform with personal modifications to suit their purpose. One factor, however, is certain. Neither the procedure nor the ideal Grecian imagery of Myron, Phidias, and Polyclitus, carried on for more than twenty centuries, is the final end. Man, rather than style, is presently the determining factor, and original solutions are the final goal.

In the age of the oxyacetylene torch and ever-improving welding techniques, new linear means are incorporated to attain unique expressions. Constructions undreamed of yesterday are now readily available. Nature may be elevated and examined through organic substances excitingly suspended in space (Figure 317). The products of modern technology, such as flexible steel, may even be richly woven into structures indicative of the contemporary era. Richard Lippold, by employing enameled steel wire and gleaming rods, richly spans and articulates space in his *Lobby Sculpture* (Figure 318). The sculpture shapes space to express cage construction and architectonic structure in the lightest possible terms. Linear webs add textural notes and suggest planes through multidimensional movements. Tensions appear and disappear as the eye, moving from jointures in space, follows other intriguing areas of the form. Thrust and counterthrust, rhythmical transitions, and the intermingling of space and gleaming matter elegantly entertain the eye. The German philosopher Schelling once contended that architecture was music in space, as if a frozen music. The same may hold true for Lippold's construction, which visually entertains through harmonic and discordant passages suspended and gleaming in space.

316   HYDRO-GYRO, *aluminum, decorating grounds of International Business Machines Corporation, San Jose, Calif., Robert Howard, 1957. (Courtesy IBM)*

317   ORGANIC TRANSFORMATION, *detail, welded steel and stone, George Zoretich, 1960. (Courtesy the Artist)*

318   LOBBY SCULPTURE, *steel, rods and wire, Inland Steel Building, Chicago, Ill., Richard Lippold, 1958. (Courtesy Inland Steel Company)*

Contemporary Sculpture: Diversified Themes and Unusual Forms

Aluminum, steel, string, plastics, glass, wire, semi-liquid metals, even machine parts now join traditional matter — clay, stone, bronze, wood — to serve as expressive material for the sculptor. Shaping this material to proclaim beliefs or reveal notions is his major aim. Statements may be brutal or idealized; interpretations purified or dissected and rearranged. Scale may be freely distorted and tactile qualities greatly exaggerated. Geometric principles or scientific or humanistic visualizations may even be presented. Indeed, most anything conceived in the recesses of the mind, experienced, or believed may be constructed in three-dimensional form.

The sculpture of Ibram Lassaw indicates his interest in natural phenomena and the structure and physical properties of the universe. His themes deal with celestial relationships, fire — with its flickering fingers probing space, even atoms and suborganisms. An awareness of geological structure, in particular the characteristics of amethyst, may provide insight into his soldered metal sculpture *Amethyst Moment* (Figure 319). The arrangement of the purple-tinted quartz in its natural environment consists of a rock mass, or geode, composed of an active and involved structure with innumerable crystal shapes. Lassaw's space sculpture is not factually descriptive, but rather an interpretation imaginatively transcribed by an inventive mind. The armature-like construction in circumscribing space identifies mass yet remains an aerated and penetrable form. Matter and space tend to become one. Dynamic contours, linear variations, and fluctuating shadows, when viewed from any angle, also assure a wealth of patterns.

The feeling of landscape, even the sensations of jungle, are suggestible in sculpture. What are the qualities associated with a jungle setting? Certainly among them are intermingling movements, diversity of shapes, and penetrating masses as foliage creeps about a jungle floor seeking shade or progresses vertically toward the sun. Thus organized complexities and wedding of detail, density of mass, divergent progressions, restricted and released movements are indicative of the setting, with strong thrusts and counterthrusts in both horizontal and vertical transitions also in evidence. Leo Amino captured such a feeling in his *Jungle* (Figure 320). He limited his material to a product of the jungle: mahogany, a fine-grained, hard, reddish tropical wood. Composed of uniquely shaped abstract symbols united into an

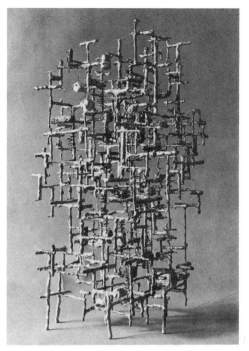

319 AMETHYST MOMENT, *metals and amethyst, Ibram Lassaw, 1957. (Courtesy Samuel M. Kootz Gallery, Inc.)*

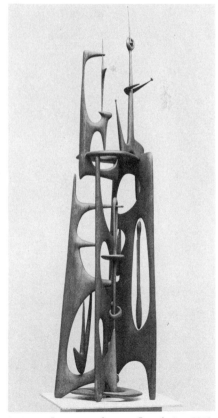

320 JUNGLE, *mahogany, Leo Amino, 1950. (Courtesy Whitney Museum of American Art)*

321   *Radiograph of Segment of Manicina Coral. (Courtesy Eastman Kodak Company)*

322   THORN BLOSSOM, *steel brazed with nickle-silver, Theodore Roszak, 1947. (Courtesy Whitney Museum of American Art)*

integrated form, the sculpture portrays a personal sensation of active growth in a warm environment. Can you visualize an informal jungle mood expressed with wire, string, and scraps of balsa wood?

Microscopic and radiographic studies of minute particles are prevalent features of modern science; for when magnified, the imagery reveals truths hidden to an unassisted eye (Figure 321). However, while scientists enlarge or distort for more adequate factual examination, sculptors do so for other purposes. The latter magnify size and distort primarily to increase emotional impact. Can you imagine a thorn blossom almost three feet in height? Theodore Roszak forged and welded steel to express his version of such a massive subject (Figure 322). Brazed with nickel-silver for rich color effects, the surfaced form is clearly and highly exaggerated. In consistency with the tactile sensations inherent in the theme, numerous shape projections and ragged edges tend to imply tortured and grasping qualities.

The use of any subject matter by an artist may often involve more than actually meets the eye. For instance, H. H. Arnason, Director of The Guggenheim Museum, offers insight into implications beyond visual factors in Roszak's *Thorn Blossom.* Arnason contends the sculpture involves a highly personal emotion and a specific intention on the part of Roszak and implies the blossom — forced, for survival, to present a shield of thorns — symbolizes an elegy to the many unprotected children who perished in World War II.

Obviously, the activities and conditions of mankind are universal and constant themes in sculpture. Portrayals may engender extensive reactions on the viewer's part, from gaiety to gloom; for content runs the gamut of all experiences, beliefs, and longings. Mary Callery strikes a note of joy in her bronze sculpture *The Seven* (Figure 323). The bronze rods, simply twisted and joined, suggest a frivolous moment captured, balanced, and retained in space. The treatment and placement of the implied acrobats convey both stability and tension. Extreme simplicity characterizes her statement of one incident in the gallery of life.

Through hacking and refining a huge section of walnut and using wooden pegs to add protruding walnut elements, Elbert Weinberg created *Captive Angel* (Figure 324). The depressing theme is somewhat akin to the subject of bound slave prevalent during the Renaissance and nineteenth century. The tragic figure, entombed within the very fibers of the organic material, can anticipate nothing but rigid

323 THE SEVEN, *bronze rods, Mary Callery, 1956. (Courtesy M. Knoedler and Company, Inc.)*

324 CAPTIVE ANGEL, *walnut, Elbert Weinberg, 1958. (Courtesy Grace Borgenicht Gallery, Inc.)*

restraint. Absolutely no liberty of movement is permitted, nor is the figure allowed more than a minimum of view. Even the hands and legs are tightly bound. Undertones of frustration can be read into the captive's facial features peering outward from surrounding feather-shaped but sturdy bars. Or is it sadness that marks the face? Rich highlights and shadows intermingle and move about the three-dimensional form, and retained chisel marks pattern great areas of the form. Both light and dark value distributions tend to intensify the dramatic mood. Though only Weinberg can fully explain his intentions in the sculpture, what do you think they were? Possibly the comment in a powerful visual manner of the lack of freedom in large portions of the world? Or maybe an indication of self-imposed restrictions when a personality is completely wrapped up in itself? Many conclusions might be drawn, but two facts are obvious. *Captive Angel* elicits strong psychological responses and deep feelings of despair.

Carving: Attainment Through Removal

Chestnut, mahogany, oak, pear, walnut, granite, limestone, marble, sandstone, and a myriad of other woods and stones are appropriate for carving. The carving process is merely concerned with cutting away all excess material to expose the desired idea. This shaping procedure, while relatively simple, can frequently be tedious, because certain hard woods and stones, selected for permanency, demand a concentrated carving effort over a fairly long period of time. Resulting three-dimensional imagery is usually defined through the removal of a minimum of material, with the remaining compact mass denoting idea. However, it would be a fallacy to conceive of carving as limited exclusively to massive and compact form treatment.

Ideas often are suggested, or subject positioning determined, by the particular shape of a substance before being carved. Following keen study, Humbert Albrizio visualized his *Seated Woman* within a long rosewood slab and made its appearance possible with deft strokes of sharp tools (Figure 325). The figure was posed in close kinship with the nature of the precarved block. The entire length, width, and thickness of the block was accounted for, and its black-streaked reddish-purple color and obvious grain sensitivity were exploited. Soft highlights and shadows enhance the three-dimensional quality of the finished sculpture. Shape curvatures cause coherent transitions and unify the entire statement. Concise directness is also highly evident; for through purification all distracting or unnecessary details have been eliminated to increase the effectiveness of the over-all mass. Albrizio permitted partially refined carved areas to exist adjacent to slick highly polished surfaces. Joined with the exciting flow of wood grain, these textural treatments act to enliven the *Seated Woman*.

Though usually associated with mobiles and stabiles, Alexander Calder has carried on extensive investigations into wire sculpture as well as carving. Unlike Humbert Albrizio's sculpture, which was formed from a single block, *The Horse*, by Calder, was constructed from three carved walnut blocks (Figure 326). This rural resident, depending on personal interpretation, appears either to be balking or eager to go. Could he be whinnying a protest or giving his master, perched on a sputtering tractor, a few haw-haws? Undoubtedly Calder had no such implications in mind, but rather intended the sculpture to extol the characteristics embodied in a horse.

325   SEATED WOMAN, *rosewood, Humbert Albrizio, 1957. (Courtesy the Artist)*

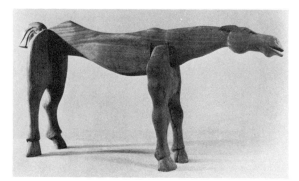

326   THE HORSE, *walnut, Alexander Calder, 1928. (Courtesy Museum of Modern Art)*

This he has nobly achieved in portraying qualities of controlled vitality, gracefulness, and suppressed power in the sleek carving. The three unified walnut segments are wonderfully balanced between simplicity and complexity. Their treatment also stands midway between primitiveness and sophistication.

Various woods, when carved, possess different tendencies toward splintering and varying degrees of hardness, but all share similar carving procedures. Wood, unlike stone, which cuts in all directions, is easier cut in following, rather than opposing, the direction of grain. Curved sharp gouges, hickory mallets, rasps, and sanding and polishing agents comprise the basic tools for shaping and finishing wood. However, particular stones, due to evolutional formation determining specific structural properties, demand specific carving procedures. For instance, granite is shaped somewhat differently than marble. Composed of fused crystals attained through great heat and pressure, granite is unlike marble and most other stones which result from stratification. Owing to its fused density and intense hardness, granite is not carved but decomposed, fragmented into dust, bruised and broken with heavy chisels struck by an iron mallet. Most other stones, including marble, are carved by slicing and chipping off small segments. In shaping stone sculpture, a pointed metal chisel is first employed to block out general proportions. Flat, broad, sharp-edged chisels or sharp-toothed chisels subsequently serve to develop more precise relationships. Following shaping, stone forms can be polished with files or rough carborundum stones and finely finished with pumice stone. It should be realized that many contemporary sculptors freely substitute power equipment for hand tools. Power tools — pointers, routers, saws, sanding disks, and others — can hasten the carving process in wood and stone.

Hans Arp's *Three Buds*, owing to both massiveness and compactness, is indicative of the usual qualities associated with carved stone (Figure 327). The theme implies latent power stretching forth, eager to burst into bloom. Thus tension is felt in sensing that the dormant form is soon to be energized. The slick surface and detail elimination places emphasis on form and also, in denying visual lingering, implies anticipated movement. Through such purification of form, completely devoid of all possible distractions, Arp captures the very essence of matter. Like Brancusi's, Arp's carvings are concise

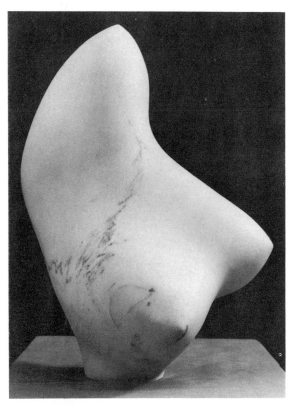

327   THREE BUDS, *marble, Hans Arp, 1957. (Courtesy Sidney Janis Gallery, Inc.)*

fluid masses which enliven cold marble. Both sculptors fuse vibrant and monumental qualities in their explicit and extremely simplified sculptural creations. When fully conceived by the viewer, their work, though cloaked with restraint, tends to pulsate with excitement.

In carving, the inherent features of density and hardness of the material in great part determine the treatment of imagery. For instance, the term "alabaster" may identify both or either of two minerals which resemble marble and are frequently carved. One, Oriental alabaster, is a variety of calcite and extremely hard, while the other mineral, also identified as alabaster, is a variety of gypsum. The latter is much softer than its Oriental kin and also softer than marble; thus, it is easier carved and sympathetic toward more intricate detailing and shaping. The use of this material enabled the sculptor Mirko to attain his splendid *Motivo Ancestrale Grande* (Figure 328). Mirko's creation completely explores and exhausts the possibilities of carving in stone. The lacy but massive form, composed of intriguing stacked segments, reaches a height of eleven feet. Through the retention of pockets of space and segment suspension, recession, and projection, the architectonic treatment activates numerous spatial and mass relationships.

Mirko undoubtedly intended the carving as a salutation to ancient forms; for its title *Motivo Ancestrale Grande* can be interpreted as the "Grand Means of the Ancients." Following a moment of contemplation, the delicately tinted and shadowed sculpture actually appears to whisper of past wonders. Being of Italian origin, the sculptor possibly had in mind homage to an accomplishment such as the Column of Trajan. Erected in A.D. 114, as a triumphal column and attaining a height of 127 feet, it still stands near the Piazza de Venezia in Rome. Commemorating Roman victories over the Dacians, the great vertical shaft is covered with relief sculpture relating exploits of armored legions in ancient lands of central Europe. Then again, Mirko may not have had a particular ancient form in mind; for his *Motivo Ancestrale Grande* does not contain specific attributes of a single structure from antiquity. Rather, it possesses qualities evident in numerous ancient practices. For instance, slight nuances in its inscribed linear treatment may imply a relationship with ancient scrolls or grand totem poles carved by imaginative peoples now forgotten. Possibly, the ornate carvings on the forward framework of Viking ships, which prowled old seas, may appear in the

328   Motivo Ancestrale Grande, *alabaster, Mirko, 1957. (Courtesy Catherine Viviano Gallery, Inc.)*

mind's eye. These visions may vanish as a suggestion of stacked ornate libation cups suddenly becomes apparent. Even Mirko's organizational solution can also be linked with ancient building practices. Greek laborers, ages ago, placed marble slab upon slab to erect their majestic columns which came to support a great segment of architectural history.

One may wonder what constructions succeeding generations will evolve to honor or recall our age. Involved sculptural forms surfaced with images of bells, books, and bridges? A cascade of ancient chrome hub caps covering great columns? Or possibly no one will remember our ways. After all, though it may wound our pride, modern man is but a momentary traveler carving a minute path from past to future.

Modeling: Addition and Subtraction

Modeling is a manner of building sculpture with pliable materials, such as clay, which permit extensive and continued change. The process offers little resistance and spontaneous modifications. Shaping procedures are somewhat similar to carving, because both treat form as mass and tend to shape all sides in unison. However, while carving moves from whole to parts to details in rigid sequence, modeling can build mass in stages or revert back to any stage by merely adding or removing portions from the mass. Carving, of course, denies addition; for what is carved away can not be restored to the remaining form. Thus, modeling has a versatility which carving lacks, and also usually requires less time for attainment. Clay sculpture, the most obvious modeling venture, has certain shortcomings, in particular, fragility, which usually demand additional steps for permanency. It is frequently transferred, by baking in a kiln, into terra cotta or, through casting, reproduced in more durable form in bronze, cast stone, or plaster. In addition to clay, other substances such as plasticine, wax, metal putty, plastic aluminum, and moist plaster are used as modeling materials. Tools which serve for gouging, inscribing, removing, adding, and shaping these pliable materials generally consist of simple hardwood blades, metal spatulas, and small wood shafts with wire-loop tips.

Plaster that has been sifted into water and stirred until developing a creamy pastelike consistency may be modeled somewhat as moist clay is. Applied to an underlying metal and wire armature, it can achieve and retain involved shapes and, when dry, provide hard unyielding surfaces. Large masses may be rapidly obtained by wrapping and partially modeling

329   HORSE AND RIDER, *plaster, Marino Marini, 1954. (Courtesy Carnegie Institute)*

330   RECLINING FIGURE, *bronze, no. 1, Henry Moore, 1957. (Courtesy Carnegie Institute)*

areas with plaster-dipped burlap. Smaller masses and details can subsequently follow by applying moist gobs of plaster and shaping with a spatula. A small amount of vinegar added to the plaster mix retards drying time and thereby secures a longer plastic state for shaping. When dry, the hard surface can be refined with chisels or filed if slight modifications are desired. The dead-white surface can also be coated with shellac and dry coloring for added enrichment. Marino Marini employed this traditional sculptural process in modeling plaster upon an underlying structure to obtain his expressive *Horse and Rider* (Figure 329).

An examination of Marini's sculpture discloses intriguing solutions in his arrangement and treatment of detailing and surface. Strong diagonals in the somewhat triangular composition provide stability while implying action. Tautness captured in the pose of both horse and rider suggests repressed fury and frustration as they appear to struggle in vain. Their expressive proportions are actively balanced, and they thrust and counterthrust in diversified and strong movements in space. Concise and exaggerated details are also given impetus through the elimination of any frivolous detailing. Notice also how mass continuations and simple contours unify and intensify sensations of plasticity of form. Deriving in great part from the ragged, rough, and semi-smooth application of plaster, the entire form appears cloaked in a dramatic fabric of light and dark. This nonmechanical surface suggests human involvement through its expressive application.

The themes of horsemen and humans with horses are frequent occurrences in paintings as well as sculpture by Marini. Deeply concerned with increasing competency in presenting the dual human-animal theme, he seeks and attains many vital and personal interpretations in a single theme. Sharing with others, such as Henry Moore, a sensitive deftness in mastering heroic and monumental sculpture, Marini ranks as one of the great artists of this age.

A modeled plaster sculpture may exist as an end in itself, as Marini intended his *Horse and Rider* to function, or it may be reproduced in bronze. It may even serve as a model for a subsequent larger carving in stone. There is no definite or specific limitation in its use; for exceptions constantly shatter any rigid notions of procedure. For instance, Henry Moore's *Reclining Figure* was originally created by applying plaster to an intriguing wire and screen form. Six copies of the plaster sculpture were reproduced in bronze (Figure 330). The original plaster figure then served an additional purpose. Shipped from Moore's homeland, England, to Italy, it acted as a model to guide stone carvers in enlarging but duplicating its imagery in stone. Working under the direct supervision of Moore, the Italian stonemasons produced a sixteen-foot-long, forty-three-ton carving in stone. This colossal sculpture now decorates a courtyard at the UNESCO Building in Paris. Thus versions of a modeling in plaster or clay may be reproduced in bronze or even stone or wood.

Imagine a cool sunny day and Henry Moore's bronze figure reclining in a garden or park setting. The monumental sculpture, with metal surfaces mellowed with age, would constantly reflect sparkling light and pocket shadows as you moved around its form. As the eyes roved over the colorful masses and examined from varied viewpoints, one's vision would naturally flow over patterned surfaces and both through and around massive shapes. Such a visual experience would add a dramatic note to any day. Visions of the intense imagery, which measures well over seven feet in height, would also be retained to appear and reappear far beyond the day. The majority of Moore's sculptures are actually designed as immense structures to be displayed outdoors in parks or adjacent to public buildings.

Two factors, primitive art and an interest in massive qualities in nature, combined, with Moore's innate sensitivities, to develop his design attitude.

Following discharge from the English army after World War I, he spent great periods of time closely studying the collection of ancient sculpture housed in the British Museum. Observing the expressive creations of ancient Samaritans and Egyptians, elongated Romanesque solutions, and compact Indian carvings of Old Mexico, Moore sensed their effective distortions. Convinced that vitality and power, rather than conventional beauty, should be his final aim, he also developed a concern with natural objects which contained those characteristics. For example, he saw that a rhinoceros or bull, though not graceful in the usual sense, possessed a vital righteousness and terrific force packed within its massive bulk. Thus great distortions and obvious exaggerations in his sculpture are explicitly and deliberately intended to attain expressive and powerful undertones. One may wonder, for example, why, in comparison with huge shapes representing other segments of the *Reclining Figure*, a much smaller shape signifies the head. The answer is found in the effects of subordination and emphasis in scale contrasts. The smaller the head the more monumental adjacent appendages — torso, arms, legs — appear to become through size comparisons.

Henry Moore's ability to transpose anatomical facts into wondrous visual relationships provides his bronzes with ageless and universal tendencies; for deliberate preconceived distortions were inherent in the three-dimensional expressions of many cultures. The British sculptor reduces humanistic sculpture to rhythmical masses and remodels in terms of power and spatial flow. A multitude of concave and convex curvatures in greatly exaggerated limbs and torsos and freely pierced areas are consistent attributes of his style. The utilization of negative spaces has also long been a prime concern of his. He contends, for instance, if one digs a cave in a hillside, it is the shape of the cave, though unoccupied, rather than the hillside, which demands attention. Thus pierced areas have a shape of their own. In addition, they fulfill another role in Moore's sculpture. Tunneling through mass, they enable the eye to explore into, through, and around, enabling more comprehensive and simultaneous views. Dynamic relationships therefore reign; for components constantly appear to expand or contract throughout all three dimensions of the sculptural imagery.

Modeled sculptures, when cast in bronze, are usually transferred by either the lost-wax method or sand casting. The former procedure involves the construction of a plaster or plastic mold. The inner

331   Box Headed Figure, *bronze, Eduardo Paolozzi, 1957. (Courtesy Carnegie Institute)*

wall of the mold or shell, containing an exact impression of the original sculpture, is then coated with wax. The thickness of the wax coat corresponds to the desired thickness of the bronze. The mold is then filled with plaster, with the thin wax application serving to separate core from surrounding mold. The wax is subsequently melted, and molten bronze is poured into the mold. The metal thus occupies the thin space between core and shell. Following cooling, the bronze reproduction is released from the mold and any irregularities are removed from its surface. The metal sculpture is then polished and, if desired, acids are employed to contribute additional color to the bronze form.

Sand casting involves a somewhat similar method. However, the mold consists of a special sand possessive of a doughy nature. In addition, the sand mold is baked to strengthen it before being removed from the clay or plaster model to act as a mold. While various modifications in both these traditional casting procedures can be undertaken, any changes generally closely relate to the older methods.

In addition to modeling clay and plaster in conventional manners, there are other means of creating imagery transferable into bronze. Eduardo Paolozzi, for instance, brings forth imaginative, heavily textured bronzes in a somewhat unusual manner. He selects discarded machine parts, flywheels, cogs, bolts, linkages, and similar industrial debris. When pressed into soft clay and removed, the metal parts leave an impression which Paolozzi then fills with melted wax. Upon cooling and removal from the clay, the wax shapes thus approximate various machine parts. Hundreds of these small wax shapes are assembled into a unified construction which is then cast in bronze. Naturally, the resulting bronze is extremely textured with innumerable craggy and wierdly blended shapes. What comes to mind in viewing his *Box Headed Figure* (Figure 331)? Some may consider it a hallucination, while others will read varied meanings. Possibly a grotesque and decadent monster unearthed from a forgotten grave? Or a mechanical dehumanized brute? Maybe even modern man, torn and unarmed, following an uncontrolled inferno of fury and flame. Many sculptors, like painters, constantly seek new and effective means for presenting forceful statements.

Obviously, semisolid metals such as plastic aluminum and sculpt metal, owing to their putty-like states, are appropriate for direct modeling. However, even solid metals, if worked in certain manners, can be modeled in freely adding, subtracting, and transforming surface characteristics of an intended sculpture. In part, welding may thus be conceived as a modeling process; for it permits areas to be burnt away or expanded when handled with plasticity in mind. With flaming torch and metal rods and strips Alberto Giacometti ventures into the realm of modeling in creating his elongated human symbols (Figure 332). Metals liquefy and, departing from their previous hardness, flow into new masses. Thin welding rods are used to attain mass rather than line and actually dematerialize to regroup into congealed rough shapes. Giacometti exploits fascinating and semiaccidental effects to achieve his figures; for the reaction of the metal to intense heat causes fretted surfaces and intermingled frenzies which refute slickness and refined details.

Giacometti's *Quatre Figurines sur un Socle* may be interpreted as four small figures resting on a base. His use of the term "figurines," which denotes small or miniature figures, in part indicates his concern with sculpture presented on a small scale. While Henry Moore, for instance, presents monumental sculptures tending to control and dominate space, Giacometti does just the opposite. His dehydrated figures capitulate to their surroundings. They convey the insignificance of matter, comprising man, in comparison with the surrounding overwhelming vastness of space. Slight, forlorn men are thus portrayed in a universe of inconceivable magnitude in great part beyond their eyes, minds, and control. A feeling of inevitable helplessness tends to permeate the cold solidified figures. Even their placement, equally distant apart, and mutual sizes and poses further a static suggestion of inactivity between the symbols and space. Only their surfaces are racy. Giacometti's style has been linked to surrealism through his dreamlike visions which stand on the verge of vanishing. His gaunt creatures, though often standing together, remain isolated and anonymous. His moods are serene and gloomy, his commentaries sad.

While various themes in sculpture may lead one to believe artists are a gloomy lot, such notions are soon dispelled in considering other works. Both pessimism and optimism are facts of life, and their interjection into art, be the area painting or literature, music or sculpture, are only natural. Some artists anticipate thunderheads and coming storms; others prefer to see the sun and sense spring. Such are men, be they engineers, lawyers, or sculptors; some point out shortcomings, while others speak of the bright promises of the future.

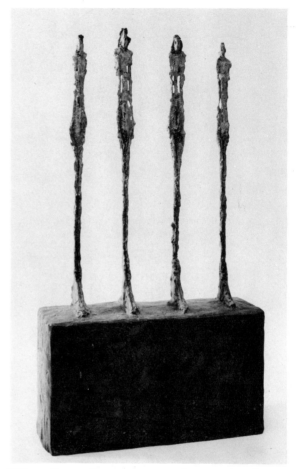

332   Quatre Figurines sur un Socle, *molten bronze, painted, Alberto Giacometti, 1950. (Courtesy Carnegie Institute)*

333   LE ROI DE LA FAIM, *metal scraps, Robert Jacobsen, 1956. (Courtesy Carnegie Institute)*

Construction: Assembled Sculpture

Robert Jacobsen ingeniously selected bits of chain, wire, bolts, pipe, and other miscellaneous metal scraps to present a humorous theme. Assembled through riveting and welding, his *Le Roi de la Faim* whimsically and expressively portrays the King of Hunger (Figure 333). The crowned and bearded monarch, enriched by an ornate neckpiece, appears to be proudly steering his mount toward a tentative feast. The use of actual eating implements, while consistent with other metal surfaces, also assists in relating the theme. The hilarious steed and horseman that emerged are clearly due to the observant eyes, imaginative mind, and gifted hands of the sculptor.

Jacobsen's sculpture resulted from a direct building method somewhat akin to the modeling process. Both are additive processes; however, direct construction differs in usually emerging in materials devoid of inherent plasticity. The use of metal rods for linear attainments and the incorporation of found objects and other solid hard substances have recently greatly extended constructional sculptural processes; also, the assemblage of sheets of metal, wood, Plexiglas, or other materials through welding, riveting, or gluing into sculptural forms is another distinct and frequent occurrence in contemporary sculpture. These areas of constructed sculpture, however, are often difficult to distinctly differentiate from modeling or carving areas. This is due to the former frequently also involving aspects of the latter two procedures.

Albert Terris welded a number of long and short steel rods to directly construct *Giraffe-Tall Standing Structure I* (Figure 334). It appears, somewhat, to have been drawn in space with sweeping linear strands presenting a concise sketch of the concept; for the sculpture, in excess of seven feet in height, does not displace but rather defines or shapes space.

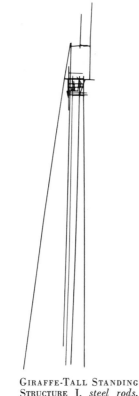

334   GIRAFFE-TALL STANDING
STRUCTURE I, *steel rods,
Albert Terris, 1954. (Cour-
tesy Graham Gallery)*

Great areas of extreme simplicity are offset with but one small complicated area. Its locale accents height as well as forces a pause, for examination, in the vertical journey of the eyes. Somewhat as a crescendo between extensive passages of serenity, the detailing further contributes visual spice and dash to the economical construction.

The duality of title evident in *Giraffe-Tall Standing Structure I* offers an opportunity to personally determine content. One may, of course, interpret the sculpture as indicative of the elongated characteristics of the giraffe. Or, if preferred, it may be viewed as a nonobjective articulation of linear pattern in space. It should not be concluded, however, that it is not highly feasible to view the welded sculpture as possessing attributes of both animal and abstract form. The title merely extends an element of choice or change. Nor should it be concluded that any title increases or decreases the worth or elegance of any sculpture. It remains a supplement, serving to provide insight into the possible intentions of the artist and acting to arouse the personal feelings of the viewer through association with similar or identical subjects or themes.

What comes to mind in conjunction with the descriptive term "northern towers"? Close your eyes for a moment and ponder its possible meanings. A conglomeration of imagery may play within the mind. One idea is soon supplanted by another. Tiny pine cones may scatter to admit sturdy trunks, that have long escaped the woodman's ax, into the mind's eye. Unending green tracts of indomitable forests and sensations of atmospheres cool and crisp may then emerge. Suddenly it is no longer spring, nor summer. Rising from a sea of white, towering northern giants stand sharply against a pale cold sky. Listen to the whistle of the wind.

The abstract wood construction *Northern Towers* is not limited to factual shapes, but is intended to germinate a variety of reactions (Figure 335). The northland's spirit of somber strength and majesty is expressed, rather than described, in its form. Its creator, Hugh Townley, used power equipment to shape and pierce the towering column. Smaller shapes were then evolved and housed in pierced areas of the abstract tower. The use of two woods, walnut and mahogany, permitted the intermingling of divergent grain and color traits. Intriguing shadows, pocketed in a variety of cavities, and exciting shapes and proportions join with these grains and colors to enrich the constructed sculpture.

335   Northern Towers, *mahogany and walnut, Hugh Townley, 1958. (Courtesy Swetzoff Gallery)*

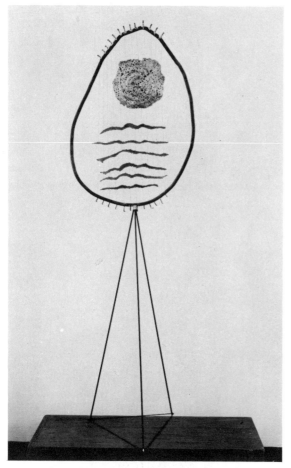

336   Sun and Water, *metal and wire, David Hare, 1953.*
(Courtesy Samuel M. Kootz Gallery, Inc.)

At times Hugh Townley, as well as other sculptors, fabricates constructions with segments and insertions not permanently linked. Versality is therefore extended; for such sculptures can be de-composed and reorganized into new constructions at the discretion of the arranger. These ventures are somewhat like do-it-yourself sculptures in encouraging participation on the part of the viewer. While intriguing and novel, such undertakings also have roots in the past. For instance, over twenty centuries ago, in the vicinity of Tanagra, Greeks produced changeable terra cotta statuettes. The figurines had movable parts which permitted the head, body, and arms to be positioned in different manners. However, rather than clay, contemporary sculptors often use large slabs of wood and produce, rather than small figurines, large sculptures composed of abstract shapes.

New constructional procedures have greatly expanded the means of presenting comprehensive ideas through sculpture. Even suggestions of landscape or seascape are now obtainable. Many of the works of sculptors such as David Hare and David Smith indicate such panoramic or even cosmic concerns. Certain of their metal sculptures also tend to refute the traditional notion that sculpture, unless as relief, must be conceived as three-dimensional form. *Sun and Water*, a sculpture assembled by David Hare, is to be viewed from a fixed frontal locale (Figure 336). The screen-like form is involved with height and width but is not concerned with depth in conveying its meaning. Hare's building stages possibly grew out of preliminary pencil sketches and subsequent thinking. The erection of the metal-rod base and the attached hoop were probably first achieved. Short metal projections, signifying sun rays, were attached to radiate outward from the large metal hoop. Fragments of metal were then appropriately shaped and treated to symbolize sun and waves. They were suspended by fine wires which were vertically stretched across the encircling hoop and attached to the small shafts indicating the rays of the sun. A variety of implications may be deduced from the theme of *Sun and Water*. It may be interpreted as indicating the actions of evaporation; for the intense heat of the sun tends to strip and raise moisture from many seas. Others may consider the sculpture as symbolizing the reflective qualities of our powerful heavenly neighbor upon the surfaces of water. Who but the sculptor David Hare, however, really knows his true intentions? Possibly he merely wished to represent in original and sculptural terms two dominant and essential allies of man.

The Challenge of
Easily Obtained Material

In a school program, or at home, the lack of particular materials or tools need not deny opportunities for creating exciting three-dimensional forms. An endless array of readily available substances can confront the would-be sculptor with distinct opportunities. Possibly an exaggerated figure or humorous creature can result from colorful bits of cloth and padding. Handled with courage and discretion, bits of plastic, wire, and wood scraps can provide intriguing experiences and worthwhile results. Even newspapers that have been read and empty tin cans can be transformed from waste if viewed with a creative eye.

Crusader merely consists of newspaper and wheat paste plus a liberal amount of talent (Figure 337). The major portions of the papier mâché form were painted with green and green-gray tempera to imply restful surfaces which permit concentration on sculptural detailing. A humorous implication appears to be contained in the interpretation of the bearded warrior nonchalantly awaiting his next campaign. One may also ponder about his quest, wondering about the besieged cities and endless travels such eyes might have viewed. While serenity is an evident feature of the papier mâché form, just the reverse is apparent in *Rooster* (Figure 338). Resulting from a diverse treatment in cutting and bending tin cans, the bird implies great action; for ragged and curved shapes and complex directional plays assure a turbulent quality. Many segment projections were directly bent outward from the main tin shell, while others were wired or soldered to serve as additional fluttering adjuncts. The cocky bird struts on wire legs and wire claws on a small stained-wood base. Bits of blue glass act as eyes. Additional color was obtained through incorporating both the exterior and interior surfaces of cans as exposed portions of the bird form. Thus silver- and bronze-like tin areas, as well as tiny accents of blue glass, intensify visual activity through contrasting color passages within this small, complex metal sculpture.

337 CRUSADER, *papier mâché, University student.*

338 ROOSTER, *tin, University student.*

There are no limitations to the ideas expressible with inexpensive material. Weird fantasies may be brought into being through a minimum of matter and a maximum of ingenuity. Even sound can be originally explored and space excitingly identified through abstract constructions (Figure 339). Indeed most any imagery conceived in the deep recesses of the mind can be clearly transferred into three-dimensional relationships. A willingness to try is the prime asset; for subsequent involvement usually unfolds its secrets to guide the solution of technical problems and attain the realization of form.

The scaly *Fantastic Creature* was designed with versatility in mind (Figure 340). It appears equally appropriate in being placed on a horizontal stand or base or hung to seem to be crawling upon a vertical wall surface. The creature was achieved through a simple construction procedure. Wire and light screen served as a basic shell. Upon this foundation plaster-dipped string was applied in linear patterns to add tactile and detail notations. The wire, string, and plaster creature was then covered with a dull-black and dark-gray tempera to add a forlorn note consistent with the theme.

Both variation and unity are harmoniously woven in space within the crisp architectonic *Space Structure* (Figure 341). While a few bits of screening and wire are the apparent ingredients, rich visual entertainment is the result. Notice how subtle and bold value and textural changes occur as the eye roves over the novel construction. A rectangular regularity contributes uniformity to the varying proportions, and linear continuums provide a fluid movement that links all members with a common bond. The somewhat simple contours allow the inherent effectiveness of the varied screening materials to fully emerge; thus, semitransparencies and overlapping passages as well as unoccupied but identified shapes are coherent and important relationships. What sorts of shadow would you imagine this sculpture could cast upon background walls? A close examination of the form discloses a great number of visual occurrences. Which of these happenings do you consider the most important in contributing visual pageantry? How would you construct an airy space screen?

Several considerations should be kept in mind if you are engaging in sculptural endeavors. Of prime importance are the natural working qualities of the materials being handled; they should not be opposed. Moments of contemplation and pure experimentation can frequently advance insight into these qualities

339 Vibrating Abstraction, *subject to sway by breeze, contact and sound, walnut and flexible rods, University student.*

340 FANTASTIC CREATURE, *wire, screen, string, and plaster, University student.*

and reveal logical possibilities. Each material has particular limitations as well as distinct advantages. One must consider its attributes, whether it is sympathetic toward being projected into space or functions best as a compact mass, how it can be easily carved or twisted, joined or cut, shaped and surfaced with textural notations. These relationships, inherent within each material should dictate, in great part, the treatment of idea and the emergence of form. Preliminary pencil sketches may also assist in conceiving of any proposed sculpture. Drawings, especially if exaggerated and imaginative, can lead toward unusual and exciting results. However, drawings should serve only to provide an initial idea, and should be freely moved away from when one is actively manipulating the materials of sculpture. Another point which should be kept in mind, when one is engaged in sculpture, is the three-dimensional factor. Sculpture is of course, unlike drawing or painting in that it can be viewed from all sides. Thus each area of the mass — front, back, sides — must be so treated that, from any point of view, visual satisfaction is transmitted. Therefore, undue attention should not be placed on any single area at the expense of others when initiating the basic shaping of the material. Frequent turning of the sculptured masses and study from varied viewpoints can greatly assist in conceiving and properly executing the entire three-dimensional form. Details can then follow to accent certain areas.

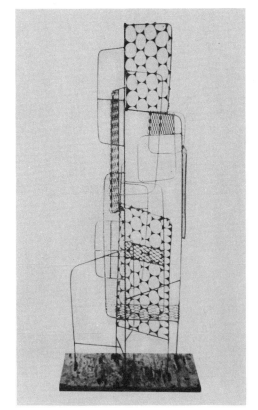

341 SPACE SCULPTURE, *wire, screen, University student.*

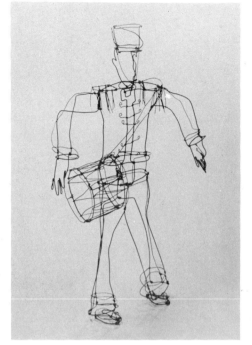

342   DRUMMER, *stovepipe wire, student, Oak Park and River Forest High School, Ill.*

343   THE WILD AND WOOLY WEST, *screen, wire, tin, and steel wool, Junior high school student, University High School, Iowa City, Iowa.*

Wire and Bits of Metal

Light wire, such as stovepipe or baling wire, is ideally suited for rapidly creating linear and bold three-dimensional forms. Its high degree of flexibility and ease of bending, twisting, cutting, and joining offer extensive opportunities. Strands can easily be joined by twisting, and when closely wrapped, they can suggest solidity in any desired area. Used separately, strands can also leap from any area to sweep into space and identify other portions essential to conveying the idea. Even the final results remain pliable and through several simple twists can assume varied positions. Action and simplicity are usually valid relationships in wire sculpture. Undoubtedly the producer spent a period of time in exploring the bending, twisting, and joining potentials of his material before creating the wire *Drummer* (Figure 342). The figure appears somewhat to have been three-dimensionally drawn in space, with sure and crisp lines concisely expressing the idea.

If desired, steel wool, window screen, bits of tin, cloth, or string dipped in plaster, starch, or paste and wrapped around sections of the form may be incorporated into wire sculpture. Such additions can suggest solidity and interesting surface variations. However, their use demands discretion and control in order that their inclusion will enrich rather than detract interest from the total form. Notice how an invigorating composition of wire, screen, and bits of steel wool suggests *The Wild and Woolly West* (Figure 343). These materials add pattern change, tactile range, and contrasting semisolid passages within the sculptural composition. The tin-hatted cowboy reigns with confidence; for he appears securely saddled upon his bucking companion. His active mount, the rearing steer, and the swirling lasso, however, greatly activate the theme. The full effectiveness of wire is stressed in the looping lasso. The wire rope tends to fulfill several roles in advancing the Western theme as well as expanding the range of the metal sculpture and unifying the symbols.

Paper and Wood Constructions

As you already realize, paper may be soaked in paste and applied to dry paper or wire armatures to obtain papier mâché sculpture. If shredded and mixed with paste, it offers another sort of modeling experience. In sheet form, properly cut, folded, or bent, paper may also imply solid forms. Properly stapled or glued, such paper sculptures may provide bright masks, animals, even the slick machines of science, *Space Vehicles* (Figure 344). Junior high school students incorporated painting with these paper sculptures to more completely express their own twentieth-century setting.

Scrappy Cat resulted from the selection of randomly cut wood scraps during a student's visit to a local wood shop (Figure 345). The odd shapes were studied, some were farther sawed by the student, while others remained unchanged. Segments were then arranged and rearranged until certain relationships were discovered. Portions were then glued and nailed to shape the fanciful sculpture. The constructional process was greatly dependent on imaginative, keen, and abstract thought. These tendencies can often assure elegant and unique forms which seem to automatically grow from a novel combination of both contrived and undetermined shapes.

Rather than wood scraps, different lengths were cut from dowel rods and glued to adjacent members to express *Flight Abstration* (Figure 346). Designed as relief sculpture, its use could contribute a refreshing and original accent to any wall. A wood base, painted white, firmly holds the lower level of dowels. Succeeding levels are actively arranged and glued to one another so that depth sequence occurs. All building members were painted a medium blue-gray. This color selection tends to subdue shadows appearing within the structure, thereby controlling an undesired complication. The concept of flight is intended to be conveyed, in the relief, through several definite factors. Strong impressions of violent and complex movements are gained through the multiplicity of directions assumed by the rods. The tempo of the construction is thus rapid, and sequences in depth, width, and height cross and recross to further the sensations of action. However, the construction retains its coherence owing to color usage and shape similarity. A quality of buoyancy, due to the projection of various levels from their underlying base, also serves to imply lightness and soaring or floating qualities which are indicative of flight. Thus an abstract notion or impression, rather than a factual episode, is recorded in the blue-gray dowel-stick relief. Color also possibly plays a role in suggesting flight; for what are the colors of the relief? And what colors often seem to both streak and coat the sky?

344   Space Vehicles, *paper, Junior high school students, La Crosse Public Schools, Wisc.*

345   Scrappy Cat, *wood, student, Wisconsin High School, Madison, Wisc.*

346   FLIGHT ABSTRACTION, *dowel sticks, University student.*

Miscellaneous Materials for Patterns in the Air

Have you ever viewed coveys of quail breaking cover to wing into rapid flight or a few busy leaves flicking their golden brown color as, swept by a hurrying wind, they swirl down city streets? Can you imagine bright kites arrayed in a brisk pale sky? During early hours, have you seen disciplined flights of wild geese crossing cold November skies, or at evening the running lights of huge metal birds, produced by Boeing or Lockheed, streaking the darkness? These, and many more, are the diverse movements of man and nature within the sky. They may, as kites, be slow and lolling, or as new atomic arrows of warfare flash at tremendous speeds to instantaneously disappear beyond the eye. How many new and shiny metal objects also pattern the sky, orbit the earth, and even reenter our atmosphere?

In order to express abstract and colorful movement in space, a student deftly twisted wire and suspended metal shapes to create a *Mobile* (Figure 347). This sculpture that moves permits constant change; for clusters of shapes can freely turn and swing about to expose new relationships. Ever-changing arrangements therefore serve to enliven space through intriguing bits of matter which appear to joyfully waltz overhead.

Materials such as balsa wood, cardboard, thin metal sheets, piano wire, dowel rods, and thread, plus a few different-colored paints, are appropriate for mobile construction. Their selection must be based on lightness of weight and ease of cutting and suspending. Methods of assembly and suspension must be prone toward movement and sensitive toward any slight circulation of air; for the completed structure should easily move into new and striking arrangements. Balance, spatial placements, and proportions are key factors in attaining proper motion and harmonious visual qualities. Discriminative judgment is essential in mobile undertakings; for a hodgepodge of conflicting shapes, proportions, and textures is not the goal. Therefore, wisely selecting and limiting the materials to be employed permits more concentration on aspects of construction and problems of shape, proportion, placement, and suspension.

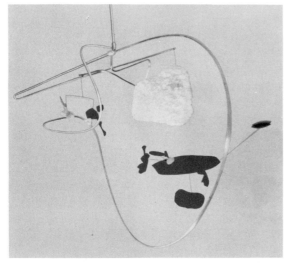

347   MOBILE, *metal and wire, student, University High School, Iowa City, Iowa.*

From Clay to Plaster and Stone

Because of its versatility, clay is extensively used in innumerable school programs. Offering a wide range of sculpture experiences, it is fitting for both very young and older hands. In a moist pliable state it permits easy and rapid handling in modeling shapes and inscribing details. The *Terra Cotta Head* retains a claylike quality in being conceived as a smooth uncluttered mass (Figure 348). Clay is highly sympathetic toward such smooth surfaces; for its plastic nature permits slick treatments with a minimum of effort. The eyes are richly entertained as they examine such coherent clay forms. One's vision tends to accelerate, in seeming to slide quickly over curved uncomplicated areas, then suddenly be retained as little areas of concise detailing demand attention. This student's interpretation contains economy and monumentality. Both are prime attributes of much contemporary sculpture.

Regarding modeling and finishing procedures, the producer of the terra cotta sculpture first shaped moist pliable clay. Following the acquisition of the desired form, the material was permitted to dry and then was baked in a kiln to obtain qualities of extreme hardness and permanency. The fired sculpture was then rubbed with colored pigments for colorful accents and finished with a coat of wax. Such a modeled clay head could also have been glazed, if desired, to achieve either an opaque or a transparent glasslike finish.

While clay is generally treated while in a moist, pliable state, it is also, when leather-hard, suitable for carving. Confronted with such a dry, hard clay block, a student employed a knife to reveal his notions of a *Carved Clay Head* (Figure 349). By carving bold and exaggerated shapes and inscribing obvious linear details, the young carver produced a highly expressive form. Its imaginative facial features suggest feelings of wide-awakeness and contentment which highly flavor the naturally distorted solution. Sharp cuts and deep penetrations result in bold shadows which enhance adjacent projections and intensify three-dimensional relationships. Obvious evidences of inscribed textural notations also mark the forceful clay carving.

348   Terra Cotta Head, *clay, wax, and pigment, student, Oak Park and River Forest High School, Ill.*

349   Carved Clay Head, *student, Pittsburgh Public Schools, Pa.*

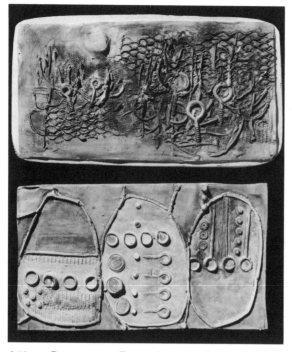

350   DESIGN FROM FOUND OBJECTS, *plaster, University student.*

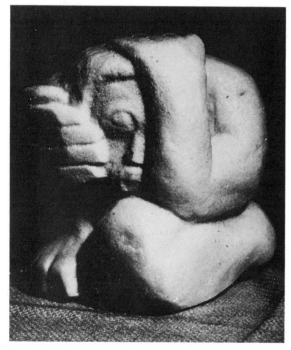

351   PEEKING, *salt block, student, University High School, Iowa City, Iowa.*

The plaster *Design from Found Objects* indicates that exciting relief sculpture can be secured from ordinary and insignificant objects (Figure 350), provided, of course, that originality is employed in their arrangement. The upper relief is reminiscent of a weird landscape, possibly a petrified forest, while the lower relief appears more formal, with strong archaic undertones. Both were produced through the use of plaster and clay. Students commenced the process with the placement of thin layers of soft clay in the bottoms of boxes. Miscellaneous objects — bits of screen, screw eyes, twigs, and buttons — were momentarily pressed into the soft clay and then removed. Their impressions remained in the clay surface. Undesired areas could be simply rubbed out and new arrangements attempted until satisfactory imagery and layouts were registered. When the desired shape, textural, and spatial relationships had been obtained, plaster was poured over the clay surfaces. Pouring ceased upon attaining a depth of about one-half inch of mixed plaster which had the consistency of light cream. Following hardening, the plaster slabs were removed from their boxes. Their underlying surfaces now contained and retained the impressions originally pressed into the clay. The transfers were thus made from clay into plaster. The latter material has more permanent features than clay, unless fired, and therefore assures more satisfactory reliefs.

In comparison with plaster only a few other materials, such as cement and clay, offer such extensive versatility. In addition to serving as a transfer agent, as in the reliefs of found objects, or as a material for molds, plaster can serve as grout for mosaics. It can also be cast in a variety of manners to attain forms, be modeled directly, or be built upon wire or screen armatures. Poured as slabs, plaster can also be carved as relief, or if shaped into large blocks, it can be carved and treated as three-dimensional sculpture. If mixed with a material such as vermiculite, it attains an excellent consistency for rapid and fine carving.

In addition to a plaster and vermiculite mixture, many other materials, from soap to stone and wood, are carvable and suitable for sculpture. Some are soft and easily carved but lack permanency. Others, extremely dense and hard, are highly resistant to shaping but last for ages. Even in a single family of materials great differences exist in hardness and properties of handling. For instance, certain alabasters, Indiana limestone, lava ash, sandstone, soapstones, and sugary marbles are easily carved and highly durable. Boulders, field stones, granite, hard and brittle marbles, and volcanic rock offer much more difficulty in carving owing to extreme hardness. In the wood family, mahogany, owing to grain and consistency of texture, and fruit woods are more appropriate for carving than are cedar, fir, or pine. Each material, be it blocks of balsa wood, dried clay, fire brick, foam glass, plaster and vermiculite, or even blocks of salt, soap, or wax, possesses limitations as well as features that are favorable to cutting and shaping. As an example, soap, while probably the easiest carved of any material, is very fragile and also not conducive to large carvings. Thus, in the majority of instances, its disadvantages usually outweigh its advantages. However, each and every material extends a challenge to discover an idea within its form.

A student more than fulfilled the challenge of a material in the carving *Peeking* (Figure 351). By displaying energy and determination and employing mallet, stone chisel, and rasp, he transformed a common salt block into a stunning sculpture. Secured from a local feed store, the approximately square block assisted in determining figure placement and treatment. But it is apparent the student marked the form with an original and forceful expression. Notice how the anatomical features are freely but effectively distorted through the removal of only a minimum of material. Both simplicity and detail are wonderfully balanced and tightly unified in the marblelike mass. Such a treatment assures that the entire sculpture, rather than particular parts, clearly provides the major impact. Thus an idea once existing only in a student's mind is now, through carving, clearly defined in a lasting form.

The Final Challenge

What ideas remain to be released from blocks of stone or pulled and squeezed from masses of moist clay? As a sharp chisel bites into wood, how shall the proportions be shaped? What impressions of imagery appear in the mind as one studies a twisted branch or feels the rough and slick transitions in driftwood? While possibly only a few, what sorts of twists begin to resolve an idea in wire? These and many more are the problems of sculpture. Both material and mind release the answers. While the material somewhat dictates tools and processes, only the creative handler determines the idea and crystallizes the final form. However, in addition to aspects of self-discovery and the active production of original sculptures, another factor bears consideration in considering the rewards of sculpture. In great part it can grow from creative sculpture activities, with their emphasis on three-dimensional relationships, yet it remains independent of such quests. Though it also deals with material, form, and appreciation, its concerns are keenness of sight and total awareness. It can be thought of as sensitivity to environment.

The intensification of sight and awareness was expressed, in one manner, by a philosopher long ago. Contending that many individuals travel through life unaware of the opportunities for sensing beauty, this philosopher implied that all his work was to help those who have eyes yet do not see. His desire was indeed a noble goal. However, in great part, such a goal must be individually attained. One must truly put his eyes to full use to adequately observe the intriguing sculptural aspects contained in man-made and natural forms; for only through seeking can regions, previously devoid of possibilities, suddenly come to life. The rewards can be endless; for new visual pleasures remain to be discovered during even the longest of life spans.

Imagine what your eyes can tell you if fully put to use. The warm vivid colors of summer or October's golden brown mobiles — have you ever really seen them? What about the proportions and glass placements of the new building in your town? Look and analyze the shapes, colors, and textures in the objects surrounding you. Study a contemporary chair, peer at the rugged trunk of an old tree. Notice the shining distortions reflected in a bright automobile fender, then note its shape. Examine closely several sculptures if contained within your town. Even start a collection of a few smooth and colorful stones washed by sea or stream, several tiny and unusual segments of wood, dried weeds. Feel them, now and then, and enjoy their varied characteristics.

The final challenge of sculpture is obvious: to more fully partake of your three-dimensional world. The means are available and the prospects vast for both shaping and enjoying innumerable forms.

TOPICS FOR CONSIDERATION

1. How has sculpture served man throughout history?
2. Have new thoughts regarding reality influenced sculpture as well as painting?
3. What relationships make up an interesting three-dimensional form?
4. Where in your state are inspirational sculptures located? What styles are they?
5. While actually existing in a minimum of space, how do certain modern sculptures imply an extensive occupancy of space? What materials are unique to twentieth-century sculpture?
6. Sculpture activities on the part of students should develop what qualities and convey what knowledge?
7. Select, from this chapter, three photographs of sculptures which you favor. Analyze them closely and determine the specific features which influenced your choice. Discuss these qualities with your friends.

SUGGESTED ACTIVITIES

1. With light baling or stove pipe wire, create a running or dancing figure approximately eight inches in height. Begin with a strand of wire about six feet in length, and bend it in the center to obtain two equal sections. This permits two extensions which facilitate subsequent bending, twisting, and wrapping, and enables the somewhat simultaneous forming of different appendages.
2. Model a compact interpretation of an animal with clay, and if possible, glaze and fire. Within the creation, stress bulk and interesting proportions in related masses. Study the form from all sides.
3. Carve a block composed of a mixture of vermiculite and plaster into an exciting abstract form. The block can be obtained by mixing an equal amount of vermiculite or silica with plaster and sprinkling the mixture into water. When a cream-like consistency is attained, the substance can be poured into a waxed milk carton or greased shoe box. Upon drying, is can then be easily carved with a knife and even sanded. Vermiculite or silica and plaster are obtainable at most any lumber yard or building supplier. If desired, a block of wood may be carved rather than the vermiculite and plaster.
4. Create a relief from scraps of metal, bolts, nuts, nails, or with scraps of wood. Employ a wood plank for a base. If deemed appropriate, areas of plank and added shapes can be painted.
5. Make a wired mask with papier mâché or burlap soaked in plaster; or try a mobile composed of light sheet metal, bits of wood, or cardboard. If the latter is undertaken, achieve active placements and intriguing balance.

APPROPRIATE REFERENCES AND READINGS

Periodical

Arts and Architecture, Los Angeles, Calif.: John D. Entenza, 3305 Wilshire Blvd.

Texts

BITTERMANN, ELEANOR. *Art in Modern Architecture*, New York: Reinhold Publishing Corporation, 1952.

LYNCH, JOHN. *Metal Sculpture*, New York: Studio Publications, Inc., 1957.

MALRAUX, ANDRE. *The Voices of Silence*, Garden City, N. Y.: Doubleday & Co., Inc., 1953.

READ, HERBERT, *The Art of Sculpture*, New York: Pantheon Books, Inc., 1956.

RITCHIE, ANDREW C. *Sculpture of the 20th Century*, New York: The Museum of Modern Art, 1952.

SEGY, LADISLAS. *African Sculpture*, New York: Dover Publications, Inc., 1958.

SWEENEY, JAMES JOHN. *Alexander Calder*, New York: The Museum of Modern Art, 1951.

10 | CRAFTS: FEATHERS TO GOLD

Art, in the fullest and most inclusive sense of the term, plans, builds, and furnishes this House of Life.

BERNARD BERENSON[1]
20th Century Art Historian
and Philosopher

352 *Pendant, engraved shell and braided cord of human hair, Australian aborigine. (Courtesy Chicago Natural History Museum)*

Unlimited Materials and Basic Needs

A probing eye spanning time and continents could view innumerable instances of man's inventive powers in handling most any imaginable material. Flingit Indians of southeastern Alaska made ornate head gear from cedar bark, while a society thousands of miles to the south in the Central Andes wove hats from bright fluffy feathers. Another tribe midway between these two worked with colored sand to bring forth elaborate geometric designs for religious rituals. Natives of the East Indies treated cloth with wax and dye for colorful dress and wove baskets and mats of local fibers. Many societies from the South Seas and America to Asia and Africa skillfully and imaginatively created masks from fiber, wood, or metal.

The urge to enrich utilitarian objects through unique construction and applied decoration is a tendency evident throughout history. Solutions frequently were based on cultural symbolisms and possessed religious implications. Many provided the possessers with great social stature. The characteristics of local materials as well as the assimilated skills of the society determined their degree of refinement (Figure 352).

[1] *Aesthetics and History* (Garden City, N.Y.: Doubleday & Co., Inc., 1954), p. 138.

Given a jungle setting and a minimum of tools, how would you shield yourself from the terrors of the environment? Confronted with such a problem, a New Guinea native blended visual richness and practicality in a coherent manner (Figure 353). The solution boldly combines a five-foot carved wood slab, paint, and fiber. A multiplicity of logic may be read into such a utilitarian device. Its size offered adequate protection, and the painted ornate pattern fostered confidence on the part of the user while striking fear in the hearts of adversaries. The fiber fringe allowed extensive arm movements in thrusting weapons while adding a minimum of weight and denying visual penetration to the enemy. The design treatment also permitted the warrior-hunter to blend within the jungle foliage, thereby securing the element of surprise in addition to assisting retreat.

Individuals of this century, conditioned to a highly scientific, mechanized society, must mentally project themselves outside their technological-materialistic environment to adequately comprehend the functional and aesthetic achievements of other eras and lands. These accomplishments are judged in terms of their physical and cultural setting; for results unfold under such influences. Regardless of origin, utilitarian objects move into the realm of art when, in addition to serving conventional purposes, they express inventive and artistic skills.

Long before the modern era, when the Egyptian pyramids were young — two thousand years before the Venetian traveler and author, Marco Polo, journeyed to China — Eastern craftsmen were achieving remarkable results in bronze. Few would disagree with Dagny Carter,[2] an authority on the arts of China, who said:

> The bronzes of the Shang people are unique in the art history of the world. Nowhere at any time have there been cast bronze objects of such magnificence and perfection, either in regard to the metal itself, the casting, or the decoration.

During the Shang Dynasty, 1766–1166 B.C., the Chinese created a great number of bronze vessels. Measuring from several inches to almost two feet in height and elaborately decorated with shallow relief, they were employed in rituals recognizing various deities. Housing sustances such as wine and grain, forms ranged from animal to abstract creations (Figure 354). Frequently securely supported through

2 *Four Thousand Years of China's Art* (New York: Ronald Press Co., 1948), p. 24.

353   *Shield, wood, paint, and fiber, New Guinea. (Courtesy Chicago Natural History Museum)*

354   *Ceremonial Vessel, bronze, China, Shang Dynasty, 12th century B.C. (Courtesy Freer Gallery of Art, Washington, D. C.)*

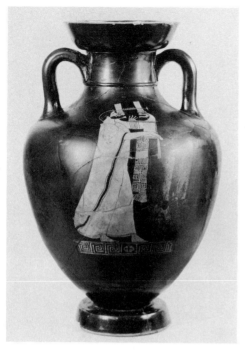

355 *Amphora, storage vessel of clay, Greece, 5th century* B.C. *(Courtesy Metropolitan Museum of Art, Rogers Fund, 1920)*

356 *Kashan Bowl, luster decoration, tin-enameled earthenware, Persia, 13th century. (Courtesy Metropolitan Museum of Art, Fletcher Fund, 1932)*

tripod construction, these libation cups were produced through an ancient casting method. An exact wax model was first constructed. The wax form was then covered and packed with clay and baked to cause the wax to melt and flow from between the fired clay shell and core. This was followed with molten bronze poured into the clay mold, permitted to cool, and subsequently removed from the mold to reveal the final form. Owing to the fusion of technical skill and expressive powers in both their design and execution, these ritual vessels, long after the decline of the Shang Dynasty, continued to receive homage from man.

Sensitive Greek fingers, assisted by rapidly spinning potter's wheels shaped exquisite pottery many centuries ago. Restraint and control marked their results. Particular forms were employed for specific purposes: the hydria, a sturdy three-handled jar, transported water; the wide-mouthed massive crater was used as a mixing bowl; the cylix was used as a drinking cup; and the amphora served to store wine, oil, or honey. The amphora decorated with a musician playing the cithara, a lyre-shaped instrument which produced deeper tones than the ordinary lyre, is indicative of Greek red-figured ware (Figure 355). Popular during the fifth century B.C., the process uses the natural color of the reddish clay to identify the figure, while lines and background mass consist of black glaze. Representations of humans were often applied as informative and decorative coatings upon pottery of this period owing to both a concern with commenting about social action and the influence of the painter and his techniques upon the potter's craft. Thus a tendency to paint rather than decorate pottery became apparent; for in concentrating on a limited field upon the form the full three-dimensional quality of the ware was ignored.

While crusading Christians and Moslems contested lands to the west, superbly decorated carpets, pottery, and metal work were being created in the Persian town of Kashan. Rather than meet more conventional needs, many of these intricately designed and colorful products served purely decorative purposes (Figure 356). Dishes and shallow bowls were often not intended as receptacles for food, but were hung on walls to enrich their surroundings. Such highly glossed forms possesive of symmetrical stylized patterns added a sharp visual note of brilliancy to Persian interiors.

It is interesting to realize that, even many centuries ago, man viewed the purpose or function of utilitarian objects in two distinct manners. A dish, for example, could assist in eating or meet its purpose by being viewed, with the stimulation of visual sensations conceived as a distinct and logical end. The great art-craft forms usually result when practicality in use and visual qualities are fused. Many products from both historical and contemporary societies possess such a duality. This is not to imply that a divorce of these factors is never warranted; for at times such ventures prove logical and rewarding. An apparent contradiction thus appears evident; however, it is resolved through the intentions of the doer and the elegance and expressiveness of the product. The producer selects the object's role; such a selection is obvious in contemporary pottery. A wheel-thrown bowl or jar can be akin to sculpture in serving as a dynamic and pleasing object to entertain the senses rather than contain peanuts or wine. Its sole reason for existence can be providing visual and tactile pleasures to the viewer, and its "utility" limited to that end.

Can you imagine a cloth wall decoration more than three-quarters as long as a football field or containing more than fifteen hundred figures in seventy-two scenes portrayed in thread? Such was the Bayeux tapestry embroidered in France during the eleventh century to ornament the nave of the Bayeux Cathedral in Normandy. Composed of yellow, red, blue, and green woolen thread sewn upon linen, the hanging measures 231 feet in length and is 20 inches in width. Thread outlines imaginary animals and foliage in a picturesque border surrounding a panoramic area which relates, among other episodes, William the Conqueror's invasion of England. Latin inscriptions offer an additional element in communication. The tapestry, now housed in a French museum, offers more comprehensive information about the habits and beliefs of the Normans than any existing literature of that period.

Though ornamental fabric used as hangings appeared in Egyptian art during the reign of Thutmose III, 1463–1451 B.C., as well as in the Far East at an early date, medieval European craftsmen devised more involved tapestry procedures to attain elaborate compositions. For instance, during the sixteenth century over fourteen thousand color variations were incorporated in some late French Gothic hangings, and their completion demanded many years. A great emphasis on minute details in both foreground and background is evident in works such as *Proceeding for the Hunt* (Figure 357). This highly treated tapestry portraying two lords, richly attired in brocaded robes and followed by a page

357 Proceeding for the Hunt, *tapestry (6 feet 5 inches wide, 8 feet 7 inches high), woven thread, France, 16th century. (Courtesy French and Co. Inc.)*

358   Breast Plate (12 inches high), Gold, Columbia, ca. 1600. (Courtesy Museum of Primitive Art)

359   Cloak (Mantle), woven wool and cotton (38 inches wide, 59 inches high), Peru, 1300-1500. (Courtesy Museum of Primitive Art)

bearing a falcon, clearly illustrates the patience and dexterity of Gothic craftsmen. The anatomical interpretation of the young page as a miniature adult rather than a developing youth conveys the medieval notion of childhood. In somewhat different forms, but sharing a mutual intent with men of the past, artists and students still employ cloth, yarn, and thread to bring brightness to walls.

We are told Spanish explorers journeyed to the new world for various reasons: to seek passages to the East, adventure, converts for the Church, a fountain of youth, or to refill the coffers of Spain. They encountered strange customs and beheld wonderful products of advanced civilizations, Aztec, Mayan, and Incan. Francisco Pizarro, the sixteenth-century Spanish conqueror of the Inca Empire, undoubtedly viewed wonders similar to the gold breast plate (Figure 358), which measures over a foot in height. Hammered into intricate relationships and richly patterned by Indian craftsman, such gold ornamentations, as well as smaller trinkets, were widely collected by the Spaniards. Gold, with its metallic luster and its buying and holding power, held great appeal for the new arrivals who diligently bartered with lead balls from Spanish muskets and the tips of Spanish swords.

At the time of the Spanish arrival, the Inca Empire extended over two thousand miles along the coast of western South America as well as far inland; it included northern Ecuador, Peru, Bolivia, and half of Chile. The Incas administered numerous coastal and mountain tribes. A system of roads more impressive and enduring than those constructed by Romans, to link their provinces, provided efficient communication and commerce in the Inca Empire. The arts flourished in numerous locales, and the craftsman's products reached a superb level of competence. The Inca's design sense and use of materials differed greatly from the then current European tendencies, which leaned toward naturalistic imagery. Indian crafts were generally more Romantic, closer in kinship with earlier European Gothic forms, bold, spirited, expressive, and imaginative. Such a factor is not a reflection of a shortcoming in craftsmanship on the part of the South Americans, but rather indicates that their solutions unfolded in harmony with beliefs and desires. The art historian Gerhard Rodenwaldt[3] indicates a meaningful reason for such imaginative and expressive inclinations when stating,

[3] Charles Seltman, *Approach To Greek Art* (London: The Studio Publications, 1948), p. 31.

When the primitive or archaic artist shows a departure from nature, he does not do so from inadequacy of vision or incompetence of hand, but because the subconscious inclination within himself and his age demands a kind of "inner truth" of form, which is not necessarily evident in nature.

Inhabitants of the western areas of South America were so skillfull that they employed mouse hair as weaving material and also created beautiful feather-covered wall hangings. In the preparation of llama wool for garments and hangings, the Peruvians were probably the most prolific dyers in the world. Tested by modern standards, many of their ancient dyes are as permanent and satisfactory as today's finest colorings. Highly inventive and expressive weavings served to cloak the natives (Figure 359). Ornate mantles were decorated with geometric symbols of deities or mythological characters directly woven into the material. Peruvians, in addition to being highly inventive in weaving and silver- and gold-smithing, were particularly gifted in pottery and allied crafts. Fanciful gardens of simulated flowers were constructed of precious metals, and pottery was such an important activity that the Chimu, a coastal tribe, buried their dead in huge clay pots. Creations in clay even included gayly decorated bird-shaped containers which, when poured from, whistled. While certain subjects were portrayed with warmth and humor, others were presented with intense and fierce characteristics. The painted wood container "keru" (Figure 360) in the shape of a tiger's head is indicative of the power and vitality of many of the Peruvians' accomplishments.

Far to the north of the former lands of the Incas, even now in our nation, one may break the earth's crust to expose a particle of an ancient crop. Though the footprints of the moccasined traveler have long been eradicated, a minute portion of his craft products remains to be uncovered. While ornate medicine pipes, boldly painted elk-skin robes, porcupine-quill embroidery, feather baskets, and expressive corn-husk masks have decayed, dissipating as yesterday's clouds, a few items still exist. In the Southwest fragments of pottery lie buried; shell ornaments may be uncovered in the Middle West; and in the Eastern woodlands a few amulets, jars, and handsomely carved stone pipes are yet to be discovered (Figure 361). Rather than plains and mountains, however, museums are now keepers of the Indian's heritage. Their displays reveal that Indian crafts can provide magnificent lessons in the useful possibilities of the natural materials of a land. Such exhibits also readily

360   *Keru, Incan painted wood container, Peru, ca. 1500. (Courtesy Museum of Primitive Art)*

361   *Pipe, carved and engraved stone, Mound Builders, Ohio Territory, ca. 1000. (Courtesy Ohio Historical Society)*

indicate that man of the past, be he Iroquois, or Inca, Pawnee, or Persian, Chinese, Greek, French, or Sioux, shaped pots, pipes, clothing, wall hangings, and innumerable other items with beauty and elegance in mind.

Dissolving Barriers: Fine and Minor Arts

"Crafts," traditionally associated with the production of utilitarian objects, designates activities such as jewelry and furniture construction, pottery, and weaving. Frequently in art history publications, these ventures are termed the "minor arts"; for their purposes, unlike those of the fine arts, encompass service factors. For instance, furniture is not made to merely provide visual joy; on the other hand, a piece of sculpture may have just that purpose. Architecture, painting, and sculpture are classified as fine arts, because they supposedly exist as ends in themselves. However; a word of caution: contrived hierarchies of value pertaining to classifications such as fine and minor arts or arts and crafts frequently breed undue confusion and false impressions. For instance, it is apparent that architecture, classified as a fine art, fulfills utilitarian needs, and many would vigorously advance painting and sculpture as useful, with numerous implications of service. Furthermore, there are tendencies to blend a craft and a fine art into a single venture in such current undertakings as ceramic sculpture. Thus it is extremely difficult if not impossible to rigidly specify domains or categorize either the value of respective areas in crafts or their relationship to the so-called fine arts. It is even feasible to conclude that many craft objects exist as ends in themselves; for does not a tapestry function as a painting?

One factor is of prime importance: any craft activity, to possess the attributes of an art form, must involve creative action. Thus a craft undertaking must go beyond mere mastery of process and technical display to qualify as an art experience. William Shakespeare's comment "Art made tongue-tied by authority" indicates that this problem is not exclusive to the crafts or of recent emergence.

Crafts in a Machine Age

Attitudes toward the role of crafts in an industrial society are dependent on three factors: one's notion of both art and technology and interest in the most suitable means of meeting the aesthetic requirements of a rapidly expanding society. Traditionalists have often questioned the imposed discipline derived from the use of machines in the production of craft objects. The view stems from a natural fear that mechanical limitations will unduly restrict expression. A firm conviction in the validity of exclusively handmade crafts has attributes both compatible and in conflict with twentieth-century mass-production techniques.

In the middle of the past century two Englishmen, John Ruskin and William Morris, instigated a craft revival. Unfortunately, both rejected the machine as a possible ally, owing to reasoning that was highly conditioned by the flavor of the era. In addition to being appalled by the poorly designed machine-made products of their time, both Englishmen viewed the machine as a dangerous mechanical monster which robbed men of pleasure in their work. The latter view is easily understood in terms of the crude belching machines of the mid-nineteenth century, located in dank sweat shops which exploited children, as well as adults, as laborers. Therefore social, as well as aesthetic factors, influenced their beliefs. Both Ruskin and Morris advocated a return to the medieval craft tradition, because so they contended, men during the gothic period derived great satisfaction from working directly with their hands. Morris actually organized a shop for the production of crafts by hand. His accomplishments included handsome hand-set books, sensitive wallpaper, and practical and simple furniture such as the famous Morris chair. In strongly advocating the crafts as a means of enriching social environment and also in personally producing well-designed objects, Morris ranks as one of the founders of the modern craft movement. His tragedy is found in his rejection of the machine; for the restriction to hand work severely limited the quantity of his offerings and made them exorbitant in cost. Only a few were therefore permitted the acquisition of his tasteful products, and thus his aim of serving an entire society was not fulfilled. It remained for men of the coming century to resolve the problem of a workable relationship between well-designed craft products and machine technology. However, the words of one nineteenth-century prophet were to ring true; the American clergyman, Henry Ward Beecher who, in "Proverbs From Plymouth Pulpit," said,

A tool is but the extension of a man's hand and a machine is but a complex tool and he that invents a machine augments the power of a man and the well-being of mankind.

Members of the German Bauhaus were the first to expound an influential and logical philosophy dealing with a fusion of fine arts, crafts, and industrial methodology. This early-twentieth-century school developed the artist-craftsman concept in great part and, when feasible, used the machine in the service of man, art, and crafts. In turning out forms, from concise but exciting chairs and dinnerware to typography, the Bauhaus crystallized the roles of artist, artist-craftsman, and industrial designer in the age of the machine.

North of Germany and across the choppy North Sea from the land of Morris lie the Scandinavian countries. By assimilating the views of earlier exponents of art and crafts as service factors in society and building upon rich native craft heritages, the inhabitants of those lands are now renowned for their contemporary craft accomplishments. The integration and glorification of utilitarian objects are keystones in the building of their twentieth-century world. Beauty, suitability, integrity, and creativity are interwoven into their fabrics, and explicit constructional solutions, blessed with excellent craftsmanship, mark their three-dimensional products. A variety of materials — clay, glass, metal, wood, wool — are shaped into beautiful and serviceable items by these northern craftsmen. Assisted by traditional looms, potter's wheels, and small hand tools, they execute innumerable products by hand. In addition, they dictate their terms to huge machines, power saws, lathes, and metal presses and also provide wise design advice to industry. The latter factor assures a flow of excellent craft forms, through industrial and commercial channels, into urban and rural life. A balance is maintained between the modern industrial production of craft forms and ancient methods of producing by hand. In Sweden, for example, numerous craft societies, *hemslojds*, preserve native methods and design traditions through encouraging local handcrafts. The societies maintain stores in the smaller towns and are nationally unified into a single organization that maintains sales outlets in Stockholm. Hand-woven fabrics, toys, jewelry, pottery, woodware, basketry, and utensils of all sorts created in home workshops are sold throughout the land. Thus, beauty permeates a society; for art is absorbed by the people in countless manners.

An examination of their products readily indicates the Scandinavians' skill and vitality in crafts (Figure 362). How would you design a chair of wood and cane? Using bottles for subject matter, could you create an interesting pattern upon cloth? Does the

362   *Scandinavian Crafts, clay, metal, wood, cloth, and glass. (Courtesy Embassies of Denmark, Finland, Norway, Sweden)*

Saarinen Chair, Eero Saarinen. (Courtesy Knoll Associates)

363

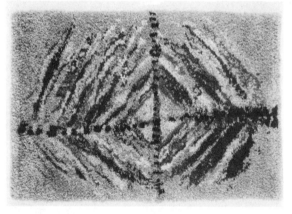

364   ALLADIN, *hooked wool rug, Sirkka Autio-Polkkynen, Finland. (Courtesy of Bigelow-Sanford Carpet Co. Inc.)*

365   *Crystal Glass Form, Steuben Ware, sculptured by Donald Pollard, engraved design by Sidney Waugh. (Courtesy Corning Glass Co.)*

glass decanter appear to be interesting? Notice how the bird motifs on the wall hanging occupy space in both an unusual and appealing manner.

In the United States the problems of tasteful craft production are being partially resolved in various manners. Artists in craft areas may work alone in individual shop or studio turning out a limited number of creative ventures in cloth, wood, or metal. Others, associated with large manufacturing concerns, function as industrial designers; standing shoulder to shoulder with engineers and other production specialists, they may have a prolific guided output. Sculptors and architects, such as Harry Bertoia, Isamu Noguchi, and Eero Saarinen, have even designed furniture for industrial production (Figure 363). While methods vary greatly, the goal remains the same: the production of sensitive and well-made craft products.

A brief consideration of several huge manufacturing concerns readily indicates interest in product design in craft areas. The Bigelow-Sanford Carpet Company recently sponsored a competition in Finland for original rug designs. Serving as an adjunct to the achievements of the company's own design staff, the foreign venture was conceived as a means of stimulating interest in keenly executed and visually exciting rugs (Figure 364). The Corning Glass Works maintains a division, Steuben Glass, which deals exclusively with the production of elegant glassware. Painters such as Henri Matisse, Graham Sutherland, and Pavel Tchelitchew have rendered designs for this finely executed crystal. The company's aim is to create original and skillfully made works of art. Each form is personally executed by hand, thus retaining the old handicraft tradition in a highly mechanized society. A recent Steuben achievement, *Moby Dick*, indicates a movement away from engraved bowls into pure glass sculpture (Figure 365). The crystal, through line engraving and form, interprets Captain Ahab and his men in mortal struggle with the great white whale. It reflects the great and tragic moment of churning sea and leaping monster which places the whalers in a precarious position.

An extensive design program in the crafts is conducted by the Aluminum Company of America. Weavers and textile and display designers, Alexander Girard, Ilonka Karasz, and Marianne Strengell, as well as architects, sculptures, and industrial and advertising designers, have been encouraged to suggest new meanings for aluminum. Concerns such as Rambusch Studios, leading American religious designers, have also been incorporated into Alcoa's far-reaching program. Rambusch craftsmen created a versatile altar group (Figure 366). In addition to direct appeal through honesty and simplicity in the use of material, certain features assure practical use of the metalware. Bases are weighted to offer maximum stability, and candle cups are removable from supporting shafts to provide ease of candle insertion. In addition, the disk-shaped catch plates, for wax drippings, may be easily removed from the candlesticks and cleaned separately. The entire group, owing to form simplicity, is also sympathetic toward mass-production methods, which assures decreasing costs and wider distribution. While craft ventures intended for industrial production may be sponsored by huge business or manufacturing concerns, other efforts are instigated by individual artist-craftsman. Many in small private studios — for instance, the ceramist Robert Turner and the master craftsman in wood, Wharton Esherick — turn out a limited number of elegantly handcrafted forms. College and university art departments partially support various artist-craftsmen who divide their efforts between personal production and teaching. Others such as Ed Secon and Roger Whitelow have associated to produce handcrafted products. Combining the price and promptness of mass production with the distinction of handcrafted production, their results have great merit (Figure 367). No matter the artist-craftsman's means, whether sponsored by industry or unassisted, the aim remains the same. The achievement of quality in his craft and its acceptance by society is his final objective.

366   *Religious Ware, Altar Group, bronze anodized aluminum, Rambusch Studios. (Courtesy Aluminum Company of America)*

367   *Table, walnut. (Courtesy Ed Secon Design Associates)*

368   *Sensing the Nature of Material and Shaping. (Courtesy Kenneth R. Beittel)*

The Artist-Craftsman; Attitude and Working Processes

Certain convictions are generally held by artist-craftsmen. Of prime importance is the belief that the creation and use of handsome utilitarian products greatly assists in raising a society beyond a savage or bare-existence level devoid of inspiration. Such an attitude thus recognizes the development of fine craft forms as a constant tendency in the evolution of civilization and as essential to its continued growth. This truism is currently obvious; for the products of our civilization — alas, both poor and fine — did not just happen, but either emerged from inquisitive manipulations of materials or were originally conceived upon drawing boards or drafting tables. Look about you at chairs and cups, consider drapery and jewelry, and the contention is apparent. The role of the artist-craftsman is to tastefully fulfill a creative function within the bounds of his field. He further realizes that both inspiration and appropriate materials exist in extensive numbers and forms throughout the universe.

Answers to the challenging problem of what can be achieved with a particular material are dependent on its inherent qualities of workability, such as its cutting, shaping, and joining characteristics, as well as on the intensity of the pursuit. During creative action, barriers dissipate between self, process, and material; for the three tend to intermingle in furthering conceptual and structural relationships. For instance, the material, during changing stages, may suggest a new direction, or at a certain moment the mind will sense a possible process modification which will offer new dimensions to the idea pursued. However, while some solutions may emerge in a moment, others may demand intense involvement over a tedious length of time.

The artist-craftsman persistently shapes his material through knowledge of its nature, mastery of process, skillful technique, sensitivity, and inventiveness. Devoted to discovering new form relationships, he may shape metal or experiment with cloth, keenly react after observing the grain pattern of wood, or dictate his terms to moist pliable clay (Figure 368).

Clay, from Banks of Earth

Widely available, inexpensive, and highly pliable, clay is easily penetrated for texturing and sympathetic to extensive glaze treatments. Owing to its features of plasticity and, when fired, permanency, it is adaptable for many craft purposes. The use of clay to form jars, bottles, cups, dishes, and trays is obvious; in addition it can function as ceramic sculpture, wall reliefs, and household objects of various sorts.

William Parry indicates that inquisitiveness, while producing wheel-thrown clay jars, led him into composing ceramic sculpture (Figure 369). Notice how surface fluctuations secured through texturing the clay, while moist, contributed intriguing accents to the monumental figure. Of his work, Parry says:

> Angel of Annunciation is the result of whim. It happened that I was making a number of covered jars — varying in each the elements of knob, lid, container, and foot. During the assembling of one set of the wheel-formed sections, I turned to scrambling the combinations. The clay was a dark stoneware and I brushed in light slip areas. Its consistency was right for impression and the additions of coils to delineate the garment. One move led to another, and perhaps somewhat in answer to the direct balance of the symmetrical elements and their inflated, pot-like form the trumpet and later the wings were evolved. In a sense it made itself and is in the nature of a performance.
>
> Where I have the concentration and the ability to recognize the character of what is emerging I am able to work swiftly and often with awareness that I cannot match again in reworking such an idea.

369 ANGEL OF ANNUNCIATION, *assembled ceramic sculpture, wheel-thrown clay shapes, William D. Parry. (Courtesy the Artist)*

370   ASSEMBLED RELIEF, *ceramic sculpture, wheel-thrown clay shapes, Harlan Hoffa. (Courtesy the Artist)*

371   SLAB CANDELABRA, *Clay, Glenn Ruby. (Courtesy the Artist)*

Harlan Hoffa speaks of the fusion of pottery and sculpture in his clay relief which, through a rhythmical arrangement of clay shapes, casts vigorous shadow interplays (Figure 370):

This ceramic sculpture is one of a series in which I have consciously attempted to bridge the gap between pottery and sculpture. The techniques used to form and join the elements which compose the piece are essentially those of the ceramist although the end result is not pottery but sculpture.

The rationale which has prompted this procedure is at least partially an outgrowth of the increasing sculptural quality of contemporary pottery. I have tried to recognize that my pots will serve fundamentally the same purpose as sculpture — that is that the ware is intended to elicit an aesthetic response rather than serve as a container. By admitting this fact to myself I am freed from the restrictions of designing for functions that will never take place and am able to concentrate on the form for its own sake. At the same time, however, I recognize that the techniques which potters have used through the centuries have been empirically developed as efficient means of manipulating the plastic clay. By combining the sculptor's emphasis on pure form and the potter's techniques of creating in plastic clay I feel that I am able to combine the qualities of sculpture and those of pottery without sacrificing the quality or integrity of either mode of expression. And I feel that integrity of expression is paramount to any artist's work.

Glenn Ruby found that a slab method of handling clay, organized with thought and discretion, can offer an exciting solution to a form problem (Figure 371). He says:

In designing this candelabra I tried to retain the slab-like quality of the clay, with little or no modeling. The design was largely determined by the nature of the clay slab in working directly with the material. Sketches were used to crystallize and choose from the various possible solutions. Variation in the design was achieved by dividing the spaces in unequal divisions allowing the candles to be placed at varying levels in the candelabra. A simple glaze treatment was chosen to allow the sculptural form to retain its unity.

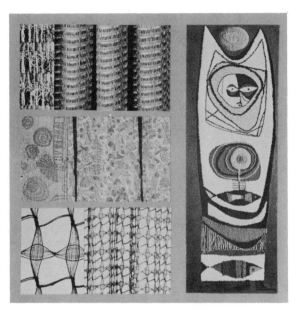

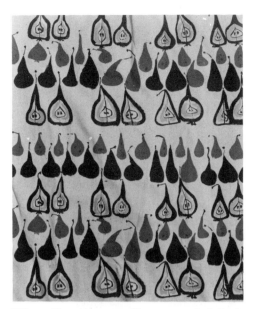

373 PEARS, *drapery, silk screen on cloth, Ruth Grothenrath. (Courtesy James A. Schwalbach)*

372 *Dress Fabric, woven, Helen Wood Pope; Drapery, printed fabric, Herbert Friedson; Drapery, appliqué, Evelyn M. Gulick; Hooked Wall Hanging, Bill Hinz. (Courtesy Saint Paul Gallery)*

Cloth, from the Looms of Man

Cloth can be easily cut, torn, joined, frayed, pierced, folded, dyed, or painted. When woven into rich combinations, printed, or sewn upon, it may serve as unique dress fabric, drapery, wall hangings, place mats, and even containers (Figure 372).

The silk screen printing process assisted Ruth Grothenrath in rapidly repeating an all-over pattern upon tobacco cloth (Figure 373). Both the interiors and exteriors of pears acted as motifs to transform the plain surface into charming and purposeful drapery. Notice how the arrangement is activated through value and size contrasts in the horizontal bands of imagery. Would not cloth printed with wood or linoleum blocks also prove appropriate for café curtains in kitchen or dining area?

Two sheets of stencil paper, oil paint, a stiff stencil brush, and a segment of duck cloth comprised the necessary tools and materials for *Variations on the Circle* (Figure 374). Created by a university freshman, the wall hanging could add a note of joy to den or recreation area. Each circle appears to have a life of its own through dexterity in paint application. Flickering and scattered intense and minute shapes radiating out from several cores contributes additional impact to the cloth banner.

Cloth upon cloth, the appliqué of contrasting burlap and felt upon muslin, denotes *Birds in Con-*

374 VARIATIONS ON THE CIRCLE, *wall hanging, stencil on cloth, University student.*

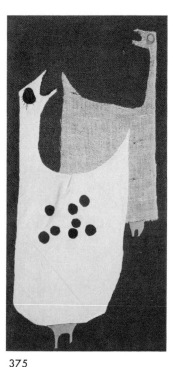

Birds in Conversation, *wall hanging, appliqué, University student.*

375

versation (Figure 375). Interest is heightened in the two bold primary symbols through the addition of small circular portions of felt suggesting eyes and body pattern. The design treatment indicates that qualities of simplicity, discretion, and ingenuity can prove rewarding in craft undertakings. Can you think of several subjects which, if treated in a similar direct manner, would serve as exciting ideas for wall hangings?

Marilyn Pappas combines appliqué, stitchery, and paint in her hanging *Beach Window* (Figure 376). Thread provides a linear element which, through a diversified application, contributes exciting directional play and textural notes. The experimental treatment of lines and shapes indicates a free inquiry into the potential of thread and cloth. An obvious naturalism is secured through exploiting ragged and frayed edges to act as inherent decorative features. Strong value counterplays and both unity and variation are apparent design factors in the solution. Passages of paint, rough-surfaced cloth adjacent to smooth-, and a controlled but active handling of space contribute additional impact. Notice how the huge flanking dark masses provide security and focus attention on the framed activated center area. The theme is reminiscent of a magic window through which one can view a blending of chaos and control. A sensitive hand planted the exciting crop.

Lorraine Krentzin often uses cloth in unusual ways for three-dimensional craft forms. Her *Pajama Bag* is a jovial fantasy composed of buttons, bright bits of felt, and scrap cloth (Figure 377). Such little people, sufficiently large to serve as storage for pajamas, would provide warmth and humor as bedroom accessories. A pocket in the rear of the bag permits the insertion of sleeping garments which add bulk to the form. Similar solutions could provide beach bags or, if filled with shredded foam rubber, decorative pillows for den or living room.

Creative weaving and hooking are excellent means of acquiring material suitable for a variety of purposes from place mats to rugs. Technical information pertaining to the construction of simple looms and a variety of weaving processes is readily available in numerous publications. Strips of cloth, yarn, and even string can be combined with twigs or reed to provide intriguing and original surfaces. Burlap stretched tightly to a wooden frame, yarn, and a hooking needle combined with a university student's skill and patience resulted in the hooked rug *Gifts from the Sea* (Figure 378). The process is uncomplicated, because the hooking needle, when inserted between the burlap fibers, deposits yarn at a determined and constant depth. Creating rugs containing unusual and interesting patterns could enrich most any art program.

BEACH WINDOW, *wall hanging, appliqué, stitchery and paint, Marilyn Pappas. (Courtesy the Artist)*

376

PAJAMA BAG, *scrap cloth and buttons, Lorraine Krentzin. (Courtesy the Artist)*

377

GIFTS FROM THE SEA, *hooked wool rug, University student.*

378

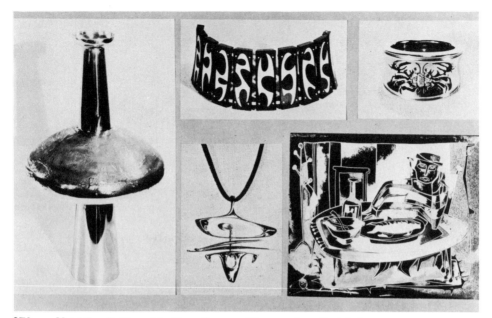

379 *Metal Can Be Treated in Many Manners. (Courtesy Saint Paul Gallery)*

Metal, from the Hearths of Industry

The physical properties of metals — solidity, malleability, tensile strength, brilliance, and permanence — provide a high degree of appropriateness for jewelry construction. Many materials and manners of shaping exquisite rings, pendants, and bracelets — from bending and piercing to forging and casting — enriched through processes involving chased, engraved, etched, and *repoussé* surfaces, have deep roots in antiquity. American artist-craftsmen continue and add to this rich handicraft tradition (Figure 379).

By stressing surface contrasts and sequence distortion for visual appeal, Donald B. Wright shaped an ancient alloy into contemporary decorative hollowware. Pewter, an alloy of tin and lead, was first employed by Romans and later used extensively in the creation of medieval tankards, plates, and chalices. Its use also continued for utilitarian objects in America long beyond our Revolutionary Period. Innumerable functional objects were formed of this alloy through melting and casting or hammering into relationships from flat metal sheets. Pewter objects can now be directly constructed upon a power lathe through rasping and burnishing or spinning, with a wooden mold controlling the shape.

By cutting a series of intriguing shapes from a sheet of silver, inlaying the metal into small blocks

380 Monster Box, *silver, Earl Krentzin. (Courtesy the Artist)*

381   BUFFET GROUP, *aluminum and porcelain, Don Wallance. (Courtesy Aluminum Company of America)*

of ebony wood, and linking each segment, Christian F. Schmidt composed a pleasing bracelet. A crab served as symbol and the intaglio process as the means for enriching the gold ring by John Paul Miller. Concise penetrations capture shadows and richly indentify the motif. Svetozar Radakovich's pendant resulted from an active composition of silver shapes and a moonstone. The employment of the cloisonné process, originated by Byzantine metal-smiths of long ago, enabled Joseph Trippetti to create a colorful plaque. His method consisted in attaching small silver fences to a copper background, filling areas with colored enamels, and firing in a kiln. The result was a glasslike surface possessing intriguing transparent and opaque passages of color.

Metal fulfills many purposes in the crafts by serving as material for containers, utensils, furniture, and even architectural detailing and room dividers. Harry Bertoia's sculpture screen for a lobby at the General Motors Technical Center may serve as one instance of the latter role. Many artists, such as Earl Krentzin, currently combine attributes of both jewelry and sculpture in their handcrafted metal creations. Krentzin's tiny, exquisite *Monster Box* protects little treasures and charges only a smile (Figure 380). Krentzin frequently gives his imagination free reign in designing craft objects which some-

what recall ancient Oriental dragons, Greek centaurs, and Gothic gargoyles. The lost-wax process served to produce his fat demon crowned with a pearl. Imagination and humor have roles to play in crafts; for varied fingers can touch the heart of man.

Recent developments in metals such as aluminum extend new potentials for the crafts. For instance, in less than a century modern technology has dropped the price of aluminum from $500 a pound to about 21 cents; therefore, the use of aluminum becomes highly feasible in numerous ventures produced by hand as well as machine. Don Wallance, noted industrial designer and author, suggested a practical use for this versatile metal in his concisely conceived *Buffet Group* (Figure 381). The solution is highly appropriate for intended machine production. The spoons are polished natural aluminum. The aluminum casserole exteriors are coated with colorful enamel, and a white porcelain covers the interiors. White porcelain also coats the interior of the large salad bowl, while the outer surface is polished aluminum. The hors d'oeuvre tree is a highly flexible grouping of interlocking serving units. Versatility and adaptability are prime factors in its solution. The tree may be easily assembled and constantly modified; for, like a TinkerToy, it offers various clusters. Thus, compact or extensive arrangements can be easily achieved, depending on the desires of the arranger. Candle holders are also integrated into the structure.

Paul McCobb,[4] well known for his elegantly designed furniture, sees a great potential in the use of aluminum in home furnishings (Figure 382). He contends:

> Aluminum has twentieth century acceptability — qualities and workability features that are unique and not comparably found in other metals. It is especially stimulating to the contemporary designer because it has not been bogged down by a traditional history of use. In other words, its very comparative newness in the design picture is an incentive to me to provide new ideas and new products, and its possibilities seem limitless in the home from almost every standpoint.
>
> In appearance, aluminum contains a design quality of its own, easily blended with other materials and pleasing to the eye. This, of course, is not enough in itself to make it useful in the best sense, but when you add its color possibilities by anodizing, and the various techniques of expanding, perforating, spinning and so on that have been developed, aluminum offers the contemporary designer almost unequalled opportunities.
>
> To be specific, the furniture group I have just designed for Alcoa is a perfect example of aluminum's qualities. Take the lounge chair, for example. Its lightness makes it a most adaptable seating unit for any family living area, and the freedom of styling that aluminum inspires has enabled me to create furniture that will fit into almost any contemporary home.

The ability to see creative potential in process and material is the mark of creative man. Even the common nail, if handled with discretion and keenly placed, can offer both a creative experience and an intriguing result. *Deployed Departure* resulted from an experimental search by a university student to discover new uses for inexpensive items (Figure 383). Surfaces were painted white to introduce a unifying element to the complicated mass and capture uniformity in cast shadows. Fluctuating placements, heights, shapes, and sizes increased the opportunities for a divergent shadow pattern within and adjacent to the metal relief.

In art there is nothing sacred about one particular process or material; silver is not necessarily superior to lead, nor is paint to clay. The importance of each lies in its breadth of creative opportunities. Thus, value judgments must be in terms of skill, design quality, originality, and appropriateness in presenting the idea, regardless of art area or material.

382   *Chair, Stool, and Hi-Fi Set, aluminum and wood panels, Paul McCobb. (Courtesy Aluminum Company of America)*

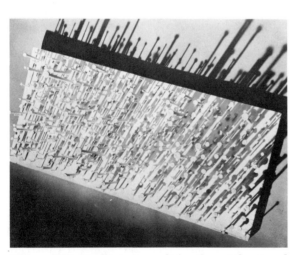

383   Deployed Departure, *relief, nails, varied sorts and sizes, University student.*

4 *Forecast,* pamphlet issued by the Aluminum Company of America, Pittsburgh, Pa.

384   *Coffee Table, walnut, oil finish, Ed Secon. (Courtesy Ed Secon Design Associates)*

Wood, the Fruit of the Forest

Before the advent of huge factories and advanced distributing techniques, young America was primarily a land of farmers and craftsmen. Needs were usually met with courage, independent action, and a high degree of inventiveness. With a few wood planks, cut and dressed by hand, early settlers carved handsome implements and ingeniously constructed furnishings. The strength, hardness, and density of ash, cedar, cherry, hickory, and walnut served them well. Resulting forms were not flamboyant but direct and uncomplicated with lush grain, keen joints, and economical constructional methods readily apparent.

Manufacturers of contemporary furniture—Knoll Associates, Herman Miller, Ed Secon Design Associates, and others — still retain the concise features of the best of early American furniture (Figure 384). Their utilitarian wood forms also often possess versatility through interchangeable units or contain pleasing blendings of contrasting material (Figure 385). They have also introduced innovations such as the use of impervious plastics and lightweight metal in conjunction with wood and the use of shatterproof glass, which through transparency denies bulk, as table surfaces. In addition, recently developed adhesives, plywoods, and veneers; heating and molding methods; and extremely capable power equipment for cutting, shaping, and constructing have extended design possibilities. However, simplicity, ingenuity, and excellent craftsmanship still remain virtues which link the past with the present.

385   *Coffee Table, plastic and wood, with interchangeable top, Lew Butler. (Courtesy Knoll Associates)*

386 THE CHALLENGE OF WOOD, *bowls in process of carving.*

Wood offers both challenge and reward. To feel its texture, sense its resistence, and direct the emergence of its final form provides an enlightening experience (Figure 386).Unfortunately, when working with wood, many students and professionals emphasize skill but ignore creativeness or design idea. A dependency on patterns or the production of predetermined results conceived by others denies essential and personal thinking. But it should not be assumed that the personal determination of design automatically assures the excellence of craft form. Creative experiences at their best are only progressive movements toward perfection. The consideration of proportions, the relationship of parts, sensitivity in handling and exploiting the material, care in building and finishing are all mandatory for success, particularly in the crafts. The inherent qualities of the material must be taken into account in cutting, joining, and finishing, and tools must be properly employed to gain the utmost through efficient means. Reference to the walnut bench (Figure 387) indicates several satisfactory as well as questionable solutions arrived at by a university student. Craftsmanship and sensitivity are apparent in the skillful production of the form and the sympathetic oil finish which stresses the warm tones and grains of the walnut. The strip construction of the top surface contributes an integrated decorative effect in harmony with the building method. The effect is naturally achieved through staggering the lengths of walnut which, when glued and doweled, compose the top surface. In addition to an interesting pattern of darks and lights, this treatment gives a buoyancy to the form; for the pierced areas permit the passage of space. The treatment also eliminates material, and thereby weight, and effectively emphasizes adjacent solid areas. One questionable relationship becomes apparent when viewing the legs. Do the legs contain undue bulk which tends to refute the implied lightness of weight in the table top by implying that great strength is essential for support? Possibly if the legs were slimmer and tapered to repeat at their extremities the identical thickness of the table top, unity or organic sequence through proportion repetition would be in evidence. What is your opinion?

The placement of aft support bars into various flanking retaining sockets enables the back of the contemporary Morris chair to assume slight or great degrees of slope (Figure 388). Thus adaptability is a contributing factor to the somewhat monumental form. The student producer freely moved away from original pencil sketches while engaged in the actual construction; for the attainment of each three-dimensional segment demanded a subsequent decision. Thus, to a great extent, succeeding stages dictated proportional relationships and placements which followed. Such a fluid working procedure assured creative range to the builder and stimulated constant thought. The chair was finished with a mat lacquer and topped with a foam-rubber pillow. The selection of a light-colored, semirough pillow covering enhanced the adjacent slick, dark walnut in adding a note of contrast. An additional pillow was also produced; if desired, it could be suspended by a strap secured to the chair's back.

Plywood, obtainable in large sturdy panels, permits ease of construction in eliminating gluing, clamping, and planing in securing large uniform building members. A range of rich veneers — birch, mahogany, walnut — available as coverings in the laminated material also permits a variety of pleasing plywood surfaces. Frequently, the problem of cost denies an extensive use of these fine but expensive

387 *Walnut Bench, a question of form.*

Contemporary Morris Chair, walnut, foam rubber and fabric, University student.

388

389 *Storage Unit, fir and birch plywood, University student.*

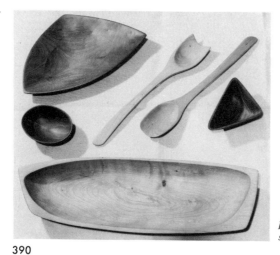

390

Bowls and Utensils, cherry and walnut, University students.

veneers. One student solved this problem by combining fir and birch plywoods in composing a concise storage unit (Figure 389). Inexpensive fir plywood serves as the outer shell. An off-white, slightly diluted enamel finish permitted a slight suggestion of grain. Birch veneer, oil-rubbed and waxed, functions as drawer fronts. These lushly grained areas added a note of richness to the entire rectangular mass. The unit achieved a practical height in being perched upon conventional metal piping secured to flanges. Painted a light value, the slender legs related to the large supported form while implying a minimum of overhead weight.

In addition to its suitability for furniture, wood is an excellent material for utensils, bowls, wall plaques, and even toys. An abundance of tools and equipment is not a prime necessity, nor need the processes be complicated. Determination and mallets, gouges, rasps, and a band saw assisted in shaping the bowls and utensils (Figure 390).

A few factors warrant consideration in the forming of a cherry or walnut bowl by hand. While both cherry and walnut are classified as hard woods, the latter, owing to less resistance in carving, is more suitable for the beginner. If sufficiently thick planks are not available, several boards can be securely glued for desired thickness. Whenever possible, cutting should be undertaken in the direction of grain. The interior hollow is usually carved before the exterior shell is shaped. This facilitates clamping, achieved by securing the wood block to table or bench with a C clamp. After the desired depth and shape are attained, the interior walls may be interestingly refined with short gouge strokes or made perfectly smooth with curved rasp and sandpaper. The outer shell can then be cut with a band saw with the

saw table tilted to the desired angle. However, before attempting the exterior cutting of the bowl, it may prove profitable to experiment in cutting several pieces of scrap wood. This provides insight into possible angles and curves obtainable with the band saw. If the bowl design permits variations in rim width, cutting will be simplified and any slight errors easily remedied. After cutting the exterior, minor refinements can be achieved with rasp and sandpaper. Several thin applications of boiled linseed oil vigorously hand rubbed into all wood areas followed with coatings of clear paste wax assure an excellent finish.

A portion of Masonite, several short sections of different sizes of dowel sticks, and an inexpensive board were the ingredients for *Scrap Relief* (Figure 391). The dominant Masonite shape, cut by a band saw into a visually active segment, activates its surroundings through a multitude of elongated probes into the background field. Mounted on several small wood blocks, it rests slightly forward of the background. This solution enables shadows to add interest. The randomly placed circular dowels also tend to enliven spatial relationships and through a sharing of identical color unify the shallow pattern.

Designed as a creative toy, *Play Board* contains numerous wooden segments painted or topped with textured cloth, fur, or patterned paper (Figure 392). Each segment, secure in the pierced-board background, may be easily removed and inserted into another area. Thus an endless number of concentrated or spread-out arrangements with harmonious or discordant passages of shapes, surfaces, and colors are readily available. Encouraging play to adult as well as child, the Play Board invites both thought and active participation. Would you like to try it? Which moves would you make first? Why?

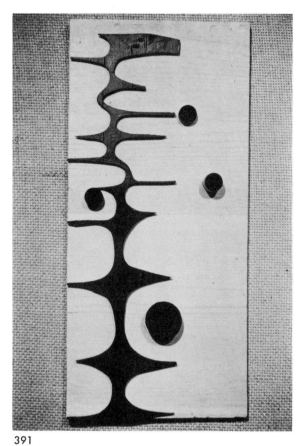

SCRAP RELIEF, *Masonite on wood, University student.*

391

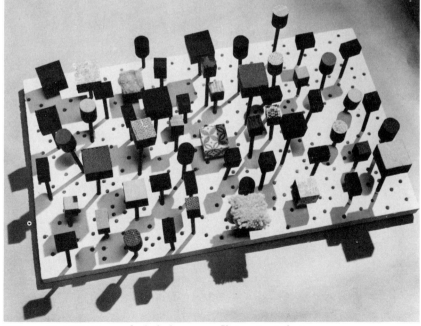

392 PLAY BOARD, *wood, cloth, fur, paper, University student.*

393 *Contemporary Hand-blown Glass. (Courtesy Blenko Glass Company)*

Glass and Tile,
Developed from Matter with Heat

Phoenicians long ago discovered that, by placing a small mass of molten glass upon one end of a hollow tube and blowing through the opposite end, bubbles of glass could be readily formed. In time men also learned to twist the blowpipe or gently paddle the glass bubble to achieve different shapes. Later, hard wooden molds were introduced to assist in obtaining uniformity in the blown forms. One of the first craftsmen to transfer such glass-blowing techniques to the New World was Casper Wistar, in the year 1739. His competent flasks and tableware, produced in the New Jersey area, were soon joined by many others issuing from the lips of numerous American artisans. In this age of huge machines and involved productional procedures in the glass industry, it is refreshing to realize that at least a few craftsmen continue the handcraft tradition of blown glass. Consider the fluid relationships and transparency of handmade Blenko ware; it reflects control while clearly fulfilling the three-dimensional potential of glass as an expressive material (Figure 393). Transparent and translucent passages within the compact decanter, as well as the elongated slender flasks, convey exciting interminglings of light and color. Such glassware can add a note of visual richness to the interior of any home.

In addition to functioning as containers, glass — stained, cut, and arranged as windows — has long contributed decoration and enlightenment. Originat-

ing in French cathedrals late in the tenth century, the process consisted of cut colored glass panels organized as patterns and inserted into lead channels for security and permanent positioning. Numerous congregations were edified by the arranged translucent windows portraying the glories of saints and related Biblical imagery. Casting a soft tinted light, the huge windows also heightened the spiritual atmosphere in numerous church interiors. The seventeenth century witnessed a modification in the production of stained-glass windows, with leading eliminated and large painted glass panels substituted. However, during the nineteenth-century craft revival, William Morris and Edward Burne Jones reintroduced the earlier traditional procedure. The large ornate windows of Holy Trinity Church, in London, are indicative of these Englishmen's finest efforts.

Stained glass is still handled by artist-craftsmen who continue to create luminous windows which speak of salvation (Figure 394).

Though neither glass blowing nor the construction of large stained-glass windows is feasible in many school art programs, other creative uses may be found for glass. Constructions incorporating colored glass, metal, and wood such as the *Abstract Space Structure* can readily be produced (Figure 395). When placed in front of a conventional window or adjacent to a wall, they reflect colorful masses and cast ever-

394   *Stained-Glass Window, Saint Joseph Roman Catholic Church, Fort Atkinson, Wisc., designed by T. C. Esser Co. (Courtesy the Architect, John J. Flad; photograph by William Wollin Studio)*

changing linear shadows. Intriguing shadow boxes, lamp housings, and miniature windows can also be easily produced by adhering pieces of stained glass to a larger underlying sheet of clear glass. Caulking compound or plastic aluminum applied along the edges of the colored glass can adhere the glass and provide an appearance of leading between the voids. Experiments in melting glass may also prove rewarding. Portions of contrasting colored glass placed upon a panel of clear glass and properly fired in a kiln yield a fused multicolored sheet. When properly framed, the sheet can serve a number of decorative purposes. Small bits from broken colored bottles as well as tiny segments of conventional stained glass may also act as jewelry. When placed on similar-sized pieces of clear glass and fired, the segments, owing to cohesion, unite into rounded glass droplets suitable as jewels for pendants or brooches. Colored glass may even be embedded in plaster or cement reliefs or, as tesserae, be used in mosaics.

The term "mosaic" relates to decorative patterns made up of small pieces of material, usually glass, stone, or ceramic tile. The segments are placed in cement or pasted upon a background material. Mosaics may vary from tiny decorations in jewelry to huge designs on floors, walls, and ceilings of buildings. Egyptian and Mesopotamian artists were the first to practice this craft. Greeks and Romans fol-

395   ABSTRACT SPACE STRUCTURE, *glass, wire, and wood, University student.*

396   GIRL WITH CAT, *mosaic plaque, ceramic tile, University student.*

397   MOSAIC TABLE, *marble and aluminum, Marjorie E. Kreilick. (Courtesy the Artist)*

lowed, using marble mosaics for floors and pavements and glass mosaics on fountains, columns, and varied architectural surfaces. Excavations at Pompeii unearthed a large pictorial floor mosaic which records in active imagery the battle exploits of the young Macedonian warrior, Alexander the Great. Later, in Christian churches, mosaics joined stained-glass windows, painted murals, and sculpture as means of informing man of the grandeur of the church and the rewards of believing. The Byzantine Empire is especially noted for the use of mosaics in religious structures; glittering accents of glass segments covered with gold leaf enhanced many of their splendid wall mosaics. The revival of interest in art of the past, evident in the nineteenth century, led to mosaics enriching sections of Westminster Abbey and the Houses of Parliament in London. During this century, mosaics add interest to the Stockholm town hall, the Moscow subway, innumerable buildings in Mexico and South America, and many hotels, schools, and public buildings in the United States.

Ceramic tiles secured from a local tile distributor, who usually employs the material for covering floors and walls in houses and public buildings, were used to create the wall plaque *Girl with Cat* (Figure 396). The tiles were broken by a hammer into small segments, arranged to express the subject matter in a personal manner, and then pasted to a section of Masonite which served as a backing. Notice how the student achieved vibrant organization through ingenuity in arranging the bits of tile. Intended for vertical placement upon a wall, the mosaic is not grouted in order to capture numerous recessed shadows which emphasize the multiplicity of pattern. Each bit of tile, therefore, appears to have a life of its own while making a minute but essential contribution to the total imagery. The use of grout, however, is mandatory to allow ease in cleaning when mosaics are used in horizontal manners as platters or table surfaces.

Mosaics for both decorative and practical purposes are often used in contemporary furniture. Marjorie Kreilick's *Mosaic Table*, composed of marble and aluminum, possesses a serving surface of strength, moisture resistance, and durability (Figure 397). Created to be adaptable to changing needs, the table consists of four separate units. The two top sections can be set adjacent to one another to act as a single large table or separated to function as two smaller tables. The sturdy aluminum supports may also be placed on their sides to lower the mosaic masses. Thus both length and height are subject to desired changes.

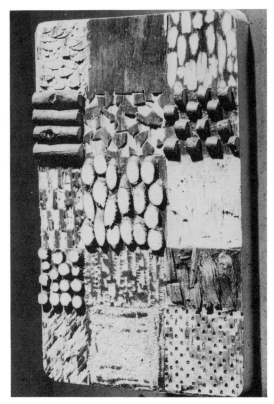

398   TEXTURE BOARD FROM NATURE, *bark and branches, University student.*

Found Material:
Gifts from Field and Stream

Exciting craft ventures can spring from frequently ignored objects found in nature's realm. Viewed with an imaginative eye and guided by an experimental hand, twigs, pebbles, and even acorns can gain new meanings. Shapes improvised from a dead limb blended with experimental probings of chisel and rasp were the means of achieving *Texture Board from Nature* (Figure 398). The treatment of branches sawed and arranged in varied manners, an expressive application of scraps of bark, and the pierced and carved areas indicate an inquisitive and revealing approach. The discovery board, while suitable for den or cabin wall, fulfilled a prime purpose in giving insight to and sharpening the inventiveness of its student producer.

Another student arranged pebbles, obtainable from beach, field, or stream bed, to produce a durable and intriguing mosaic. The decorative slab is serviceable as a large planter coaster or as pattern accent adjacent to fireplace or upon a patio. Large and small, craggy and slick, light and dark stones, embedded in the concrete slab, clearly vie for attention in the *Pebble Mosaic* (Figure 399).

399   PEBBLE MOSAIC, *stones and cement, University student.*

400 FEELING OF THE FOREST, *relief, acorns, University student.*

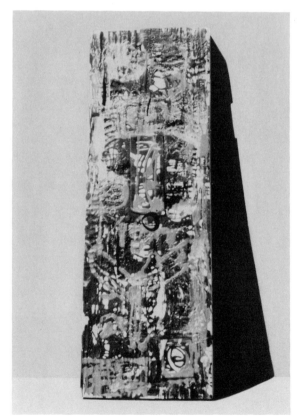

401 ABSTRACT PLAQUE, *carved and painted, wood, paint, and bits of metal, student, Wisconsin High School, Madison, Wisc.*

Under the capable hands of a student the fruit of an oak tree blossomed into the *Feeling of the Forest* (Figure 400). The acorn relief reveals its theme in obvious fluctuations in height and intense interminglings of shapes and space, qualities common to a forest environment. The student found design appropriateness in acorns for several reasons. Their smooth elliptical forms capped with scaly involucres, which when removed result in contrasting concave shapes, offered distinct organizational possibilities. Also, color proximity when massing an abundant number of the small hard objects permitted a quality of restraint. Several were broken, cut, crushed, burnt, or filed to analyze obtainable modifications in size, shape, and surface. The subsequent decision to restrict their use to their original state was due to a desire for both naturalism and visual directness. Placements upon a wood base were then determined. Different levels resulted in gluing acorns directly upon the base as well as supporting others upon snipped nails of various lengths which acted as posts. Pockets of retained space resulted from the use of the upper concave sections of acorns, while the pods — concise spheres — hastened spatial movement. Shapes, color, textures, organizational method, and space were thus utilized to convey the poetic rhythms of the forest.

The world is full of new meanings. Both man-made city environments and nature's streams, fields, and forests hold an inexhaustible abundance of subject ideas and materials awaiting creative hands. Look about you and then toward the horizon.

A Point of View

The purpose of crafts may be twofold: to provide society with well-executed and visually pleasing products and to offer revealing experiences and satisfaction to the constructor. In school programs the stress should be on the latter. The development of skill and spirit and the achievement of unique personal solutions are, however, mandatory. Cloth, pebbles, leather, strands of reed, pine, clay, copper, silver, a walnut plank, colored glass — these and others are but the basic materials. They remain formless until ingenuity extends them meaning (Figure 401). The problems of tools, processes, and materials as to availability and appropriateness are dependent on the drive of both teacher and student. The final answers, however, remain the obligation of the student. Education is only to indicate the way, with the pace and final directions determined by the student.

Certain craft ventures offer success through simple procedures and a minimum of equipment; others may involve rather complicated processes, many tools, and extensive technical information. Explicit instructions relative to everything from loom construction and weaving procedures through jewelry processes and glazes suitable for ceramics are contained in many specialized publications. If required, these publications, both texts and magazines, may be found in school or public libraries or secured directly from their publishers.

Though knowledge and proficiency are essential, they are but the foundation. Idea is paramount. Frequently it emerges as one studies the nature of a material. This is particularly evident in working with clay, because it is highly sympathetic toward immediate and extensive form modifications. It can be easily pinched, pulled, rolled, parted, and joined into various shapes. Remaining as it does in a pliable state for a relatively long period of time, clay also offers an extensive working period. Constructions may result from simple clay coils or slabs, with the resulting forms susceptible to new relationships through twisting or turning actions. Success is dependent neither on many tools nor on complex processes, and even for the beginner, it is relatively easily obtained (Figure 402).

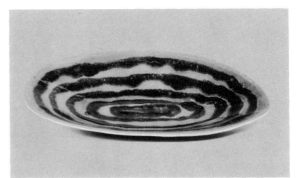

402   *Glazed Dish, clay, Junior high school student, State College Area Schools, Pa.*

403   *Necklace and Earrings, silver, Senior high school student, Hampton Township Schools, Pa.*

404   ANTEATER AND STILL LIFE, *wall hangings, stitchery, yarn on burlap, Junior high school students, University High School, Iowa City, Iowa.*

405   *Stained-Glass Windows, Zion Church, Milwaukee, Wisc., Peter Recker, 1960. Subtle and bold colors intermingle with clear glass and sturdy wood mullions to contribute an inspirational pattern. (Courtesy the Architect, William P. Wenzler)*

In comparison with clay, many other materials encompass a somewhat tedious forming process. For instance, silver, owing to hardness and resistancy, as well as its cost, usually demands premeditated planning in the manner of preliminary sketching. Specific knowledge of process is, of course, also needed. Skill, however, in tune with such knowledge, grows only from actual participation in working processes (Figure 403). Thus, experiences in designing, cutting, soldering, setting stones, and polishing implants particular secrets and unfolds a personal touch or technique. However, this unfolding skill factor, achieved through doing, is certainly not confined to silver or metal in general, but holds true for all materials and art areas.

Strong evidences of self-discovery are apparent in both *Anteater* and *Still Life*, stitchery wall hangings created by junior high school students (Figure 404). Thought and control assured clarity, while adventurous attitudes contributed impact to their treatment. Variations in stitches, value and color interplays, accents of solidity, implied textures, and the wise use of available space guaranteed visual excitement.

Youthful discoveries in expressing ideas and handling materials, no matter what their elegance, are not the final end. They mark but the beginning, as probes amassing insight and courage and reinforcing inventive attitudes. These attributes can constantly serve to intensify reactions and more adequately influence the structuring of all future endeavors. Dependent on inquisitiveness and invention, art both recognizes and encourages the superiority of man over formal rules and binding reasons. Thus the cultivation of the uniqueness of individualism and the pursuit of personal excellence are two of its major purposes within a school program. Bent not on destruction, but rather on positive construction, art experiences should foster a strong desire which continues beyond maturity deep into the twilight years. That desire, an eagerness for brilliance, tempered with sensitive restraint, in all the products of man.

406 CROWN OF THORNS, *oil painting, Alfred Manessier, 1954. Linear tensions and spacial clashes provide dramatic grandeur to this ageless theme. (Courtesy Carnegie Institute)*

408 *Fountain, plastic, ceramic, and metal, West Hill Library, Akron, Ohio, Luke and Rolland Lietzke, 1960. An unusual accent in an urban environment is gained through this fountain arrangement which provides invigorating sprays, patterns, and reflections. (Courtesy the Artist-Craftsmen)*

Mosaic, Venetian tesserae, Edmund D. Lewandowski, 1959. A recent addition to the façade of the Milwaukee County War Memorial Building, the large mosaic numerals convey the periods when youths fell to enable the nation to stand. (Courtesy the MILWAUKEE SENTINEL*)*

407

In Conclusion

Expressive hands and imaginative eyes currently shape an endless number of materials. They richly compose glass and wood, actively guide paint to proclaim and reveal, develop gleaming mosaics from bits of matter, or bring forth creations in innumerable other substances (Figures 405, 406, 407, 408). Though solutions are both diverse and comprehensive, one factor remains consistent. The process is always demanding. Regardless of classification, be it sculpture, graphics, or painting, crafts, architecture or drawing, each area presents challenges towards attaining effective forms. Each, also, has many reasons and many means.

In parting, let us keep in mind Voltaire's contention that all the arts are brothers for each is akin to the other. Furthermore, each and all only emerge through constant search and self-discovery (Figure 409).

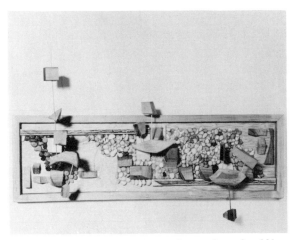

409 VARIABLE RELIEF, *pine, walnut, rods, and pebbles, University student. Position of rods and suspended wood shapes changeable as desired.*

TOPICS FOR CONSIDERATION

1. In what ways can the crafts beautify and intensify life?
2. What can be the roles of hand craftsmen in a machine age?
3. When is a craft activity not an art form?
4. Do you think the majority of Americans sensitively select the objects that are contained in their homes? What qualities, do you imagine, usually determine their choices?
5. Select several craft objects, or photographs of objects, which, in your opinion, appear to be well designed, and indicate reasons for your judgment.
6. Can you think of a few historic and contemporary craft objects which display extreme degrees of integrity or directness and honesty? Think in terms of the handling of material and the treatment of surface.
7. What crafts would you include within the general classification of art, and how can originality be assured in each of these activities?

SUGGESTED ACTIVITIES

1. Carve a bowl from wood or create a cloth bag suitable as a container for beach accessories or similar purposes. The cloth bag can be enriched with a stencil pattern, thread stitchery, or applique.
2. Model a jar or bowl from clay using the coil, slab, or wheel-thrown method. Glaze and fire the article.
3. Create several pieces of jewelry composed of copper wire, enameled copper, or pierced silver. Cuff links, pin, or necklace are but a few of the objects which can be devised.
4. Construct a miniature stained-glass window approximately one foot square, employing a geometric pattern. Frame the window and use it as an adjunct to a conventional window through suspension or placement on a sill.
5. Execute a mosaic from ceramic tile or pebbles. It can be intended for placement on a wall or serve as a flat platter upon which potted plants can be placed.
6. Create a plaster plaque. The slab can be directly inscribed and carved or derived from a richly textured sheet of clay.
7. Build a toy or creative plaything for a young friend. Incorporate features that provide actual movement. It can be composed of bits of wood, metal, plastics, wire, Masonite, or other suitable materials. Upon completion, the toy can be brightly painted.
8. Produce a wall hanging by stenciling oil paint on duck cloth. Possibilities for imagery may range from creatures of the forest or feathered friends to a nonobjective arrangement or a figure or city caricature.
9. Prepare a wall hanging using stitching. Sew thread, yarn, and small segments of cloth upon burlap. An exciting theme could be a fantastic garden.

APPROPRIATE REFERENCES AND READINGS

Periodicals

Craft Horizons, New York: Crafts Horizons, Inc., 29 W. 53rd St.

Design Quarterly, Minneapolis, Minn.: The Walker Art Center.

Texts

"American Jewelry." *Design Quarterly*, 45-46, Minneapolis, Minn.: Walker Art Center, 1959.

"American Pottery." *Design Quarterly*, 42-43, Minneapolis, Minn.: Walker Art Center, 1958.

"American Weaving." *Design Quarterly*, 48-49, Minneapolis, Minn.: Walker Art Center, 1960.

BASSETT, KENDALL T., THURMAN, ARTHUR B., and D'AMICO, VICTOR. *How to Make Objects of Wood*, New York: The Museum of Modern Art, 1951.

COX, DORIS, and WARREN, BARBARA, *Creative Hands*, 2d ed., New York: John Wiley & Sons, Inc., 1951.

DOUGLAS, FREDERIC H., and D'HARNONCOURT, RENE. *Indian Arts of the United States*, New York: The Museum of Modern Art, 1941.

DUCAN, JULIA HAMLIN, and D'AMICO, VICTOR. *How to Make Pottery and Ceramic Sculpture*, New York: The Museum of Modern Art, 1947.

HALD, ARTHUR, and SKAWONIUS, SVEN ERIK. *Contemporary Swedish Design*, New York: Pellegrini & Cudahy, 1951.

JENKINS, LOUISA, and MILLS, BARBARA. *The Art of Making Mosaics*, Princeton N.J.: D. Van Nostrand Co., Inc., 1957.

KARASZ, MARISKA. *Adventures in Stitches and More Adventures, Fewer Stitches*, New York: Funk & Wagnalls Co., 1959.

KRUM, JOSEPHINE R. *Hand-Built Pottery*, Scranton, Pa.: International Textbook Co., 1960.

LINTON, RALPH, and WINGERT, PAUL S. *Arts of the South Seas*, New York: The Museum of Modern Art, 1946.

LISSNER, IVAR. *The Living Past*, New York: G. P. Putnam's Sons, 1957.

MANLEY, SEON. *Adventures in Making: The Romance of Crafts Around the World*, New York: Vanguard Press, 1959.

MARTIN, CHARLES J., and D'AMICO, VICTOR. *How to Make Modern Jewelry*, New York: The Museum of Modern Art, 1949.

WALLANCE, DON. *Shaping America's Products*, New York: Reinhold Publishing Corporation, 1956.

WINEBRENNER, KENNETH D. *Jewelry Making: As an Art Expression*, Scranton, Pa.: International Textbook Co., 1953.

INDICES

Name Index

Washburn, Gordon Bailey, 236
Washington, George, 12, 238, 245
Waugh, Sidney, 284
Weiler, Joseph, 31, 32
Weinberg, Elbert, 252, 253
Wenzler, William P., 6, 247, 306
Whitelow, Roger, 285
Whitman, Walt, 94
Wilde, John, 132, 133, 176
William the Conqueror, 279
Wirth, S. S. Captain, 196

Wistar, Casper, 300
Wood, Grant, 187
Wordsworth, William, 49
Wren, Sir Christopher, 68
Wright, Donald B., 292
Wright, Frank Lloyd, 62, 80, 82, 90, 92, 93, 94, 96-102, 112, 113, 125
Wright, Lloyd, 84
Wyeth, Andrew, 189, 203

Zingale, Santos, 218
Zoretich, George, 161, 249

Subject Index

Abbey of Saint Denis, 73
A-Bomb, 191
Aboriginal art, 276
Absolute inventiveness, 164
Absolute reality, 161, 236
Abstract art, 35, 151, 152, 186, 202, 262
Abstract expressionism, 177, 187, 188, 191, 200, 202
Academics, 144, 183
Accent, 155, 262
Acropolis, 63
Action painting, 177; see also Abstract expressionism
Activities, suggested
    architecture, 85, 127
    crafts, 308
    design, 58
    drawing, 148
    general, 19
    graphics, 234
    painting, 181, 214
    sculpture, 274
Adaptability
    architecture, 50, 96, 97, 103, 104, 120
    furniture, 295, 302
    nature, 25
Advancing color; see Color
Adversaries, natural, 221
Advertising, 6, 27, 33, 57
African art, 164, 242, 243
Ahab, Captain, 285
Alabaster, 256
Alcoa Forecast Collection, 46, 47, 57, 285, 293, 294
All-over pattern, 51, 289
Alphabets, early, 129
Aluminum, 38, 47, 246, 249, 293, 294
Aluminum Company of America, 285
American Indian art, 239, 240, 241, 281
American scene painters, 76, 150, 187
Amethyst, 251
Amphora, 278
Amulet, 241
Animals, symbolic usage, 11, 128, 129, 240, 241

Appian Way, 243
Applied decoration, 23, 66, 79, 105, 113
Applique, 290
Apollo, 222
Appreciation, 3, 8, 10, 273, 306
Archeology, 53, 239
Architectonic, 164, 194
Architecture
    as an art form, 113
    challenge, 127
    Chicago School of, 90-93
    formation of styles, 61
    future, 124
    Gothic, 73
    Greek, 63
    historical forms as inspiration, 55, 68-72, 76-81
    international, 106-111
    logic of revivals, 82
    nineteenth-century revivals, 68, 74
    organic, 93-105
    present, 87
    Roman, 66
    suggested activities, 85, 127
Armed Liberty, 244
Art
    for art's sake, 36, 192, 202
    benefits derived, 3
    elements, 15
    historical forms as inspiration, 52-57, 94, 256
    materials, 13, 21, 40, 118, 134, 213, 226, 265, 287, 306
    purpose of, 5, 28
    range, 3, 118, 151
    role of performer, 2, 16-18, 180
Art Nouveau, 106
Artists and industrial design, 284
Assembly Hall, University of Illinois, 118
Assur, 222
Assyrians, 222, 243
Athena, 63, 65, 72
Athens; see Greece
Atmospheric, 14, 49, 194
Auschwitz, 196
Automatic drawing, 174

Color *(Continued)*
  symbolic associations, 208
  usage, 207
Colosseum, 55, 73
Columbian art, 280
Column of Trajan, 256
Columns, Doric, 63
Communication, 6, 190, 193, 242
  instantaneous, 57, 170, 171, 191
  spiritual, 74, 84, 242-245
Comparison of styles; *see* Style comparison
Concave and convex shapes, 248, 258, 259
Concrete, usage in architecture, 46, 97, 98, 107,
      108, 118, 120
Congressional Library, 245
Consistency, 49, 136, 159, 200
Constructivism, 35
Containers, 28-30, 241, 277, 278, 281, 290, 293
Container Corporation of America, advertisements,
      33, 57
Contemporary realism, 191, 194
Contour drawing, 136
Contrast, 15, 143, 156, 185, 191, 259, 290;
      see also Color
Contrived and undetermined shapes, 174, 269
Correlation, in architecture, 97, 103, 117
Cost-saving methods
  in furniture, 297-298
  in residential architecture, 87, 108, 116
Crafts
  artist-craftsman, 286
  as an art form, 282
  craft materials and processes, 287-304
  crafts in a school program, 305
  final aim, 306-307
  function of, 284
  production procedures, 282-285
  suggested activities, 308
  traditional methods and purposes, 276-281
Crater, 278
Crayon etching, 142
Creative action, 3, 124
Crockets, 74, 78
Crystal Palace, 35, 62
Cubism, 164, 186
Cut and torn paper
  in design, 40
  drawing, 142
  graphics, 227
  painting, 209
  sculpture, 268
Cylix, 278
Cypriote art, 55

Dadaism, 36, 186
Danish crafts; *see* Scandinavian crafts
Declaration of Independence, 244

Decline of Greece, 65
Decline of Rome, 73
Decoration
  in architecture, 113
  in furniture, 23
Dedication, 172, 192
Deliberation, 137, 174, 209
Depression, American, 195
Design
  in art, 27
  artists speak of, 29-33
  current influences in, 22
  early American, 23, 95, 295
  effectiveness of primitive works, 276, 277
  judgment, 23
  materials and methods, 35-57
  meaning of, 21
  in nature, 25
  process, 21
  sources, 35
  suggested activities, 58
De stijl, 106
Differentiation, problems of, 132, 199, 260
Dinnerware, 5
Direct printing, 226-227
Directional play, 156, 165, 290
Directness, 57, 170, 255
Discords, 152, 249, 263
Distortion, 16-17, 164-173, 193, 252, 259
Drapery, 51, 289
Drawing
  benefits, 133-134
  contour, 137
  form, 138
  function of, 133
  gesture, 136
  ingredients, 137
  line, 136
  suggested activities, 148
  texture, 140
  tools, 134
  value, 143
Dream imagery, 132, 187, 199
Ducco printing, 230
Dynamic form, 129, 247
Dynamic movement, 35, 165, 177, 186, 249
Dynamic symmetry, 63, 174

Eagle, American, 64, 247
Earth
  aerial photographs of, 58, 162
  contour sculpture, 124
Easter Island, 238
Economy
  in architecture, 106, 110
  in design, 32, 57
  in drawing, 130, 146

Plywood, 295, 296

Pointed arch, 73

Pointillism, 185

Poland, invasion of, 196

Polynesian sculpture, 238

Pompeii, 302

Positive space, 40, 51

Post-impressionism, 185

Post and lintel, 73, 116

Power equipment, use of
    in architecture, 87, 108
    in crafts, 282
    in sculpture, 255

Pottery, 28-30, 278, 287, 288, 305

Prefabrication, 87, 108, 115, 118

Pre-Raphaelites, 52

Pressure, in printing, 217

Primitive art, 8, 55, 128, 239, 242, 276, 277

Primitive painter, modern, 190

Processes
    art; see each specific art area
    technological, 44-47, 106, 110, 118, 249, 293, 295

Projection, for appreciation, 277

Protest, art as, 195

Psychology in art, 199

Punic War, 196

Purification of form, 27, 107, 111, 254, 255

Queen Victoria, 78

Quest, constant, 307

Radiograph
    of coral, 252
    of sea shell, 93

Reaffirmation, art as, 9

Realism, 160-163, 183-185, 194

Realistic representation, 189-191

Reality
    divergent views, 158-159
    new visions, 161
    science and art, 161-164

Rearrangeable form, 34, 46, 123, 264, 295, 299, 302

Recall, 18, 131, 256

References and readings, 19, 59, 85, 127, 149, 181,
    215, 235, 275, 309

Regionalism, 187

Rejection of past, 53, 91, 164, 176, 188, 247

Relief
    printing, 218
    sculpture, 9, 36, 37, 64, 66, 75, 243, 246, 272

Religious art, 285; see also Gothic and Churches

Renaissance, 11, 35, 61, 243

Repetition, 15, 51, 155, 179, 289, 294

Reproduction, comprehensiveness of, 217, 259

Research, visual, 164

Research Tower, 100

Residential architecture
    problems of, 113
    solutions; see Houses

Restricted form, 87, 253, 255

Results of experimentation, 43, 134, 209, 226

Revelation, 159

Revival
    age of, 52
    current tendencies, 53-57
    dangers of, 82
    logic of, 82

Rheims Cathedral, 74

Rhythm, 15, 29, 162, 224, 259

Richmond, Virginia, 68

Rockets, 26, 165, 269

Rodent, X-ray of, 167

Roman
    architecture, 66
    crafts, 302
    sculpture, 185, 243

Romanesque, 61, 73, 80

Romantic
    architecture, 76
    painting, 76, 175, 183

Romanticism, 62, 74

Rome
    decline, 73
    growth, 65

Roux, E. T., Library, 99

Rubbings, 140, 145, 220

Rugs, 49, 284, 290

Salvation columns, 242

San Francisco Palace of Fine Arts, 62, 70

Sargassum fish, 25

Satire, 195, 222

Scandinavian crafts, 283

Scale contrast, 132, 191, 218, 242, 247, 259, 261

Science and art, 44, 125, 161-164, 252

Scrap materials, use of
    in crafts, 303
    in design, 40
    in drawing, 140, 142
    in graphics, 226
    in painting, 171, 206
    in sculpture, 265

Scratchboard, 142

Sculpture
    ancient forms of, 236-245
    carving, 254
    constructions, 262
    final challenge, 273
    imagery determinates, 237
    modeling, 257
    nationalism, 244-247
    new materials and forms, 251